Just *Lassen* to Me!

A First-Generation Son's Story: Surviving a Survivor

Book 1: Survivor Indoctrination

Harvy Simkovits

Just *Lassen* to Me!

A First-Generation Son's Story: Surviving a Survivor

Book 1: Survivor Indoctrination

Edition 3.1

Copyright © 2019 Harvy Simkovits

Published by Wise Press

ISBN-13: 978-0-9773957-1-2
ISBN-10: 0-9773957-1-5
Library of Congress Control Number: 2019900344

Praise for *Just Lassen to Me!*

Harvy's exquisite novel-like prose is a remarkable story of his quest and struggles to unlive his father's dreams. With unbridled candor, recall, and penetrating self-reflection, he shares his story suitable for a screenplay on the rewards and tortures of family enterprise.

> ~Paul Karofsky, Executive Director Emeritus Northeastern University Center for Family Business, family enterprise consultant, and co-author of *So You're in the Family Business: A Guide to Sustainability.*

Harvy brilliantly describes the seesaw tension created by the joy and privilege of sharing in a wealthy father's favor and fortune, while bearing the burden of his dad's financial secrets that only he knows. He writes a powerful, candidly written account of his family's complex and turbulent history, and his father's financial finagling, that will resonate with all readers who suffer the psychological costs of frightening family dysfunctions. Harvy's journey of personal struggle and seeking redemption will resonate with readers from all walks of life.

> ~William J. Hurley, former District School Board Chair, retired Superintendent of Schools and School Principal, Graduate School Instructor, Educational Leadership Consultant, and School Psychologist.

The mystic poet Rumi asked this: "And you? When will you begin that long journey into yourself?" Harvy Simkovits has begun his journey inward, reviewing the ways his larger-than-life father shaped him, and reflecting on the damage done by family secrets. His writing poses the questions many of us ask as we move into adulthood and authenticity: How have family stories and struggles shaped my inner struggles? How do I love my family and be free to become my authentic self? This book can serve as a model for anyone embarking on that journey of self-reflection and personal growth.

~The Rev. Mary Margaret Earl, Executive Director and Senior Minister, The Unitarian Universalist Urban Ministry.

Harvy's work is remarkable. He shows courage by plumbing the depths of his family secrets, revealing how his upbringing caused him to shape, even twist himself to survive his family. This memoir is an act of self-healing, a coming to terms with a past that helps make peace with where one has been and currently is. This story will resonate with people who are digging themselves out of tumultuous histories. It's a story of redemption, of finding value in the struggles that life has given you. I marvel at the effort Harvy has put into it and admire what he has accomplished.

~Jay Vogt, Founder of Peoplesworth, and Author of Recharge Your Team: The Grounded Visioning Approach.

The second son in an immigrant family, the young Harvy grew up in Canada. Harvy was his flamboyant father's favored child and confidant. How this thoughtful, yet naïve, young man reconciles his love of—and admiration for—his dad, with the unwanted knowledge of his father's wild life and shady business dealings, makes for fascinating reading and results in a heroic twist.

~Audrey Friedman Marcus, former Executive Vice President of A.R.E. Publishing, Inc., and author of *Survival in Shanghai: The Journals of Fred Marcus 1939-49.*

"Just Lassen to Me!" is an engaging, touching, and very personal memoir of growing up navigating the complex relationships in an Eastern European immigrant family. Harvy Simkovits' father is a survivor of service in four armies on both sides of World War II. He also escaped beneath the Iron Curtain with his Hungarian wife to a new life

in Montreal. Dad becomes a successful businessman and pulls young Harvy into an orbit of sometimes-shady deals and family conflicts. Harvy's entertaining story has twists and turns, including a fascinating revelation from his mother.

~Walter Leutz, Professor, Heller School for Social Policy and Management, Brandeis University.

Harvy's tale, remarkable and so interesting, feels very real—as if you were right there living it with him. The stories about his father, mother, and their families are so incredible; one could not make it up. The characters are bigger than life with all of their warts. They are believable, lovable (for the most part), even with their sad or tragic flaws. The story of his mother's family survival and success is amazing. I could picture the situations he narrates as if I had been there myself.

~Jim Bourdon, Former Founder, Owner, and President of AMS, Former Board Member of Small Business Association of NE.

Harvy's memoir is exceptionally well written and astonishing in its detail about events, places, and people going back so many years to his childhood, adolescence, and young adulthood. This effort is an important vehicle for liberating himself and confirming his integrity and decency. It's an extraordinary telling of a highly personal and complicated journey.

~Calvin Melmed, BSc., MD, FRCP(C), FAAN. Emeritus Chief, Dept of Neurological Sciences, Jewish General Hospital. Associate Professor, Neurology and Neurosurgery, McGill University; and Carolyn Melmed, BA, Cert Ed., Cert Conflict Resolution and Mediation.

A truly fascinating tale about a unique and colorful immigrant father, an immigrant mother with deep secrets, and the powerful impact they had on their son. It's a wonderful story and honest!

~John Levine, Chairman and CEO, Pinsly Railroad Company, a third-generation family business.

In Harvy Simkovits' memoir of his complicated father, the son has assembled the weight of memories to impress upon the reader the stamp of this forceful man he loved and endured. Simkovits unknots the kinks of this big-hearted swindler, affectionate brawler, chivalrous womanizer, and solicitous browbeater with panache. The author's searing honesty about his complicity as a potential beneficiary of the shenanigans of this tax-evading, deal-cutting entrepreneur makes for an extraordinarily fascinating memoir. It is as much about the son's struggle to uncouple from the sin and resolve the guilt as it is about a freewheeling father who could very well be the protagonist of a Canadian immigrant version of Mad Men.

~Tom Daley, author of *House You Cannot Reach—Poems in the Voice of My Mother and Other Poems* and instructor in memoir writing at Lexington Community Education.

Simkovits recounts his struggle to come to terms with his father's morally questionable financial dealings in this first memoir in a series. (It's) a thoughtful consideration of the limits of familial loyalty.

~Kirkus Review

Dedication

This book is dedicated to sons and daughters who have had to live up to great life promise and confront deep family shame, and to my mother.

Contents

Excerpt – Book Two: Survivor Teachings

Acknowledgements
About the Author

Why *Just Lassen to Me!*?

Is it possible to admire a man's accomplishments but abhor what he stands for, to seek his blessing but spurn his legacy? What if that man is your father?

In 2005, I began writing stories about John and Anna Simkovits. It was five years after my father passed away after a lifetime of drinking like a Russian fish, smoking like a Canadian chimney, and working and playing hard as the driven Hungarian-Slovak immigrant he was. It was seventeen years after my mother died of a broken heart. Until that time, I had hidden—and thought I had banished—my troubled family history from my mind and life. Little had I realized how much I had to say and how much I had to reconcile within myself for my father's fiascoes and my foolish failures.

Some have asked me why I chose to write about the dark and disturbing relationships between my flamboyant yet flawed father, my devoted yet disaffected mother, and my honest yet defiant older brother. My blind desire for Dad's love and acknowledgment led to my calculated gambles and blatant complicity in my father's continual finagling with money, friends, and women. "Why not lay the past to rest?" people have asked, and "Is this the way you want your family, and you, to be remembered?"

Had I been angry at my family? For sure! Had I been mad at myself? Even more!

I needed to reconcile with my dark past and to reveal the truth about what I knew and did with this gregarious, successful, yet deeply imperfect man of a father. I had to come to terms with the parts that members of my family had played, including me, in enabling his chicanery. I wanted to show not only the close connections but also the insidious impact that Dad had had on those who worked for him, on his colleagues and so-called friends, and on our failed family.

Johnny Simkovits had lived a carefree nightlife of entertaining business colleagues and Eastern European cohorts in the barrooms, classy restaurants, and cafes of Montreal. But his home life became peppered with screaming matches, not only with my distraught yet sharp-tongued mother but also with his other wives and women.

Dad had founded and led a legitimate business as a major manufacturer within the Canadian record player and console stereo industry. He had also helped to precipitate the last vestiges of that industry. He churned his legitimate profits into Montreal real estate while maintaining a clandestine offshore enterprise and money empire that skirted the taxman.

My father had lived a charmed personal life of liquid libations, lively admirers, loose ladies, and merry ethnic melodies. But he continually berated his factory employees, and he discarded wives, mistresses, and even good friends when they no longer suited him.

I was one of the few who saw many of my father's fancies, facets, and failings. I was possibly the only one whom he trusted with the greatest knowledge of his nighttime cavorting, cash-making shenanigans, and money-hiding and tax-avoiding ploys.

For decades, I went along with my father's underhanded wheeling and dealing, and his playing around with his gang of merry Montrealers. I allowed my blind admiration of and unwavering loyalty to him to obscure my judgement when he told me about his latest mischievous adventure, money-making venture, or tax-evading endeavour. I knew about his other women, but I neither did nor said anything to stop him from his flagrant transgressions—except to eat myself up regarding his deceitful plays and abusive ways. I kept his offshore empire concealed from the government and his clandestine cavorting hidden from my family. My intense desire to become Dad's chosen son may have even caused me to dirty my fingernails in a Johnny Simkovits money-making maneuver.

The moral and ethical dilemmas I faced as I took part in Dad's daytime scheming and nighttime seducing had a burgeoning life of their own. I was compelled to wrestle with my conscience and put down my complicity. I needed to acknowledge and accept the insidious impact this charismatic yet conniving man had on me, his closest son.

Others have asked, "Isn't your relationship with your father, mother, and brother three separate and distinct tales and not one interwoven memoir series?"

They raise a valid storytelling point, and I make the argument, "Don't we all grow up in separate but related worlds where our parents have families and kin of their own? Aren't all of us the product of blended families, which creates blended histories, perspectives, and life stories?" I couldn't fully comprehend my multifaceted life and its complex evolution without understanding my entire heritage, including my predecessors and their life-altering experiences. I, like many, can't untie that entwined mesh. So I offer you my total narrative for you to wonder about and tease apart as you may.

The story and characters presented in this memoir are based on events, e-mails, and interviews, both with my family members and with my parents' family, friends, and close colleagues. Many shared stories about my father's achievements and tales about his mischief—some to get it off their chest. A few of Dad's chummy companions, business colleagues, and Eastern European cohorts were not willing to be a part of my project, and I understood and accepted their decision.

I especially thank my stepmother and brother for reading and commenting on many chapters of my manuscript. They stirred and clarified many of my memories and offered their truth to my perspectives.

The names of many organizations and individuals mentioned here (outside of Dad's companies and our immediate family) have been changed to maintain their privacy. Some people have been intentionally left out. I ask their forgiveness but suspect they might prefer it that way.

I have worked to keep my narrative focused on my relationship with my father, mother, brother, and stepmother. I aim to tell my story in the way I saw or imagined events around my family had unfolded. It is not my purpose to shame or blame individuals and organizations that intentionally or naively played along with my father's furtive finagling. My goal is to shine a light on the dark truths and shady dealings surrounding my father and me. And I want to show the power of my family's history to define and shape my life, whether I wanted it fashioned that way or not.

This book is the first volume in a series that chronicles my efforts to survive my tumultuous family, especially my finagling father. Come! Meet my colourful dad, John Simkovits, and the rest of my thorny family, and make your determinations. Dad was a captivating yet blemished man affectionately known to his Canadian friends and colleagues as "Johnny" and to his homeland family and comrades as "Jani." Make of us what you will, but for good and bad, Johnny left an indelible mark on every man, woman, and child who knew him.

Harvy Simkovits

Note to U.S. Readers

This narrative uses typical Canadian writing conventions. The British "our" ending is employed for words like "labour," "favour," "colour," etc. The colour "gray" is used instead of "grey," "judgement and acknowledgement" are used instead of "judgment and acknowledgment," "jewellery" instead of "jewelry," 'moustache instead of mustache," "pyjamas" instead of "pajamas," "travelling" instead of "traveling," "service centre" instead of "service center," "bank cheque" instead of "bank check," "meagre" instead of "meager."and so on. "Practice" and "licence" are utilized as the noun form of those words, while "practise" and "license" are employed as the verb form.

Instead of "breakfast, lunch, and dinner," in my Canadian environs, it was "breakfast, dinner [a formal midday meal, unless it was an informal meal like in a 'box lunch' or 'cafeteria lunch'] and supper [the evening meal]." Also, what are "sodas" in America are "soft drinks" in my country of origin.

For some Canadian English words, the more typical American forms are employed. For example, "toward" and "afterward" are employed instead of the British "towards" and "afterwards," and so on.

Canada converted all its measures to metric during the 1970s. British units were employed before 1970 and remained the custom in certain areas, like in the size of a wood cabinet. This memoir works to utilize each type of measure where appropriate.

Personal Notes

Though my story brings to light the less than ethical practices of one global bank and one fundraising arm of an independent university, it is not my intent to disparage all multinational banks or private universities. I only wish to shed light on the dubious financial practices of some entities, which most likely exist all around the world, that collude with wealthy individuals to skirt paying a fair share of tax to the country in which they reside.

At least fifty percent of the profits from the sales of this book will go to support non-profits that work to help victims of domestic abuse and violence.

Book One

Survivor Indoctrination

Part I:

Oh, My Papa!

1

My *Fader's* Ambiance

April 2006.

Kathy Varga e-mailed me unexpectedly. I hadn't heard from her since my father's funeral six years earlier. I had no idea where her brief note would lead regarding my deceased dad.

Both of our Hungarian fathers had been strong-willed, opinionated, and self-absorbed diehards. They loved to listen to their voices, were always peddling something, and rarely let a pretty face go by without trying to grab her attention. They enjoyed telling you what you should do with your money and life—to become more like them! Dad started his opinions with, "Just *lassen* to me!" He said that in his deep, Hungarian-Slovak-accented voice as he pointed his fingers at your chest and looked you straight in the eyes.

Kathy's e-mail offered a message from her father, now over ninety years old. In his prime, Jiri Varga had been an under-ten handicapper on the golf course. He pitched financial schemes to every person with whom he played—though usually off the course.

I never had an affinity for the guy. He talked about his latest bigwig clients and pushed his newest "legitimate" tax shelter schemes. He bragged, "I made millions in the insurance business, then doubled my take by investing with the biggest and best Montreal investment firm."

I expected it was Jiri and my dad's big egos, on top of their parallel stories about surviving WWII in Hungary, escaping the Soviet takeover, and immigrating to Canada, that attracted them to each other. But there was more.

Kathy's message said, "My father received a call from a Mrs. Beliveau in Montreal. It seems she knew your dad from the Troika days."

Though my dad had been underground for half a dozen years, and I hadn't lived in Montreal for the last seventeen, the memories flooded back.

The Troika had been a swank Russian restaurant and bar in the heart of Montreal's Crescent Street nightlife area. That upper-class establishment was situated several black granite steps below street level. In the days that I had gallivanted with Dad and his assorted and sordid male business colleagues, we entered that belowground grotto from a large, black stone landing at the bottom of those steps.

Behind a wide, heavy, iron-plated wooden door was a dark, foreboding, burgundy-walled alcove. There squatted a small, black-enamel table, set with a fan of Troika business cards and a couple of Troika-embossed coasters. Snug against the table sat two black iron chairs turned toward each other—as if they were waiting for an intimate conversation to happen.

Beyond those chairs, and through a second thick, dark wood door with a small see-through window, we obtained a quick glimpse of the action that was going on inside. We pulled open that heavy door and walked into a large, dimly lit room richly decorated in bright burgundy wallpaper above a waist-high wall of red brick.

Strategically placed were large mirrors that made the cozy restaurant look larger, and to allow the men and ladies to check and groom themselves after doffing fancy hats, silk scarves, and wool coats. Colourful paintings of Russian scenes covered the restaurant's walls. A bronze coq stood straight in a clear acrylic box attached to one wall.

We stepped into this oasis for thirsty men and a wannabe gentleman like me. We were ushered inside by a tuxedo-wearing maître d' or a pretty green-eyed hostess in a tight black dress with red accessories. Our host or hostess efficiently took our London Fog trench coat or Montreal-made fur, and our fur and felt hats. They then whisked us into a world of Russian drinks and delicacies, lively Eastern European folk music, and people of every European ethnicity. Men sported dark three-piece suits and women wore low-cut cocktail dresses.

As soon as we heard a rendition of the restaurant's energetically played theme song *O Da, Troika!* (Oh Yes, Troika!), our ears perked, our chests protruded, and everyone forgot the concerns they had contemplated in the parking lot. You might quickly forget your problems too! This old, aristocratic Russian world of strong, virile men—with appealing ladies on their arms or by their sides—was not where the meek shall inherit the earth.

On the restaurant's back wall hung a large painting. It portrayed an ornate Russian sleigh pulled by three prancing horses. The owner of the restaurant had named his establishment after such a vehicle. This painted troika held an aristocratic family that snuggled together under warm wool blankets as the horses pulled them through a winter countryside scene—like out of *Doctor Zhivago*.

The restaurant's logo, embossed on the menus, drink coasters, and business cards, featured the heads and forelegs of those three frolicking horses. Their manes rose as one large aura above their heads. The image appealed to my father because it reminded him of how he and his closest comrades lived it up in lively tandem.

Troika's ambiance represented my father well. Dad regularly invited his friend Jiri, among other Eastern European comrades, for evenings out at that extravagant hideaway. They raised a ruckus by night while keeping their wives waiting at home. It was the women's job to tend to the children, and to wash and iron their man's white dress shirts for their "business meetings."

Lots of funny business went on at that place, Dad being the general manager of the shenanigans. He knew how to take care of his cohorts, especially the repressed Canadian Anglophones, showing them a whooping gypsy time. More than once, I saw Jiri raise a glass to my father and say, "Johnny is the best entertainer of his friends." Another fond friend, Aras, noted, "The party never starts until Johnny gets here."

These entertainments were often a screen for their extracurricular activities. It was a rare evening when women guests didn't crowd around my father's Troika table, cozying up to one or more of these virile men, especially my father.

I wondered how much Jiri told his daughter, Kathy, about the joint, which had sat at the same Crescent Street location for over fifty years. I think most fathers would keep their daughters away from a place where roving male eyes undress female objects of pursuit.

Kathy concluded her message with, "My dad knows you are writing a book about your father. He thought you might want to contact Mrs. Beliveau. She might be a source for you."

Hmmm, I thought. I had seen and heard a lot about my father's underground Troika activities, possibly more than most, but not necessarily everything. *This connection could be interesting.*

At the end of Kathy's e-mail was Mrs. Beliveau's number.

* * *

A few days later.

"Hello, Mrs. Beliveau. I'm Harvy Simkovits, the son of John Simkovits."

"*Allo*, Harvy. It's nice of you to call. *S'il vous plait*, please call me Lucie. Your *fader* is not alive anymore, *n'est-ce pas?* I called his good friend, Mr. Varga, recently, and he told me so."

"*Oui.* Dad died of cancer in October of 2000. It was six months past his eightieth birthday."

"*Tant pis*; that's too bad. I knew your *fader* a long time ago from the Troika—him, Jiri, and his other good friend, Aras." She paused then added, "There was an East German fellow too, and others. It has been so long; I can't remember all their names."

"I believe that fellow was named Hans."

"*Mais oui*, Harvy!"

Those gents had been a jovial bunch when out together—like four Eastern European musketeers. They had made up Dad's regular "Troika gang," and joined him there for nighttime diversions. They brandished their Cross pens to sign tabs and copy down a name and phone number on the back of a Troika coaster. Dad's compatriots especially looked forward to being there with their good friend, Johnny, for he always picked up the tab.

I was ready with my questions for Dad's old acquaintance, or might she have been more? "Lucie, I got your name and number from Jiri's daughter, Kathy, after you talked to him recently. May I ask why you have been calling my father's old companions?"

Her voice projected sureness. "I was trying to get in touch with old friends that I met thirty years ago *trew* your *fader*."

Johnny had been a Troika regular for decades. The place reminded him of the months he had spent in Russia near the end of the Second Great War. Though Dad detested the Soviets, he loved to party like a Cossack.

He knew how to flip the switch from daytime businessman to evening entertainer. After he had locked the door to his Montreal manufacturing company, near the end of a busy week of purchasing and production headaches, he headed straight to the Troika. His motto was, "Enjoy tonight, for you don't know what comes tomorrow."

Sometimes my father entertained out-of-town customers or suppliers there for several nights in a given week, especially when he needed their good graces. After one long workday of negotiating with a vital Toronto vendor, Dad turned to the other company president and said with a wink and smile, "If you agree to this price on my order, I'll take you out for a good supper at the Troika." Because "a good supper" could mean much more than a meal, Dad got his way.

Lucie continued her musing happily. "We had such good times together with your *fader* and his friends, and then I lost touch. I called Mr. Varga recently to know if *dey* were still alive. Sadly, I heard from Jiri that Aras died too."

"Yes, Aras passed away a year or so after my father; he was ten years older. But it's quite amazing that Jiri is still alive. He's well into his nineties and 'still kicking'"—my imitation of a phrase my father liked to employ for elderly people.

After all their late-night toasting and singing like comrades, and fooling around with lively Montreal "broads" looking for a good time, I was impressed that any of them lived to reach old age. Into his retirement, after having had a few, Dad could squat down and kick out his legs in a Cossack dance. But I guessed that the elder Jiri had paced himself a little better.

"By the way, Lucie, can you tell me more about how you and my father knew each other?"

"*Sûrement!* It was so funny how we met back then. It was 1976, the year the summer Olympics were in Montreal. I think he told me you were at MIT at *dat* time."

"That's right, Lucie. It was between my bachelor's and master's degrees."

By then, Dad had introduced me to the Montreal Playboy Club. He had given me both a Playboy keycard and a company American Express credit card as a twenty-first birthday present. Boston had had its own Bunny Club back then. Emulating my father, I used my father's gifts gladly with my college chums.

Lucie continued. "One night that summer, I was having supper with my daughter at the Troika to celebrate her birthday. Your *fader* and Aras were there too, sitting a few tables away. During supper, *dey* sent over drinks, and then *dey* asked if they could sit with us."

Unlike timid me back then, those two had had their moves! No doubt, Lucie must have had a pretty face and a nice figure, accentuated by a sexy dress and deft touches of make-up—things Dad and his friends couldn't resist.

Over the years, Dad had taken me to the Troika to show me some of his ropes. He wanted this son to grow up just like him, and I obliged awhile. I had taken in the Russian food, the French wine, the Eastern European music, and the classy immigrant people. It was intoxicating!

Sometimes Dad allowed my bringing along a school buddy or girlfriend. My father was generous to everyone, buying drinks and meals, and sharing smokes. If put to the test, he could outdrink anyone with his favourite Russian vodka, then be able to walk a straight line and drive his car home without mishap.

I had admired my father for his hearty belly laugh and his deep baritone voice, which resonated throughout the club when he sang Eastern European songs. He told funny and sad stories of his old-country that had everyone at his table howl with laughter or cry in their bowl of borscht. I had smiled at my father's amusements, and I still did today.

Lucie was engrossed in her remembrances; she spoke as if all of it had happened last week. "My daughter and I accepted your *fader* and Aras's invitation. But the funny thing was that they thought my daughter was my sister—she looked much older than her age." Her voice elevated. "We laughed and laughed after they found out who she was. We had such a good time with them that evening."

Perhaps Lucie didn't realize how much of a high-class pick-up place the Troika had been. Many ladies went there looking for quick companionship or something more. More than one of my father's colleagues found "the woman of his dreams" at the Troika's bar. Those fellows sought a one-night flirt, or a regular out-of-town fling, or to tie a new eternal knot that required them to break bonds back home.

Lucie continued, "I liked your *fader* because he was so nice and respectful, a real gentleman."

I bet she hadn't heard the one about how he once arrived late at night with mixed company. Because he was not able to get his regular private table in the back of the restaurant, he and his friends had to sit in a more crowded part of the room. They spoke and laughed so loudly that a fellow at an adjoining table became annoyed. The patron started to flick salt from his place onto Dad's table.

As the story goes, Dad asked him calmly to stop, claiming, "Everyone's talking loud in the restaurant." After the third or fourth time that salt had flown over, Dad rose from his chair, went over to the guy, and punched him right in the nose, bloodying his face.

The man was immediately whisked off by his friends to a hospital emergency room. He subsequently hired a lawyer and charged my father for assault and battery.

For months, Dad and his Troika colleagues debated as to who had been right and wrong in that altercation. Privately, I wondered if my father's short fuse had gotten the better of him. In the end, Dad won the case. After hearing from the witnesses, the judge ruled that the other fellow had provoked the incident with his salt assault.

My curiosity was peaked. "Lucie, do you mind if I ask how long you knew my father?"

"*Pas du tout,* not at all. I knew him for maybe a year. We became friendly from the beginning. After my first husband died, I moved to the city; I could walk to the Troika from my place. Every time your father went there with his *chers amis,* he called me to join him and Aras. That's where I met Jiri and Hans. We had such good times together."

I smiled into the phone. "The Troika was certainly their fun place away from home."

Sometimes, at the restaurant's customary two o'clock closing time, the manager locked the front door and pulled the curtains shut while the booze continued to flow. The more venturesome ladies nuzzled a little closer to Dad or a member of his gang.

More than once, my father confided to me that he paid a woman to be "nice and friendly" to an important customer. And in the caretaking of a close colleague, he'd turn to him, wink, and say quietly, "Be careful what you do with her. You don't want to catch anything."

Dad loved the Troika so much that he recreated its décor—the brick, burgundy wallpaper, and wooden bar—in his mistress's basement (later his third wife) after he left my mother a final time. He then "borrowed" ashtrays, drink coasters, snifter glasses, and whatever he could lift from the real Troika to make his basement look authentic. My father figured the restaurant owed him for the business he had given the place over the years. I later learned that the Troika's owner knew my dad was stealing, but the proprietor never confronted his best patron.

Lucie broke my reverie. "For a while, Harvy, I was there almost every Thursday night, sitting with your *fader's* friends at his large table in the back."

I wonder if Dad had told Lucie how he had gotten that private table for himself; it wasn't exemplary of his best Troika behavior. Not wanting to be taken for a sucker after one of the bartenders padded his bill, Dad exploded. He threw obscenities as well as a shot glass that smashed the large mirror behind the long, dark lacquer bar.

By way of appeasement from the owner, Dad was seated in grand style at "his table" every Thursday night. There, he gathered his companions regularly to celebrate the near end of the workweek. The cozy table was on a platform, a bird's eye perch to the whole restaurant. From there, Dad and his comrades kept an eye out for a classy "spring chicken" (something they said among themselves with a chuckle and a nod) that walked into the place.

"Or, if it was late into the evening," Lucie added, "we'd sit at the big table by the bar, in the front."

At that other table, tucked away in a quieter corner of the bar area that occupied nearly a third of the restaurant, my father and his gang had hoisted many liquid suppers. Dad once recounted that a loose woman they hosted showed the boys—them glaring down the side of their crowded table—how she could smoke a cigarette from between her legs.

Lucie went on. "Harvy, I met lots of interesting people there through your *fader.*"

Some of my father's out-of-town colleagues had kept a lady friend tucked away in Montreal. The colleague paraded her out at the Troika, joining

Dad and his gang for drinks or supper. Over the years, they kept on returning, like lions to a favourite watering hole, for the restaurant's special *je ne sais quoi.*

In particular, Dad's friend, Hans—a muscular and gruff immigrant—had been a boisterous fellow. Dad told me that Hans had had an altercation with another Troika patron while they were obtaining refills at the crowded bar. The two men started to push and shout at each other.

At the bartender's demand, they took their fight outside, angrily accusing each other as they exited the front door. Ten minutes later, they returned jovially, their altercation resolved, and they bought each other drinks.

Hans was one to become more rambunctious after a few. Dad recounted, "One night, after I left the Troika for the evening, Hans got into trouble for shoving another patron who had bumped into him—though Hans claimed that the other guy pushed him first."

My father smiled and winked at his friend's high-spirited nature. "In the middle of the night, Hans had to call home and be bailed out by his peeved wife [a proper French woman] while their young son slept alone in the house."

I sympathized with their son, for I imagined the boy's German and French parents playing out WWIII at their house after Hans returned from a late-night jaunt. Similarly, in our home, I recalled my Catholic father and Jewish mother conducting an ongoing Hungarian inquisition about Dad's nighttime whereabouts and Mom's nagging nature.

Lucie's voice elevated with excitement. *"Ton père* was a generous man, always paid for his comrades and me. He was a good man, a real European gentleman. We both liked to laugh and enjoy life. We shared a special *joie de vivre."*

The old conniver did have his admirable qualities. He reveled in being the big shot and having fun, especially with a lively lady around. My father never allowed a colleague to pay when he was hosting—just like you would never ask a supper guest in your home to pay for the food and refreshments. Dad would get angry at the waiter, threatening him with the loss of next time's tip if the server ever handed the check to anyone other than my father.

When Dad paid, he used his American Express card. It showed that he had been an AMX member since 1960. My father once told me, "After I started my business in '53, it took me seven years of keeping my credit good to become a privileged card-carrying member."

Lucie stayed with her recollections. "After our nights out, your father drove me home in his fancy red Mercedes sports car."

"Yes, Lucie, it was a 450SL."

That large 2-door roadster, complete with both removable hardtop and retractable soft top, had been my father's midlife pick-up-mobile. The police sometimes stopped him for excessive speed or erratic driving. Dad would puff his cigar in the officer's face to mask the alcohol on his breath.

On another occasion, when he realized an unmarked police cruiser was following him, he drove straight to the police station. The maneuver gave him extra time to light a cigar and steady himself. At the station, he self-assuredly told the pursuing officers, "I was afraid to stop because I didn't know who was following me. You could have been robbers trying to force my expensive car off the road."

In both cases, the officers let him go. When Dad told me those stories, I could only smile at his quickness and shamelessness. I wondered if I could develop his kind of moxie.

Because my sibling had not been as good at his studies as I had been, Dad enticed my brother into college by buying him a Mercedes 280SL roadster. Going to MIT in Cambridge, MA, I hadn't needed a car.

But I did snag my brother's "green machine" for a semester or two when he went off to foreign lands for extended adventures during the years he had worked at Dad's company. My brother's wheels, with their fancy hubcaps, recognizable by their 3-point star logo, were perfect for carting my bookish college friends to Boston's Bunny Club.

I could feel Lucie's exuberance for having been a part of my father's crowd. For a time, they had drawn me in too. She continued. "Your *fader* was the boss at the Troika. They did things for him there. The musicians came to his table, and the chef would make something special for him. Your *fader* loved to sing many Eastern European songs. He was very entertaining."

They'd kiss your feet too if you had spent the kind of money he did there. The chef made him his favourites, like osso buco (veal shanks) with the edible marrow still in the bone. Or he prepared a tender rack of lamb so that Dad could chew the meat right off the rib.

In 1975, Dad had had a Christmas party at the Troika that cost him more than half my annual MIT tuition. As a souvenir, he kept the cancelled company cheque in the top drawer of his office desk. It was proof of his commitment to the establishment, in case the restaurant's staff or owner ever gave him a hard time for being rowdy.

Each night he went there, Dad put cash discretely into the hand of Sasha, the restaurant's lively and wide-smiling guitarist. Dad's money kept the musician coming back to his table to play and sing. Accompanying Sasha around the room was Vladjec, an accordion player who could follow any tune.

Sasha, Vladjec, and Dad taught each other many risqué songs in any number or mix of Eastern European languages. Together, they had everyone laughing and clapping. With the vocalizing of a song's single verse and refrain in my father's deep Eastern-European voice, Sasha and Vladjec caught on. They then had Dad's whole table lifting glasses and loosening wallets in praise.

With my dad's language capability, he could alter vowels and consonants in a song lyric. A Russian *How are you doing?* transformed into a Ukrainian, *What are you screwing?* Those who understood responded with hoots and howls.

One night, while he entertained important out-of-towners, Dad tore a hundred dollar bill in half. He gave Sasha one of the halves early in the evening, saying, "If you play good tonight, I'll give you the other half when we go home in the morning." Sasha earned his money by closing time.

Lucie laughed. "Once your *fader* took something from there for me, and no one said anything. It was a crystal tray with peppermints that I liked so much."

Dad bragged about how he and Aras, on a given night, would pinch a giant cordial snifter from the joint to impress and gift to a new acquaintance. One time after supper, Aras's girlfriend (later his second wife) put a massive snifter—large enough into which to enclose a child's head—under her dress. She then walked out of the restaurant pretending she was pregnant.

"Lucie, did the waiters show you how they pour digestifs into those big snifters?"

"*Bien sûr*, Harvy. It was so exciting when they did that."

When Dad had ordered cognac and Grand Marnier after supper, the waiter wheeled an after-supper drink cart to the table and removed a few giant liquor glasses from high off the wall. The server skillfully twirled one glass at a time on the flat top of his cart.

As the snifter spun around-and-around on its base, Sasha strummed his guitar rapidly. The waiter then held the bottle of alcohol 30 centimeters, then 60 centimeters, then 90, above the twirling glass, and he poured a healthy measure. He never spilled a drop, and everyone at the table applauded his dexterity.

I wanted to get the whole picture of Dad and this lady friend. "Lucie, did you do any other things with my father?"

"*Oui!* One weekend he took me to Toronto, and he let me drive his Mercedes. It was a sunny day, and your *fader* took off the hardtop. I drove over a hundred and fifty kilometers an hour on Highway 401, my hair blowing all over. It was so much fun."

She kept going. "Another time, your dad invited me to see his manufacturing company in Ville St. Laurent. I never saw a factory before; I found *très intéressant*. He had many people working for him."

He must have been attracted to her to parade her at his place of business for everyone to see.

"He showed me his private office, where I saw pictures of you, your brother, as well as your dead mother."

What? Oh, mein papa!!

She went on. "Then there was the time when Johnny invited my three kids and me to go skiing over the Christmas holidays at his chalet in St. Adele. He couldn't be with us because of a business trip overseas, but he let us use the place."

I had held myself back from divulging much of what I knew of my father's Troika world. But my temperature now rose. "Excuse me, Lucie; you said you saw a picture of my dead mother. I'm afraid she was still very much alive in 1976. She didn't die until '88. They had been separated a few times over the years, but they were still together in '76."

Her voice expressed surprise. "Oh! Johnny told me that she had died, that he was a widower for some time. He wore no ring."

The conniver probably slipped it into the vest pocket of his three-piece pinstriped suit.

An eerie silence permeated our conversation for several long seconds.

I broke the quiet. "Did my father say anything else about himself?"

Lucie's voice was meek. "He did talk a lot about his sons, you and your *broder*. He said you were *un bon etudiant*, a good student."

Dad had adored his kids and tried to be an example of working hard and playing even harder. I'm sure he became disappointed by seeing me grow out of his late-night lifestyle, though I had enjoyed the Troika's ambiance awhile. My big brother typically stayed away from such places. In becoming a profoundly religious man, the constant drinking, smoking, and off-colour kibitzing repulsed him.

Having seen and heard our mother weep at home on long and lonely nights, and not being able to hold my liquor and play the dual life Dad did, I eventually cut out early from my father's late-night "business meetings." When I became more self-sufficient, I gave Dad back his company's American Express card and let my Playboy Club membership expire. I didn't want his lifestyle and money anymore, nor have him keep tabs on my social life.

Lucie offered more. "Your *fader* mentioned that he was a pilot during the war and fought with Russia against the Germans."

"Yes, that's partially true, Lucie. He also fought for the Germans and Hungarians against the Russians, until he defected in '43."

"I did not know that part."

Dad had preferred to keep his controversial sides hidden in mixed company. Though he had told me about his past life in addition to his nightlife, I suspect there were things I didn't know.

There was a long breath at the other end of the phone. "Funny that your *fader* told me he was a widower."

I guess that had been his customary line at the Troika. "What an old fool he is!" my mother many times exclaimed, especially after she realized he wasn't coming back to her after he had left her a final time. I wonder if Mom might have been the fool herself in having had any faith in such a man.

"Yes, I understand, Lucie," I remarked coolly. My curiosity kept me going. "Do you mind if I ask whether you and he ever got romantically involved?"

She obliged without hesitation. "*Non.* We were just good friends. He was interested in me, but I was twelve years younger than him, and he was not my type. We just laughed a lot and had lots of fun."

Only twelve years younger? His last wife had been twenty-four years his junior! He probably hoped to turn this woman around, thinking she was a good investment. "So why did you stop seeing each other, Lucie?"

She took a long breath. "Johnny and I stopped getting together when I met my second husband. *Malheureusement,* he died a couple of years ago, so I was trying to reach out to old companions. Too bad about Aras dying too; he was *un homme gentil.* We always joked about that first time we met, with their thinking my daughter was my sister."

I smiled again. Aras and my father had been partners in ladies, lyrics, and libations. Both of them enjoyed Montreal's nightlife and its high life. They went out regularly to several of Montreal's Eastern European clubs that had their kind of flair. It was a rare week that Aras wasn't right by Dad's side, unless a woman sat between them, sharing their company and Dad's generosity.

I added, "Like my father, Aras was a good singer too."

Lucie came back quickly. "Harvy, I never heard him sing at the Troika."

"I guess that's because he preferred standing in front of a crowd—something he had done at the Hungarian Tokay."

Before they moved their business to the Troika, Aras and Dad had frequented the Tokay Restaurant, two blocks over on Stanley Street. The latter was famed for its imported gypsy music quartet and rich Hungarian fare. The style of the restaurant was of an authentic Hungarian cellar restaurant, or *pince* as they call it. After the Tokay had closed in the '70s, Dad and Aras moved their nighttime gatherings to the Troika.

I went on. "My father liked to sing at the table. Perhaps Aras didn't want to stand up at the Troika and steal the show from Sasha." Maybe he also didn't want to steal Lucie's attention away from Dad. "Aras was quite the guy, Lucie," I added.

"Yes, I could tell, Harvy," she lamented.

Lucie didn't know the half of it! It seemed as though Aras and Dad were on their best behaviour with her and her daughter. I knew Aras to be a chauvinist magician.

When I was seventeen, Aras showed me a magic trick. He took a wooden match and broke it almost in half so that it was held together by only a few fibers. He placed the broken stick on a table and then dabbed a drop of water at the crack. As the two legs of the match spread apart, Dad's companion smirked and chuckled. He then said something crude about the workings of a woman's anatomy when in the throes of hot passion. As an adolescent, I became enthralled; today, I cringed at the remembrance.

I could hear Lucie sigh slightly. "Harvy, I miss those good times we had."

I'm sure my dad did, and a part of me did too. When my father, at seventy-four, left his last wife after a seventeen-year relationship, Aras' spouse wanted nothing to do with Johnny. She was so angry with my dad for making a mess of his marriage to a woman she liked that she stood in the way of Aras going out with his long-time friend. From then on, Dad and Aras talked only over the phone. The Troika never saw those two together again.

I took another breath. "Yes, Lucie; those were the days, as they say."

My questions were exhausted. I didn't want to divulge more about what I knew yet suspected Lucie didn't. "Well, it has been good to talk to you." *I think*. "I wish you and your daughter well. *Au revoir*."

"*Au revoir*, Harvy. *Merci de m'appeler*, and my good wishes to you too."

Lucie and I never spoke again. But I continued to wonder how Johnny, the great pursuer, felt in losing his catch to another after such a patient pursuit. I'll never know since he's currently entertaining St. Peter at that greater Troika in the sky. No doubt, he has one eye scanning what's coming through the Pearly Gates while he orders refreshment to wet the old saint's whistle.

* * * *

Part II:

Days of Reckoning

2

Beginning of an End

October 1999.

I shivered as I stood in the large, dimly lit conference room of the prestigious Canadian law firm, Elliot Trudell. It was I who was cold and not the place. The firm was in the Canadian Imperial Bank of Commerce Building, one of Montreal's tallest skyscrapers. The English "Elliot" and the French "Trudell" names suggested the bilingual nature of the firm, essential for attracting national corporate and wealthy personal clients.

A wall of glass revealed a breathtaking view of the city's core. My eyes followed the straight streets rising steadily to meet the sheer face of Mount Royal, the erosional remnant of bedrock that stood behind the city's center.

It was a cloudy and chilly fall day outside as the year was rushing into the last winter of the twentieth century. The summer greenery of what the locals called "The Mountain" had radically shifted into the bright orange and vibrant red of fall. Decaying leaves blew in the wind. I wondered if this autumn day would create a radical shift in the course of my Canadian first-generation Simkovits family.

A young, slender, blond woman, dressed in a dark suit, had led me into this large meeting room. Though her name, Sylvie Dubois, written on her badge, was typical Quebec Francophone, she spoke in perfect Ontario Anglophone. "Mr. Simkovits, please wait here for Mr. Lefebvre. He will join you momentarily."

"Yes; thank you, Ms. Dubois," I said. I tried not to show my angst.

"Please, call me Sylvie." She gestured with an open hand toward a sideboard. "There are water and glasses there if you like."

I was impressed with her manner as much as with her flawless English, probably as perfect as her French. Was she showing her genuine, caring nature and natural voice, or did her tone come from years of ingrained training and working at this firm? I figured that Elliot Trudell was very selective in hiring staff that represented the professional image and bilingual mix of its international law practice.

"Thank you, Sylvie," I said hesitantly. I tried to smile but wasn't sure if I was succeeding.

She nodded, offered a small grin, and then turned back to the living-room-sized reception area from where we had just come.

I looked down at my hands; they were sticky with sweat. I could feel a rise of sourness in my stomach.

The trouble with my insides was a malady I might have inherited from my father. He was prone to an acidic stomach, which led to ulcers during his early manufacturing years.

Or perhaps my weak gut—along with battling excess weight at times of my life—had come from my mother who hadn't been adept at speaking English. She once batted her hand at me and cackled, "When the pediatrician asked me if I wanted to nurse you as a baby, I right away said no. I thought he had asked me, 'Do you want a nurse for the baby?'"

Dad had treated his acidic belly by sucking Tums tablets during the week and polishing off bottles of carbonated Vichy water on the weekends. When his pain had become intolerable, he chewed doctor prescribed horse-sized biscuits that he said, "Tastes like goddamn chalk."

With sufficient care and treatment, his ulcers went away. But his tummy troubles persisted, especially after eating the rich Slovak and Hungarian food he enjoyed. He kept a roll of Tums in his suit pockets, to use after a night of business entertaining. At Elliot Trudell today, I wished I had both Tums and Vichy water to chase away the gnawing feeling in my abdomen.

I shivered again. Whether my troubled gut had come via Mom or Dad, I had found out I didn't have the stomach for my father's decades of money mischief. I poured myself a glass of water, took a swig, and walked around the conference room to steady myself. Though I had turned forty-five years old a week earlier, I felt like a misbehaving student sent to the principal's office, or perhaps an accused waiting for a judge's verdict.

On the wall were wood-framed pictures of current and former senior partners of the firm. Included were Supreme Court justices, foreign ambassadors, federal cabinet ministers, and a Prime Minister or two. They hung above glistening, well dusted, lacquered wood sideboards. Eskimo soapstone sculptures, symbols of Canada's native people, decorated other tables. The carvings looked heavy, probably needing two sure hands to lift. Though I had the urge, I didn't want to try today.

I had emigrated from Canada to the U.S. over a decade ago, chased away by the rising Separatist mood in my home province. Though I had left my country, I still felt a connection and responsibility to the nation of my birth.

I was different from my immigrant father, who had been born and raised in Czechoslovakia between the Great Wars. He had fought on both sides during WWII and then escaped his country after the communist takeover. Unlike him, I felt a strong allegiance and obligation to my Canadian homeland.

In the middle of the room was an oval, dark mahogany, conference table. It was large enough to seat a TSE100 (the top 100 Toronto Stock Exchange companies) board meeting, along with a small militia of lawyers—something I was sure this firm could provide. I imagined multi-million dollar business deals consummated here. With the political and business influences of this firm, many may have revealed personal secrets in this very room. Perhaps today would be no exception.

I continued to wait for my recently re-acquainted friend, André Lefebvre. He was one of the firm's senior attorneys and a prep school chum of mine. Soon he would become a close confidant. What will he say about what I would reveal to him today? These were secrets I had been privy to for nearly three decades, but I now wanted freedom from their decades-long hold on me.

Would André remain a friend once he fully comprehended what I had known for most of my lifetime? Or might he make a summary judgement and ask me to depart this conference room unsatisfied?

Sweat started to form under my collar. I thought of my father and the circumstances that had brought me here to visit my lawyer friend. In my inside jacket pocket were two sets of documents. For years, Dad had hidden them not only from the Canadian government's eyes but also from my mother and brother's view. Only he, I, and his clandestine offshore bank knew about them and what they meant for him and me.

I came to see André today to relieve myself of the illicit weight I had carried for so long. That burden brought kinks to my spine and pangs to my gut. Today would be a day of reckoning between me and the money secrets I had kept for Dad every day of my adult life.

While I paced the room, I thought of the first document I was going to divulge to my friend, and how my finagling father had consummated that agreement.

* * * *

3

Father's First Love

November 1991.

Dad was waiting for me in his old factory office. The long, warm days of Canada's short summers had turned into the brisk air that signaled the cold and darkness of the coming winter. Two years earlier, in 1989, I had said my farewell to Montreal, the city where I had been born and raised. At 34, I had relocated to Boston to continue my career in the city where I had completed college.

I hadn't been willing to stick it out with the declining and discriminated English population in my predominantly French home province. Like my father, I disliked the nose-in-the-air Quebec government that only wrote and spoke in French to its citizens—unlike in the rest of Canada, where federal government correspondence was bilingual. Many English professionals had departed Montreal during the '70s and '80s, and I followed suit in 1989.

Besides leaving Quebec, my new life in the States allowed me a greater distance from my father's shadow and reach. No matter how much time I spent with him, he pressed, "Can you stick around a little longer, son?"

Though I breathed a little easier in Boston, I still wanted to stay in touch with Dad and be in the know about his business undertakings and investment activities. I regularly dropped in on him at his suburban office when I routinely returned to Montreal on business trips.

Today, as I walked to the office entrance, I noticed a new sign in the stackable signboard that held my father's holding company's name, JHS Industries, and his factory tenant, Gusdorf Canada. The new name on the sign was Canexco Enterprises. My insides shook as I wondered about the new business venture my father had conceived.

That new name was similar to CANEX Company, an offshore corporation Dad had opened in the 1970s. He had created CANEX to shelter his international corporate dealings from Revenue Canada (Canada's IRS). A decade later, my father told me that he had closed CANEX and moved his hidden money elsewhere.

Seeing the Canexco name on Dad's office sign, I hoped the new company had no relation to the previous one. Dad rarely told me in advance what was next up his slippery sleeve regarding his business and money shenanigans.

I walked into JHS's front office. It was one of three adjacent rooms that Dad maintained in the corner of his 50,000 square-foot factory building. The office walls were of dark-walnut veneer. A false ceiling held recessed fluorescent lighting. On the floor sat four desks of durable oak. Most of that furniture had been a part of Dad's business life since he had started his company in 1953, the year my big brother was born. I smiled as I thought about the stories those nearly 40-years old desks would tell if they could talk.

My father was bent over one of the desks, blueprints covering its surface. I looked at my dad, now approaching 72 years old. His figure was ten centimeters shorter and perhaps ten kilograms stouter than mine. His twenty-four-year younger wife had dyed his straight-back greying black hair to a dark Grecian Formula brown. It better matched the woman he married after divorcing my mom, now deceased.

Dad's presence—like his girth—loomed largely. A cigar burned between his fingers. My father looked pensive as he perused a blueprint. His mind appeared to be turning slowly and deliberately, like gears in a grandfather clock.

When my dad turned to look at me, his eyes widened, and his voice boomed, "Hello, son!" Before I could give him a customary kiss on both cheeks, he motioned toward what he had been perusing. My father continued to talk, his voice tones modulated by his heavy Eastern European accent.

"Come and see *dis*!" Dad exclaimed. "We had a *beeg* meeting here this morning with the Czechoslovak Consul, a few business people from Bratislava, and government representatives from Quebec City. We've started a new company, Canexco. It will be incorporated both here and in Czechoslovakia to build and market prefab, insulated particleboard panels." He hardly took a breath. "The panels can be used to knock together inexpensive homes and office buildings within days instead of weeks or months."

Weeks earlier, over the phone, my father had mentioned, "My latest project for Czechoslovakia." That didn't stop him from now telling me again. But this was the first time I heard the official name of his new venture. I let out a breath, now knowing that Canexco seemed unconnected to his former offshore CANEX Corporation. I hoped there wouldn't be overly egregious money misbehaviours with the fledgling company, but who knew for sure with Johnny Simkovits.

I walked to the desk and saw drawings of the structural panels and mock-ups of boxy-looking buildings. I knew that if I didn't pepper my father with questions, he'd tell me more on his own. He continued. "We're applying for reimbursement from the Quebec government for our start-up costs. The province is making cash available to companies like ours that can help stimulate exports to previous Soviet satellite countries."

The prospect of making a double killing—both in Czechoslovakia and here in Quebec—had my father grinning from ear to ear. His round, smiling face and slicked-back hair reminded me of Paul Sorvino in the role of crime-boss Paulie Cicero in the 1990 *Goodfellas* movie. Unlike Paulie, Dad never carried or owned a gun, which gave me relief.

I pointed outside. "So that's what that new Canexco sign is about."

"Yes, son, I had it put up this week."

I was interested in my father's business deals, especially his legitimate ones. I looked at the drawings. "So how much funding is the Quebec government giving you? And how did you arrange this Canexco project with them?"

Dad grinned. "I know one of the ministers in the provincial government; he's a Slovak fellow and a member of our CSPBA (Canadian Slovak Professional and Business Association). The minister made the connection for me to the people who run the Quebec export program. They'll pay us 50% of Canexco's marketing and start-up costs—up to $75,000."

He winked my way. "But you know me, son. I'll work on stretching that money further."

I smiled again, though my heart skipped a beat. I knew my father's ways of padding bills and asking for kickbacks. I suspected he would spend considerably less than his requisite 50% in that Quebec government assistance program. Dad did such things as if they were business as usual.

Unlike my brother, I never confronted my father about his money manipulations. Steve's complaints about Dad's deceptions never changed our father's MO. Unlike he did with me, Dad stopped telling Steve about the maneuvers he was enacting or planning.

Though I felt uneasy about my father's financial mischief, I wasn't going to waste my breath and risk not being in the know. Part of me admired Dad for his ballsiness. Anyway, his screwing of the provincial government was not yet a *fait accompli*, and it was up to Revenue Quebec to police its cash.

I dodged Dad's deception. "It's good you are keeping busy in your retirement. And it must feel good to help your country."

If my father didn't keep his mind busy, he might wither away behind that old office desk. In his JHS heyday, he had had nearly a hundred people working at his beck and call. His factory could pump out five hundred, 40- to 60-inch console stereo units in a given week for major Canadian manufacturers and retailers.

I had worked in Dad's factory both for many college summers and for two-and-a-half years after I dropped out of business school. Attending Harvard B-School had been my Dad's dream for me, but not mine. I now was in the organization and management development field, and glad my JHS days were a faded memory.

Dad sighed to my comment as he pointed to his forehead. His voice was mocking. "At my age, I need projects like this like I need a hole in my head." He took a breath. "I'm only doing this for Czechoslovakia. They are still a poor country and need more industry."

My father's tone rose. "Even though forty years of communism has ended, it's the same damn politicians and bureaucrats running my country. They just changed their shirts the day after their Velvet Revolution of '89 and then called themselves social democrats." He pointed at me and offered a small smile as he kept his voice raised. "And the younger generation there, kids like you, know nothing about business and making money."

Though I had recently turned 37, Dad saw those half his age as youngsters.

Dad's voice calmed a tad as he raised his hand like a general ready to make a speech to his troops. "My country now needs people like me to make serious investments there. Because the Czechoslovakia consulate here knew I ran a woodshop and cabinet-making factory, they came to me for help." He pointed to the drawings. "This panel business could be a big moneymaker and help Czechoslovakia get back on its feet. The communists destroyed the people's spirit there, so business people and expatriates like me need to get involved."

All my life, I knew where my father stood both with making business and with the former communist rulers of his homeland. While I was growing up in Montreal's West Island community, he told my brother and me, "Canada's was still a young country when your mother and I decided to come here after we escaped the bloody Soviets." He took a breath and added, "The population of Canada in 1949 was only thirteen and a half million people. I felt we would find more opportunities here than in the U.S."

Dad was right about Canada. Four years after he had disembarked the immigration boat, he was in business for himself, running his Montreal Phono Company. Dad later renamed it to JHS Electronex, those three initials representing the first names of Dad, my brother Steve, and me. And the *ex* at the end of "Electronex" had been Dad's way of avoiding the Quebec language police. They would have prosecuted and fined his company if he had employed an English moniker for his business.

Dad's electronics training during WWII, his cabinetry-making background derived from his father, his long days of nose-to-the-business-grindstone, and his unwavering spirit had helped him to build a sizable home electronics manufacturing business. Large manufacturers like RCA Canada and retailers like Sears Roebuck had been his most prominent customers.

But his business hadn't lasted. Twenty-five years after he had begun Montreal Phono, Asian component manufacturers began to supersede the console stereo market. My father wasn't able to latch onto the next big consumer electronics wave, causing his sales to decline. After thirty-one years of being "the boss," my father closed his company and retired at the end of 1984, just before his sixty-fifth birthday.

Now seven years into his retirement from manufacturing, Dad kept his mind and money involved in smaller business and real estate ventures, including the Czechoslovakia project, which he was now crowing about.

"That's great, Dad," I said. "I hope you make a million of those building panels. And it's good you can help Czechoslovakia. Who expected communism there to be over in your lifetime?"

Dad and I had had separate holiday trips to his homeland in the fall of '89, a month or two before the Iron Curtain came down. Except for the talk of "glasnost" (policy of openness) by the Secretary-General of the USSR, there were no signs of the tumbling down of communist walls.

Dad looked at me again. "All my Eastern European friends and I were flabbergasted when the CSSR [Czecho-Slovak Socialist Republic] lowered its flag, and the Russian Soviets walked out of the country." He banged his palm on the table as his voice became stern. "Good riddance to them! The communists killed the spirit and ambition of the people there."

A small bell hung from the ceiling inside the front-office entrance. I had placed that bell there, after Dad had renovated his building's other offices and rented most of them, including the attached factory building, to a tenant.

The bell chimed to announce someone was entering. Dad and I turned to see a tall, handsome, hefty man walk in. He looked more than ten years younger than my father, though he was as tall as I was and huskier than Dad. My father's face brightened, and so did his mood. He smiled and said with exuberance, "*Hallo* Ralph."

"Hi, Johnny," the debonair, dark-haired fellow began. "It's getting dark outside, and I saw your car in the parking lot. I wanted to drop in to say hi before I went home." He looked at me. "But I see that you are with someone."

My father pointed to me. "Ralph, this is my younger son."

Dad turned my way. "Harvy, say hi to the new President of Gusdorf Canada, Ralph Lieb. Since earlier this year, his company has been renting our factory building."

Dad's face held a soft expression. "Ralph drops in often to see me. We have known each other for years, all the way back to when he was Gusdorf's sales manager." Dad looked right at me. "If you remember, Harvy, we built knockdown [ready-to-assemble] furniture for Gusdorf a few years before we closed JHS."

I reached out for the man's hand and said, "Hello Ralph." He took mine and gripped it firmly. I added, "Yes, I remember hearing about you and Gusdorf; it's nice of you to visit my father." I smiled. "That must mean he's a good landlord."

Ralph smiled back. "Good to meet you, Harvy. And, yes, your father treats us very well." He pointed toward the factory part of the building. "He keeps the premises in great shape for our production."

Dad jumped in. "Last year, I helped Ralph with a loan to buy out Gusdorf's Canadian subsidiary from its U.S. parent. Then we moved his new company into our building here. They are growing like gangbusters, now running two shifts."

Ralph raised a hand in my direction. "One day, Harvy, you should come to see our operation." He looked at my father. "We may have to go to three shifts soon, Johnny. It's not been easy keeping up." He turned again to me. "We sell most of our products into your big U.S. market. The cheap Canadian dollar gives us a big cost advantage, but my management team is getting stretched."

My father was quick to see an opportunity. "Harvy can help you, Ralph. He's a big business consultant in Boston, and he has clients here in Montreal too."

I looked at Ralph and softened the proposition. "I work exclusively with owner-managed companies to help them become their best and succeed more in their business." I didn't say, *and run their companies a heck of a lot better than we did in our family business.*

I raised my hand. "I'm on the lookout for success stories for my company newsletter. Maybe I can see your operation and interview you." I grinned. "Anybody who works his way from sales manager to company president to run a booming business must have a good story to tell."

Ralph grinned back. "That's kind of you, Harvy. Give me a call when you plan to be in Montreal." He took a business card from his jacket pocket. "I'd be happy to talk."

I took his card and handed him mine. "Will do, Ralph."

Ralph nodded at me and then turned to my father, "Johnny, I see you are in good hands, so I'll say good evening."

"Thanks for dropping in, Ralph. Have a good night, and say hi to Nancy for me."

"For sure," Ralph said. He waved goodbye, turned around, and walked out.

The door closed behind him. "I can tell Ralph's a nice guy," I offered. "Hope he'll stick around a long time as a tenant in your building."

Dad raised his hand. "There's no one better; he's a real gentleman. We've helped each other a lot over the years. The loan I gave his business was for $250,000 at prime-plus-one. My only regret is that I didn't insist on becoming his partner."

I was surprised by my father's statement. I knew how hard he could be on close associates. He always advised me never to get into a minority position with business partners. Over the years, some of my father's business cohorts left his office with not more than the shirt on their backs.

Dad continued. "Ralph's a good manager. He has many long-time employees and is making good money in his production." He paused. "And his wife, Nancy, is a real gem too. They often invite Elaine and me out for supper." (Many years had passed since Dad had divorced my mother and married his next wife.)

I admired how my father enjoyed mixing business and pleasure, socializing with customers, suppliers, tenants, and the like. Elaine enjoyed that ride too. She was not only able to talk shop with the guys, but she also became friendly with the wives. Unlike Dad and Elaine, I preferred to keep my clients and personal world separate. But for my father, it was as if those two domains were one.

Dad continued. "Ralph and Nancy are such nice people." His tone turned serious. "But Ralph tells me that he has problems with some of his staff, so maybe you can help him. You should go see him."

He lowered his voice and touched my arm. "Ralph also told me that his health is not the best. Don't tell him I told you, but he's having heart problems. I even sent him to my doctor so that Nancy wouldn't know about it." He glared at me. "Please talk to Ralph soon. Maybe you can help him reduce his stress by getting stronger people under him." He touched his chest. "I would hate to see him have an attack."

I nodded, looked back at my father, kept my face staid, and said, "I will, Dad. Thanks for the connection. I'll call him when I schedule my next trip to Montreal."

My father had impressed me again. He showed concern for an old friend to whom he had given financial support for a business pursuit. At the same time, he offered a prospect to me. Maybe he was also seeking a bit of an insurance policy on his company loan to Gusdorf by having me help Ralph and his company. Through his business career, Dad had conducted many aboveboard business deals and made many good faith connections with and for business friends. I was proud of the legitimate side of my father's business personality.

With colleagues like Ralph, who my father knew well and respected, he was never greedy like a loan shark. But from the time the Soviet government of Czechoslovakia confiscated his first business in 1948, Dad detested any government's reach into his private pockets. He was quick to complain, "The government is my business partner, whether I want them to be or not. Every year, they take half of my company's profits and give me nothing in return."

On the other hand, my dad reveled in the prospect of having it the other way around, as he now did with the Quebec government helping to fund his new Czechoslovakia venture. He saw that as a small return on the sizable annual business and personal taxes he and his company had paid over the decades.

The air stood still in my father's front office. Dad looked at me as if he wanted to say more. I stayed quiet and waited, knowing that my father was more forthcoming if not pressed. He raised his hand in my direction. "Harvy, I need to ask you something before we *foot-scoff*."

Foot-scoff was his word-play for "fuck off" or "get the fuck out of here." All my life, I had heard him use the term. His male business colleagues had acquired the expression from him, using it when they were in mixed company so no one would be offended. When asked by an unsuspecting wife about the term's meaning, the knowing husband said, "It's just a Slavic word Johnny taught me for 'get the heck out of here.'"

Dad motioned for me to follow him into his back office. His private domain contained the same dark walnut wall paneling as the front office sported. Instead of an oak desk, there was a larger, glass-covered, cherrywood desk in the middle of the room, one side snug against a wall. Rather than the linoleum that covered the main office floor, this room had a rich burgundy carpet. Instead of metal chairs with thin cushioned seats and backs, the chairs here were of solid wood with well-cushioned red-vinyl seats and backs.

This desk and these chairs had been with Dad for nearly forty years. They showed nicks here and there, but Dad had held onto them. Perhaps they reminded him of his grand manufacturing days, or maybe he didn't like replacing things that still served him well enough. I imagined my father dying behind this desk, a contract or cheque ready to be inked under his limp hand.

My father leaned back against his old desk. He pointed toward a chair. I sat down where I had always sat for our private conversations ever since I had been a teen.

My dad's voice was low, almost in a whisper. "*Lassen* to me, son. I need you to come with me to my bank one afternoon this week, the place that holds my money over there." He took a breath. "Can you make it? I want you there so you can get some benefit after my death."

My curiosity heightened. I knew Dad's "money over there" meant his cash hidden in an offshore bank. My father's coyness meant he wanted to keep this knowledge just between us, as he had done in previous conversations concerning his clandestine cash.

My eyes glanced at the walls to Dad's left and right. There hung oil portraits of Dad's father, Jan, and maternal grandfather, Gabor. My mother's brother-in-law, who could craft an accurate likeness directly from a photograph, had painted the former.

The portrait of Jan portrayed the elder Simkovits as an urban man wearing a dark suit and tie. He sported a short black moustache, similar to Adolph Hitler's, though I knew they didn't have more than that in common. I never met or knew my father's father; he died in Czechoslovakia before my brother and I were born. Dad had told Steve and me that his father had been a strict but fair man with both the young Jani and his younger half-brother, Edo.

The latter portrait, of Gabor, hung on the opposite wall. A Montreal Slovak who knew our father well had painted it, also from a photograph. It showed Gabor dressed in his Sunday best. Dad's grandfather had been a farmer, having lived in the rural countryside outside of my father's hometown of Košice (*Ko-she-tsay*). The elder sported a long and thick, curly-end moustache that went out beyond his cheeks.

I knew Dad admired his grandfather, many times recounting, "During his over twenty-five years of retirement, Gabor crossed fruit trees to make new types of fruit." My father would grin. "And every night before bed he took a shot of strong plum brandy. He buried three wives and lived well into his nineties."

On the wall behind me hung a third portrait; it was of Dad in his early forties. It, too, had been painted by my mother's brother-in-law. In the picture, Dad wore business attire. His penetrating eyes looked to one side as he stared into the distance. Like the other two portraits, Dad presented no smile. His face looked intelligent, powerful, and determined.

I glanced briefly at my grandfather and great-grandfather's portraits. I pondered whether my face might hang here side-by-side with these Slovak men. I wondered what might stand out about me.

Dad's statement—about giving me some benefit after his death—caused me to sit straighter. My 37-year-old mind felt honoured. I suspected I was going to be taken into my father's confidence once more on a secret financial matter. His offer of going to his bank "over there" suggested my entrance into the hidden money realm he had built outside Canada. I had known about his offshore stash for nearly twenty years, but neither did my brother or my mother.

It wasn't that Dad loved me more than Steve; our patriarch just trusted me more with his secrets and hidden assets. I was his special son, the one closest to him. I even knew more than Elaine did about his offshore investments. For Dad, this son's allegiance trumped any woman's affection. All I needed to do was stay patient, vigilant, and deferential. If I kept my mouth shut about what he was going to tell me, I'd get to know more about what he had in store for my financial future.

Though I felt uncomfortable whenever my father employed his cryptic approach of *I'll tell you how much I want to tell you when I want to tell you*, I nodded as I always did. I spoke calmly and quietly. "Okay, Dad. What if I come by here on Thursday afternoon before I head back to Boston?"

"That's good, son." He leaned more toward me. "Can you be here at two o'clock so we can make an appointment at three? This way, we'll have time to talk before we get there."

"Sure, Dad," I replied. I instinctively knew not to ask or say more for now.

My father stood straighter and resumed his full, deep voice. "So are you coming out to supper with Elaine and me tonight? We can go back to that nice Italian place near us. They have great osso buco, and good veal *limone* that I know you and she like."

I reverted to my usual tone. "Italian sounds great."

"Okay, son; give me a couple of minutes to close the place, and then we can *foot-scoff*." He smiled warmly.

I smiled back.

* * * *

4

Legal Light Beacon

Various times in 1999.

Two months before I walked into the Elliot Trudell law firm in October of '99, in the warmth of Montreal's short summer, André and I had reconnected. It was at a bar mitzvah for the son of a mutual friend, Geoff Levi. Before André arrived at the reception, I had read his nametag next to mine at our designated table.

I thought how amusing it was that we would be here together, sitting right next to each other. We hadn't seen each other in twenty-five years. I didn't realize at this celebration that I would soon seek out André on a very personal and private financial matter.

Before André arrived at our table, I had hidden my place card to see if my old chum would recognize me. When he came and sat down, he didn't seem to know me. I grinned, grabbed his hand, and ribbed, "André, I can't believe you don't know who I am!"

When I saw the dismay on his face, I pulled out my place card and showed it to him. His expression went from befuddlement to deep warmth. We both laughed. "What a surprise and a real pleasure to see you again, Harvy," he said.

"André, I can't believe it's been—let me count—twenty-eight years since I last saw you at Bishop's. You look terrific, just the way I would have imagined." He was the same tall, well-built, thick black-haired fellow I remembered.

One year my senior, André had been a fellow student at our small, private high school, Bishop's College School, in rural Quebec. Before the end of our time there, both he and I had had our names imprinted on the school's wood-paneled dining hall walls for having reached a high level of academic proficiency as juniors and seniors.

I remembered André being a hard worker and a serious student as I was. During class sessions, our arms were full of textbooks and notebooks. His even-keeled disposition was especially present after school, as a captain of the football team, and a high-ranking officer in our part-time cadet corps. He rarely raised his voice to anyone, even the youngest among us. He enjoyed talking to the younger classmates and had an open ear for struggling and homesick students.

André gestured toward me and offered a big smile. "You're looking great, Harvy. I see you've stayed in shape."

"Thanks. I've done my best." I was at a stable weight now but could gain ten to fifteen pounds during times of distress or depression.

Before André and I could say more, the emcee announced the entrance of the bar mitzvah family. Everyone stood and clapped to the lively music. The bar mitzvah boy, preceded by his siblings and parents, walked in and waved to everyone.

After shouts of joy and more clapping, the Levi boy greeted the crowd and thanked our participation on this, his special day. Assisted by the rabbi, he blessed the bread and wine. He then asked us to enjoy our meals.

"Such a nice family," I said to André.

"Yes, it's been a pleasure to know them," he responded.

I grabbed the breadbasket, offered André a roll, took one myself, and passed the rest around. André now took his turn to rib me. "You've changed a lot, Harvy." He winked. "That may be why I didn't recognize you."

I had been a husky boy when I started Bishop's, fattened by my mother's Hungarian cooking. Over the five years I spent at the school, I slimmed down through school sports and bland cafeteria food. Then again,

André might be referring to my thinner, metal-rimmed glasses as opposed to the thick, black-rimmed, Coke-bottle-lens glasses of my adolescence.

My school chum grabbed the bottle of white wine sitting on our table, poured us healthy portions, passed the bottle along, then looked back at me. "How do you know Geoff, Joanie, and their family?"

"We met in the early 1980s," I replied. "We were in the Y.E.A. together for a couple of years."

"You mean the Young Entrepreneurs Affiliation?"

"Yes, Geoff and Joanie were on our local chapter's board when I joined. I got onto the board right behind them. We've been good friends ever since. How about you; how do you know them?"

André nodded toward the table where the Levi boy sat with his friends. He smiled. "My son and Geoff's son are close companions. Our two families became good friends through our kids. By the way, how's your brother Steve doing? I think I've only seen him once since our BCS days—at an early reunion."

André and my brother had been classmates. In our small high school of about fifty students per class across six grades, André may have spent more time with Steve than I had spent with my brother back then. Unlike me, who had played second-team then first-team soccer, they had played football on the school's top teams.

Students often bantered as to which of the two school sports was more macho. My brother might exclaim, "Soccer pussy!" when we passed each other in the school hallways. I'd retorted, *"Duhhh, foootbaalll!"* Irrespective of our preferred sports, both the soccer and football students came out to root loudly for each other's teams during interschool matches.

"Cheers, everyone!" I said and lifted my glass to all those at our table. I turned and leaned closer to André. I pointed to my drink and offered quietly, "I need a little of this before I talk about Steve." I wanted a moment to ponder how much I wished to say about my brother to his long-ago peer.

We spent the next few minutes talking to the other guests at our table. We made introductions and shared our connections with the bar mitzvah boy's parents. As couples went back to talking in pairs, André and I gravitated back to each other.

The seat on the other side of him was empty, as was the one next to me, so it was easy for the two of us to chat. We started on the salad. "You asked about my brother," I said.

André's eyes opened, and his ears perked up. "Yes, Harvy; I had seen a lot of him at Bishop's. I'm sorry I've lost touch."

That distance probably was as much Steve's doing as André's. My brother had found new cohort pastures in which to graze, and he rarely stayed in touch with previous barnyard colleagues.

I started with a factual summary. "As you probably know, Steve had a hard time with school." André nodded as I spoke. "He quit college midstream and worked as a purchasing agent for our father's manufacturing company here in Montreal." I took a sip of my drink. "About a dozen years later, Dad closed the company and retired. Steve then found similar positions at a couple of other manufacturing companies in the area."

I didn't say that Dad had helped Steve find those positions through his Montreal business connections. To me, at that time, my brother was the type who felt our father owed him a job or should support him outright if he didn't have one.

"I see," André said. "What's your brother doing now?"

I took a breath and glanced around the table to make sure everyone else was in other conversations. "I need to say something else first," I replied. I continued to eat my salad as my voice turned a little cynical. "Steve converted to Mormonism fifteen years ago."

My brother had made that change without any forewarning to our family. It unsettled our Catholic father, Jewish mother, and agnostic me. From my perspective, Steve had fallen off the deep end with his new religion.

I continued. "Steve married a Mormon woman, had two kids, left his last job, and now works full time for his church as a family historian and church elder." I tried to keep my tone from being sarcastic, but I didn't know if I was succeeding.

André looked at me with his eyes open wide. "From what I remember about him at Bishop's," he offered, "your brother seemed to be looking for something." He raised his hand slightly off the table. "And it sounds as if the two of you still don't get along."

I bit hard into my bread roll and took a bigger sip of my drink. "We took very different paths," I said. Though I felt the muscles in my jaw tighten, I worked to maintain a straight face. Whether I wanted the feelings or not, something grated on me whenever I talked about my brother.

Steve was only thirteen months older than I, but it felt as if two separate families had raised us. He and I had not gotten along as kids. We had poked, punched, or bugged each other continually. Our parents tried to keep us close, with Mom dressing us as twins while we were youngsters, and Dad enrolling us into summer jobs at his company when we became old enough to work. But Steve and I were as similar as an owl and a mule, him the latter, of course.

André was perceptive about my brother's search for a higher power throughout his young adulthood. But for me, Steve's religious conversion was the icing on the multi-layered sibling-rivalry cake that both of our parents had helped to bake.

I had seen a "Mrs. Anna Lefebvre" nametag at the empty chair next to André. Pointing to the open seat, I asked, "Is your wife not here?"

André looked away for a moment. "Unfortunately, I had to take Anna home because she felt ill after the bar mitzvah service. She has not been well lately." His eyes glanced downward.

I found myself doing the same. An image of my mother—also Anna— came into my mind. Though she had died over a decade earlier, I still felt pangs of her sudden and unexpected death. Almost every day since, something triggered my thoughts about her, making me sigh inside. Today's trigger was the place card next to André.

I looked at my school chum. "Sorry to hear about your wife's illness. I hope she feels well soon."

He took a breath and looked back at me. "Thanks, Harvy. Unfortunately, it's been a long haul for her." He didn't say more. His face turned pensive for a moment, and then he returned his focus to me. "What about you, Harvy? I see you are here alone, but there's a wedding ring on your finger."

I smiled. "My wife Beth couldn't make it to Montreal. She stayed home in Boston to take care of our three-year-old son."

Deep down, I hoped to raise my boy differently from how my dad had raised me—maybe even in ways I wished Dad's father had raised him.

André's face brightened as he lifted his glass. "Congratulations on your son."

"Thanks." I raised my glass to meet his. "Having a kid has been fun, but my wife and I are now tired all the time."

"Yes," André countered. "I know what that's like." I wasn't sure he was connecting his tiredness to his growing kids or his ailing wife. In a quiet tone, he added, "To tell you the truth, Harvy." He took a deep breath, and his voice turned somber as he pointed to his wife's place card. "I'll have to cut back at my work, or I'll need to find a less demanding position so that I can be around more for Anna."

"She must be very special to you."

André nodded. He was very unlike my father, who would never have sacrificed his work for my mother. Mom once told me, "Your father was too busy at his company the day you were born. When I was ready to give birth, he sent his friend to drive me to the hospital."

I felt touched that André and I could share personal details after not seeing each other for many years. I suspected that our boarding school bond made us feel as if we had stayed longtime friends.

The music started again; the tune was "Hava Nagila." People were up and clapping once more. Many couples and kids got out on the dance floor and danced in a circle. Concentric circles of guests held hands and surrounded a smaller circle of the bar mitzvah family. Everyone danced vigorously around the Levi family in one direction or another. Guests held white handkerchiefs that they either flicked into the air or grasped between two people as they danced. Everybody was laughing, some even shouting with glee. The Levi family, jackets peeled off the father and son, were bursting with glee.

I thought of my mother again and smiled inside. She would have been happy that I was experiencing a fun part of her Jewish heritage. During WWII, she and her family's survival in Budapest, Hungary—employing false Christian papers—certainly hadn't been fun for them.

Raised in my father's Catholicism, my brother and I hadn't known about our mother's Jewish heritage until we were in our late teens. After my mother's death, I began to enjoy Jewish traditions, especially celebrations like this one. Having an analytical mind and little penchant for languages, I figured I would never have made it through Hebrew school.

Standing by our table, André and I clapped to the music. I knew that he was Catholic—we had attended Sunday services while at Bishop's. Though I had danced at Jewish weddings, it felt odd to jump out there now and join the circle. I was without my wife, and André's Anna was missing too.

André and I watched the dancing from our table, smiles on our faces, our hands clapping to the melody. I leaned over to him and raised my voice over the music. "What have you been doing professionally since Bishop's?"

André grin widened, and he leaned toward me. "Ever since high school, I wanted to be an international corporate attorney and live overseas." He leaned closer. "After I had passed the bar here in Montreal, I got a great opportunity at Elliot Trudell. They transferred me to Hong Kong to build our firm's international corporate tax presence there before that city changed hands from the Brits to the Chinese. Anna and our two young kids came with me."

"That must have been exciting," I almost shouted, my voice straining over the music.

His tone matched mine. "We had a great time there, Harvy. We stayed a few years and travelled the Far East as much as we could while our kids were small. Afterward, I made partner with the firm. We then relocated back to Montreal to get the boys started in a bilingual school." His face dropped. "I still travel a lot—probably too much." Maybe he was thinking of Anna again.

The music stopped. As people headed back to their tables, André and I resettled in our chairs. He turned to me. "What about you, Harvy? I heard through the Bishop's grapevine that you went into engineering at MIT."

It was my turn for my face to drop a bit. With top marks in high school math and science, I was encouraged (perhaps pushed) by my father's "*Lassen* to me, son." He had told me, "You are smart enough to go to the best engineering school in the world."

I turned to André. "I got both my Bachelor's and Master's Degrees in Electrical Engineering and Computer Science at MIT." I took a breath. "But I had gone there mostly because my father wanted me to. Though I was good at engineering, I didn't have a passion for it. I didn't see it as a lifelong career."

"I see, Harvy. So what happened after that?"

"I exercised my technical credentials for a couple of years after I graduated. I worked at Procter & Gamble's engineering division in Ontario."

"So you made soap and detergent?" he quipped with a grin.

I smiled back. "Those and more."

I explained that I was in charge of installing and maintaining instrumentation for P&G's manufacturing processes that made Crest toothpaste, Head & Shoulders shampoo, Crisco oil, in addition to soaps and detergents. I offered, "The two years I spent there was kind of dull."

My voice rose. "The bright side was that I did have two steady girlfriends." They had been back-to-back relationships, unlike my father, who was rarely satisfied with exclusivity.

André brought his thumb and first two fingers of his right hand together and pointed them upward, and said, "Yes! It takes us flamboyant Montreal men with our *je ne sais quoi* to bring out the fire in those Ontario Anglophone women."

We both laughed. I didn't reveal that, for several years, I had been pretty dry in the women department until Ontario helped me out.

The bar mitzvah parents had been walking around to the tables; they now reached ours. The short but svelte Geoff was well suited to his even shorter but beautiful wife. They were full of smiles.

Along with the others at our table, André and I shook hands firmly with Geoff and gave big hugs and kisses to Joanie. After the customary bar mitzvah congratulations, Joanie asked, "Are the two of you getting to know each other? We thought you might enjoy each other's company."

"Even better," André said. "We know each other from private high school over 25 years ago."

"That's amazing," Geoff said. "You'll have to tell us more."

"Yah!" Joanie beamed another grin. "I want to know about the juicy stuff."

"We'll be sure to save the best for you guys, once we figure it out ourselves," I offered with a grin. "We both spent five years at an all-boys high school situated in the sweet-smelling pig and cow pastures of rural Quebec. It was pretty dull stuff."

"Couldn't have been that bad if you two guys came out of it," Joanie said with a smirk.

André and I chuckled. Geoff and Joanie waved farewell and continued to the next table. None of us, including me, knew yet about the juicy stuff that would come from our unexpected meet this evening.

André and I sat down. "Such nice people," he repeated.

"Yes, the best," I said.

André topped off our wine glasses. He looked my way again. "So Harvy, where did you go after P&G? It sounds like you got out of engineering."

I took another sip of wine and held onto my glass. "Unlike you, André, I meandered in my career."

I told him how, at my father's urging, I had gone to Harvard Business School, but dropped out midstream. "Business school was a big transition from engineering. It took me only a month at the B-school to realize that Harvard wasn't for me, though I stuck it out for half the first year."

I told him how I then worked with my father and brother in our family business until I figured out what I wanted to do next. "It was good that I worked in the factory while Steve had an office job. He and I got along in the beginning, but by the end, we couldn't agree on anything." I raised my hand. "And our father yelled at his employees too many times for my liking."

"Family businesses can be like that." André's tone was calm and kind.

I gulped down most of my second drink, or was it my third? I looked at André. "What I finally figured out was that my father wanted me to do was go to engineering school, then to business school, and then to law school as you did. Then he wanted me to work for our family business, where he would tell me what to do because he had 'many more years of experience.'" I made quotation marks with my index fingers as I said that last phrase, my tone mocking.

"Sounds like he wanted you to live his dream rather than find your own."

"You're so right and perceptive about that, André." I grinned. "I think you could have been a psychologist in addition to a lawyer."

He smiled back. "In my client situations, I've seen similar stories. And, I remember seeing your father when he came to visit you guys at Bishop's."

André held his hand open, chest high, and then shook it in the air as if he were gripping a softball firmly. "There was this intensity about your dad." He looked back at me with a soft expression in his eyes and face. "It's not easy to have a father like yours."

"You're right about that!" I blurted.

I didn't say it, but I wondered if I could survive my father's intensity. He certainly had had big hopes for me, and I wasn't sure if I had or hadn't lived up to those expectations.

I didn't add more. I didn't want this happy occasion to turn into a father-, brother-, or self-bashing one. Though it felt as if I were doing more of the talking, André seemed to be genuinely interested. I suspected that his natural curiosity made him a lawyer who was a cut above his colleagues.

My voice reenergized. "During the time I worked for my father, I discovered the field of human resource and organizational development." I smiled. "That specialty appealed to me more than engineering or business. I later went back to college in Washington, DC, to get a master's in that field."

The waiters served the entrée—beef bourguignon. *"Bon Appétit,"* I said to everyone at the table as I lifted my near-empty glass. We clinked glasses once more and dug in. Realizing I was starting to get a buzz, I put my glass aside. I didn't know if I was pleased or disappointed that I couldn't hold my wine as my father could hold his vodka at my age.

After a few moments of table conversation, André and I turned to each other again. "You were mentioning your master's program, Harvy. How is organization development different from an MBA?" He slowly chewed the beef, showing an umm, umm good look on his face. He pointed to himself. "I completed an MBA jointly with my JD in law."

"That's a great combination, André. I guess you are a sucker for education like I am."

He chuckled. Maybe his father had urged him to collect university degrees as my father had done with me. I didn't ask if my notion was correct.

I chewed a little more aggressively on my meat. "To answer your question, organization development (or OD, which is what the people in the field call it) was my way of saying no to my father's dreams for me and in doing something for myself." I explained, "OD is like the organizational behavior subject you took in business school but expanded into a full master's program, with courses on how to train people and consult to organizations. That's the work I now do. My focus is on educating owner-managed-business executives and managers on how to operate their companies better."

André nodded. "It sounds fascinating. Glad you were able to break away from your father. Where did you go after obtaining your masters?"

"While I was completing my degree, I got in on the ground floor at a startup management education firm that opened offices in both Montreal and Boston." I pointed toward him. "Later, I became a junior partner there."

"What's the name of the firm?"

I lowered my voice. "It's a small outfit; you probably haven't heard of it." I didn't want to mention its name, for it now was my direct competitor. And I hadn't left the firm on the best of terms with some of the partners. "Anyway, André, I decided to leave and go independent. I've been on my own for nearly ten years."

"It must have been challenging to make those changes," he said. I sensed his sincere attention and deep respect, unlike how I sometimes felt toward my circuitous career path.

"You can't imagine," I responded, half-smiling and half-serious. "Though my latest master's program was a lot more book reading and paper writing, I was glad to have made the change." My grin broadened. "I guess I like to work more with people than with things."

"It sounds as if you are now enjoying what you are doing," André offered.

"Yes, I'll drink to that." I poured only two fingers of wine into my glass and raised it to my reacquainted friend. "And, it's particularly good to be on my own, especially to be independent of my father and his business."

"Here's to finding yourself," André added, lifting his glass to mine. We both downed our drinks.

Music started again. André and I smiled and clapped along with everyone else.

My unexpected meeting with André at that celebratory evening kindled my trust and respect for my old school colleague turned big-firm lawyer. Over the years, my businessman father had warned me, "Bigshot lawyers have a licence to steal. You need to be careful because they try to take advantage. They enlarge their projects and complicate their advice so they can charge more."

I remembered my father shouting obscenities over his office phone at his lawyer about his inept legal advice or large legal bills. Dad might refuse to pay. I once asked him about those money skirmishes. To my inquiry, my father offered a slight grin. "He and I have been doing business this way for years. Sometimes, he wins; sometimes, I do."

André didn't fit that gamesmanship mold. When we said our farewells at the end of the evening, we agreed to meet again on one of my future trips to Montreal. Little did I realize how soon that would be.

* * *

I continued to stare out the Elliot Trudell conference room window as I waited for André to arrive. It was taking so long that I felt as if I were the main character in *Waiting for Godot*. In those slow-ticking moments, I stood, walked around the room, and perused the pictures on the walls and statues on the tables. I looked out the window again to view the city's downtown, and then I sat back down.

I repeated my motions to keep my nervousness at bay. The moral and legal offences I planned to divulge to André today rivaled what one might confess to a family priest. Though my father owned those money hiding and tax-avoiding transgressions, I had complicit knowledge of them. I tried to quell my shivering ribs and tightening gut by remembering the good time André and I had had at the Levi bar mitzvah.

I stood once more and looked again out of the large conference room window. I pondered the other quirk of fate that had led me to André this day.

Since early in '99, I had been talking to an American lawyer, Jay Henry, about my father's furtive finances. Dad was 79 years old, and his health had been waning for several years. A stroke in '93, at the age of 73, had left him partially disabled. Every muscle on his left side now slumped; he could only manage a three-quarter grin, and he needed a cane to walk.

My father had had a lifetime of strenuous workdays and late nights of "business gatherings" at the ethnic clubs, bars, and restaurants of Montreal. In his prime, he had smoked up to five packs of cigarettes each day and polished off a bottle of vodka with friends while gallivanting at Montreal's lively establishments. He had had several wives and many live-ins. Dad seemed to have burned through his God-given case of candles. How much longer he had left on this earth was a matter of medical debate. It might not be too long before he would be with the angels or perhaps the alternative.

Jay Henry, a tax attorney from New York City, was researching and writing a book on managing and preserving family wealth. The daughter of one of the famous and wealthy Bronfman brothers had referred me to him.

She and I had met at a Boston seminar on the transfer of family wealth between generations. When I shared with her, with subtle hints, my concerns regarding my father's money shenanigans, she mentioned Jay and put me in touch with him.

The first time Jay and I talked was on a sunny but cool spring day in Boston, while he was in town researching his book. We met over breakfast at the Ritz Carlton. I sat waiting for him in the hotel's elegant restaurant.

The restaurant's lighting was as soft as the fine linens on the table. Polished silverware sat on the table. The walls were full of original scenic New England prints. While I looked around the room, I saw others wearing business attire as I was. I wondered if anyone else would be divulging family secrets this day.

Jay entered, and I waived him to our table. He was about ten years my elder. He wore a simple two-piece navy blue suit and tie. I expected a New York City lawyer to wear a shiny suit with gold cufflinks and diamond tie pin. He sported none of those, looking more NYU professorial than a Wall Street professional.

We shook hands, and Jay sat across from me. To put me at ease, he pulled a quarter from his pocket and put it on the table in front of me. "Please take the coin and place it in my hand," he said.

I did.

He added, "You are now paying me for this legal consultation. Everything you tell me will be held in strict confidence according to U.S. law."

Though it seemed as if I might be in a scene from the *Godfather* movie, I felt relief. Jay's gesture was unusual in my understanding of big-city lawyers.

Over breakfast, I gave him cursory details of my father's offshore financial affairs. Though Jay's manner had loosened my tongue, my voice still quivered. "Now that I'm living in the U.S., I'm concerned that my father's 'financial shenanigans' will affect me here with the IRS." I used my fingers to put quotes around those two crucial words as I worked to keep my face sober. There was still a part of me that admired my father's money-hiding brazenness.

I could hardly look into Jay's eyes. "I've read that the IRS goes after suspicious tax-maneuvers more aggressively than our Revenue Canada. I don't want to have a mess on my hands after my father passes away. I want to clean up anything shady that he has created, even if it has to wait until after his death." I kept my eyes earnest. "I need to know whether I can and should do something now while he's still alive. And I need to figure out how to involve my older brother in what I know."

Jay raised and swung his hand slowly in the air, like a college professor or caring preacher. He urged, "Harvy, you need to distance yourself and your brother from your father's suspect finances as much as legally possible." His voice was calm but firm. "Get your names off of any suspicious accounts, and have yourselves removed as the co-executor of your father's will."

He urged, "Find a close professional or family friend you trust to play that role. That way, any questionable tax-maneuvers or suspect financial accounts your father has created will stay connected with him in Canada. The U.S. tax authorities will see no direct connection between you and his affairs."

Jay's tone quieted. "How much does your brother know about your father's suspect business matters?"

It was a crucial question. I sighed. "Because Steve is very religious, my father never trusted my brother regarding his offshore dealings." Dad had kept him in the dark all these years. "From what my father told me, Steve knows little to nothing about it."

I looked down at the table and added, "But I don't know what he truly knows. He and I have never talked or even hinted to each other about what we know or suspect of our father's money maneuvers."

"So it looks like you have to carry this out on your own until the time is right to include your brother more fully."

"I guess so," I said. "My luck, right?"

What Jay had said was the understatement of my life. Dad had made me promise not to divulge to Steve anything I knew about his offshore money. But the weight and pressure of that knowledge were crimping my shoulders and pounding my head. I hoped I wouldn't burst a blood vessel in my brain and end up half limp like my stroke-affected father.

The corner of Jay's mouth rose to my quip, but his face stayed serious, and he didn't respond. After paying for breakfast, I thanked him for his time and generous advice. We agreed to meet again in a few months, on his next research trip to Boston.

* * *

I looked at the leaves swirling in the autumn wind outside the Elliot Trudell building. My sides shivered again. I had attempted this past summer to follow Jay's advice. On one of my business trips to Montreal, I visited my father at the small suite of offices he maintained in his old factory building.

Now fifteen years into his retirement from manufacturing, Dad still needed a desk to sit behind where he could manage his one remaining building and the many landholdings his company still owned. He had had a stroke six years earlier, which paralyzed his whole left side for a time.

After that hit to his health, my father stopped investing in new business ventures, including the prefab building panel project he had started for his home country. His office was now a place to host old business colleagues who still came around to visit.

It had been late in the day when I arrived at Dad's office. My father was alone; his long-time bookkeeper—perhaps now more an old-man sitter—had departed the premises before rush-hour traffic.

My father sat behind his hefty, now nearly fifty-year-old, wooden office desk. His cane leaned against the corner of the wall behind him. His bad left leg, never fully recovered from the stroke, was buttressed on an open bottom desk drawer as he leaned back in his tall, cushy office chair. His face looked long and tired, with the skin and muscle on his left side slumping a bit more each time I saw him.

He was watching the early news on a small, rabbit-eared TV that sat on a desk across the room. His glassy eyes made me wonder how much of the newscast was sinking into his psyche.

When my father saw me, he offered a big *"Hallo* son!" in his gruff voice, made that way by the stroke. He engaged both of his hands to place his bad leg on the floor, but he didn't stand up. I returned the hello, walked over to him, and bent down to exchange kisses on our cheeks. "How are you, Dad?"

"I'm still kicking, son. And I'm so happy to see you."

Though Dad had regained strength on his weak side after years of physical therapy, his left leg was only useful to stand on. There was no kick left in that one.

My father motioned downward. "I want to show you something." He extended his good right leg and presented a platform shoe that he had obtained for his right foot. "This new shoe I got will help me to walk better."

"Looks good, Dad," I fibbed. He had shown me the special shoe the last time I saw him, which was a month earlier. Even with the platform under his right foot, he still dragged his left leg as he walked with a cane. I thought he might soon need a wheelchair.

I turned down the TV volume. Dad then started on his customary questions. "How long are you staying in Montreal?"

"Just another day; I'm driving back to Boston tomorrow."

"Can you come for supper tonight?"

"Yes, I can. I'll follow you home in my car."

I actually had to lead Dad home, for he was becoming more confused and forgetful. When he drove the three kilometers from his factory office to his apartment each weekday, he sometimes got lost. A simple wrong turn would lead him onto the highway ramp and many kilometers out of his way. My father then called Suzie from his car cell phone. (Suzie was Dad's eight-year younger significant other who he now lived with after he had divorced Elaine.)

Suzie had been living with Dad for four years. They had gotten together six months after his marriage to Elaine had failed, as predictably as his thirty-year marriage to my mother had dissolved. After Dad's call home for Suzie's help, she'd come and find him parked on a side street in North Montreal. She then led him back to the assisted living apartment where they resided.

"That's great," my father said to my affirmative response to his supper invitation. "I'll call Suzie in a minute and let her know." He looked at me again. "Are you staying with us tonight?"

I sometimes stayed with my father and Suzie in their spare bedroom. Staying with them allowed me not only to spend more time with Dad but also to keep my travel costs down for my Montreal clients. "Sure, if you have room for me." I quipped with a smirk.

His straight face told me he didn't quite get my wisecrack. "We always do, son. You know that."

I just nodded.

Dad changed the subject. "How's everybody at home?"

"Everyone's doing fine. Your grandson Mathew will be starting pre-school in the fall."

"That's great," he said. "Do you know when you will be coming to Montreal next time?" It was another one of his regular questions.

"Not sure right now, maybe next month; I'll let you know."

"So let's go then. I'll call Suzie and tell her we're coming home."

I looked at my father and said, "Dad, before you call, I have an important question for you."

He didn't hesitate. "Sure, Harvy, what is it?"

I shuddered. From the time I had moved to the U.S. ten years earlier, it was unlike me to ask my father for anything. Unlike my brother, who regularly asked Dad for cash handouts to help support his family, I wanted to show my father I could make it on my own.

According to my recent meeting with Jay Henry, I had to get this special request out of my mouth. I consoled myself that it wasn't money for which I was asking. "I want to ask you if it would be possible to remove Steve and me as co-executors of your will."

My father's eyes looked troubled as he took a few seconds to take in my question. He then looked at me with intensity in his face. "Why are you asking that?"

I took a breath and responded calmly. "I don't want any disagreements between Steve and me in carrying out your last wishes." I took a long breath. "Would it be possible to ask your notary, Peternik, if he would be your executor? You've known him a long time, and he helped us rewrite your will after you had your stroke in '93."

Six months after his debilitating illness, my father had asked me, and not my brother, to help him rewrite his will. I continued. "If Peternik were your executor, Steve and I would have little opportunity to disagree about anything written in your will."

My father knew how my brother and I rarely agreed on matters related to his JHS holding company, though Dad had wished it was otherwise. He now was resigned to see his two sons never getting along, and us rarely being together in the same place.

My father stared at me for a long moment. "Are you sure you want to do that?"

I felt a little surge of confidence. "Yes, Dad, I think it would be a good decision for all of us. I don't think you'd want Steve and me to argue after you're gone."

I was giving him my best line, and I hoped he would take a loyal son's lure. I couldn't be straight with him about needing to distance myself from his hidden estate and questionable investments. That was counter to his longtime plans of having me take over his offshore legacy one day. He many times had put his hand on my shoulder and told me, "If and when something happens to me, son, you know where my money is over there. I'm leaving it for you."

If he knew my real motives for asking him to change his executors—my growing fear of getting caught and prosecuted by tax authorities—he'd assure me loudly. "There's absolutely nothing to worry about," he'd insist. "Only you, I, and my offshore bank manager know what I have over there."

But I was no longer confident. I was growing weary of my father's years of hiding money and evading taxes. Recent newspaper articles had mentioned that both Canadian and U.S. authorities were going after tax evaders more rigorously. More so, in recent years, Dad had added my name to some of his illegitimate assets and agreements. Those moves contributed to my uneasiness about being associated with his hidden hoard.

My father looked down at his desk and then back at me. His voice was calm. "Okay, son, if it makes you feel better, I can call the notary."

I was surprised and relieved. "Thanks, Dad," I said with a calm voice. I left the topic there.

The next morning, while Suzie was in the kitchen making breakfast, I quietly reminded Dad of his promise. He again said he would call Peternik.

I sensed Dad's capitulation had been too easy. A month later, I called the notary. He shared that my father hadn't asked him to make any changes in his will.

I sighed. I figured my father wanted no one besides Steve and me to oversee his estate. Maybe he didn't want our spending money on a professional executor, or he plain forgot.

Though I felt discouraged by his failure to keep his promise, I assumed there was nothing more I could do. I wasn't going to push my father any further regarding the change Jay had wanted for me.

I guess I'll have to wait for Revenue Canada or the IRS to knock on my door. I hoped there wouldn't be jail time in store for me. Twenty-four years earlier, my father had risked such on himself when Revenue Canada caught him in a corporate tax dodge. He had been lucky to get away with just a steep fine but no jail time.

I stood and walked around the Elliot Trudell conference room once more. I wondered if I could have said or done anything different to make my father comply with my wishes to change his estate executors. I closed my fist and pounded it lightly on the conference table. I found it hard to come up against my father, even in his old and tired age.

My brother had less trouble confronting our father—though Dad rarely listened to either of us no matter what approach we took. Dad may have wanted to keep things simple regarding his will, but he certainly made things more complicated for me with his concealed offshore money.

As I continued to wait for André, I thought of Jay once more. We had met again at the same Ritz Carlton restaurant in September of '99, a month after the Levi bar mitzvah, where I reconnected with André. I told him about my unsuccessful attempt to change the executors of my father's will.

Jay had looked right at me. "The best thing I can tell you, Harvy, is that if you and your father ever got caught by the tax authorities before your father's death, they'll most likely view him as the primary perpetrator and you as an unwitting accomplice. You would have less to worry about, as long as you don't have your name on his suspicious accounts or your signature on suspect contracts."

I gulped hard. Jay's words had consoled me a bit, but I still felt guilt-ridden and open to prosecution. One illegitimate money agreement Dad had executed had my name written as the beneficiary. I also held a power of attorney over one of Dad's smaller offshore accounts—in case he needed me to get cash for him. Might my stained fingers have come too close to my father's dirty hands? Had I gotten his black money muck under my fingernails?

Jay then added, his voice firm, "In the eyes of the law, you wouldn't be accused of tax evasion as your father would be, as long as you have distance from his affairs."

I nodded. *And what about in my own eyes?* Could I rid myself of my own self-loathing for what I had known for the last twenty-seven years?

Jay looked at me; the intensity in his eyes muted. "As a U.S. attorney, I don't think I can help you further with the Canadian side of your father's finances."

My tone was pleading when I asked, "Might you know anyone in Canada, preferably Montreal, who could help me?"

He viewed me with caring eyes. "I'll look into it and get back to you."

"Thank you," I said. We ended our conversation there.

Within a week, Jay e-mailed me a name I hadn't expected. His message said, "Go talk to André Lefebvre at Elliot Trudell. He's a good international tax lawyer."

Borrowing an old expression from my father, *I was flabbergasted.* Of all the tax lawyers in Montreal, and even at Elliot Trudell, Jay pointed me back to my school chum with whom I had recently reconnected at the Levi bar mitzvah. I called André that day and made an appointment to see him on my next trip to Montreal.

Was this a sign? Could André become a legal light beacon to help me navigate the illicit waters of my father's furtive offshore fortune?

* * *

I walked once more to the window in this Elliot Trudell's conference-room and stared down at the cold city streets. I kept reaching for and glancing at the sensitive papers I had tucked away in my breast pocket. Late the previous night, I had "borrowed" these papers from my father's private office. Dad concealed those incriminating documents behind a dropped ceiling panel above his hip-high cast-iron office safe.

Years earlier, while I had been visiting him at his office, Dad pulled up a chair next to that safe. He had me stand on the chair as he pointed upward with his cane to a loose ceiling panel. He then told me to move the panel up and back to retrieve and then re-hide his secret documents. He said, "Only you and I know where they are."

I wasn't sure if Dad's assertion was correct. *Might that be the first place a Revenue Canada officer would look if they ever raided Dad's office?* What I was sure of, was that my father, with his bad leg and deteriorating balance, could no longer risk standing on a chair to get to the papers on his own.

Those precarious papers now filled my inside jacket pocket. They detailed my father's secret offshore bank dealings. For the first time, I was going to share this evidence with an outsider. No one, not my wife, my brother, or my closest confidants, knew what I knew or what I was about to reveal. I stood alone at Elliot Trudell with these Johnny Simkovits skeletons tucked into my jacket. Dad's decades of illicit money hiding caused my chest to swell with dread.

My father was still lucid and mobile in his older age, but his mental and physical decline was accelerating. At social gatherings, he might ask Suzie or me, "Who was that person I was talking to?" His health now seemed more in the hands of his maker than his doctor.

I felt privileged to know about my father's offshore finances these last twenty-seven years. I was lucky to have been promised ownership of his legacy after his death, but I loathed continuing to conceal his offshore stash. Keeping these secrets from my wife and brother made me feel soiled, as if cow dung forever clung to my shoes.

After Dad's death, his hidden stash would be placed squarely at my feet. That offshore money felt like the papers stuffed in my jacket—awkward, burdening, and needing protection. I only hoped my years of growing angst could survive Dad's years of denial of any wrongdoing.

I had to act prudently. My father would be livid if he knew I was disclosing knowledge of the hidden assets that he had painstakingly assembled over most of his life in Canada. I felt a void in my chest for breaking the trust he had bestowed upon me. If he knew I was here today at Elliot Trudell, he'd hit the roof, condemn my manhood, and perhaps disown me. Though Dad was a shadow of the man he once was, and I could probably push him over with a sturdy fly swatter, could I ever again look him straight in the eye?

The frightened child in me wanted to flee this conference room, but the moral and ethical man in me made me stay. I looked at my watch; I sat down and stood up again; I tugged at my collar, trying to loosen my necktie's grip. *Where the hell is André!?*

After what seemed an eternity, though perhaps had been only thirty minutes, my friend entered through the conference room door. He wore a big grin and offered a robust "Hello, Harvy." He grabbed my hand firmly. "Sorry to keep you waiting. I was on an international call."

"No problem." I lied, trying not to show my unease.

For a moment, we remained standing, chatting about family. André asked about my wife and son. He said his wife, Anna, was doing better. He confided again that he was planning to make a professional change to spend more time with her. I felt honoured by his trust in me. I hoped my friend would feel the same after he heard what I had come here to disclose.

I thought again of my mother. If she were looking down from the heavens today, she would have been glad to see me here with my friend. She received few benefits from Dad's growing wealth after they had come to Canada from Czechoslovakia post-WWII. That was fifty years ago, almost to the day.

During her over three decades of marriage to my father, Mom had washed and ironed her husband's dress shirts every week. She cooked his favourite Hungarian goulash and Slovak *halusky* when he was home on the weekend. And my mother Spic 'n Spanned and Cometted their home to a spotless clean. She sewed her dresses from scratch, and patched rips and replaced missing buttons in our family's knock-around clothes to save every penny she could.

A professional seamstress, Mom had supported Dad during his early business years when their money was tight. From the time she gave birth to my brother in '53 and then to me in '54, Dad was doing better in business, so she became a housewife fulltime.

While my father had grown and prospered as a Canadian entrepreneur, Mom stayed home to raise us kids. She told Steve and me, "I saved on myself so that your daddy could have more money for his business." She also had to plead with him to obtain a few more dollars for her weekly house expenses. Little did she know, as I did, the details of the underhanded monkey-business and nighttime funny-business in which her husband was involved all these years.

After countless fights and two separations in their three decades together, Dad walked out on Mom for the last time in 1980. He later married the much younger Elaine.

I understood my mother's profound and deep sadness for having lost the person she called, "My only true love." But what I was doing with André on this wind-swept October day was more for my peace of mind on earth than for hers in heaven.

André motioned us toward two chairs by a sideboard next to the window. Feeling the heat and sweat under my collar, I wanted to take off my jacket but didn't want the bulky, clandestine papers to tumble onto the floor.

How well my friend handled the first two-page document that I was about to show him would determine whether or not I'd present him the second thicker wad. I didn't want to fan out all my troubles in front of him at once.

After another moment of chit-chat, André asked, "So tell me how I might be of help to you, Harvy."

I took a deep breath and looked at my friend. "I brought some sensitive documents on which I need a legal opinion. Can you look at them and give me your advice?"

"Sure," he said with a slight smile yet serious face. "Show me what you have, my friend, and I'll do the best I can."

"André, can I trust you'll keep what I show you just between us?"

"Of course, Harvy." His face turned serious. "Consider us now bound by attorney-client privilege." He didn't make me give him a quarter as Jay Henry had done. Maybe the rules in Canada were different from those in the U.S., but I didn't ask. Even with André's assurance, I tried not to show my nervousness as I took the first document from my pocket and handed it to him.

He took the two pages from my hand, unfolded them slowly, and started to read. The door into my father's secret financial world was now cracking opening. My 27-year shadowy pledge of silence to my dad was coming into the light. For the first time in my life, I was crossing a threshold of actively plotting against my father.

Would light or darkness come through the cracks I was creating? Either way, there was now no going back.

* * * *

5

What Kind of Investment?

November 1991.

That Thursday, two days after Dad had asked me to come with him to his offshore bank, I honoured his request by arriving at JHS precisely at two o'clock. Unlike my brother, but like my father, I respected punctuality.

As soon as I walked in, my father stood and said, "Let's go, Harvy. We'll talk in the car." He handed me the keys to his Lexus. He glanced at his bookkeeper and said, "Rob, Harvy and I have a meeting downtown and will be back in a couple of hours. Just close the place as usual if you leave before we get back."

Rob nodded from behind his desk and then went back to his JHS paperwork. I wondered what Dad's bookkeeper of eleven years knew about my father's offshore affairs. My father had assured me many times, "Rob knows nothing about what you and I know."

But there was no way for me to test that statement without divulging something to Rob about what I knew, and I didn't want to do that. I felt a shiver as we departed Dad's office. Wasn't it the testimony of Al Capone's bookkeeper that finally got that famed Chicago crime boss behind bars for federal tax evasion?

I chauffeured Dad into the city. Now seven years into his retirement from manufacturing, Dad preferred his silver Lexus to the various Mercedes he had driven during the height of his business years. "With a Lexus, you get a lot more car for your money," my father had told me after he had switched brands. How much car he got never seemed to concern him during his company's heyday when he had been chasing more than just business in his sporty Mercedes.

After we had sat the car, Dad spoke matter-of-factly, "Son, take us to the Alexis Nihon Plaza; you know where it is, near downtown Montreal. We'll park in the indoor lot and take the elevators upstairs."

I knew that office and shopping complex. I had worked in one of the office buildings when I had been a junior partner in a startup executive and management education firm. I noted that Dad hadn't said which one of the Alexis Nihon office towers we would enter. He'd point out the building when we got to the plaza.

I headed to the highway. I knew not to ask Dad questions about our excursion. It was better to let him set the pace of our conversation. I felt nervous. I didn't know what my father had up his scheming sleeve.

I had never before gone to Dad's offshore bank here in Montreal. Over the years, he had talked to me about it privately, saying, "Unlike the banks in Switzerland and the Cayman Islands, my new bank has a branch right here in Montreal. I can get access to my money just by driving downtown; I don't have to fly to Timbuktu."

I had no idea how any onshore bank could perform such money magic here in Canada. I guessed I was going to find out today.

As we merged onto the highway, Dad lit a fat Cuban cigar with his gold-plated Dunhill lighter. He took several puffs. I disliked my father's billowing smoke, though I tolerated his smoking.

My father cracked open the passenger window to suck out the fumes from our moving car. He then turned slightly toward me and pointed his stinking stogie in my direction. "Do you remember Ben Cohen?"

I thought for a moment. "Wasn't Ben the guy who assisted you and JHS about ten years ago, when JHS was still in operation? Didn't he help you get business from Consumers Brands back then?"

"That's the guy!" Dad exclaimed. "He's since passed away. But I had owed him a favour because he introduced me to the furniture buyer at

Consumers. Ben got JHS into Consumers when we needed business to keep us going awhile longer."

I remembered a hot and sticky summer day in 1982. Between graduate school stints, I was working at my father's company. In those days, Dad had had a large front office. It held a row of filing cabinets along one wall along with seven desks for him and his office staff. One afternoon, I was sitting behind one of those desks doing production paperwork when a short, thin, older man walked in unannounced through the front door. He wore a loose shirt and baggy slacks.

The elder's face and shirt collar were wet from the outside heat, and perhaps from carrying an oversized, leather briefcase. He seemed to be over 75 years old. His face was dark, wrinkled, and leathery, that of a road-warrior salesman.

Walking as tall as his small, boney figure allowed, the guy eyed the room and the people sitting at their desks. In a deep, raspy voice, he barreled out, "My name is Ben Cohen." He raised a finger. "Who's the proprietor of this establishment? I want to speak to him!"

My 62-year-old father was sitting behind his desk, about three meters from the stranger. Dad typically turned such unexpected travelling salespeople right around, telling them to make an appointment with his secretary if they wanted an audience. But he seemed drawn to the older man's chutzpah and exuberance. From across the room, I could see my father quick-eye the old guy up and down. "I'm the person you're looking for," he said. "My name is John Simkovits. What can I do for you?"

Ben fired off questions in rapid succession. "Is this a factory? What kinds of products do you make here? How long have you been in business?"

Dad stayed polite and calm. "We manufacture console stereos for big department stores like Sears and Woolco." He took a long breath and kept his eyes on the fellow. "We have been in business for nearly thirty years. We build the wood cabinets and assemble the electronics into them." While Dad indulged this peppy, timeworn man, I watched from two desks away. I wondered where this conversation was heading.

Satisfied with my dad's answers, the old fellow stepped forward and placed his briefcase on a chair next to my father's desk. He raised a finger again and boomed, "I want to show you a big opportunity." He opened the case and pulled out a miniature wooden table and matching chair. The furniture pieces were up to fifteen centimeters tall or wide, appearing like what one might see in a giant dollhouse.

One-by-one, like a grown kid with building blocks, the elder gently placed the miniature furniture on Dad's desk. My father and everybody else in the office watched in silence.

Mr. Cohen spoke proudly, "I'm looking for a manufacturer to build these pieces for me." He took a deep breath and patted the leather case with his hand. "I have more unassembled here in my briefcase. I've designed them to be sturdy and good-looking. Low-end furniture stores will buy them."

His voice rose to a crescendo. "There's a huge market out there for this practical and inexpensive furniture." He pointed his finger at my father. "All I need is someone like you to make it."

Sensing an opportunity, but keeping his face expressionless, Dad turned to me. "Harvy, can you please take Mr. Cohen into my private office and let him assemble his pieces. I'll join you shortly."

Though I felt uneasy about this overly exuberant ancient who smelled of snake oil, I ignored my senses for the moment. "Please come with me," I said. We walked down the hallway to my father's private office.

The old guy and I didn't say much to each other; he stayed focused on his task. Within minutes, he had taken over the top of my father's cherrywood desk to display his models. He fit together small wooden parts and meticulously assembled a set of simple but sturdy-looking miniature chairs, couches, and tables. He placed his prototypes into configurations that one would see in a living room or den. He fussed with the items, arranging them until his eye was satisfied.

A moment later, my father walked in. "Let's see what you have here." Dad bent over the desk, examining the pieces with a critical eye and a hand to his chin. After another moment, he turned to Ben. "Those look nice, but who exactly is going to buy them?"

Ben exclaimed loudly, "I have connections at major furniture distributorships! I only need a manufacturer," he pointed at Dad, "like you, to make them!"

I was a little taken aback by the elder's brashness, but it didn't faze my father. He looked long and hard at the guy. "Before I commit my factory to build these items, is there a way you can help me?"

The savvy salesman fired back in his raspy voice, "What have you got to sell?!"

My father then turned Ben around and gave the old guy a tour of JHS's factory and warehouse. They then made a deal. Ben would help JHS get into Consumer's Brands, a national retail chain that sold low-end furniture and consumer electronics. Ben said he was friendly with the furniture buyer there and would make a spirited introduction of JHS and my father to them. In return, Ben expected a quid pro quo regarding the building of the pieces that he had displayed on Dad's desk.

I continued to drive Dad to our bank appointment near the city. The fumes from Dad's cigar thickened, even with the car's window cracked open. I let out a few coughs, but it didn't deter my father from enjoying his stogie.

He took another drag, and smoke billowed out of his mouth as he continued to refresh my memory. I didn't know everything that had transpired between Dad and Ben, because, in that summer of '82, I had departed JHS to work on my third graduate degree.

Dad offered, "After we had started selling products to Consumer's back then, Ben asked me to build full-size samples of his furniture pieces."

Dad looked down and tapped the cigar's growing ash into the car's dirty ashtray. "At first, I said okay to Ben's venture." He took a long breath. "But we soon realized that JHS would need to buy special lathes and other equipment to manufacture his furniture pieces. I didn't want to take on the additional capital costs, so I abandoned his project. Instead, I asked Ben if there was something else I could do for him."

Dad's smoke, maybe his story too, began to irritate my insides. "Okay," I said abruptly, letting out another sizable cough. Ben's style had rubbed me the wrong way. He was the kind of guy you couldn't get rid of once you owed him. For years after that Consumer's referral, Ben dropped in at my father's office regularly and unannounced. Dad invited him to his private birthday parties and company Christmas gatherings. For the years I had known him, Ben continued to converse with great crescendo and allowed little legroom for listening. Maybe that was why he and my father had gotten along.

On one occasion, when my dad had still been in manufacturing, I dropped in to see him at JHS. Ben was there. Dad invited him, my brother, and me to have lunch at a local deli not far from the factory.

While the four of us crowded into a booth, Ben couldn't stop talking about the old, paunchy chef who stood behind the counter. That fellow wore a full-length butcher's apron and held a barbeque-sized cutting knife and fork. He carefully and efficiently hand-sliced the hot meat for each smoked meat sandwich—a popular delicacy in such Montreal establishments.

Waving his index finger in the air, Ben spoke with gusto. "That smoked meat chef *must* be the owner! Look at the way he carefully slices the meat, cuts out the fat, and lays the lean, juicy pieces onto the rye bread. Only the business owner would take so much care with every sandwich. This guy knows about customer service and how to feed people right." He raised his finger even higher in the air and shook it more. "I'm certain he's the owner."

After our lunch, as we departed the deli, I stayed behind for a few seconds so I could ask the chef if he was, in fact, the restaurant's owner. When I asked, he looked at me funny and shook his head.

I said nothing about it to Ben or Dad but smelled a bigger whiff of know-it-all coming from that brazen old businessman. I wondered if he would cause trouble for my father.

Getting closer to Dad's clandestine bank in the city, I blurted out, "What did Ben now want in exchange for introducing you and JHS to Consumer's?"

To my hasty question, my father replied, "Just *lassen*, son. I'm getting *dere*."

I let out another big cough, hoping Dad would get the message about his smoking. My father continued to puff away, though he opened his window a centimeter more. I stayed quiet as he continued. "Ben told me that instead of giving him something, I should go with him to his bank where he would show me what I could do for him. I said, 'Okay,' and we soon went there together, like you and I are doing today."

Into what kind of money manipulation had Ben gotten my father, or is my father just making it sound as if it were Ben's idea? And into what was Dad now getting me involved?

For years I had known my father to be involved in various money schemes, including tax-deferral and tax-avoidance trickeries. Some were legitimate, but others were sketchy, legal, and perhaps criminal.

Dad's face turned solemn. "I don't know if you remember, son, but Ben and his wife had lost their children to hereditary kidney disease."

A pang of guilt rose in me for mentally dressing down that man in my mind. My tone softened. "Yes, now that you remind me. It was regrettable."

My father spoke calmly, but loud enough to be heard over the wind noise coming through the partially open window. "Because Ben had no legal heirs left alive, he gave money to the Canadian Kidney Foundation." He pointed his cigar again. "He also made a big donation to the Independent University through the bank that I'm taking you to today. It's the Montreal branch of the Global Trade Bank."

Dad jabbed his cigar in the air in front of him, as if he were pointing to someone. "Ben introduced me to the bank manager and a representative of the university."

I had never heard of this unusual bank. My father had mentioned a bank in Luxembourg, where he had placed his money. Was this Global Trade Bank situated there, and this university too? I held back from asking, for more would be revealed when we got to this mysterious place where he was taking me.

Dad continued. "Ben wanted me to get involved in a similar financial arrangement that he had done for himself years earlier. It's called a charitable gift annuity. The Global Trade Bank was able to provide special tax benefits to make it an excellent deal."

The details were billowing out of my father's mouth like the smoke from his lungs. Little did either of us realize that Dad's unhealthy habits would precipitate his stroke within two years. Had I known, I might have yanked that cigar out of his fingers and taken his smokes away for good. But, at this time, I was still too timid to risk my father's disfavour.

Dad turned again toward me, smiling as he talked. "Ben wanted me to donate money to that university through the bank. As with any charitable gift, the university would give me a tax receipt right away that allowed me to deduct the donation from my income taxes. The bank would then invest my money gift, and I could choose the fund in which to put the cash. I would then get the income annually for as long as I lived."

The grin on my father's face grew. "When I eventually die, the money I gave them would be passed to the university." He chuckled. "My estate would then get a nice thank you note from that institution." He chuckled and then took another big inhale of his cigar.

From what I knew, there was nothing unusual about such charitable vehicles. As long as the annual income from the annuity was declared in Dad's tax returns, and the requisite tax paid, the deal was legit. Hearing my father's laugh, I said, "Okay, Dad, so what's the trick?"

He continued to suck on his cigar. "The Global Trade Bank works it so that it pays the annual annuity income in cash. I can go to any of their branches around the world to withdraw those earnings. The bank never provides tax receipts for the income; they never file income reports with the Canadian and Quebec governments." He was grinning ear to ear. "I don't have to declare any of the income, ever."

I said nothing as I worked to keep Dad's car steady on the highway. Something else was beginning to stink besides his cigar. I could tell that he was giddy, possibly intoxicated on his murky money maneuver. He glanced my way and added, "With the double tax savings—from the initial tax deduction and the tax-free annual income—my investment in that annuity eight years ago has so far cost nothing. And the cash income will continue to come every year until I die."

"That's interesting, Dad." I tried to stay nonchalant so that I could uncover more. "How much money did you give them?"

My father looked proud as he said, "It was $80,000 Canadian, which they converted to $69,000 U.S. back then. Because of the immediate tax deduction at my income tax bracket, it cost me less than half of that.

Depending on interest rates, the investment makes four to five thousand U.S. each year for me." He grinned wide. "As I said, I pretty much got my original investment back so far. The additional income I'll get over future years will be pure profit."

My chest felt heavy, my throat dry. My father's $80,000 donation eight years ago had been double my annual salary at the Montreal consulting firm where I had worked at the time. I was surprised he gave away such a sizable amount to a faraway university. It was dramatically more than the $1,000 he gave each year to both the Montreal Slovak Church and the Canadian Slovak Professional and Business Association in which he participated.

I was apprehensive about Dad's cavalier attitude regarding the wool he was pulling over the taxman's eyes. I held my concerns in check because I had known that such wool pulling was in my father's sheep shearing repertoire.

Like Al Capone, would my father one day get thrown into the clink for his tax skirting? For the last twenty years, Dad's financial furtiveness had taken him from Europe to the Caribbean. He was now working with an obscure global bank, perhaps located in Luxembourg. Once again, he was dragging me into his offshore chicanery.

I came forth with another question, asking it casually. "So, why are we going to the same bank today?"

He turned his husky body toward me. "I want to help you in the same way, and to protect the assets in my estate when I die." He pointed his cigar my way again. "The people at the bank will explain it to you."

Dad's words grated on my psyche as much as his fuming cigar irritated my lungs. He turned back to look out the car's window, put his cigar in his mouth once more, and ended our conversation there. I knew there was nothing more to be gotten from him for now.

* * *

We exited the highway and entered city streets. My father stubbed out his cigar in the ashtray and then pushed the stub through the open window. We parked in the garage under the Alexis Nihon Plaza high-rise complex and took the elevator to the ground floor.

Water fountains sprayed in the marble lobby, and people hustled across the large foyer. Dad motioned in one direction, and we grabbed an elevator heading up the north building. I was glad we didn't go up the south building where my former employer was situated. I didn't want to bump into anyone I knew there and then have to deal with awkward looks or questions.

Dad pushed the button for the seventh floor. *Might that be a lucky or unlucky number for me today?* When we reached our floor, he and I were the only ones to step out into a quiet lobby. To one side, on a large wooden office door was written "Global Trade Bank" in modest-sized brushed-aluminum lettering.

Dad walked to the door and pushed a button. Someone buzzed us into a small entranceway that held nothing but a security camera placed high in one corner. After a few more seconds, he or she buzzed us again through another large, windowless, wooden security door that opened into a small reception area.

This place is no ordinary bank!

Inside this bank's compact lobby hung large, framed travel posters of Luxembourg's lush forests, its centuries of castles, and its capital, Luxembourg City. The captions were in multiple European languages.

So this is the Lux bank my father had mentioned to me these last few years. I was getting a fuller picture of his money maneuver of moving his stash to an offshore bank within fifteen minutes from Dad's old factory.

Hallways ran short distances in two directions to what looked like offices and conference rooms hidden behind solid cherrywood doors and opaque glass. A svelte woman, perhaps in her sixties, came out from behind a reception desk.

The elegant-looking older lady wore a silky, beige blouse and dark-brown conservative skirt that hung just below her knees. Her hair was short and well-sculpted around her face. Her shapely figure and legs belied her age by at least twenty years. I'm sure Dad enjoyed the graceful way this woman carried herself.

The receptionist held out her hand and greeted my father with energy and a heavy accent, "Hello, Mr. *Shimkovich.*" I noted that she articulated our family's last name in its original Hungarian-Slavic pronunciation. Maybe that was her country's pronunciation too.

"Hi, Hilde," my father said. He took her hand, raised it to his mouth, and gave it a peck.

Wow! My father must have been here many times to be so intimate with her. It never took him long to get friendly with a good looking woman with whom he had a connection.

Hilde giggled softly. "It is good to see you again," she offered. She retracted her hand gracefully and looked at me. "This must be your son."

"Yes, this is my youngest," Dad replied with a grin. He turned to me. "Harvy, say hello to Hilde. This wonderful lady has been with the bank for thirty years, and here in Montreal ever since I've been with them." He grinned. "And she will be with them another thirty years," he kidded.

"Hello, Hilde." I nodded her way but didn't take her hand.

She smiled at me and then turned back to Dad. "You are so charming, Mr. *Shimkovich.*"

"I wish you would call me Johnny. All these years and you still don't call me by my first name?" He said that with a tone of disappointment.

There was a school teacher's expression on her face, half stern and half loving. "You know that's not proper for me to do." She pointed toward the entryway. "Out there, I might call you that, but in here, it's *Mr. Shimkovich.*"

His eyes bright, and his face adoring, my father nodded his understanding. Though it was unusual for him not to get his way, he rarely argued with a mature and pretty face.

Hilde turned again to me. "It's nice to meet you, Harvy. Your father has mentioned you many times."

My gut felt uneasy being at this bank of potentially ill repute. I had no idea what money surprises my father had in store for today. I hoped my discomfort wasn't showing. I focused on Hilde's attractive face and forced a smile. "Hopefully, my dad has said good things about me."

"Always!" she exclaimed.

She turned back to my father. "Mr. *Shimkovich*, you are a bit early. Please sit here in our waiting area for a few minutes; I'll bring you into a conference room shortly."

"No problem, Hilde. You know my philosophy. I'd rather be ten minutes early than one minute late."

"Yes, I know that of you." She said that wryly, with a nod of her slightly tilted head. "Would you like coffee now or wait until you meet with Mr. Simon."

I suspected Mr. Simon was the bank manager.

My father looked at me. "Harvy, would you like anything?"

"I'm okay for now," I replied. I looked at Hilde while pointing down the hallway. "If you have club soda, I'll take one with no ice when we go inside." I figured I needed to calm my shaky stomach here on foreign banking turf. Asking for a club soda was a little more suitable than requesting a glass of warm milk.

My father turned back to Hilde. "I'll also wait." He grinned and winked. "And you know what I like."

She looked at me. "Yes, we have club soda, Harvy. I'll be pleased to get that for you."

She turned to my father. "And I'll get you your usual black coffee with no sugar, Mr. *Shimkovich*," she raised an open palm, "and with coffee liqueur, *n'est-ce pas?*" She smiled. "Or would you like to try the chocolate orange flavour this time?"

My father lifted his hand. "Please not more than this much," he said. His pinky was extended horizontally from his fist to indicate the measure he wished. "It's not past 5 o'clock. And I'll stick with the coffee flavour; the orange is too sweet."

"With pleasure!" Hilde exclaimed, and she turned to leave us.

Dad and I sat in the small reception area. It had just enough seating for four well-showered people sitting in a cramped space. Scattered on a coffee table were Canadian business magazines and Luxembourg journals. I rummaged through the pile and came across one that struck my attention. My growing discomfort about being here may have led me to pick out that particular publication. "Look, Dad! Here's an article about a bombing that happened in Luxembourg some years ago."

"Yes, I heard about it," he acknowledged. "Such attacks are horrible." He raised his voice a tad. "There are people everywhere who want to destabilize governments, even well-established ones. It can happen anywhere and at any time." He raised a hand. "And that's another reason why people like us need to protect ourselves."

He put his hand on my arm. "Don't worry, son; this bank is safe. Though the bank's head office is in Luxembourg, it has many branches over the world."

Dad was working to alleviate my concerns about this bank being a suitable place to put his offshore money. Was he naïve, or was he asking me to be?

Hilde returned to usher us into a small, sparse room at the end of one hallway. It contained not much more than a conference table and half-dozen chairs. One wall had another poster depicting the Luxembourg countryside.

Sitting and waiting were two men. One wore a navy blue suit, while the other sported a dark grey one. Both had white shirts and nondescript dark ties. They stood as we entered.

Hilde said, "You know everyone here, Mr. *Shimkovich*." She gestured toward the forty-something-year-old man standing at the head of the table. "Harvy, this is Mr. Simon, our bank's manager." She then turned toward the other man who looked a decade older. "And this is Mr. Schmit, the Director of the Canadian Supporters of Independent University."

Okay, Harvy; Dad's latest money-hiding game has now begun. As always, just watch, listen, and learn. There was no need to get frightened or upset. As I had done before in Dad's clandestine world, I would patiently wait until I heard and understood the whole picture.

We said hello, shook hands, and passed out our business cards. We sat down in comfortable tilt-and-swivel, low-back office chairs while Hilde served the refreshments. Like Dad, both Simon and Schmit received coffees in decorative china cups. I didn't know if their drinks were spiked, or maybe this bank saved the liquor only for its clients. On the surface, our gathering felt like an every-day business meeting, but my gut told me there would be more.

Dad took a sip of his brew and turned to Hilde. "Thank you very much. It's just the way I like it, and not too hot."

She nodded at my father, turned to leave the room, and closed the door behind her. I glanced around and saw no security cameras. *I wondered how much Hilde knew as to what would transpire here.*

Mr. Simon jumped in. "Harvy, I hear from your father that you have lived in Boston for the last couple of years. How do you like being there?"

I was accustomed to Dad having other people ask me questions on his behalf. He may have told Mr. Simon how his sons tell him little of their lives and plans. Though I was nervous inside, I played along, trying to stay light. "Our Boston winters are shorter and more temperate. And it's nice to be close to the ocean."

The banker glanced at my business card in his hand. He leaned forward in his chair. "And how is your work going there? I see that you are a consultant." He was edging into his real line of inquiry.

I leaned back in my seat and worked to project a confident voice to someone I wasn't sure was friend or foe. "Boston's a great place for new ideas in my field. I can stay at the forefront there more than I can here in Montreal. And I don't have to work or learn in two languages." I offered my statements as much for Dad's ears as I did for Mr. Simon's.

Mr. Simon looked at my father and then back to me. "But you still come to Montreal, don't you? Your father tells me you have clients here too. And you speak French?"

I nodded and smiled. "Yes, my work is split between Boston and Montreal. And I speak enough French to get along socially here. But I coach managers and consult to organizations better in English, my first language." It was irrelevant that I could understand conversational Hungarian from the time I had been a kid. I was sure Simon knew our family's background from my father.

The manager smiled back. "I do hope that you stay connected to your home city. We will then have a chance to get to know each other a little better."

This fellow seemed friendly, but this social foreplay was getting tiresome. I couldn't wait until Mr. Simon took the focus off me and got down to our banking business. But this turf was my father's. I didn't want to push the conversation too fast. Knowing Dad's ways, I would uncover more by going with the flow and asking my questions when an appropriate opening arose.

My father came into the conversation. "Son, Simon has been with this branch office a few years already." (Dad had a tendency, perhaps customary for his heritage, to call people he knew well by their surname as if it were their given name.) He looked at the manager and said lightly, "And he's planning to stay a few more, huh Simon?"

The banker answered politely. "The bank will eventually move me elsewhere, or back to Lux, but I am here for now with my family. I am enjoying Montreal, and your father and I have gotten to know each other very well." He grinned again. "He has taken me to his Troika restaurant and his Slovak Business Association parties. I'm getting to know your Slavic community well."

What else had my father shown this Simon fellow at his favourite Montreal watering hole? The Troika was known for more than its Beluga caviar, Russian vodka, and roving Eastern European minstrels. I could imagine the introductions that my father was making for this banker to the well-to-do businessmen—and perhaps the lively ladies—who frequented that place.

My father leaned forward and put his palms on the table. "Simon and I have become good friends, in addition to the good professional work that he and his bank have done for me."

What bank needed a marketing campaign when it had guys like Ben Cohen and Johnny Simkovits working on its behalf? I was anxious to hear more about the business arrangement that brought us here today. Though a part of me wanted to run out of this place, I stayed glued to my chair until this dubious banking ride was over.

Simon eyed his associate. "Mr. Schmit, here, is also from Lux. He lives in Toronto, where he represents Independent University in Canada. He often comes to visit us in Montreal to help our best customers like your father."

Schmit's head raised a centimeter. "Unfortunately, our Toronto does not seem to be as exciting as your Montreal, yet it's also not as cold in the winter." He smiled. "It takes Europeans like me a couple of years to become accustomed to your extreme Canadian seasons."

"Yes, I know!" I exclaimed, speaking from nervous anticipation. "Quebec is very cold in the winter and has plenty of mosquitoes in the summer. I guess that's why I really moved south to Boston."

Simon and Schmit chuckled. My father forced a smile. I knew he wished I had remained in Montreal as my brother had done. Dad may have thought my introduction to these banking charlatans and his money shenanigans would keep me coming back here to visit him. Though it troubled me to think so, he wasn't entirely wrong.

Schmit continued. "And maybe from Toronto, we can bring good ideas for your father's money here in Montreal."

My abdomen tightened. The university representative was getting to the business matter at hand.

My father piped in. "Yes, Schmit; please explain to Harvy what we are doing. I want him to get the full picture. He knows about the annuity I arranged years ago with your university." Dad didn't say that he had told me about that investment just today, during our car ride to the bank.

Schmit clasped his hands on the table and nodded to my father. His face turned serious, and his tone was matter-of-fact. I held my breath as he began. "The agreement your father will sign today will authorize a gift payment from his estate to our university when he passes away."

Schmit made a fist with his right hand and placed it toward my father's side of the table. He then slid that fist toward Simon. "Money we obtain from your father's estate will be invested in an account that Mr. Simon will open and manage here at the bank." He unclenched his fist and moved his hand toward me. "These funds will then give you, Harvy, annual tax-free income for the rest of your life."

I felt my heart pound. There were those magic words, "tax-free income." Were they the hook and line that Ben Cohen used to reel in my father to this hush-hush banking haven? And was Dad now orchestrating his reeling in of me?

My father jumped in. "Harvy, I want to shelter my Canadian pension money from Canada's high income taxes when I die. I don't want you to have to pay too much tax on my estate. Because I'm in an over fifty percent combined tax bracket here in Canada and Quebec, my estate will save a lot of money with this annuity idea."

His voice was calm, and his face was serene, like a father telling his child a bedtime story. "I'll leave instructions for you and your brother, as my estate executors, to make this donation to Independent University after I'm gone."

Dad gestured toward Schmit then looked back at me. "Yet, you alone, Harvy, will get the benefit from the annuity. Your brother won't know about this arrangement among us." He made a circle with his finger to indicate those of us in the room.

Like times before, my father's trust in me trumped his love for his first son. I was privy to Dad's clandestine money arrangements; my brother wasn't. At this time, I felt no reservations about it.

Over the years, Steve had proven his inability to let tax-dodging dogs lie sleeping offshore. He vigorously admonished our Dad if he suspected our father was doing something unethical, or he would tell our mother (when she had been alive) and perhaps confess such things to his Mormon bishop.

I demonstrated my steadfast loyalty to Dad by keeping quiet about his money maneuvers, as he had asked of me. My goal was to reap the rewards of my father's hidden treasure chest while my brother wouldn't. But was I fooling myself? Was it my father's offshore stash that I was craving, or was it something more?

This Independent University deal was unlike Dad's previous offshore tricks. This occasion was the first time his secret shenanigans directly involved me. I would no longer be at arms distance from his hidden stash but a direct beneficiary of his clandestine dealings. I was less sure about this arrangement. My head ached about the prospect of Revenue Canada or the IRS chasing me, even jailing me, for unpaid taxes. I grabbed my glass of club soda and took a big swig.

Schmit continued. "Harvy, as you collect the income every year from your father's donation, you'll not get any annual tax receipts from our university or this bank. You won't have to declare the amounts on your tax returns, no matter where you are residing."

The university rep offered that information as if it were nothing to worry about. "You'll get a choice of investments," Schmit added. "You can go more conservative with bonds and CDs, or slightly more aggressive with a percentage of equities. You'll decide how much you want to risk, and in what ways. Every year, you can withdraw any interest and capital gains over and above the original donation amount." He paused for a second and eyed me carefully. "As long as the original amount stays intact in the account, anything above that is yours to withdraw."

My uncertainty about the arrangement made me look for a hole in the net that I saw closing on me. I looked at Schmit. "What if the investments lose money?"

Simon answered. "We limit the amount of risk you can take with the funds. We have money managers who choose and oversee the investments. If there is no return or a slight loss in a particular year, then you won't be able to take any cash withdrawals that year." His eyes stayed focused on me. "But the bank takes the risk on the principal. If by chance, there is a loss in your father's original investment, then the university will see that much less from the donation."

Dad spoke up. "You don't have to worry too much about that, son. The annuity I currently have has paid me steadily these last eight years. That money has not seen any losses."

I kept my eyes on Simon. I could tell he was checking my reactions just as I was checking his. I held myself together, my hands clasped in my lap.

Seeing no red flags, Simon continued to speak calmly. "We try hard not to see any reductions in principal. We work, first, to give you a good return, and second, to see that the original capital is transferred to the university when you pass away many, many years from now." He batted his hand in the air as if I would live forever.

Though I felt the money lure, I worried that Dad's financial net would further entangle or even drown me in illicit waters. I looked at Schmit and kept my voice calm. "So how does this work? We can't just transfer my father's pension funds here when he dies. Don't we have to pay Canadian withholding tax on them first?"

Schmit showed a wry smile, looking as if others had asked him such a question before. "It's quite simple, Harvy." He raised a hand. "Rather than take you through the mechanics of the money ins and outs, it would be easier to think of your father's final income tax return when his estate files them. In Canada, an estate can do that up to six months after a person's death."

Employing his index finger, Schmit drew an imaginary rectangular box in the air in front of him. "Let's say this is your father's final tax returns. On the income side of that return, you will see a line for the—let's say for discussion purposes—$1,000,000 income from the money remaining in his RRSP [Registered Retirement Savings Plan, like an IRA in the U.S.]." Schmit drew an imaginary line in the top half of his imaginary box. "That income, of course, is fully taxable."

He lowered his finger a few centimeters and continued. "However, by then, your father's estate will have paid us the annuity amount. We also would have given his estate a charitable receipt. So you will have a $1,000,000 charitable contribution in the deductions section of your father's final returns." Schmit drew another imaginary line in the bottom half of his imaginary box. "The two amounts in the income and deduction lines will, for the most part, cancel each other out in your father's combined federal and provincial tax returns. That will leave you, in effect, paying little to no tax on that $1,000,000 of your father's RRSP funds."

A slight smile came to his face. "And, the beauty of it is that the whole $1,000,000 will be here with the bank earning income for the rest of your life. Neither the government will know, nor will you have to pay taxes on those earnings."

He took a long breath and continued. "If you didn't take advantage of this annuity vehicle, then your father's estate would be left with less than $500,000 from his RRSP after his estate pays Canadian and Quebec taxes. Any earnings on that smaller amount would then be taxable each year in his estate, unlike here where the whole one million would earn tax-free money for you."

I handed it to Schmit; he had skillfully explained his annuity tax dodge. I turned in my chair and looked at my father. My heart thumped a little harder, and I felt my collar get hot and sticky. I worked to stay collected and asked casually, "Is that how much you plan to pledge to the university in this arrangement?"

"Yes, son. Right now, I have well over $1,000,000 Canadian in my RRSP account. Anything over the million dollars that my estate would give to the bank will go directly to you and your brother, and you'll have to pay income taxes on that portion."

His voice became excited as he repeated what Schmit had said. "But my estate will immediately save half a million in taxes by our enacting this university annuity through this bank. And the income earned from the whole one million will come to you, and only you, tax-free each year."

His tone was confident. "The Canadian and Quebec governments don't have to know anything about it, and neither does your brother. By the time you die—30, 40, or even 50 years after me—you will have recouped the initial investment many times over." He grinned as he wagged his finger at me slightly. "The longer you live, the more you'll get, so you better stay healthy."

I nodded at my father then looked at Schmit. "Is the university willing to wait until my death, perhaps decades from now, for it to receive the donation proceeds?" I turned to Simon. "What if Revenue Canada audits your bank? Don't you have to divulge the income we are earning with you?" I was still looking for escape holes in this slimy money web.

Schmit replied first. "Our university is very patient. Your donation is guaranteed future money for our programs. Whenever it comes, it will help us a great deal. We have many people who do such things with us, and it acts as a private endowment for the university." He gestured toward Dad and me with his open hand. "Until that day, our annuity program is a big financial help to you and your father."

Simon spoke right behind his colleague. "Revenue Canada cannot audit us like a regular Canadian bank. We have foreign incorporation, and our head office is in Luxembourg. We don't have to disclose our Canadian customers to your government, or even how much Canadian assets we hold in our bank. You are protected here; the banking laws of Luxembourg, not Canada, regulate our institution."

Dad opened his wallet and pulled out a black credit card. The grey letters embossed onto the card spelled out "Global Trade Bank of Luxembourg," and a series of numbers were underneath the name. "See this?" He put the metallic-looking card on the table. "With this, I can come here anytime, or go to the Global Trade Bank branches in New York or Miami, to obtain the cash income from my current annuity."

My father looked slightly flushed as if he were revealing a super special birthday present. It was like the Mercedes sports car he had given my brother twenty years earlier, to entice his working hard in high school to get accepted into college. But the enticement he put in front of me was going to sit undriven in a bank showroom until Dad was in his grave. That event wouldn't happen until many years from now.

He continued. "This bank has many branches in Europe and over the world. All you need are this card and your code number. Any teller will then give you your money with no questions asked. As long as you don't remove more than $10,000 cash at one time, there is no government paper trail." He grinned again. "It doesn't even have to be you getting the money. With this card, somebody else can do it for you, but it's better that you go yourself."

Simon came in. "You pay such high taxes here in Canada. We are trying to help you keep more of what your father has earned in his lifetime." He looked around at all of us. "You win, your father wins, the bank wins, and the university wins." He didn't offer that the Canadian and Quebec governments would lose, and my brother too.

Dad's eyes were penetrating, and his voice firm. "*Lassen* to me, son! A lot of wealthy people do this. We should not be any different than the rest."

Schmit echoed his words. "We have many Canadian customers like you who want to protect their assets and lifetime of earnings. Our annuity program is a very prudent way to do so. Your money is safe here, earning tax-free income for the rest of your life."

Dad was always ready to cast his money into tax-avoidance waters—seemingly a regular sport among wealthy Canadians. My father's previous financial tricks—ones that I knew about—had shown how even our Canadian banks and accounting firms colluded with people of means to skirt federal and provincial taxes in this country. I had also read in newspapers how wealthy

Canadians and Americans sheltered assets in tax-free havens like Switzerland, Cayman Islands, and The Bahamas, just as my father had done over the years. But this was the first time that I had heard of a seemingly prestigious university in on the game.

I was amazed by how courteous and professional Schmit and Simon were about deceiving our Canadian governments, making their scheme sound ordinary and acceptable. Then again, their sales pitch was clearly for their institution's benefit.

In my younger days, my father's tax-avoiding plays had enticed me. But keeping his secrets and holding the shame of potential exposure now roused the acid in my stomach. If I agreed to this Independent University annuity deal, I would be directly involved in his criminal pastime. *What the hell am I going to do?*

I felt I had little choice. I had been a long-time spectator, even player, in my father's money-hiding sport. I felt there was nothing I could say or do to disentangle myself or avoid swallowing one more illegal lure.

The assets in question were my father's funds, not mine. He didn't need my permission to do this money manipulation. He just needed my acceptance and willingness to continue playing his sport after his death. Would I have my father's gumption to collect clandestine and untaxed investment gains out of offshore bank branches over the frigging world?

I felt ensnared. There was little I could do without risking Dad's trust and confidence in me concerning the rest of his offshore legacy. It had been nearly twenty years since he first let me in on his overseas stash. I expected that his offshore wealth would one day become mine if I kept my mouth shut and went along with his tax-avoiding ploys.

If I made a fuss about this university annuity deal, Dad might go further underwater, telling me nothing about other hidden money excursions he had already taken or would subsequently take. He could then leave me high and dry as a non-beneficiary.

Part of me didn't want to take the risk of losing my father's favour. Another part questioned why his trust and confidence were so important to me. *Was it only his money to which I was attracted, or was there something else?* Indeed, there had been a high cost to my head and gut in being Dad's confidant.

My stomach felt uneasy as I nodded my understanding of the annuity arrangement. I had run out of concerns to air, except for the ones I had already lived with for decades. I looked down at the table. "Okay," I said to no one in particular. *Shit!* I had allowed Dad's net to close on me again; another damn hook was lodging into my gut.

Dad turned to Schmit. "Harvy agrees. So, let's do it."

I consoled myself. With me as beneficiary, my father might be less likely to deplete his retirement funds if he earmarked them for me through this annuity. Might this arrangement be his calculated way to ensure that his pension funds wouldn't be "pissed away" by his offspring after his death? He had many times voiced those words in a caustic tone. He was worried that Steve or I wouldn't wisely spend either the money he had bestowed upon us over the years or the assets he planned to bequeath to us at his death.

From his briefcase, Schmit retrieved two copies of a two-page agreement. He put them in front of my father, and Dad signed where Schmit indicated. Schmit then countersigned underneath Dad's mark. He gave my father a copy and took the other for himself. He concluded by saying, "You have made a good investment in both your son's future and the future of Independent University. We thank you for your support."

How the hell can this place get away with such blatantly tax-skirting baloney? Wouldn't they get caught eventually?

It would take years for my discerning a plausible answer. I eventually realized that the Global Trade Bank and Supporters of Independent University only needed to claim that it was up to their account holders, individual donors, and annuity beneficiaries to declare the proper income and pay the relevant tax from their offshore holdings. The bank could easily claim no wrongdoing for what was the taxpayer's responsibility. What a sly sport they played!

We stood and said our goodbyes. I shook Simon and Schmit's hands quickly, nodding but saying nothing, working not to show how knotted I felt inside. It had taken only moments to transact the crafty contract. Dad had set the bait and cast the line, and then Simon and Schmit reeled me in. All I needed to do was to be the good son and swallow the hook. They didn't even require my signature on the agreement, just my knowledge and acceptance of a promised future transaction.

Dad grabbed Schmit's hand firmly and smiled sincerely. "When you are here in Montreal a little longer, you must come out with Simon and me. I'll show you the best nightlife in the city."

"Yes," the university rep said with a bright face. "I would be very pleased to do that with you. I will let you know when I will be in Montreal and have the time to join you."

Schmit might have heard from Simon how gregarious and generous my father could be to his favoured guests, especially those visiting from more lackluster Toronto. There the city locked restaurant doors and rolled up its sidewalks at one o'clock in the morning. In more spirited Montreal, Dad enjoyed treating out-of-towners to their desired vices up to our city's customary two o'clock bar closing time, even later for generous and loyal patrons like Johnny Simkovits.

I followed my father out of the conference room and back toward the bank's entryway. He looked at Hilde and gave her another big grin as we walked past her desk. "Thank you, Hilde, for everything. The coffee was excellent. I'll see you next time."

She smiled back and said, "It will be a pleasure to see you again, Mr. Shimkovich."

Still feeling unsettled, I only nodded in her direction. I again wondered how much she knew of what was going on in this bank, where she worked to make the customers feel welcome.

I followed closely behind my father and out the double security doors. I desperately needed fresher air. I prayed that Dad wouldn't smoke another cigar on the ride back to his office.

Though my gut was tight and my head spun regarding our hidden-money talk, I figured it was better for me to know than not know about my father's latest dubious deal. After Dad's death, either years or decades from now, I could choose to declare the annual income and pay the required taxes on that Independent University annuity. I certainly would have more control over Dad's money at that time. If I wanted to, I could even include my brother in sharing the proceeds. *Time is on my side,* I told myself.

Dad and I waited in the barren hallway for the elevator. He turned toward me but kept his eyes on the elevator door. "Harvy, please keep what happened today just between us. Don't tell Steve or anybody else. You know we can't trust your brother to keep such things in confidence."

My brother's staunch beliefs about right and wrong caused him to resist or denounce our father for anything Dad enacted that wasn't 100% legal or ethical. If Steve had been at this bank today, he would have criticized our father in front of Simon and Schmit, and he probably would have stormed out of the meeting at the first mention of "tax shelter" or "tax-free."

To stay in my father's favour, I never crossed him in front of others. If I had differing opinions, I kept them for private conversations. Dad seldom took my advice, but—if approached right—he did offer his ear rather than his ire.

Steve and I were very different people. Unlike my brother, I listened to our father's perspectives about money and business, whether I agreed with them or not. Unlike Steve, I had never loaned and lost large sums to unscrupulous friends and colleagues. My brother had spent his annual JHS bonuses on world travels, abandoning our father and his company for up to six months at a time. Steve gave 10% or more of his income to his church, those earnings having come from Dad and JHS. Many times, Dad had complained to me, "Your brother cares more about himself and his church than about the company that supports him and me."

Counter to my brother, I worked to emulate my father who saved every penny in his business. I frugally squirreled my company earnings and bonuses into secure investments like whole life insurance and retirement savings. I prudently maintained my money-saving path so that my father would see my being more like him. Or was I a staunch saver because I feared my father's abandonment, as he had unabashedly deserted my mother?

Decades ago, Dad stopped telling Steve about his financial secrets because he feared my brother might "put them on the drum for everyone to hear." Dad said that he was keeping my brother ignorant of his offshore affairs. I held onto Dad's secrets as if my future would depend on it. I ignored the growing tightness inside me about his sordid offshore mischief.

But that tightness had worsened over these last years. I was coming into my own, growing more successful in my independent consulting practice, and I prided myself on my honesty and integrity in my client dealings. I became more uneasy with my father's dubious ways—even though every wealthy Canadian might have been doing the same.

I had tried to be a loyal and trusting biblical Isaac to my revered Abraham father. At some juncture, I started to feel as if I were being led up a mount for my sacrifice to a false money god. Every year, I felt a heavier weight on my shoulders, especially for knowing more about my father's intentions than the supposedly naïve Isaac may have known about his father's. I felt apprehensive that my Ishmael brother knew little of what I knew. I wondered if my father had other clandestine sacrifices planned for me.

I drove us back to my father's office. In the car, I again pondered why my father's money, and my being his trusted confidant, was so important to me. *Why couldn't I say no to him?*

As we neared the JHS parking lot, my dad turned in his seat to look at me. "Harvy, I'm giving you most of my Canadian pension money through this university annuity. But after I'm gone, be a good brother by helping Steve out if and when he needs it."

Considering the continual angst and jousting that had gone on between my brother and father over the years, Dad still felt responsible for his first son. Maybe he was expressing his unconditional love for any child he bore, as he might also do for me with my sibling.

"Okay, Dad; if that's what you want," I said for now.

But I didn't want to be an extension of my father with my brother. I didn't want to have to "help out" Steve for the rest of his life. Time would tell how I would deal with my brother after our father's death.

I had plenty to gain from my father's current generosity with me, and little to lose in remaining quiet for now about his unconventional estate planning with Global Trade Bank and the Canadian Supporters of Independent University.

No one was going to get shot or die with this university deal. No one—not even Steve—was going to get hurt knowingly. I could still be fair to my sibling after Dad's passing, by giving him a cut in the annual annuity take. Only our government was going to get a little short-changed years from now, and then only if I completely carried out Dad's secret plan.

There's lots of time; I consoled myself as I had done times before. *There's nothing to be overly concerned about right now.*

* * * *

6

Deal Defying Act

October 1999.

I glanced out the large windows of Elliot Trudell's large, dim conference room as I sat motionless in front of André. The Montreal sky remained a dull grey on this autumn morning; no sun peeked out. My friend's face expressed an intense curiosity as he perused the first document I had handed him.

I pointed to the papers and worked to keep my hand from shaking. "This is an annuity agreement my father signed in 1991 for my benefit with the Canadian Supporters of Independent University." I offered the name because it was present on the document.

I felt naked and exposed. I was grateful that André's attention was on the agreement and not on me. He leaned forward in his chair, his elbows on his knees. His eyes scanned the paperwork as he held it in his hands.

"I want to be able to get my father's estate out of this commitment," I said. "My father got himself into this charitable annuity arrangement to tax-shelter his pension funds and to give me income for the rest of my life after his death. The problem now is that he no longer has the retirement pension money to fund this annuity."

André raised his head and looked directly at me, a stunned look on his face. "I hope you don't mean your father's broke!" he exclaimed.

"No, not at all," I replied. "My father still has assets in his business. It's now a holding company that's mostly owned by my brother and me, though my father remains the controlling shareholder." It felt odd that Steve and I owned the majority of our father's JHS holding company assets, but we had no legal say over them until Dad would be two meters underground.

I continued. "My father also gets a sizable income from many life annuities he arranged decades ago when he sold various properties he owned. But that income will terminate when he dies." I stopped there, not wanting to babble. I waited for more questions from André.

After a moment of rereading the document, André put the paper on the table and looked at me. "Okay, Harvy; tell me more about your problem with this agreement."

I offered, "To make a very long story short, my dad had a stroke two years after he signed this agreement."

"Is your father okay?" my friend asked, his eyes wide.

"He's well enough now," I said as kindly as I could. I didn't want to get into my father's disability, a conversation that might have been more appropriate for a therapist than a lawyer. "But a year after his disability, he separated from his third wife. They made a divorce agreement to transfer the bulk of his pension assets to her."

Dad's marriage to Elaine, after his divorce from my mother, didn't last the way I had hoped. Though charming when chasing the opposite sex, my father was a hard man with whom to live.

There was a hell of a lot more to that story, as there always was with my father. What I had said to André was enough for his getting the gist. He continued to listen as I spoke, his face expressionless. "The problem now is that what little my father has left in his pension can't fund this annuity agreement." I looked pleadingly at my friend. "What can I do to get my father and me out of this arrangement?"

To keep my account simple, but perhaps more to save face, I didn't share with André that I would clandestinely obtain, only if I chose to, the tax-skirted income from the university annuity after my father's death. I didn't tell him that my brother, André's classmate at our private school, knew nothing of

103

this agreement. I also didn't say that, as the years passed, I felt a growing weariness about my father's tax-avoiding shenanigans.

I had not become the world traveller my father had been. Dad had traipsed off to Europe, Asia, and the Caribbean for both business and pleasure. Conversely, I was a family man, staying close to home and building my consulting practice in only Boston and Montreal. I couldn't envision going covertly from one Global Trade Bank branch to another to retrieve annual annuity cash earnings. Over these last years, I decided that I would rather have less money in my pockets, give the government its rightful due, and remain clean in my business and financial dealings.

Dad had once been caught, prosecuted, found guilty, and paid hefty corporate fines for falsifying his company's tax returns. He had spent a small fortune on a pricey corporate attorney who helped him to avoid personal criminal prosecution and jail time.

I wanted to avoid the pain and shame of being caught by either the IRS or Revenue Canada. I didn't want either of those government agencies to arrive at my doorstep one day, the way they had unexpectedly landed at my father's factory door twenty-four years earlier.

This Independent University transaction was just one among a cadre of money hiding and tax-avoiding games that Dad had played during his near fifty-year professional life in Canada. My knowledge about his Caribbean property deals, his offshore shell corporation, his loans to crooked characters, his hiding of funds in offshore tax havens, and his myriad tax-avoidance schemes weighed on my conscience. I felt that weight every time I visited him in his old factory office.

Dad was now pushing 80. Over six years had passed since he had had his stroke. It had wrecked half his body, and perhaps as much of his mind. There were increased signs in him of the effects of a lifetime of deception and failed relationships. His once vibrant face was increasingly void of smiles. He seldom laughed or sang as he had done for decades at his favoured Hungarian Tokay and beloved Russian Troika venues. He now didn't have more than one vodka drink at supper, and could hardly carry a tune from his half-sagging face. Like the Tower of Pisa, he leaned to one side every time he shuffled along with his cane, dragging his almost useless left leg to catch up with his better right one. No one knew how long the special sole on the shoe of his able foot would continue to prop him up before he would need to sit in a wheelchair and then lie in a grave.

Despite his stroke, Dad was smoking again, consuming over a pack-a-day to pass the time. He was reluctant to exercise or do physical therapy, and he rarely walked further than from his office door to his car or from his apartment door to the building elevator. My father could sit at his old company desk for hours playing gin rummy with his longtime company bookkeeper. He still came in four days a week to old-man-sit his nearly twenty-year employer.

And Dad complained continually about the various women he had lived with, saying, "They never really cared about me, only about themselves. They only wanted my money." He also confided, "Your dear mother was the only one who took good care of me; she didn't want me for more than love."

At least Dad acknowledged that his longest relationship had been his best. He hadn't treated my mother well, leaving her several times for younger women. He then returned into her perpetually open arms after his affairs had soured.

But Mom never got to hear these appreciative words from her husband of thirty years. She had died of a broken heart two years after Dad had divorced her and eight years after he had left her the final time. Over and over, my mother had gotten the blunt end of the love arrow from Dad.

These last years, I found myself increasingly wary and exceedingly weary of being involved in Dad's sordid money secrets. I did appreciate my father's long-term investment in me. He had paid for my three university degrees and my short stint at Harvard Business School. For many years, he gave my brother and me annual bonuses from his company.

But his money schemes and failed relationships aggravated me more each passing year. I didn't see that his wealth offered him (or me) any greater peace of mind or improved relationships with women. Whenever I looked at his half-drooping face, tired-looking eyes, and cane-led foot, I thought, *I don't want to wind up like him!*

I felt ashamed about dishonouring the trust my father had put in me regarding his offshore money, but I felt right about seeing André on this day of personal reckoning. My heart thumped hard and fast as I quietly watched my friend study the university annuity agreement once more. After what seemed like many reads, he looked at me. "I'll have to double-check with one of our estate experts on this, but I don't believe this is a binding contract."

My heart nearly jumped out of my chest. "What do you mean?!"

He looked into my eyes. "This agreement makes a declaration upon your dad's death. In Canadian law, and by the laws of most countries, such declarations can be made only through one's will, and not through a side agreement like this."

André looked down at the paper once more. "Give me a moment to make a call to one of our estate experts to double-check my thinking on this." He raised his head again and looked my way. "Don't worry, Harvy. I won't mention your name or the name of the organization involved." He took another breath. "By chance, do you know if your father wrote this agreement into his last will?"

I brought my hand to my chin and thought for a few seconds. "No, not that I know." I searched my memory. "My father asked me to help him write his last will six months after his stroke in '93." I pointed to the agreement. "That was a couple of years after he signed this annuity deal." I shook my head as I continued racking my mind. "I don't believe he made any such declaration in his will."

Dad must have missed or forgotten to do so, or he hadn't wanted to. And I must have overlooked or forgotten that stipulation to make the university annuity fully binding. I looked at André. "I doubt that my father changed anything in his will since then; his notary would have told me."

Yes, Peternik would have said something. I had called him to see if my father had followed up on my request to change the executors of his will. The notary told me that my father hadn't changed anything since we had written and consummated his last will in 1993.

André dialed his colleague from the conference room phone. When my friend reached him, he described my situation briefly, mentioning no names. After a few moments of back and forth, it became apparent that the university annuity agreement was non-binding unless my father had written its instructions into his last will.

A sense of relief grew in me. I was starting to feel confident that I was coming out of one neck of my father's illicit woods. The Canadian Supporters of Independent University deal no longer bound me to an offshore tree. After Dad's death, I could ignore subsequent appeals from the university, or tell their representative, Schmit, that my brother and I wouldn't honour the arrangement. The university couldn't encumber Dad's estate or me, except to say that we had a moral obligation to follow-through on Dad's wishes. I could easily sidestep that argument; there would be no legal recourse for them.

I could divulge to my brother, my co-executor in our father's estate, just enough about the history and circumstances of this annuity agreement so that he would see its lack of integrity. Steve wouldn't want to deplete Dad's after-tax estate to fund the sizable annuity solely for my benefit. On the other hand, if I told him that our father wanted only me to get this portion of his estate, he might feel disowned by Dad and cheated by me. I had to be careful about what I might say to my brother about this.

What about Schmit and Simon? By signing the annuity agreement, my father had made them my confreres for the rest of my life. Wouldn't I be screwing those future siblings, the Global Trade Bank and the Independent University, out of a million dollars down the line by reneging on Dad's deal? Then again, wouldn't I be cheating the Canadian government of half-a-million in taxes from my father's estate if I went along with the arrangement?

My father alone had signed the agreement. I no longer wanted the clandestine tax-free income after his death if it meant screwing my sibling and skirting the taxman for the rest of my life. I could rightfully declare the annuity income, and even share half of it with Steve. But then, wouldn't we be enablers of an underhanded scheme designed by representatives of an offshore bank and university that posed as helping wealthy Canadians avoid income taxes?

Dad had wanted his pension money to be used for that donation after he passed away. But there weren't enough of those funds left to invest in the university annuity. If Dad had wanted this donation to happen, he would have made sure that he put the gift into his will and kept his pension money intact.

André now handed me a legal opening to break a shady deal that my father seemed to have broken on his own. Part of me had no qualms about walking through that opening. But was I becoming a cheat like my father, using a legal loophole, albeit a good one, to potentially get out of an agreement Dad had signed? Dad could fund that university annuity through his other taxable assets.

My mind was getting overwhelmed, my head was starting to hurt, and my gut began to twinge.

I needed more time to ponder this contractual conundrum. My father wasn't dead yet. I could wait to make my decision until Dad was closer to or in his grave. Nothing illegal, immoral, or unethical had happened so far. There might be other options available to honour his wish or clarify this money riddle. I had time to think, especially since my brother didn't know about this annuity agreement, and my father seemed to have forgotten—or was he purposely not saying anything about it? Might he divulge his final wishes to me on his deathbed?

My eyes glanced past André as he continued to talk to his colleague on the phone. I looked up at the conference room ceiling. Would my mother, now underground for twelve years, want me to go through with this annuity arrangement? She would certainly want my brother to receive a fair share of my father's fortunes.

A touch of lightness came to my chest and shoulders; a semblance of warmth came into my hands. I now felt more control over this sordid investment situation. I could better wrestle with this annuity problem later, and I could include my brother carefully in that wrestling. *How much will I have to tell Steve?* I or we could consult with a lawyer like André when the time came.

Okay! A small problem is somewhat solved, and a big one is left to go.

My friend ended his call and looked at me with an air of satisfaction. Relief in my voice, I said, "Thanks, André. It seems like we got that one under control pretty quickly."

"I'm glad I could help an old chum," he said with a pleased tone followed by another grin.

André cut our celebration short, and his voice became lawyerly again. "You said there was another thing you wanted me to see."

My heart started to thump again. I felt my face get flushed. I pulled a second, thicker wad of paper from my breast pocket. "André, I guess that this other situation I have to show you won't be as simple and easy to resolve as the last one."

His face turned serious as he beckoned with one hand. "Let me have a look," he said.

* * * *

Part III:

Adolescent Lessons

and Lesions

7

Where We Came From

July 1968.

Dad was pushing 160 kilometers per hour on the autobahn between Salzburg and Vienna, Austria. *Wow! The world is flying by.* He was keeping up with other Mercedes and BMWs heading east. We whizzed past hay and grain fields that waved to us in the breeze. We left behind "old farts," as Dad called them, doing 130 km/h in the slow lane.

My brother and I were in our early teens and on summer vacation with our parents. For me, Dad's highway speed was exhilarating. I knew he was an excellent driver; he had never had an accident or close call during my young life of close to 14 years. He had told us there were no speed limits on Austrian highways. He was testing the car's limits, and perhaps his own. I sat still next to him and watched the white lines blur. *Go, Dad, go!*

From her backseat perch, Mom shouted over the car's revved engine. "Jani, do you have to drive as fast as those *bolondok emberek* [crazy people]?" She blurted out her Hungarian rather than search for English words.

Mom hadn't learned to drive. For as long as I could remember, she sat in the back seat with either my brother or me when we went on vacations that involved driving, like this one. Even in Montreal, when Dad drove us in his '98 Oldsmobile to Sunday church or for a countryside excursion around the city, Mom regularly sat in the back by herself. On those occasions, my brother and I would sit on the front bench seat, with me squeezed between Dad and my brother.

Because our father worked six days a week, perhaps he allowed Steve and me to sit in front with him so that we would have more time together. Or maybe it was Mom who did the allowing, for Dad was in a better mood when his kids were right next to him.

Our Mercedes rental only had front bucket seats. So, today, I took my turn in the front while Steve hung out in the back with Mom. "Don't worry, Anna. I'm just keeping up with the others," my father bellowed over the engine roar. "I know what I'm doing and want us to get to Vienna before the day is over."

"Please, Jani, there's no rush."

Mom (left), Steve (right), and Harvy (with toy camera) with Uncle Edo (2ⁿᵈ from left), Aunt Ilonka (middle), and other family friends in Sliač, Low Tatra Mountains, Slovakia, 1960.

Dad paused for a moment. He turned his head and shoulder slightly toward Mom, his voice still roaring. "We only have tomorrow to spend in Vienna before we cross the border into Czechoslovakia. I want us in bed early tomorrow night, so we can get up first thing the next morning, hit the road to Bratislava, and arrive at the border before it gets crowded. It could take hours to make the crossing."

His voice turned irritated. "The border guards will want to open our luggage to see if we are smuggling anything into the country. They'll make us change money at the official government rate and go through who knows what other baloney."

Like my brother, I stayed quiet as our parents hashed things out. Dad usually got his way in these skirmishes.

For the first time, our whole family was heading to Czechoslovakia on holiday. Twice before, in '60 and '64, Steve and I had accompanied our mother on summer visits to our relatives in Slovakia. We had spent two months with her, both in Košice, my parents' hometown, and in Sliač, a spa village in the Low Tatra Mountains that Mom's family enjoyed. This trip would be Dad's first time back to his homeland after Mom's and his escape from their country nineteen years earlier.

"We are going to spend only four days in Slovakia," Dad offered. "We'll spend one day and night in the Tatra Mountains and three days in Košice." His voice lowered. "I don't want to be there too long."

Mom (second from left), young Steve and Harvy, and (left to right) Aunt Irén, Aunt Ilonka, Dad's stepmother Maria, Uncle Edo, Uncle Viktor, and other family friends. Košice, Slovakia, 1960.

"How come, Dad?" my older brother shouted over the engine roar.

Dad turned his head a little more in my direction; his voice still elevated over the din of the thundering engine. "You boys remember how I told you that Mom and I had run away from Czechoslovakia in the spring of '49. It was the year after the Soviet Communists took over our country."

"Yah," Steve and I said simultaneously.

Dad's tone turned serious. "In those days, I owned and operated a radio retail and repair store in Košice. With a partner, I also ran a public-address installation business there. Because I was a capitalist, I became an undesirable person in the new communist regime."

Left to right: Old Geza, Aunt Ilonka, Uncle Geza, Mom, Steve, Dad, Aunt Irén, Harry,
in Sliač, Slovakia, 1968.
This family trip was Dad's first time back in Czechoslovakia since he escaped the country in 1949.

Dad held our Mercedes at an even speed as he passed a VW. "Soon after the Soviets took over our country in '48," he continued, "the new government sent me a letter saying that the communist state now controlled my business. I was no longer the owner but just a manager of my company." He paused for a second as he stared out at the highway, his face becoming tight and red. "I was flabbergasted, but there was nothing I could do."

The car's cabin turned silent except for the sound of the engine and the tires whirring on the road. I watched Dad while he glanced in his rearview mirror as he moved the car back to the slow lane. After a moment, Steve asked, "What's the problem with us going back to Košice now?"

My father eased back on the accelerator to 140 km/h, letting a couple of faster BMWs jet past. I wasn't sure if his maneuver was because of my mother's request to slow down or because he was thinking about my brother's question. From my front seat perch, I could see Dad gaze forward into that distant past.

He raised his right hand off the steering wheel momentarily and continued. "Back then, I had a country place in the High Tatra Mountains that I went to for winter skiing. In early-'49, when I returned to Košice one Monday morning after a weekend away, I was picked up by the local police." He inhaled deeply. "They threw me into jail and didn't even explain why they arrested me."

"Wow! That must have been scary," I shouted.

Jani and Mom's brother, Geza, cross-country skiing in the High Tatras. Winter of 1948 or 1949.

"Did Mom know?" Steve asked.

"No," Mom replied with energy. Her voice was not as elevated as before. "We were a steady couple at that time, yet I had no idea he had been taken away until after he got out. He was gone only a few days."

Dad divulged more. "On my last day in jail, my cousin Lutsy came to get me out. He told me what had happened and why I was there."

My eyes widened in anticipation. I jammed my cold hands under my armpits in our air-conditioned car.

Dad took a long breath. "My company's electrical crew had recently finished installing a new public address system in the Košice sports stadium." He raised his hand off the steering wheel again. "The following weekend, while I was away in the Tatras, that system went haywire. A Russian Communist dignitary had come to speak there on that Saturday, and a Red Army band was performing too. My cousin heard that when the dignitary spoke, and the band played, their words and music were drowned out by cracking noises coming from the loudspeakers."

While clinging to the top of the steering wheel with both hands, Dad demonstrated what he was saying. He stretched out the index and middle fingers of his left hand and crossed them with the index finger of his right hand. "Lutsy told me that when the police investigated, they saw that a loose wire had caused a short circuit across the speaker connections. That shorting of the wires produced a loud *CRACK, CRACK, CRACK* in the speakers."

He jabbed his index finger into his chest and shouted, "The police thought that I had created the problem." He lowered his voice a tad and pointed away from himself. "My cousin came with me to stand before the police captain. The officer told me, 'Jan Simkovits, you are charged with sabotage against the communist state. What do you say for yourself?'

"'I'm not guilty,' I told him." Dad's voice was confident, even arrogant. His voice elevated once more. "'Explain yourself!' the captain shouted at me."

Dad's tone steadied but stayed firm. "I told the captain, 'You can't hold me responsible for what I didn't do. It was the people from my electrical crew, and not me, who did the wiring for that stadium installation.'"

Dad's voice rose again as he blurted with bluster, "The captain then yelled at me, 'You are in charge of your people, aren't you?'

"'I can't watch over everything and everybody all the time.' I told him firmly. 'Somebody from my crew may have caused the problem. It was without my knowledge.'" My father jabbed his finger into the car's steering wheel. "'I wasn't even in town when it happened. You can't hold me responsible.'" Dad said that as if the police captain were standing right in front of him.

I quivered in my seat. *How could the Czechoslovak police do that to my father?* But I had a clue. During the summers that my brother and I had visited Slovakia with our mother, my Košice relatives spoke in quiet voices whenever they talked about their communist government.

When I later asked my mother about it, she said quietly, "My brothers and sisters don't want any communist sympathizer to overhear them. Sympathizers could be anybody, anywhere, at any time. Those people could report my relatives to the authorities." She pointed away from her. "If your uncle or aunt ever spoke against the government, the police could put them in jail or send them away."

Dad turned his head slightly toward me but kept his eyes on the road. His voice calmed. "The Košice police captain couldn't prove that I was the guy who created the speaker problem, so he let me go." His voice rose again. "But the captain told me, 'Let this be a warning to you, Jan Simkovits. If you create any trouble from now on, I will throw you in jail for good.'"

Over the years, I had overheard my father share parts of his story with our Eastern European Canadian friends. Now that I had a fuller picture, my ribs felt an icy chill on this summer day. I repositioned my AC vent to push the cold air toward the back of the car.

I asked sheepishly, "Did the police ever figure out who created the short circuit?"

Dad glanced at me and spoke calmly. "As far as I know, son, they never did." He took another breath. "But on that day, after I walked out of the police station with Lutsy, I said to my cousin, 'I have to leave Czechoslovakia.'"

He patted the steering wheel and added, "Lutsy then asked me, 'Jani, are you sure?'"

Dad's voice turned soft as if his relative were there sitting between us. "I said to him, 'I have to leave the country because there is no future here for me. If they're going to watch me all the time and accuse me of things I didn't do, then I can't live like that.'"

From the back seat, Steve asked, "So what happened then, Dad?"

My father accelerated and passed another slowpoke doing under 140 km/h. He eased back into the right lane and said, "Rather than waiting for the Communists to accuse me again of some other phony baloney, I quietly collected debts from friends. Then, on the black currency market, I exchanged the Czechoslovak cash I had to U.S. dollars and German marks." He pointed my way. "I needed hard currency for when I'd be out of the country, for Czechoslovak korunas would be worthless anywhere else."

He then pointed to the car radio. "As I was driving to Bratislava to get to the Austrian border, I heard over the radio that the police were looking for my car, a black Mercedes. I figured that someone from Košice squealed about me wanting to leave the country."

"That must have been scary," I said. "What did you do?"

Dad took another long breath while his eyes stayed fixed forward. "On a country road heading to Bratislava, I ditched my car in a farmer's field. I took my rucksack, walked to the train station at the closest village, and took the next train to Bratislava." He took a long breath. "I waited until nighttime, found a woman on the street, and then I paid her to come to the outskirts of the city."

He grinned. "That woman and I pretended to be boyfriend and girlfriend." He gestured forward with his hand. "When we got close to the frontier, I let her go back to the city while I continued through the woods."

He spoke with apprehension. "I walked throughout the night and into the next day. I crossed the border and walked to the outskirts of Vienna, fifty kilometers away. There I took a streetcar into the city." His voice hesitated and then continued. "I was lucky at the border too. I nearly fell into a big ditch that had been dug by the communist military to catch escaping refugees like me."

My body shivered again. *How might I have dealt with my father's situation?* It must have been terrible for him to flee his country in 1949 at the age of 29. I wondered what future he might have had in his homeland under communist rule, and what future my brother and I would have had there as his sons.

I had seen how most of my Czechoslovak relatives lived in small apartments and how they waited in long lines to buy bread, butter, meat, and clothing. Many of their homes held onto the lingering smell of cooking oil turning bad. Television sets and chocolate bars were a luxury, and jean pants and Superman and Batman comics didn't exist. I was glad our family lived in Canada, where we could get five English-language television channels—three American and two Canadian networks.

Dad glanced again into the car's rearview and side-view mirrors as he followed another fast-moving vehicle in the passing lane. He kept talking, his voice now lighter. "Before I left the country, I asked your mother to marry me so that we could go together. I didn't want to leave the country alone."

Mom spoke. "By then, I had fallen in love with your father, so I agreed to go with him. We had a quiet civil marriage on April 5th. I then left later that month for Vienna, ahead of your father. It was easier for women to get out of our country back then. I was able to get on a special bus filled with Hungarian refugees leaving southern Slovakia through Bratislava to Vienna."

She raised her hand. "Vienna was a free zone controlled by the Americans. So, unlike your father, I left Czechoslovakia legally. That's why I could go back home to Košice in '60 and '64 with you boys."

Dad allowed Mom to speak. "After your daddy escaped," she continued, "he found me in Vienna at an apartment hotel where we had arranged to meet. We were happy to be together and free from the Soviets."

I turned around to look at my mother. She was smiling, her cheeks rosy. She continued. "Later on, your father saw posters in the city that said Canada was looking for domestic couples, so we decided to immigrate there."

I wanted to ask Mom and Dad more about their time in Vienna, the city where we were now heading. Dad glimpsed at Mom in the rearview mirror and then jumped back into the conversation. "We had to escape again from Vienna to Salzburg because the Russians still occupied and controlled the area around the city. We joined a group of refugees. For three nights (we slept during the day), we walked cross country until we got to the American zone near Salzburg."

Dad's tone turned deadly serious. "After travelling through the woods and back roads with only the stars to guide us, we arrived hungry and tired at the American zone. We were lucky not to get caught by the Russians. Had they captured us, we would have been sent back to Czechoslovakia and maybe to a work camp in Russia."

Anna and Jani in Austria after they escaped from Czechoslovakia. Spring of 1949.

He patted his open palm on the steering wheel. "Thankfully, the Americans helped us by giving us food and taking us to the center of Salzburg, where we could register for the Canadian immigration program. There, we were finally free of the Iron Curtain."

Mom spoke again. "Boys, that's why we wanted to go back to those cities on this trip; we wanted to show you those places. They are beautiful sites, and they bring back a lot of memories for us, especially about how we had escaped from Czechoslovakia."

Though there was more to know about my parents' chilling adventures, my mind whirled with a history I hardly knew. I reached between the front seats for my jacket, put it over me, and stared at the fields whizzing by.

Dad continued to speed down the autobahn to Vienna. He passed more cars and then moved back to the right lane to let faster drivers go by in their massive Mercedes and flashy BMWs.

Steve then asked a question that was also on my mind. "If it's still dangerous for you, Dad, why are you going back to Czechoslovakia now?"

Mom looked at my big brother and smiled. "You heard us talk about First Secretary Alexander Dubček, the new leader of the Communist Party of Czechoslovakia?" She raised her hand again. "He's a reformist. His communist government has been lenient in permitting more visitors to go into and citizens to come out of our country."

"People are calling it The Prague Spring," Dad offered. "Because of the more open relations, I was able to get an entry visa to visit. I haven't been back since I left there in '49," he repeated.

Mom added, "There was only one other time that your father ever wanted to go back."

Dad scrunched his face and tightened his lips, looking a bit annoyed. He grumbled, "It was when my father died in '51, two years after we had come to Canada."

Mom ignored Dad's discomfort. "Your Daddy wanted to go back home for his father's funeral. The Slovak priest in our Montreal church had to come and talk him out of it. The priest and I were worried that the communists would shut the door behind your father, throw him back in jail or send him to a work camp, and I would never see him again."

"So, there's nothing to worry about now?" I asked.

"We're okay," Dad responded, "But because tourists have to register with the local police when they stay over in a Czechoslovak city, I don't want to give the local authorities too much chance to check the national records. They might then see that I didn't have official permission to leave the country in 1949."

He took a long breath. "To be safe, I don't want to spend more than three days in your mother's and my hometown. I don't want to give the police the time to come looking for me."

* * *

Many happy reunions ensued during our short Košice stay. In my parents' small city of their birth, Dad had only a couple of cousins from his father's side, and no one remained from his birth mother's family. She had died young from tuberculosis when my father was a toddler. Dad's father remarried a Slovak woman a few years later. *Nagymama* (grandmother) Maria was from a family of twelve brothers and sisters, and many of them lived in Košice with their families.

Three of Mom's five siblings and their spouses still lived there too. One of her brothers lived in Prague. A second brother had followed Mom and Dad to Canada in '50, with his wife.

At our Kosice hotel, my brother asked Dad why most of his and Mom's family still lived in their hometown.

Dad looked at Steve and me. "Other than during the recent Dubček era, the Czechoslovak Communist Party hasn't allowed its citizens the freedom to move from city to city unless they get official permission to do so." He pointed his finger like a teacher giving a school lesson. "If people want to change jobs, they need to get a signature from both their old boss here and their new one over there." His face stayed somber. "That's difficult for most people to do because many bosses want money under the table as compensation for their written permission."

"Oh," I said. "We don't do that in Canada, do we?" At 13 years old, I hadn't yet learned our country's employment ropes.

"No," Dad offered. "Canada is a free country. You can work where ever you want, as long as you are capable. That's another reason your mother and I left Czechoslovakia to go there."

In Košice, we visited one set of kin after another. Quoting a Hungarian expression, "We were up to our necks in relatives."

Most of them lived in compact apartments in stark concrete block buildings built by the communists. Specks of grass and sparse trees surrounded the stark structures. Within, we walked up flights of dingy and dimly lit staircases. We rode noisy, cramped elevators. I smelled the musty odors of dust and lubricating elevator grease mixed with the pungent fragrances of spicy Hungarian and Slovak cooking.

It was tight quarters in the small apartments that housed our extended family. There were smiling older men with missing teeth and zaftig women who Dad affectionately called *stara babas* (old bags in Slovak), though he never said that in their presence. Crowded within petite living rooms were space-saving wall units and modest furniture that left little space for standing or walking around. Kitchens had little elbow room if more than one family member wanted to cook.

A tight standing-room-for-one bathroom, with a tub and sink but no toilet, was situated in the hallway by the front entrance. Next to the bathroom was a smaller toilet compartment, entered via a separate hallway door. Sitting in that broom-closet sized *véce* (water closet, or literally "WC" in Hungarian) felt like being in an indoor outhouse where one's bowed head almost touched the door.

Dad had forewarned us about the bleak concrete panel exterior and cramped insides of Košice's dreary communist buildings. "Boys, you have to realize that no one owns their home in the communist world. They rent it from the state, which builds and owns everything."

His face looked serious as he spoke in a somber tone. "The kind of home we have in Canada—a three-bedroom, split-level house with a den and two bathrooms—is almost unheard of here." He grinned. "We are lucky not to be squeezed into a small apartment like canned Canadian herrings."

He raised a finger. "Please don't say anything that will embarrass our relatives or us. If they ask you about Canada, talk about the things you do at home but not what we own."

I understood my father's concern. At our Montreal home, my brother and I were not allowed to whine about sharing a bedroom. My mother scolded us if we complained about brushing our teeth together in the bathroom, or if we grumbled about one of us being at the sink while the other was taking a bath. I was grateful that Dad had the foresight to cross an ocean and not remain in a country of cramped water closets.

We split our time in Košice between my father's torrent of Slovak relatives and my mother's Hungarian siblings and their smaller families. My brother and I understood Hungarian. Mom spoke that language to Steve and me at home, and we had acquired more during our previous summer trips to Košice.

From Mom's brothers came joyful pokes and squeezes. From her sisters came teary hugs and sloppy kisses.

When *Irén néni* (Aunt Irén, my mother's middle sister) first saw us this time, she burst forth with joy. She put her crossed hands over her heart, shed a tear, and proclaimed how happy she was to see us. It was as if she had lost us for a lifetime, and we now came home to her.

Irén was a short, heavy-set woman; she reminded me of the *stara baba* woman I saw in Canadian TV commercials for Italian pasta and spaghetti sauce. She lived with her professional artist husband, Maximilián Buš (Bush).

My brother and I referred to the short, stout man as *Busie bácsi* (Uncle Bushie), just as both Mom and Irén did. He was a handsome man, yet no taller than I was at thirteen years old. He sported a narrow forearm that ended in a deformed, stubby hand with tiny fingers, that way since birth. He kept that hand in his pants pocket so no one would stare at it, especially us kids.

Irén was full of excitement when surrounded by family. She hardly sat down or closed her mouth to either words or food. She had no children of her own. She showered my brother and me with her home cooking, all sorts of local cookies and chocolates, and continual attention. She stroked our heads as if we were cherished pets, calling us, "Nice boys! Nice boys!" Those were possibly her only English words, and she had a habit of repeating herself as she talked. It was all a part of her love and adoration for her nephews.

My mother's family congregated at Irén and Max's larger-than-average apartment. It was situated on Košice's main street, next to the opera house where my uncle worked as a set designer.

Max was an accomplished painter and had filled his and Irén's apartment with his stained-glass creations and oil paintings. The largest painting hung behind their long, wooden dining room table. It showed a nearly naked man bleeding to death as he lay dying on a luxurious, red cloth canopy bed covered with an animal skin blanket. An attractive, almost entirely naked woman looked on with her arms and hands held up in surprise or despair. *Busie bácsi* explained in Hungarian, "It's 'The Death of Attila' on his wedding night. The woman is his bride, Ildico."

My zaftig *Irén néni* placed her hand on the backside of her head. She turned her head to one side as if she were mimicking Ildico. She offered in Hungarian, "Busie used my likeness and physique for Ildico." Because my aunt's girth was many times that of the svelte woman in the painting, everyone chuckled, including me.

Similar to this likeness, my uncle, Max Bus, copied the original painting
"The Death of Attila," created in 1855 by Paczka Ferenc of Hungary.

Over the next days, Irén treated us to her Hungarian suppers of goulash, chicken paprikash, and stuffed cabbage. She fried big *szilvás és turós gombóc* (cheese and plum balls) for dessert. By the end of each meal, I felt like one of her stuffed balls and was ready to curl up for a long nap. Not even the endless chatter among Mom's family could keep my eyes open.

We spent the rest of our time in Košice with the larger clan of Dad's stepmother. Many of those Slovaks also spoke Hungarian, especially the older folks who were born before WWII. Younger Slavic- and Russian-speaking parents urged hugs and *Ahoys* from their young kids. Old *nagymamas* and middle-aged *nénis* pecked and patted our cheeks. Dark, leather-skinned *nagyapák* (grandfathers) and *bácsis* wielded firm handshakes and solid back slaps.

Dad's relatives seemed less well-to-do than Mom's. They invited us just for mid-day snacks instead of big suppers. They served buttery, cucumber and cheese-filled finger sandwiches, syrupy soft drinks, brittle cookies, and chocolate-sprinkled biscuits.

Our parents encouraged my brother and me, both pudgy teens, to eat the food that their family served. Perhaps still stuffed on Aunt Irén's home cooking, Mom and Dad only picked at what Dad's relatives had prepared. While my parents spoke to Dad's family in Slovak, a language Steve and I didn't understand, my brother and I indulged in the sandwiches and biscuits until the buttons on our pants nearly burst.

The hours of chitchat wore me down. I felt suffocated by the food and bored because I didn't know the language. (My parents spoke Slovak at home only when they didn't want Steve and me to understand what they were saying.)

By the end of our last visit, Steve and my eyes turned glassy. I felt like a beached Canadian seal lounging on a hard and scratchy couch. We melted into the thin and hard Czechoslovak furniture cushions to wait out the remaining food and seemingly unending chatter.

On our last full day in their hometown, Dad wanted to give us an experience of Slavic folk culture. He followed a car caravan of his relatives to a *salaš* (sheep farm) in the countryside. We spent the afternoon in a large cabin where Dad and his kin consumed *bryndzové halušky* (sheep cheese fried with little dumplings) and knocked back gallons of raw sheep milk. Dad looked at my brother and me. "My parents used to take me to places like this when I was your age."

I found the soft sheep cheese too salty, and it squeaked between my teeth. The sheep milk was warm and bitter. *Yuck!* All I could eat was the salty white bread rolls. Steve and I sat for hours watching Dad and his uncles get into that sheep stuff as they talked nonstop in Slovak.

Realizing we were bored, Mom took us outside to look at sheep getting sheared. Though the scrawny, naked animals were fun to watch, I couldn't wait to get back to my mother's relatives in Košice and the Hungarian fare I found more palatable.

Though Mom and Dad's families were happy and excited to reunite with ours, conversation dipped to whispers whenever anyone talked about the communist government or the lack of decent goods in the local stores. When Dad asked about First Secretary Dubček, our relatives glanced out windows and toward open doors to see if anyone else was listening.

Later, I asked my father, "If it's the Prague Spring, why is everyone so careful with what they are saying? I thought life in Czechoslovakia was now freer."

Dad's face looked grim. "No one knows for sure if the Soviets will let Dubček continue his reforms. Everybody's afraid of what the USSR might do. No one here wants to make an enemy of the old-line Stalinists."

His face turned grave. "I don't blame them; you can't trust those Russians. Stalin and his successors have imprisoned and killed many who spoke against them. Whole families could disappear, and no one would know what happened to them."

From then on, in parks and public places, I too found myself looking around to see who might be overhearing our conversations.

After each extended visits with my father's family, Dad slipped American dollars to husbands and fathers as we said our goodbyes. I was touched by their joyful faces—complemented by the bitter-sweet, watery eyes of their spouses—as they palmed Dad's cash. It seemed as if everyone looked up to my father.

After we had left the last family, Mom turned to Dad and spoke in Hungarian. "Why do you give money to every one of your relatives? You are not that close to these people. Who are they to you?"

My father shrugged and responded in their language. "They talk to each other. If I give to one, then I have to give to the rest." He looked at my brother and me and switched to English. "Having a few dollars, they can get a lot of Czechoslovak koruna on the black market. This way, they can eat a little better this month."

Mom said nothing more, but her tight face showed her feelings about my father's giving habits, though he gave cash to her siblings too. I liked that my father put smiles on his relatives' faces. I wished that Mom and he wouldn't fight about it.

For our last night in Košice, Dad rented the back room of our hotel's restaurant to host a private party for thirty-five relatives. He had the manager arrange long tables in the shape of a T, with our family sitting at the top of the T. "That way, we could see everyone, and everyone could see us," Dad said.

He wanted to return the hospitality to those who had fed us during our days in Košice. I suspected that Dad wanted his relatives to celebrate with us for a final time and to show them how well our family was doing.

My father didn't want our party held in a public place. He knew how rowdy things could get among drinking Slovaks. He told us, "I don't want to attract too much attention while we are here."

None of Mom's family joined in that evening; I gathered that they were not the party-goers that Dad's family seemed to be.

Dad was right about his kin. Many of the men grew loud voices and wobbly legs after knocking back shots of Slivovica, a potent plum brandy that was 50% alcohol. They partook in 76-proof Becherovka, a digestif of herbal bitters that they downed after supper with or in their coffee. Wanting to educate his sons about life, Dad let us taste those spirits. "Try it, but don't get loaded," he said.

I took small sips. Those strong drinks burned three times—on my tongue, in my throat, and in my stomach. I then realized why Hungarian-Slovak fare was much spicier here in Košice than what Mom cooked at home. The way these Slovak men drank throat-burning Slivovica and smoked lung-choking Russian cigarettes, the food needed to be overly spicy for them to taste it. I wondered if they would spend Dad's money gifts on those vices rather than food for their families.

As the evening wore on, the noise in the room got louder, and the air became dense with cigarette smoke. To keep up with the rest, Mom slowly nursed a drink, and one of Dad's Canadian cigarettes burned between her fingers. With a big smirk and hearty laugh, she chatted with the men and ladies who came up to her. Carrying his drink, Dad stood and walked around to visit with every guest. He shared smokes and, along with them, toasted to good living and long life.

Being too young for adult vices, and perhaps too shy to engage our home-grown Hungarian, my brother and I played with the candles that sat on the table. We employed a knife to see if we could make the candles drip hot wax down their sides, but without the drops reaching the tablecloth. After a time, a waiter came and took the candles away. All we could then do was order and down more syrupy soft drinks and sugary biscuits.

The next day, as we checked out of our hotel, Dad boasted that the whole previous evening's affair—a three-course supper including drinks and tip—had cost a little over 4000 Czechoslovak koruna. That was about $140CAD at the black market exchange rate my father had gotten from a close relative. Dad said, "For $4 Canadian per person, or about $3.50 U.S., any Westerner can be a big shot in this poor country." He smiled. "Yesterday's supper would have cost me ten times more in Montreal."

Back then, I was proud of my father for his largesse and for knowing the money trade of Czechoslovakia's black market. Today, I'm relieved the communist police hadn't caught his exchanging money illegally and then sent him to an Iron Curtain jail.

After our three filling days in Košice, my father drove my brother and me to Switzerland. There, Steve and I were to stay for three weeks at a French-language camp. We would take classes every morning—to help improve our French for school in Quebec. Dad told us, "I want you guys to learn good French and not what the Quebec farmer speaks."

For the weeks we were to be in Switzerland, Mom would remain in Košice with her relatives. The plan was for her to join Steve and me in Zurich near the end of August so that we could fly back to Montreal together.

There were no hassles in Bratislava when we passed through the Czechoslovakia frontier into Austria—unlike the over two hours it had taken to cross the other way. Leaving the border station, Dad said, "I'm glad we are out of Slovakia. With the Soviets, anything could happen without warning."

* * *

Steve and I attended a Swiss camp situated on the hillside above Lausanne. It overlooked deep blue Lake Geneva. The French Alps, looking dark green and gray in the distance, jutted out behind the long lake.

It was the morning of Wednesday, August 21, 1968. It was Steve's and my last week of camp. On that warm and partly cloudy day, we had finished our morning French classes and were heading for a well-earned dinner. The camp director's assistant saw us in the hallway and said, "Harvy and Stephen, come with me, please. Madame Director wants to see the two of you."

My brother and I stared at each other with an expression of "Did we do anything wrong?" (Or maybe each of our faces projected, "What did *you* do wrong, brother?") Neither of us said anything as we followed the assistant to the director's office.

When we arrived, the director—a large, dark-haired, Czechoslovak-born woman—was speaking vigorously over the telephone. We knew that her voice could turn icy stern if one weren't where one should be during the school day. Now, she was half crying and half screaming into the large, black receiver. "Where is my brother? What happened to my brother?" she cried.

I was taken aback by her frantic tone. When she saw Steve and me, she lowered her voice, converted to her native Czech language, and turned away from us. She wiped some sweat from her brow with a handkerchief. Soon she hung up the phone and turned to look at us. "My brother is a political activist in Czechoslovakia. He recently went missing."

Her voice was edgy. "Dubček's Prague Spring has ended. Last night, Soviet, Polish, Bulgarian, and Hungarian troops entered and occupied Czechoslovakia. People have disappeared; telephone communication has been cut off; the borders are closed. No one is getting in or out of the country."

Without waiting for our reaction, she retrieved a note from her desk. "Your father called earlier today and said he wants to talk to the both of you." She glanced at her watch. "He's calling you from Montreal any minute now, at noon. Just sit here and wait." She gestured toward two chairs in front of her desk.

The hands of the wall clock showed a minute to noon. My brother and I glanced at each other, said nothing, and followed the director's orders. I suspected we didn't want to upset her any more than she was.

Seconds after my bottom had hit the chair, the phone rang, its loud ring startling me. The director grabbed the big, black phone receiver, said hello, and then spoke in her native tongue. She then handed the phone to my brother, saying, "It's your father."

As Steve put the receiver to his ear, I leaned toward him and put my ear near the earpiece. Dad said, "Hello, son. Do you understand what's happening in Czechoslovakia? Has the director explained it to you?"

My brother said, "Yes, Dad, she told us. Have you heard from Mom?"

Dad was calm. "No, not yet, but don't worry." I didn't know if my father said that because there truly was nothing to be concerned about or if he just didn't want us to worry. "Your mother will get out on her own when she can. If she can't get out of the country by the time your camp ends in a few days, you two will have to go by train to Zurich and then to the airport by yourselves."

Dad's voice stayed composed, unlike Mom who could get upset at the hint of any family strife. "I left your Swissair flight tickets and money for the train with the camp director. She will give them to you on the day you leave so you can get to Zurich and then fly back to Montreal." His tone remained matter-of-fact. "I'll alert Swissair about Mom's possibly not flying with you, and about you guys being on the plane as unaccompanied minors."

"Okay, Dad," we said simultaneously.

"Good! And don't worry about Mom; she'll be okay. Now let me speak to the Director."

After she had hung up the phone, the Director offered, "If you boys want to, you can take the rest of the day off from your camp activities."

Steve and I looked at each other and then back at her. "No, we don't have to," both of us said, and we exited the room. I, and perhaps Steve too, didn't want questions from our campmates as to why we were not participating in activities.

For the ensuing days, I wondered what it must be like for Mom and her family in Košice. Did Russian tanks surround them? Were Hungarian troops pointing machine guns at them? I wondered what had happened to the director's brother. Was he beaten and behind bars in a Soviet Socialist prison? Maybe no one, except the Soviet authorities themselves, knew what had become of him. Then again, perhaps I had seen too many war movies, and nothing terrible had happened.

It took me a long time to get to sleep that night. A day or two later, I developed painful stomach cramps that had me running to a bathroom both day and night.

The Tatransky sisters (left to right, Aunt Irén, Aunt Ilonka, and my mother) together at Sliač, in the Low Tatra Mountains of Slovakia.
August of 1968, just days before the Soviet reinvasion of Czechoslovakia.

On the day before my brother and I were to leave for Zurich, the director stopped us in the hallway. She said, "Your mother has called." The stern-faced woman spoke matter-of-factly. "She has made it out of Czechoslovakia and is now in Vienna. She will meet you tomorrow at the train station in Zurich. We'll put you on the morning train from here."

She said nothing about her brother. I surmised that her unemotional tone meant he was okay, but I didn't know for sure and was afraid to ask.

Mom was crying with joy when she greeted us at the Zurich station. She hugged and kissed us repeatedly, as Aunt Irén had done after not seeing us for years.

Over supper at our hotel, she told us about the rumbling Russian tanks and the marching Hungarian troops coming down Košice's main street to reoccupy the city. She blabbered, "My family and I were scared; we didn't know what would happen. The government closed the Košice airport and railway station; we couldn't make any international calls; I didn't know if I could get out of the country." She hardly took a breath. "For days, we stayed indoors and listened to the radio. We didn't know what else to do."

She put her hand to her head and continued to talk fast. "After a while, we heard that the authorities were telling foreign tourists and journalists to leave the country. I was able to take a train to Bratislava and then a bus to Vienna—the first place I could call your camp. I was then able to get a flight to Zurich early this morning."

She looked longingly at us, put her hands on ours, and blurted. "I'm so happy to see the two of you." A big sigh came out of her as she looked down. "No one knows what's going to happen to our Czechoslovakia."

Over the next weeks, Mom received letters from her relatives that told us they were okay. She began to shrug off her ordeal. She publicly celebrated Dad's trip behind the Iron Curtain by putting an announcement in our small-town newspaper:

Canadian immigrant, John Simkovits, recently returned from visiting his Czechoslovakia homeland after nearly 20 years of separation from his stepmother and family.

Because of her limited English, Mom had asked for my help with the announcement's wording. I asked her, "Why are you doing this, Mom?" I didn't understand why she was making Dad's reunion with his family such a big deal.

"Because we should be proud of your father," she responded.

"So why didn't you put the announcement in the paper before we left for Czechoslovakia?"

She looked at me as if I were naïve. "I couldn't. What if word of your daddy's visit to his homeland got to Czechoslovak communist authorities? They might have detained him and made it hard for him to come back to Canada."

When subsequent letters to Mom arrived from her Košice family, she never shared their contents with my brother or me. Perhaps she wanted to protect us from her family's hardships as a renewed Soviet winter descended upon their country. By then, Steve and I had returned to boarding school and were at an even greater distance from our parents' homeland.

By the end of that summer, my head and gut better understood my parents' paranoia about the communist rulers of their country. I better comprehended why our Slovak-, Polish- and Hungarian-Canadian friends spoke with frustration and tears about their overseas relatives living not only with a shortage of goods but also with a fear of the Soviets.

I appreciated my father even more for immigrating to a country where tanks didn't rumble down our roads, where people didn't have to whisper in their homes or on the street, and where we could live and work where we wanted to. I felt that both my brother and I owed our father for having escaped his country to give our family such freedoms.

* * * *

8

My Father's Devotions

I was glad Sunday services were over. Now we could eat!

My belly had made hunger noises through another boring Latin Mass that possibly nobody except the priest could understand. The dull part of the day was over. I was ready to feast on my mother's dinner of meat soup, chicken paprikash, cucumber salad, and apple strudel for dessert. My brother and I, now in our mid-teens, were home from boarding school for the summer. Our father had taken us to the local Roman Catholic church while Mom stayed home to make our meal.

To Dad's chagrin, Steve and I had been fidgeting, poking, and prodding each other in the pew during services, acting like the young teenagers we were. After several times of saying "Shush!" to us, Dad stood, stepped in front of me, motioned me to move over to his spot, and then sat down between Steve and me. He then looked sternly at us but said not a word. It was easy to feel his irritation.

Dad said little during the car ride home. As soon as we arrived, Mom told us, "Boys, go wash your hands." She looked at our father too. "Dinner is ready."

By the time we came to the kitchen table, Mom had placed her hot *húsleves* (meat and vegetable soup) at everyone's place. We sat and chewed on the chunks of beef and slurped the vermicelli laden broth. While he ate, Dad bent his head so low that it looked as if it might drop right into his bowl.

Dad could be funny during a family meal. He once came down for Sunday breakfast and looked very unusual. His face stayed blank, and he said nothing, but I could tell he was holding back a smirk or snicker. It took us a minute, but we suddenly realized that my father had parted his hair to one side instead of combing it straight back. He looked as if he were a much younger version of himself. We all pointed to his head and burst out laughing, and Dad chuckled along with us.

But at today's dinner, Dad was in a serious mood. His eyes unexpectedly looked up at Steve and me, and he began to speak. "Boys, my parents were very strict with me. My parents expected me to go to church every Sunday and behave during services." He spoke slowly and deliberately. "My father made me become an altar boy at St. Elisabeth Dom in Košice. If I ever misbehaved, the priest would say something to him after services."

My brother and I slowed down our soup slurping, and I stared into Mom's broth. I felt as if my father—and maybe God too—were looking down upon Steve and me for having shoved each other in church.

Steve and I knew that Dad had been born in 1920 in the newly formed Czechoslovakia. His parents raised him in the dominant faith of his Slovakia province. During one of our summer trips there, in 1960, when my brother and I were kids, Mom had shown us Košice's St. Elisabeth's Dom.

That over 600-year-old gothic cathedral towered over the small city and was the spiritual centre for Eastern Slovakia. During our visit, we passed through the Dom's cool interior structure full of massive stone columns that supported a central dome. We walked by small chapels with massive stained glass windows that brought multi-coloured light into that enormous edifice. Rows of lit candles in small and large red jars were at the base of every sculpture and holy figure.

Under a statue of Mother Mary, my brother and I had dipped our fingers into holy water and made the sign of the cross. Below a figure of St. Elisabeth, the Hungarian Empire's patron saint, we dropped Czechoslovak koruna into collection slots. We lit candles, knelt, and prayed silently—our hands clasped tightly together—for departed relatives. The kind face of St. Elisabeth, like Mother Mary's, gave me calm in this enormous stone house of worship that seemed to touch the sky. It felt as if God, Jesus, and all the Slovak and Hungarian saints were eying my every move. I wanted to have them think of me as "a good boy," worthy of their blessings.

When I later walked down the outer stone steps of the cathedral, I tripped and skinned my knee. I cried while my mother and her relatives consoled me. They washed my wound with a wet handkerchief and patted my head and cheek. I wondered why St. Elisabeth hadn't looked out for me as I departed her house of worship. *Didn't I pray well enough for her and Mother Mary?*

Our father took in a hefty spoonful of Mom's soup. His face scrunched as he turned to her and said, "*Nagyon forró!* [Very hot!]" His voice was irritated.

Mom went to her fridge and fetched a few ice cubes to stir into the broth. She then sat down to join us.

Dad looked at my brother and me. "When I was a child," he offered, "I was never permitted to fool around in church. If I did, my stepmother would grab and shake me. After services, my father would take me to the shed and spank me good with his belt."

My brother and I remained quiet. Contrary to his upbringing, my father never laid a heavy hand on me. He once raised a belt to my older brother for disobeying our mother, but he later felt terrible about it; he never spanked Steve again. But he still could let out an ear-shattering bellow if we ever crossed him. I never wanted to get him angry.

Dad looked again at Steve and me. He offered, "Boys, I want you to put your best attention to your Catholic studies and on our church services. I want you to be good Catholics."

My father didn't explain what a "good Catholic" was to him, other than implying that Steve and I shouldn't bug each other in church. He didn't realize that many students in our Catholic public school hadn't quite seen our religious studies as he did.

My brother and I had attended Catholic elementary and junior high schools in the Montreal suburb where we lived. Religious Education classes occurred weekly, but its homework was minimal, rarely challenging. Being a conscientious, eager-to-please student, I did my Bible story reading, showed attention and respect to the attending priest, and raised my hand in class. But not every student was as diligent.

Every Friday morning at our Catholic junior high, students participated in a Mass. It was performed in the school cafeteria and led by a newly minted priest, Father Michaels. He was a young and soft-spoken man. He was also a very practical pastor.

At the beginning of our first service, Father Michaels had the students pass both a silver plate and an empty golden chalice through the rows of the student congregation. The plate contained quarter-sized, unleavened bread hosts.

As the 150 students passed those items from kid to kid, starting from the back row to the front of the congregation, Father Michaels stood behind his makeshift cafeteria altar and offered his instructions. He spoke in a soft tone. "If anyone wishes to receive the Holy Sacrament, please take one host from the plate and put it into the chalice as it passes along."

With his thoughtful plan, Father Michaels would have the exact number of hosts he needed to bless before the offering of the Blessed Sacrament. Since the priest had to consume every blessed host before the Mass concluded, his instructions would allow for not wasting any of the hosts.

It seemed that some students became bored with our morning service. The chalice became filled with hosts, but very few kids went forward to receive Holy Communion. The unsuspecting Father then had to spend many minutes stuffing his cheeks full of those dry, cardboard-flavored wafers. Having just one of these hosts melt on your tongue was manageable. Having to consume dozens at a time, over and over again, could be torturous to one's saliva glands.

I could see the astonishment and pained frustration on Father Michael's face as he eyed his filled chalice at the Communion conclusion. He consumed the pile of hosts slowly in his bursting mouth, using what little holy wine available to wash them down. He never said a harsh word about it to the student and teacher congregation. *Holy mackerel!* crossed my young mind as I watched the innocent priest struggled, without a whine or a whimper, with his laden cup.

Father Michaels repeated this practice for several Fridays. As the Masses continued, more students got into the act. Being an obedient student, I never added more fuel to the chalice by placing an unnecessary host into the cup. But others did.

Not a single student dared to laugh or giggle through this procedure for fear of being accused of stuffing the chalice. There was utter silence in that cafeteria, by teacher and student alike, while the Father's host consumption continued to its complete conclusion, crumbs and all, week after blessed week. I held back snickers and felt awful for Father Michaels, but I didn't know how to help our priest with his holy host quandary.

After weeks of painfully pondering his predicament, this puzzled priest finally recognized the flaw in his host allocation. At subsequent services, just before the start of Mass, the Father laid the plate and chalice right next to his altar. He then gave his instructions for desiring pupils to come to the front of the room to place a wafer into the cup. Now that there had to be a student face behind every blessed host, only those who wanted the Sacrament got the Sacrament.

I continued to devour Mom's homemade soup, as tasty as ever.

I thought about my father's religious practices. Dad was a faithful Catholic, but he wasn't the most devout follower. We didn't go to church every weekend, though we rarely skipped Mass on the holy days of obligation. My brother and I in tow, we went to services on Christmas, Easter, Good Friday, Palm Sunday, and other important days.

Sometimes Mom came with us, especially for the Masses at Montreal's Slovak Church or St. Patrick's Basilica in downtown Montreal. Other times she stayed home to have dinner prepared for when we returned.

Our father's greater devotion was to his consumer electronics business. He produced kids' record players (he called them "lunch boxes") and adult console stereos, enjoyed in tens of thousands of homes throughout Canada. For most of our growing up years, Dad "made business" six long days per week and rested only on Sundays. Outside of church, he spent much of his downtime snoring like an elephant on the living-room couch to sleep off a hard week's work.

Dad was a cold-weather Catholic. When it was warm enough outdoors, instead of putting on a Sunday suit and sitting and sweating in a hot, humid church, he played golf with his business friends and colleagues. He left home at sunrise for a prompt seven o'clock tee off. Steve and I received church reprieves on those days too, rising late and watching television all morning in our pyjamas. When we became old enough, Dad took one of us to the golf course to be his caddy or cart driver.

During my turn shadowing our father on the fairways, I closely followed his instruction. I kept the right distance from him when he hit his golf ball. I cleaned those white balls in the ball cleaning machines, swishing each dimpled sphere up and down until it sparkled like new. I watched out for the direction of his every hit, helped him find a lost ball in the rough, and kept track of everyone's score. Every time my father approached his ball, I said a quiet prayer under my breath, "Please, God, help him hit a good shot." He prayed too, saying *"Hesus Maria!"* in sync with his duffs, slices, and hooks.

Coming off the 18th green, Dad put his hand on my shoulder and said, "You're a good golf caddy, son." I filled with pride. Our golf outings were much more fun than going to dreary church services conducted in dull Latin.

Coming back home after clubhouse sandwiches, Dad hugged the couch for the rest of the afternoon. He rose for a mid-afternoon snack of back bacon with rye bread and green pepper slices. He woke again for Mom's supper (paprika chicken, stuffed cabbage, stuffed peppers, or Wiener schnitzel) that we ate at the coffee table as we watched *The Wonderful World of Disney*. Mom and Dad were in good moods whenever the television and her Hungarian cooking were involved. It made me warm inside.

After supper, our father lay down to watch *Bonanza* and to have another snooze if it came his way. While Mom cleaned the kitchen, Steve and I hung out in the living room with Dad. Elephant snores again emanated from him as he slept.

Encouraged by our father, and guided by our Catholic elementary school, my brother and I were confirmed and had our first communions. Dad rarely talked to us about those Catholic ceremonies and their significance, or what being Catholic meant to him. He only offered, "As my parents had wanted me to do, you two need to pay attention to your religious studies in school."

Not wanting to cross Dad, I did.

Mom never said much about our family's religious rituals; she followed Dad's lead or lack thereof. While we were growing up, her most significant contribution to our religious upbringing was to serve us fish sticks or breaded sole on meatless Fridays.

After we had finished Mom's soup, she served her main course of chicken paprikash. It swam in her delicious creamy tomato sauce that also topped her petite potato dumplings. Sides of sweet and sour cucumber salad completed the presentation. We dug in.

Dad was in a teaching mood this day, and he had our undivided attention. He continued his luncheon sermon. "Like all young Czechoslovaks, I had to start my compulsory military service right after my 18th birthday, in 1938."

He took a deep breath as he looked down at the kitchen table. "But six months after I joined the forces, the 1938 Munich Agreement was signed by Germany, France, Britain, and Italy." He counted the countries on his fingers, starting with his thumb. "That Munich accord was an act of appeasement by the British and French toward Adolf Hitler who wanted to expand the Nazi regime."

Ire now rose in my father's eyes. His left hand—clenched in a fist—hit the table with a thump. "Nobody could believe it. Without our Czechoslovak government having any say whatsoever, parts of my country became annexed to Germany and Hungary. What remained was the smaller, fascist-led state of Slovakia and the Nazi-controlled Protectorate of Bohemia and Moravia."

Dad stopped eating. He glanced at Steve and me for a moment and then added, "Yet Hitler had a bigger plan. The Slavic people were to become workers for the Third Reich, or the Nazis deported them east, further away from Germany."

He raised his voice again. "Hitler planned to enslave us, sterilize us so we couldn't have children, starve us, and then discard us like we were nothing." He flung his free hand toward the floor. "Those Nazis bastards wanted to use us up and kill us off for their master Aryan race and new German order."

I sat still in my chair; I didn't lift my fork to my mouth until Dad would calm down. After a moment, he grabbed the edge of the table with both hands and continued to speak with force. "While the ink was still wet on that Munich Agreement, Hitler immediately expanded Germany's empire by annexing the largely German-speaking Sudetenland that bordered Bohemia and Germany."

From previous conversations, I knew Dad was sympathetic toward the Sudetenland Germans. The winning allied powers of World War One, led by President Wilson of the United States, had carved Sudetenland out of the Austrian-Hungarian Empire in the formation of the multi-ethnic state of Czechoslovakia. Dad had told us, "The Czech police sometimes brutalized those Sudeten Germans by killing innocent women and children during their demonstrations for independence."

Nevertheless, Dad stood with his Czechoslovakia, reminding us, "Between the Great Wars, Czechoslovakia was the first and longest-standing democratic republic in Europe. Even though there was discord, Masaryk, our first president, gave all regions and minorities a voice in the government." I saw my father's proud smile for his once democratic homeland.

My brother and I stayed quiet as we continued to fork down Mom's paprikash. Dad now spoke calmly, talking as he chewed. "The 1938 Munich Agreement changed everything in my part of the country." He pointed his finger like a school teacher. "That agreement led to southern Slovakia becoming annexed to Hungary. It was a deal Hitler had made with Hungary's Regent, Admiral Horthy."

My father's voice sounded compassionate for the former Hungarian ruler. "In the years after Hitler had come to power in 1933, Horthy decided to side with Germany. Horthy hated and feared the Soviet communists more than he did the Nazis." Dad took a long breath. "He counted on his Nazi alliance to protect Hungary from Soviet Russia. He also wanted Hungary to regain the empire it had lost in World War One." He sighed. "In 1938, Hitler obliged."

Dad shook his head, clenched his fist, and pursed his lips. "With the stroke of a pen, without the people of Czechoslovakia having any say, the major powers of Europe dismantled our democracy by way of that Munich Agreement."

I was impressed with what my father knew about his country's history. I was also disturbed that the Axis powers cut up his homeland like meat for growling dogs.

Dad looked away and then back at us. "Because of that accord, my military comrades and I, who were from the southern part of Slovakia, had to report back to our hometowns. We were to be transferred from the now-defunct Czechoslovak forces and into the Hungarian military." He glanced at Mom. "Our city of Košice was renamed Kassa (*Ka-sha*)—as it had been during the Austrian-Hungarian Empire—and it became a part of Hungary again."

Mom jumped into the conversation. "All the Hungarians in our region of Southern Slovakia celebrated our re-annexation. There were parades in Kassa." She raised a hand. "The main street filled with cheering people."

While staring at Dad, my brother asked the question I was thinking. "Could what happened to Czechoslovakia happen here? Could Canada ever get invaded and annexed?"

Compassion was in Dad's eyes as he looked at my brother. "We don't have to worry about that here, son. Canada has been an independent democratic country for over 100 years, and we have a good, strong neighbour in the United States. It's one of the reasons why your mother and I came here. America wouldn't let anything happen to us if the Soviets tried to invade us from the north or west."

He pointed his fork at my brother. "Our bigger problem here in Quebec is the growing animosity between the French and the English. Some French people want Quebec to be a country separate from Canada."

My bold older brother came forth with another question. "Dad, what would happen if Quebec did separate from Canada?"

"That would be a big problem, son." Our father raised his right hand and sliced the air with his knife. "It would divide eastern and western Canada. *Les* bloody *Québec separatists*,"—he said those words with a Slovak version of a

French accent—"want to destroy our country. It's going to cause a lot of English people to move out of our province. We may have to leave too."

Mom poked my father's shoulder while she stood behind him, ready to swoop in for finished plates. "But that may not happen for a long time," she piped in, "if it happens at all."

I wasn't sure if I should feel safe or not where we lived. My mind felt bursting with what I was hearing. I kept my attention on Mom's dinner, filling my stomach with her soothing fare.

I was glad my parents had come to this country to have my brother and me. Who knew what would happen if our province were no longer a part of Canada. My kid's mind wondered if we would be forced by French marauders or militia to leave our home. I trusted that my father would know what to do if something terrible ever happened in Quebec. He had survived many ordeals. By his side, our family would survive too.

Dad glanced at Mom, his brows raised, and his face turned perturbed. He took back the conversation. "After the Czechoslovak army disbanded, I had to prove to the Hungarian command that my Christian background went back for many generations. Without that, I could have been thrown out of military service and thrown into a Hungarian forced labour camp with other undesirables and enemies of our new regime." His voice rose. "I had to prove that my family had been Catholic for many generations."

Mom stayed quiet as she moved her serving dishes back to the stove and placed our empty plates next to the sink. Dad kept on speaking as he ate, pointing his fork at us as he continued his dinnertime lesson. "Some members of my extended family in Kassa, from my mother's side, were Nazi sympathizers. Others were volunteers for the Slovak SS or members of the Hungarian Arrow Cross fascist party." He pulled on the front of his white shirt. "I remember them in their green shirts. They had a pair of crossed arrows as their badge." He demonstrated by crossing his two index fingers.

His voice hardened. "The thought of those people makes me sick. They hated Jews, and they terrorized everyone. They executed many Jews, military deserters, and escaped prisoners." He looked upward and pointed with his fork. "Near the end of 1944, when the Russian Soviet Army was knocking on the door of Slovakia, the Arrow Cross fanatics went so far as to hang those people on the lampposts in downtown Kassa."

I stared at my plate, my gut knotted from the horror.

"Yet my parents were not fascists," Dad added. "They were just swept up in the Nazi craziness. We had to pretend we were not against them."

Dad didn't say more about what he meant. I wondered if he and his parents had to stand aside, trying to ignore the atrocities the Nazis perpetrated on its people. Or might my grandparents have had to participate in some terrible way? Though I was glad my father said his parents hadn't been fanatics, I couldn't bring myself to ask him more about it, and neither did my brother.

Jani as a pilot. The date of the photo is unknown.

Dad continued his Sunday dinner sermon. "Before the war broke out against the Russians in '41, I was redeployed to attend air force flight school in Germany. I became trained as a reconnaissance pilot." He took another deep and long breath. "After the Eastern Front had become established, I flew missions over Russian territory." He looked away and then back at us. "A couple of times, my plane was shot at and hit as we flew over the Russian front."

He smiled slightly. "But I was lucky. I never got hurt bad and was able to get myself back to German or Hungarian controlled territory."

My father paused. For a second, he stared at the kitchen wall behind my brother and me, and then he continued calmly. "In '43, the war started to turn against the Axis powers."

Steve and I continued to chow down on Mom's delicious meal. I couldn't help but think about my father's other devotions that may have helped him cope with that terrible war.

Dad revered cigarettes, as I suspected many of his military comrades did. He could chain smoke up to 100 of those sticks per day. While having visited my father's factory office, I saw my dad light the next one, already place in his mouth, with the last embers of the one he was finishing. When a burn hole appeared in his white shirts or dark suits, he scolded himself, an English or Hungarian obscenity emanating from under his breath, but it never curtailed his habit. A cigarette always burned somewhere around him, like candles or incense burning in a church.

Dad was a religious drinker too. He took in scotch or vodka with his friends as if those spirits were mineral water. I imagined that during their off-hours in the Hungarian or German armed forces, he and his military buddies had played a variety of drinking games. Dad demonstrated his alcohol prowess during his birthday or Christmas parties with our family and 80 of his closest Canadian friends, many being Eastern European immigrants like him and Mom.

At one of my father's parties, at his favourite Hungarian restaurant in Montreal, the Tokay, Dad was in especially good form. After everyone had had a few, he took a 6-oz drinking glass and filled it to the brim with his favoured Stolichnaya vodka. My dad held and balanced the full glass on his head. Next, he crouched down low to dance like a Cossack to the musician's spirited Russian tune. He kicked his legs out from under him to the beat of the music. His expatriate countrymen yelped, and they applauded his agility. He then placed the glass onto the back of his flat hand placed in front of him.

As the accordion played and singing began, my father brought the edge of the glass to his mouth. Without touching the glass with his other hand, he slowly drank, his head tilting back gradually to take in the spirits. As he swallowed the potent contents, he was spurred on by spirited Slovak chants from his comrades in rhythm with the music, "*Pij do dna! Pij do dna! Pij do dna!* [Drink to the bottom!]" The chorus ended with loud applause and happy cheers as he polished off every drop. With Dad's arms stretched up and out, the glass was held high and upside down in his mouth, its rim secured firmly between his teeth.

After Dad had finished downing the alcohol, the edges of his lips curled in a proud grin as his teeth still held onto the glass. Seeing even one drop flowing down his cheek would have been a stain on Dad's manhood. I never saw my father spill.

As those party evenings wore on, many of Dad's English Canadian friends gradually took their leave. Dad then sat down around the table, surrounded by his Eastern European colleagues and comrades, all of them having their filled glasses at hand. Dad raised his vibrant baritone voice to start a Hungarian or Slavic song, and the musicians elevated their instruments to follow.

This time, the lead violinist didn't know the tune. Dad sang it slowly, using his index finger to conduct the high and low notes. The musician could mimic the melody within a verse or two, and the other players followed along. One after another, Dad's buddies chimed in on the chorus, following my father's choral lead. Watching from a table or two away, I smiled and piped in too, humming the tune or mouthing the words I didn't understand.

At a point in the song, a Slavic "arm," "leg," or "Russian egg," turned into a cloaked male body part. Those who knew the language offered a "Woo," "Whoa," or "Ah" of surprise, or roared with laughter. I couldn't join the celebration because I understood only Hungarian and English.

I admired the jovial mood my father created and the camaraderie he garnered from his colleagues and friends. And everyone was Johnny's friend when he was the host. As a young teen, I didn't consider whether Dad's addictive devotions might catch up with him one day.

Though I began to feel full from Mom's delicious Sunday dinner, I kept scooping up her paprikash sauce using the fresh deli rye bread she had put on the table. She said little one way or another about what Dad was offering regarding his war experiences—possibly because she had heard his stories before.

Mom knew Dad didn't like to be interrupted when he had the floor. If any of us said more than a word of agreement or amazement, or unless we asked a question to clarify, he'd turn to us and ask gruffly, "Who's supposed to be talking now; you or me?"

Our father went on with his recollections. He explained. "In late 1943, I decided to take my fate into my hands. Many Hungarian military men were getting fed up with the war, and things were turning against the Germans after they lost big battles in Russia and Ukraine."

His voice rose again. "Those Nazi bastards treated us Hungarians as second class. They made us work like dogs for their precious Fuehrer, requiring us to do extra shifts and crappy jobs." He looked down at his open hands. "Once I had to peel potatoes until my hands were so cramped and raw that I couldn't grip another one."

He glared at us. "It was becoming more dangerous to fly; the Russians were shooting down our planes more and more. Some of my countrymen decided to defect. I thought about it too, but the German officers were telling our Hungarian forces how the Russians were immediately killing any captured or surrendered troops, so I and others were afraid."

I shuddered but kept my eyes on my father.

He clasped his thick hands. "Then one day in early '44, two of my Hungarian friends and I became fed up with the German commanders. We decided to stick together and take our chances with the Soviets. On our next mission in Ukraine, we ditched our planes behind enemy lines and waited for a Soviet patrol to find us."

I could see Dad's glassy eyes staring into that past. He continued. "When the patrol came, I went out first with my hands up. I waved a white handkerchief so I could talk to the lieutenant in charge. I spoke to him in Slovak, a language related to Ukrainian. After the officer had spoken to me, he asked me to call for my two friends. When I did, they came out from their hiding place among the trees and bushes."

Shock and disbelief filled his voice. "While those two guys stood behind me, the officer tried to speak to them." Dad looked down. "They couldn't answer his questions because they only spoke Hungarian."

His voice hesitated, but he powered through. "The Russian officer then took his gun and shot and killed them on the spot—BOOM!—BOOM!" With those last loud words, Dad made the shape of a gun with his fingers and pointed to each side of him to demonstrate where his two companions had fallen.

I don't know about my brother, but I was stunned. We stayed affixed to our seats, our eyes down, and not uttering a word.

Dad continued. "The Soviet officer kept me alive because I spoke Slovak." His voice rose again. "Because the Soviets were afraid of Hungarian spies, that bastard lieutenant immediately killed my friends."

Oh my! My brother and I might not be here today if Dad weren't both Slovak and Hungarian.

Years from now, our father would reveal to us, "In 1943, the Russian Soviets were working on a pact with Czechoslovakia's exiled President Benes. He had set up his exiled government in Britain. From there, Benes prepared Czechoslovakia to work with Russia to fight against the Nazis."

I then realized that the Soviet lieutenant who captured my father might have kept my father alive because he was no longer part of the Axis enemy. Perhaps at the stroke of a treaty pen, my dad had become part of the Allied resistance movement. My father had been lucky in the timing of his defection. Months earlier, the same Soviet lieutenant might have shot him dead too.

Dad put his fork down and sighed. "The Russians then transported me to a POW camp that held many Czechoslovaks. It was in Odessa, near the Black

Sea." His lips formed a hint of a smile. "There was farmland around that camp, and the place smelled stinky from animal manure, but you could see the sea." Dad's stretched out his arm as if he were pointing to that body of water. "In Odessa, I thought the war was finally over for me."

I released my held breath. I was glad Dad was now safe and away from the fighting.

My father took a large swig from his glass of Vichy that Mom had poured for him. L'eau de Vichy was his favourite carbonated mineral drink for settling his acidic stomach. After he had let out a hearty burp, he said, "*Yoy!* That's good."

He continued his story. "During the six months I was in Odessa, I learned to speak Russian and Ukrainian. Because I could speak several Slavic languages, like Czech and Polish, the Soviet guards employed me as a leader and go-between among the POWs."

He looked at my brother and me. "You never know how important it could be to speak different languages." He was referring to our giving attention to our bilingual studies in Quebec.

Dad grabbed a piece of rye bread and dabbed it into his paprikash sauce. His face was tense. "But by the middle of '44, the Czechoslovak First Army was formed in Russian-occupied Poland under Czechoslovak General Svoboda."

He stuck his thumb out to indicate the number of his regiment. "The Russians pulled the Czechoslovak citizens out of the POW camps. They made us join Svoboda's new army to fight against the Nazis." He took a long breath. "The plan was to conduct an offensive with the Soviets to push back the German forces from Slovakia."

He looked at my brother and me, but I couldn't meet his eyes. I wondered if the Axis military had forced our father to fight and kill people.

He went on. "After we left the POW camp, we got organized and ready for our first battle in eastern Slovakia. But the Russians were not giving our new Czechoslovak forces the military support they had promised. So when my division passed close to Košice in the fall of '44, I escaped from them too. I found my way back to my parents' home to hide for the remainder of the war."

Dad's voice became edgy. "By then, I was sick and tired of the fighting, and I didn't trust the Russians!"

It's one thing to be brave but another to be smart. Our father knew the odds for him weren't favourable under the Soviets. He had found a way out.

Between his final bites of Mom's main course, Dad added, "What those Russian Soviets wanted was to decimate our Czechoslovak Army and Slovak resistance movement. That way, they could more easily take over our country after the war."

Decades later, I found out that Dad's assertion was correct. I learned that, in late '44, The First Czechoslovak Army was a part of an invasion of Slovakia through the Dukla Pass, less than 100 kilometers north of my father's hometown. Massive German resistance and subsequent counteroffensive killed tens of thousands of attacking Czechoslovak troops. The battle was one of the bloodiest at the Eastern Front and in Slovakia's history.

Luckily, Dad was not involved in that battle. He was safe by hiding at home in Košice. I now understood more of my father's deep distrust of his so-called Soviet liberators.

My dad took several long breaths and handed his plate to Mom. Though he had finished his meal, his tale wasn't complete. He looked at my brother and me again. "When I arrived home, my father was happy to see me, but my stepmother was worried about harbouring a deserter."

He took another long breath. "But my father put his foot down and said I could stay. He could understand my situation." Dad raised a hand. "As a Hungarian artillery soldier in the First Great War, my father had been captured early and spent nearly that whole war in a POW camp."

Dad looked away for a moment and then right back at us. "My father arranged for me to sleep in a barn near our home. For months, until the war was over, my half-brother Edo brought me food every day."

Born in 1931, and eleven years younger than Dad, Uncle Edo had been too young to fight in WWII. I had met my uncle during our family trips to Košice. He always smiled and happily played street soccer with us. Though he was in his late-thirties at this time, Edo still lived with his mother in Košice. Unlike our father, Uncle Edo never talked about the war to Steve and me.

Dad's voice became subdued. "I was involved in four militaries: The Czechoslovak (before the war), the Hungarian, the German, and finally the Czechoslovak Soviet military. But during those awful years, I wasn't fighting for any country or religion or anything." He pinched his forearm. "I was fighting only for my own skin."

I again sat stunned. The war movies I had seen as a kid pitted the good-guy Americans or British against the bad-guy Germans or Italians or Japanese. The Hungarians and Russians were rarely involved. I wondered how anybody could fight for more than one side. I found it hard to believe what my father had done. I said nothing and continued to stare at my empty plate.

Mom put out her hand. "Give me your dishes, boys, and you can have dessert."

My mind wasn't with her but with Steve McQueen in the movie *The Great Escape*. Could I have been as cocky with captors and as courageous with a getaway as the brave McQueen had been with his POW jailers? Could I have survived a military defection and a POW camp, and then escaped a bloody battle as my father had done?

Dad may have been self-conscious about having fought for the Axis side during WWII. When once asked by a Canadian colleague about what he had done during the war, I overheard his saying that he was part of the Slovakian resistance movement. He added, "I flew as a pilot for the exiled Czechoslovak President Benes." He later pulled me aside and asked me not to say otherwise.

I nodded my understanding. I guessed my father preferred a connection with the "good guys" and the winning side. Though the Benes part of his story was maybe over the top, how could anyone easily explain what my dad had experienced? When I once or twice bragged to a new friend, "My father fought for both sides during World War II," the Canadian kid asked, "Was he a spy?"

Dad's luck in surviving dire straits had started in infancy. He had more than once told us, "When I was one year old, I came down with pneumonia. My mother became worried and thought I could die."

Dad batted the air with his hand. "One day, during my illness, there was a knock on the door. My mother rushed to open it. She expected to see my father coming home with medicine. Instead, she was greeted by an old gypsy with a bag of goods over her shoulder."

Dad's voice rose a tad. "My mother right away told her, 'Go away, old woman! My baby is sick; I have no time for you.' But the gypsy pushed her way into the house, saying, 'Your child is sick? Let me in. I will cure him!'"

Dad raised a hand. "The gypsy showed my mother how to cook strong garlic and milk soup, which my mother carefully fed me. Soon afterward, my fever broke."

Dad showed a boyish smirk. "When I was older, my father told me I survived my sickness because of that old gypsy woman, but my mother never saw her again." He grinned. "But from then on, I've loved the smell and taste of fresh garlic; I could eat it every day."

On workday mornings before leaving the house, my father rubbed raw cloves of that pungent herb onto slices of rye bread toast that Mom had prepared for him. He dunked the toast into his black coffee to help wash it down. Not wanting to linger at the breakfast table, he stood the whole time—leaning forward with his foot propped on a chair, one arm placed on his propped up knee. Dad had told us, "The garlic toast and coffee calms my stomach and helps me get going in the morning."

I understood my father's home-grown medicinal practices. When a doctor diagnosed him with an ulcer after years of late-night entertaining, he soothed his stomach by chasing milk into his scotch. But the things he did to settle his stomach could churn mine.

* * *

Mom cleared the remaining dishes and readied the kitchen table for dessert. She set down warm apple strudel and retrieved vanilla ice cream from the freezer. Dad lit a smoke, took a big puff, blew it into the air, and then pointed his cigarette at the dessert and us. "Have all you want of that sweet stuff." He raised his cigarette. "I have my dessert right here."

Steve and I were chubby kids who took after our full-figured mother. Like her, we rarely said no to dessert.

Dad kept talking as the rest of us dug in. "After Czechoslovakian democracy became reinstated in 1945, a friend and I started our radio retail shop and public-address-system installation business in Košice. Some of our military friends were working for the new government. Through them, we were able to get business."

He smiled. "As small towns and villages across Slovakia became connected to electrical power, we obtained contracts to install speaker systems in town squares and public stadiums. My partner handled the contracts and government people while I managed our Košice operation and crew."

His grin widened. "Through my retail store in Košice, we also smuggled in radios from Western Europe and sold them on the black market for a good profit."

In addition to his devotions to garlic, cigarettes, vodka, music, wordplay, and nighttime revelry, my father was a fervent capitalist. At my young age, I felt proud of his devotions, as long as they didn't involve a church.

"Wasn't that dangerous?" my brother asked.

My father grinned again. "You just needed to know how to pay off the right customs officials. Everybody has a price to close their eyes." His grin widened. "How do you think we got those government contracts? My partner and I knew which palms to grease." Dad chuckled.

I looked at him and smiled. I hoped I could grow up and be as smart and cunning as he was.

Dad watched us gobble our dessert as if we hadn't had any dinner. He said, "I think I already told you that in '48, the Czechoslovak Communist Party seized the government and then took over the private businesses, including mine."

Jani and Anna somewhere in Slovakia soon after the Soviet takeover of their country in 1948.

His face stiffened again, and he held his lips together tightly. He repeated what he had told us many times before. "The communists hated capitalists like me. I didn't want those bums to tell me how to run my affairs, so I decided to escape Czechoslovakia."

He took a deep breath, glanced at Mom, and then looked back at my brother and me. He pointed his cigarette at us once more. "Six months after we had escaped, we arrived in Canada by ship. I was happy that I no longer had to look over my shoulder for the police to grab me again."

I nodded but said nothing as I felt my father's words once again reach under my skin. Mom stood between Dad and the stove, a serving spoon in her hand, no telling look on her face. Steve nodded too and then asked, "What about your parents, Dad? Were they okay with your leaving the country?"

Dad's lowered his eyes. "They didn't know, son. I didn't tell them I was escaping; I couldn't. If I had mentioned anything, they could have gotten into trouble with the police for not stopping or reporting me. I didn't say a word to them until I wrote them from Vienna." He looked away again and then back at us. "They wrote back to tell me they were heartbroken but that they understood."

Mom reentered the conversation. "That's why your father wanted to go back to Košice in '51, for his father's funeral. Your father's father unexpectedly died of a heart attack. Your daddy felt bad about not having said goodbye." She looked down at the table. "Thank goodness that Father Billy talked him out of it.

When I was a kid, I had gotten to know our Slovak Church's Father Billy during one of Dad's Christmas parties. I remembered the priest being a jovial, heavy-set guy who liked to sing and tell people what they should do—all qualities Dad shared. Though Father Billy had a big belly laugh, his loud and gruff voice unnerved me.

Dad enjoyed the Father's company and liked the way the priest did his spiritual business. He had once said, "Father Billy came to visit my factory office because I couldn't make it to Mass for a while." A smirk came to his face. "I invited the Father into my private office. There, we had a scotch together, and I made my confession and took the sacrament. Then I put money into the Father's hand. 'For the church,' I told him."

Despite his staunch Catholic upbringing, Dad didn't carry disdain toward any religion. He held a particular fondness for Jews. He had told us, "After the war, I got to know and do business with a few Košice Jews." He looked at Mom and smiled. "In '48, one of those friends introduced me to your mother."

On some Saturday mornings, Dad took my brother and me to his factory office to give Mom a break. I overheard his conversations with his Jewish Canadian business colleagues—ones who didn't adhere to Saturday Sabbath rituals. They were capital investors, material suppliers, or critical customers to Dad's company. Over coffee, my father joked with them on the inherent differences between Jewish rabbis, Catholic priests, and Protestant ministers. I was too young to make sense of their animated and laughter-filled conversations, but everyone seemed to enjoy Dad's quips.

On one Saturday, on the car ride home from his office, Dad had volunteered, "Most Jews are smart, hardworking, and good business people." He added, "No two Jews think the same way about their religion; they're always debating." He chuckled. "If you ask two rabbis the same question, you'll get three opinions." His tone turned a touch terse as he pointed a finger. "If the Jews didn't have a common enemy in the Arabs, they would forever fight among themselves."

I was too young to differ with my father's views, but today I know that he could have said similar things about almost any religion, including our Christianity.

Regardless of his levity toward other faiths, my dad never refused any man of the cloth who came to his company door to look for contributions. He told us with a smirk, "I give money to every religion. This way, when I die, I'm covered by them all."

Dad took another puff of his cigarette "dessert" and blew the smoke upward. He said nothing more about escaping his country.

It would be decades before our father would confide in my brother and me of his more insidious reasons to leave his homeland. He'd say that many fascists, those who hadn't died in the war or hadn't fled before the Soviet invasion, were caught and prosecuted by the allied armies. He then offered, "From my mother's side, I had an uncle who became the mayor of Košice in '44. He and his brother were big shots in the Arrow Cross Party."

He raised a fist. "In their short time in power at the end of the war, those Arrow Cross bastards sent over 500,000 Hungarian Jews, gypsies, and military deserters to their deaths. Many Jews were removed from the ghettos in Budapest, shackled together in pairs on the city's Chain Bridge, and then shot in the head so that they would fall together into the Danube." His voice was harsh. "Many Slovak and Hungarian undesirables, including gypsies and criminals, were sent to Auschwitz, where the Nazis gassed nearly all of them to their death."

Dad looked down at his hands on the table. "Just before the Russians occupied Košice in January of '45, my uncle and his brother escaped with their families. They fled to Argentina, and we never heard from them again."

I was relieved to know that my father wasn't a heartless fascist. A close friend of his once confided to me, "Because your father hates guns, he never owned one." I was glad he never possessed one of those killing devices.

Jani (right) with his business partner, Gabor, and their plane. 1947 or 1948.

Before finishing my dessert, I got the gumption to ask, "Dad, what happened to your friend who was in business with you in Slovakia? Did he escape Czechoslovakia too?

Dad took the last puff from his cigarette and stubbed it out. "My partner, Gabor, was a pilot like I was. Together we bought a five-passenger plane for our business. We used it to fly to the state capital, Bratislava, to meet with government officials. We also flew across Slovakia to check on our technical crews and electrical installations."

My chest rose with pride for my aviator father.

Dad raised one arm above his head and pointed upward. "Our plane could perform aerial tricks." His eyes followed his hand down to the table. "But on a beautiful Saturday afternoon, Gabor and a few of his friends had dinner together, and they downed too many drinks. Afterward, he invited everyone to go with him for a joy ride.

His voice turned somber. "Our plane could do loops, but with a maximum of two people and half a tank of gas." He looked down into his open hands. "That day, five of them got into the plane with a full tank."

My dad took a long breath and lifted his head. "A little while later, a country farmer saw them attempt a loop in the air." He raised his hand and moved his index finger slowly to trace out the pattern of the plane's loop. "The plane made it to the top of the loop." Dad's finger reached the pinnacle of its arch; then he dropped that finger into the open palm of his other hand. "They never were able to get out of it. They crashed nose-first into the farmer's field. All of them died instantly.

Dad's voice quieted. "I lost a good friend and business associate that day." His voice turned harsh. "But because of Gabor's negligence, I never saw a penny from the insurance company for our plane." He let out a sigh. "After his senseless death, I never wanted to fly again."

Oh, my! It felt as if someone had punched me in my stomach. My father's face looked pained as if he, too, had been hit square in the gut.

He glanced at Mom then back at us. "Another one of my other good school chums had been deeply affected by the war." He took a deep breath. "One day, he just walked into the woods, cut open his stomach with a knife, and bled to death." Dad shook his head slowly. "I couldn't understand why he did that. The war was over, and his whole future was in front of him." He paused, and then added, "As with my business partner, his death was pointless."

My mind turned numb. What had that other friend been a part of that made him take his life? That question would resonate in my mind for a lifetime.

Dad added, "With many of my friends now dead, most of my relatives gone from Košice, and my business controlled by the Soviets, I had very little left to keep me in Czechoslovakia."

Mom joined us for dessert. She smiled, maybe to compensate for Dad's sad story. "Boys, we were lucky to come here to Canada," she offered. "The Canadian government had a program for new immigrants.

"After we had arrived here from Germany in October of '49, we spent a month in an immigration camp in Ajax, Ontario. The people there found jobs for us in Pembroke." She raised her hand and waved it over her head. "It's a town way up north, past Ottawa."

The ship, MS Scythia, on which Jani and Anna arrived at Quebec City, Canada. October 5, 1949.

She took a long breath. "For a year, your father was a cook at a restaurant while I was a housekeeper for the manager's family." She looked at us with bright eyes. "Boys, you remember the McCanns, don't you? We visited them once when you were small."

"Yes, Mom," my brother and I blurted out together. "They were very nice people, and they had a lot of kids," I added. I remembered their warm English Canadian hugs and pecks—more subdued than the bear-hug squeezes and sloppy kisses provided by our Czechoslovak kin.

Mom continued. "I had to wash, iron, and mend clothing for the McCann family's six children." Her voice turned strained. "They were mostly boys. It was hard work."

Dad placed his hands flat on the table. "The McCanns were like adopted parents to us." His voice turned hard. "But your mother and I were stuck in that Ajax immigration camp for more than a month before the immigration officials there found us work contracts in Pembroke." He glanced at Mom. "Your mother didn't put down enough skills—like cooking—onto her application. She only wrote that she was a seamstress and could do house cleaning."

Mom glared at us, her eyes looking peeved. "I didn't want to lie on the application."

Dad gazed at her. "I would have taught you how to cook, which I did anyway in Pembroke." I heard the irritation in his voice. "The McCanns became pleased that you could do more than just clean and sew."

Mom didn't respond to Dad's comment. She gathered other finished dishes and carried them to the sink.

My brother turned to our father. "Dad, I didn't know you could cook."

"Your father is an excellent cook," Mom proclaimed. "I never had the opportunity to cook at home in Czechoslovakia."

She raised a hand. "After my mother died when I was twelve, my eldest sister, your auntie Ilonka, did the cooking for our family. Then, after the war, I was too busy as a seamstress to learn." She glanced at Dad. "Your father's too busy with his business to ever cook at home." Her tone was a touch bitter as if someone had put spicy paprika on her tongue.

Dad didn't look her way but kept his eyes on my brother and me. "After I learned to speak enough English in Pembroke, Mr. McCann allowed me to put a sign in the window that said 'Expert Radio Repair.' During the war, in addition to being a pilot, I learned electronics. In Pembroke, that window sign helped me find customers. That's how your mother and I started to collect and save money."

Dad grinned. "Even at the Ajax immigration camp, I got known for my electronic repair skills. When the camp commander found out what I could do, he moved your mother and me into an apartment on the base. I set up a repair shop in the living room to fix radios, toasters, and other electronic things. It was good because, in the barracks, your mother and I would've had to stay in separate men and women's quarters even though we were married."

"How did you learn English?" I asked.

Mom grinned. "During our one year with the McCann family, we took English classes. We improved by going to see movies every week."

Dad grinned too. "Sometimes, we stayed in the theatre to see the same movie twice, or even three times, for the fifty cents we paid."

Mom is taking a break from kitchen duty at the Ajax, Ontario immigration camp. October 1949.

Mom offered, "After we completed our contracts with the McCanns in 1950, we resettled in Montreal." She looked at Steve, her eyes holding a soft expression. "It took us until '53 to give birth to you, Stevie."

She turned toward me and offered a big smile. "So we started as soon as we could with you, Harvy, and you came right away. That's why you two are only thirteen-and-a-half months apart in age."

Unlike my mother, I felt little warmth or pride from what she was saying. I wasn't sure what was good about Steve and I being so close in age. During our single-digit years, Mom had dressed us as twins. We slept in the same bedroom, even in the same double bed when we travelled on vacation with Mom and Dad. It seemed that Steve and I did everything together, even going shopping with our mother.

Steve and I became known for our raucousness. When Mom took us to the local mall, we played "catch me if you can" between racks of clothing in the department store. We grabbed delicate things off shelves, moving stuff from one place to another, and then pointed fingers at the other for having messed up those things. One store manager begged, "Mrs. Simkovits, please keep your children out of my store."

Mom as she works in her and Dad's first Montreal home; c. 1950

Steve bugged me regularly by poking his finger into my side or thumping his fist into my shoulder to get me riled. Even worse, he taunted and annoyed me by placing his finger or fist just centimeters from my body and not touch me. My parents once told me, "Stevie stopped bugging you only when you started to fight back."

I recollected that my brother didn't stop bugging me until we entered boarding school, where we lived separately from each other. At home, Mom yelled, even screamed at us when we crossed a line with her due to our seemingly endless fighting. But my brother's and my unruliness never stopped while we lived at home.

Steve and I had been at each other again in church this Sunday. He had poked me with his fingers, and more than playfully punched me in the thigh. To my father's dismay, I poked, punched, and shoved my brother in return. It led to Dad putting himself between us in the pew and now filling us with his dinnertime lecture turned long tale.

Maybe our father wanted us to put aside our petty bickering and be grateful for what we had by his and Mom's immigration to Canada. I wondered if my brother and I could ever get past our intractability with each other.

We finished Mom's strudel and ice cream. My mind wandered to what else my father had tried to teach my brother and me about his spiritual devotions.

After our family had moved into our suburban home in Montreal's West Island in 1959, Dad hung a crucifix on the wall above his and Mom's bed. I was five years old, and he told Steve and me, "Don't play or fool around in Mommy and Daddy's room."

The dire looking, dying Jesus looked down upon my parent's room. His image made that space feel sacred to me, where we should never play or else He might judge me poorly.

Years later, my brother told me that Dad had hidden a stack of Playboy magazines under his and Mom's bed, and that had been the reason why he didn't want our playing there. Once, when Mom went shopping without us, I snuck into my parent's room for some under-the-bed spiritual education.

Dad tried to guide us through other significant adolescent issues—drugs and sex. He told Steve and me, "If I ever catch you smoking, I'll punch your nose!" He'd say those words, his hand raised in a fist, whenever he lit a cigarette among his friends while Steve and I were watching.

Our father had odd ideas on how to teach his sons about sex. Once, when Steve and I were in our mid-teens, we spent a Saturday afternoon with

Dad. After he had completed some business with a travel agent near the then shady St. Lawrence Street area of Montreal, we went for a walk along the main drag. Dad unexpectedly said, "You guys know about the birds and bees, don't you?"

Steve and I nodded and timidly said, "Yes." Saying anything else felt awkward and embarrassing. Dad then walked us to an X-rated movie theatre, bought tickets, and we went in to catch the show.

Throughout the performance, I squirmed in my seat as a couple cavorted and contorted on the screen. Dad probably noticed my discomfort, and maybe my brother's too, and he took us out before the movie ended. Outside of the theatre, he changed the subject. He never again took us to such a film or said another word about our sex education.

Mom's Sunday dinner was winding down. The last big crumbs of her apple strudel were sitting on my plate, no room left in my stomach for them. Dad pulled out another cigarette and lit it. He inhaled the burning tobacco, tilted his head back, and blew the smoke toward the ceiling. I could see the pride and self-confidence in his eyes for what he had undergone, overcome, and become in his life.

Years later, as I looked back upon that meal, I realized that I, too, had aspired to be a "larger than life" man like my father, though hopefully with fewer trying experiences. I wondered how I might have made it through a horrible war or responded in seeing my extended family side with a fascist regime.

Would I have had the wherewithal to ditch a plane across military lines and defect to another side? What might I have said or done in front of an enemy lieutenant? Might I have had the gumption to escape a horrific battle at the front lines, survive senseless deaths of close friends, and then escape my country after a communist takeover? Could I work as hard as Dad did six days a week and then take on late nights of drinking, smoking, and entertaining? I wondered where the awe and admiration I had for my father would take me.

Would I have to duplicate Dad's devotions to endure?

* * * *

9

Sweet and Sour

Hungarian Memories

"**C**'mon! It's time. Let's go!" Dad blared in his deep, heavily-accented voice. He grabbed his coat and car keys. "I hate to be late!" he bellowed.

Mom spoke up. "Okay, boys, put on your shoes and jackets, and we can go." There was a hint of annoyance in her voice. "I still need a minute to finish my face, but I want you two ready."

Our whole family had dressed in our Sunday best. Dad, Steve, and I sported our dark jackets and ties; Mom wore a handmade brown jacket and skirt. We were headed for a regular pilgrimage to the city, as we did almost every month since we were old enough to sit still in a restaurant. We were to take a trek back into my parent's Hungarian heritage.

Steve and I sat on the front bench seat of our father's car. Dad seemed more subdued when his two sons were beside him, and I felt special to be right next to him. Seated alone in the back, Mom seemed to rate second class, but none of us said anything.

I reminded myself of the tasty midday meal we were going to have after the unintelligible Latin services in St. Patrick's Catholic Church (later raised to Minor Basilica) in downtown Montreal. Dad was attracted to St. Patrick's high-domed sanctuary, immense gothic columns, and musty incense smell, which reminded him of the celebrated St. Elizabeth's Dom in his Slovak hometown. Enormous religious frescos, giant stone statues, and colourful stained glass windows inundated St. Patrick Church's several adjacent chapels. It took this kid's breath away. Dad kidded, "They make a lot of holy smoke in that big place."

For the long 75 to 90 minutes of the Mass, I would need to endure the dull service without fidgeting. This time, Dad would sit between Steve and me from the beginning to the end of the Mass, and Mom would sit on the other side of me. After hearing a preponderance of *"Dominus vobiscum"* and responding like robots, *"Et tu spiritus sanctus,"* we would be transported into my parents' appealing Hungarian world for a well-earned dinner.

I felt uneasy as Dad drove us into the city. Not only was my suit a little tight around my chubby middle, but my stomach felt seasick because of Dad's driving. He drove fast and wove his way across lanes to get the best advantage over other drivers. I hoped to get through the day without a major mishap on the road, in church, or over dinner.

More than once, my father had told Steve and me, "In 1950, after we had finished our government contracts in Pembroke, Ontario, your mother and I decided to settle in Montreal. Quebec was a Catholic province, and Montreal was the largest and most cosmopolitan city in the country. Immigrants were coming from all over to resettle here."

Montreal provided a vibrant mélange of French brasseries, Irish pubs, English taverns, Italian restaurants, Jewish delis, Greek bistros, Chinese eateries, and Eastern European clubs and cafes. Waves of my parents' Slovak and Hungarian countrymen had come here since the early 1900s. Dad offered, "In Montreal, we quickly made new friends through the Slovak *Leaga* [League] and *Magyar Klub* [Hungarian Club]. In those places, it felt as if we were home in southern Slovakia."

After the lackluster Sunday services in St. Patrick's, I couldn't wait for our visit into my parent's ethnic milieu, especially the Hungarian Tokay Restaurant that we all enjoyed. Though the Tokay was situated on the first floor of a nondescript downtown office building, entering the restaurant felt as if one were walking into a secluded, elegant basement grotto.

The restaurant's interior was dark, made that way by the dim lighting, the crimson curtains at the doorways, and the dark walnut wood of the vestibule where we hung our coats and hats. Crimson velvet paper hugged the walls, and rich, red tablecloths covered each table. The pungent smells of traditional Hungarian cooking—loaded with paprika, garlic, cayenne, and black pepper—filled the air. The odors reminded me instantly of my mother's kitchen and her family's cooking back in Czechoslovakia.

Years earlier, during our first family visit to the Tokay, Dad had looked at my brother and me across our dinner table. "This place is named after a famous brand of sweet dessert wine called Tokaji ['of Tokay' in Hungarian] that is produced in northern Hungary." He pointed to a map on the wall. "The Tokay region crosses into southern Slovakia, near to Košice." He gestured toward us. "During the time the Hapsburgs ruled Austria-Hungary, the Tokay region became famous for producing 'the wine of kings and the king of wines.'"

Dad had gone on to say that, in 1960, a Hungarian family launched Montreal's Tokay Restaurant. "It's one of several Hungarian cafes and clubs that opened in Montreal after 1956," he said. "Many Hungarians came to Canada after their revolution failed against the Communists." He raised his finger. "The Tokay is a little more special than the rest."

Mom added, "It gives us very nice memories of the home we left behind." She pointed her finger too. "Hungarian painters did these paintings; they are similar to what your uncle Buš is known for in Košice." She gestured to another wall. "See those colourful painted wooden plates and spoons? They are typical of our homeland."

I spoke up. "It's like the things we have at home that we got from Košice when we visited there."

"That's right." My father grinned. "The restaurant's owners brought these decorations with them when they emigrated from Hungary." He further explained, "The manager is Mrs. Magyar. Her name means Mrs. Hungary in Hungarian." Neither Steve nor I asked if that was her real name or just what Dad called her.

Dad gestured toward the servers and the area where the restaurant's small orchestra played. "All the waiters, along with the band of gypsy musicians, have come here from Hungary to make money for their families back home." Dad turned a little more in his chair. "Do you see that big instrument on the floor that looks like a miniature grand piano?"

Steve and I nodded as we eyed a big, decorative wooden box that stood on four legs and was situated next to the restaurant's small dance floor.

Dad continued. "In addition to a violinist and accordion player, the restaurant has a cimbalom player." (A cimbalom is similar to a dulcimer.) He went on to explain this unusual percussion instrument. "It has many string triplets, like on a piano," he offered. "But instead of piano keys, the cimbalom player uses two long sticks that have masking tape wrapped at one end. With that tape, the musician can strike the strings hard without damaging the instrument."

I nodded again. My father always impressed me with what he knew. "When are they going to play it, Dad?"

He grinned and winked at me. "Now that we are here, son, it will be anytime soon."

Dad was right. Within minutes, the Tokay's musical trio walked out to the dance floor. They wore black pants, white dress shirts, and traditional red-on-black embroidered Hungarian folk vests.

I watched closely as the group started on a melody. The violinist slowly strolled between the tables to serenade guests. The accordion player closely shadowed him.

The two men came to our table early, and they bowed their heads a little as they greeted Dad. He returned their greeting with a big smile and a calm voice. They chatted for a moment in Hungarian as if they were pals.

Dad introduced Mom, my brother, and me. The violinist bowed again as he said, "*Jó napot; Örülök, hogy megismerhetem.* [Good afternoon; it's a pleasure to meet you.]" Dad then requested several of his favourite songs. The violinist raised his instrument, and the other players followed his lead.

Mom and Dad were all smiles, and they sang along while Steve and I listened to the mesmerizing music. Between the pieces, Dad told us the names of the songs in both Hungarian and English. They first played the vibrant "Hungarian Csárdás," and then the rhythmic "Hungarian Waltz." The musicians then performed the lively "*Forró Kanári* [Hot Canary]," where the violinist drew his bow rapidly across the strings to make his instrument sound like a chirping bird.

During that song, the cimbalom player struck his instrument with great gusto, his hands moving fast to maintain pace with the violinist. I got worried that he'd break a sweat or his instrument, but he seemed to have no trouble taming his apparatus to his will.

When they finished those renditions, everyone in the restaurant vigorously clapped their approval. The players then turned toward all the patrons and played the lively "*Az A Szep* [That Is Nice]." It was a popular Hungarian song that had every guest singing, humming along, or tapping their feet. In English, the refrain of this lively version went:

> *That is nice, that is nice,*
> *The one who has blue eyes,*
> *The one who has black eyes.*

After the song had ended, Dad turned to us. "Although Hungary has been conquered many times over the centuries, lorded over by Turk, Nazi, and Soviet regimes, the Hungarian people always find something good to sing about."

Dad slipped a ten-dollar bill into the violinist's hand that was held open below table level. The suave gentleman bowed his head and kicked his heels. "*Köszönöm tehát nagyon szépen.* [Thank you so very much.]"

After the violinist and accordionist walked away to play for other customers, Dad once again looked at my brother and me. He spoke softly. "It's good to give the players money so that they not only play well for us but also come back to play again. These guys are here for only six months before they return to their homes in Hungary." He raised a finger. "They need our dollars to help feed their families a little better."

Steve and I nodded our understanding. "Why can't they stay longer in Canada?" my brother asked.

Dad reached his hand out toward my brother. "They come here only to work. The communist government permits them to be out of Hungary only that long. When they go back, a new group of players will come."

Mom added. "I'm sure many of them would like to bring their families here, but the Hungarian government doesn't permit it."

"The only way for them to do that is to escape their country as we did," Dad said. "But if they refused to go back to Hungary after their time here is up, they'd not only stay isolated from their families, but their families could get persecuted by the communists."

I nodded but said nothing. I felt bad for these men's kids who didn't see their fathers for half-a-year at a time—or perhaps for years if those fathers defected. Though I rarely saw my father during the weekdays, I felt lucky to be with him not only on weekends but also for Sunday dinners like this one.

As the musical entrepreneurs walked around and played at other tables, I noticed that they gave more attention to the tippers, like my father. Many people sang or hummed along to the melodies. The musicians did get around to every table, offering every customer a spirited time in exchange for uplifted eyes, lively applauses, and the possibility of a few dollars.

My brother and I could speak in our parents' Hungarian. I felt like an adult when I understood what the Tokay's waiters and musicians said, and when I ordered my meal in our family's native tongue.

For her Sunday meal this time, Mom ordered the *lecho* appetizer (a stew of spicy Polish sausage, green peppers, tomatoes, onions, and rice) and the Wiener schnitzel main course. Dad went for the peppery goulash soup, followed by the veal paprikash.

My brother and I followed suit, choosing one or the other of our parents' main courses—Steve and I rarely ordered the same dish for any restaurant meal. When the appetizers arrived, my brother and I tasted our parents' dishes, along with a good dose of rye bread to cut their fiery taste.

On previous occasions here, we had tried the stuffed cabbage, stuffed green pepper, and chicken paprikash, contrasting them to Mom's version of those dishes. Mom's cooking won this contest, even though we never found fault with the Tokay's offerings.

Dad once ordered the *fa tányér* [Wooden Plate] for us to share. It was a mix of several kinds of grilled meats and sausages served on a large, three-level, revolving wooden platter. It filled the center of the table and was possibly enough food to feed a hungry Boy Scout troop. We rarely finished it, and Dad had the waiter wrap the extra meat to take home.

My favourite Tokay dish was the crispy Wiener schnitzel, Mom's preferred one too. A piece of succulent veal was pounded thin and wide. The chef then breaded and skillet fried it to make a crispy crust. When done, the meat was served on a large oval plate and hung beyond its edge. The buttered mashed potatoes, the sweet red cabbage on the side, and a good dose of juice squeezed on top from half a lemon, made this meal a kid's delight. I remember feeling like a stuffed Hungarian cabbage after eating one of those creations, enough to put me to sleep during the car ride home.

The Tokay's cheerful and subdued Hungarian music went well with our soaking up the hearty Tokay soups and sauces with the tasty deli rye bread accompanying the meal. After dinner, Dad bought a loaf of that fresh bread, along with Hungarian kielbasa, from the adjacent Hungarian coffee shop that Mrs. Magyar also managed. Along with our father, my brother and I loved that dried and spicy kielbasa wrapped in rye bread and combined with a slice of tomato or green pepper. It made for a tasty late-Sunday-afternoon snack before Mom's supper was ready.

Once Dad's business became financially solid in the '60s, he held many of his big birthday and Christmas parties at the Tokay. Almost every year, Dad invited over 80 guests to partake. He took over the whole establishment for an evening of music, drinking, and laughter in celebration of another milestone. Customers, suppliers, colleagues, trusted employees, and friends from as far away as Toronto and Quebec City rarely passed on one of Dad's parties.

Dad greeted every guest with a broad smile, along with a big, genuine, and energetic "*Hallo!*" He gave everyone a warm handshake with his thick, strong hands. During the evening, he had a drink with every man and said something charming to each woman about how great she looked.

My father was versed in how to comment on a woman's appearance, generating pleasurable giggles, sighs, and blushes from the ladies. He had the charisma of Pierre Elliott Trudeau, the flamboyant Prime Minister who was famous for his light-coloured suits and a red rose in his lapel.

Trudeau was known for using obscenities in the House of Commons, but he once claimed that he said "fuddle duddle" instead of a more piquant alternative. Dad liked this about the Prime Minister, and he adopted Trudeau's terminology as his own. "Go fuddle duddle yourself," he'd say with a smirk to a wise-cracking jokester. In return, my father received a happy howl.

During his birthday party, my father only nibbled at his food and headed off to chat with every guest. The gypsy musicians played energetically throughout until there was hardly a guest remaining. Dad initiated another tune and slipped the musicians extra cash to keep them lively and on their feet.

As people took their leave, no gentleman departed without a manly hug. For the Canadian ladies, there were two kisses—one on each cheek. For his Eastern European guests, Dad smothered them with three kisses on their two cheeks, and sometimes a fourth on the lips, regardless of sex. After having their fill of food and drink, no one minded where and how many times Johnny kissed them, though he might say to a wisecracker, "Don't expect me to kiss your ass."

Mom and Dad are stepping out for one of their infrequent parties. Mom is wearing a dress she had made herself. C. 1960, a decade after arriving in Montreal to start their new life

When it was time to say goodnight to his dearest friends, Dad gently took the right hand of every female who had come to the party. He bent slightly at the waist as if he were a member of a royal court. He then raised his hand to kiss the top of their hand, either gently with his lips or playfully with a big smack. Dad had once told us that his maternal grandfather, Gabor, had been a *Nemes* (nobleman) in the Austria-Hungarian Empire. From Gabor, Dad acquired gentlemanly European manners that were pleasurable to English and French Canadians.

If a woman's husband pretended to be riled by Dad's hand-kissing, my father grabbed the jealous husband's hand. He brought the man's hand quickly to his face but turned his wrist over mischievously to kiss the top of his hand instead of the fellow's. This "Slovak kiss" drew a big laugh from husbands and wives alike. Dad had a knack for adapting and blending his old-world ways into his new world surroundings.

Mom circulated with guests too, but she was more sought out than seeking. Many of the Canadian-born men enjoyed bantering with her and nudging up against her beautiful Rubenesque figure—as if they had never seen or touched a full-bodied Eastern European woman before. Mom took the attention in stride, with a big smile, glowing eyes, and a bounce in her step.

Mom and Dad were good dancers. They mixed it up with other partners on the Tokay's dance floor. Even when people packed the floor, it didn't stop Dad from picking a few ladies, including Mom, to dance with among the tables. Not wanting to be outdone by Johnny, other men followed suit. Everyone grinned and laughed as if the night would never end.

Steve and I hung around our table during these festivities. We sat next to Mom and watched everybody have a grand time. We ate our Hungarian favourites until we could consume no more, and then had apple strudel and vanilla ice cream for dessert. We poked each other here and there, but Mom raised her voice if we took it too far.

It was nice to see both of my parents enjoy themselves on these occasions. Broad smiles, hearty laughs, and big smooches emanated from them—at least for as long as their love lasted.

Mom wasn't as big a drinker as Dad was. He could polish off a half bottle of spirits in an evening with colleagues. She would start to lose her energy when she got into a second Dubonnet, needing to sit down until the effects wore off.

While I was a kid, straight Scotch was Dad's favourite spirit. He later switched to vodka, explaining to his friends, "If the cops stop me on the way home, they can't smell the alcohol on my breath, especially when I puff a big cigar in their face."

Dad could smoke a package of cigarettes in an evening out, on top of the several packs he consumed at work during the day. He'd top off the evening with a cigar or two. On the other hand, a couple of cigarettes were about all Mom could handle at a party; she smoked only to be social.

As he drank more, Dad's voice became louder, his laugh rowdier, and his behavior more boisterous. He worked his deep baritone voice to sing an off-colour Eastern European song.

His mastery of Eastern European languages helped him change original song lyrics to the name of a hidden body part, creating snorts and laughter from his countrymen in the room. When he made a toast in Hungarian and changed a critical vowel, "To your health" transformed to "To your ass." I overheard him quietly translate these phrases for the English-folks, causing the men to snort and the women to blush. Everyone hooted, raised their drinks, and worked to mimic my father.

Dad followed suit by raising his glass and amassing a big grin. He then spoke the toast with such a heavy accent that one couldn't tell which vowel he was using. His verbal and facial expressions led to another chuckle from those around him. I smiled, too, at my father's charming crudeness.

Though Dad could be loud and a bit uncouth, blowing his nose into his handkerchief like a horse, I never saw Dad do anything embarrassing in front of his guests while high on alcohol—except for rebuffing Mom's requests to slow or calm down. One evening, after one of her ill-timed comments, I saw him lean over and tell her quietly but firmly in Hungarian, "My drinking and manners are none of your business."

After one too many times of being bothered by Mom, he yelled that statement at her in English; his words slurred slightly. Others at our table overheard. They glanced at him and Mom, but no one said anything to dampen the evening's mood. Mom turned to talk to other friends, saying nothing more about Dad's drinking. Though I felt as if a grenade were about to go off in the restaurant, I pretended as if nothing terrible had happened. My brother did the same.

Years later, Mom told Steve and me, "Your Daddy might have loved me more if I could smoke and drink as he does."

My brother and I rolled our eyes and didn't respond. Though she may have spoken truthfully, I felt that her tendency to say such inappropriate comments sent our father's attention in other directions.

After Dad's regular Thursday nights out at the Tokay with his business customers and colleagues, he was still able to drive himself home without serious mishap or incident. Occasionally, the cops stopped him for speeding, but he knew to act politely with them.

On the way home from one of his big parties, while our whole family was in the car, Dad talked innocently to the policeman who had stopped him for changing lanes haphazardly. Dad said, "Good evening, Officer. . . . Really, Officer? . . . I didn't realize, Officer! . . . I'm sorry, Officer. . . . Yes, Officer; I'll be more careful. . . . Thank you so much, Officer." His comportment helped him to play the cop not to give him a ticket.

After he had closed the car's window and started on his way, Dad smirked, looked at the rest of us, and said, "One time, a police officer stopped me, and he asked me to get out of my car to walk a straight line." He chuckled. "I was able to do it, and he allowed me to continue without a ticket or warning." He batted his hand in the air. "The guy could do nothing."

Until seatbelt laws came into existence years later, my father never wore one. Even after those laws became enacted, he only looped the shoulder belt over his left shoulder, not buckling it in place.

Dad did receive costly speeding tickets and seat belt violations, but this didn't deter his drinking and driving habits. Some nights, he came home so late from wining and dining people, he just changed his shirt and tie and headed straight back to his factory office for his customary 7:00 start. He saw it as a part of his work hard and play hard lifestyle.

In the middle of one night, after another Thursday night "business meeting," I overheard Mom speak harshly to him. "Johnny, you shouldn't drink so much. You'll get in a car crash."

Dad immediately raised his voice. "I know what I'm doing! I know how to manage my alcohol."

The following weekend, my father confided in me. "I didn't remember how I got home last Thursday night." He chuckled in a soft tone so Mom wouldn't overhear him. "I had to check the garage to see if my car was there." He smiled. "Luckily, it was."

Back then, I never worried about my father's drinking and driving. He never fell asleep at the wheel, swerved on the road, or really forgot where he had put his car. I admired him for his ability to stay in control. He told me, "I drink as long as I feel I'm in command of what I'm doing. I know when to stop." Later in life, I knew he had been taking dangerous risks, especially when he had our family in the car after his big parties.

The thing that worried me more was seeing my father get loud and belligerent when he was intoxicated. He could shout, "Leave me be!" at Mom in Slovak, Hungarian, English, or in all three languages. He might hit his fist on a table, or drop something that then broke, though I never saw him punch anyone or throw anything when under the influence.

What enraged my mother most was my father's late nights. Once, I heard her wake in the early morn, Dad neither sleeping in bed nor snoring on the couch. She paced the living room, frantically repeating to herself, "What should I do? Should I call the police?" When he finally arrived home, she cornered him and raised her voice, "Johnny, I was scared. I was afraid you were hurt or killed in an accident."

Dad responded in Hungarian, his voice slurred. "If you don't get a call from the police or the hospital, then you know I'm okay."

She kept at him, her tone far from warm or welcoming. "You give more attention to your business friends than you do to us, your family."

Dad raised his voice enough to make the ceiling and my spine shiver. "Stay out of how I do my business! I'm doing this for you and the family. I don't tell you how to run the house!"

Nervous shakes and cold sweats came upon me as I lay in bed. I pulled the covers higher over my head. I was thankful when Mom retreated in silence to their bedroom. I kept my eyes closed and pretended I was somewhere else. I went to sleep only after I heard Dad snoring from the living room couch.

After my father had come home late on another night, Mom pleaded once more. "The boys need you around more."

He responded harshly, "It's your job to be with them and raise them while they are still kids. I'll be there for them when they are older and ready to go out into the world."

I stayed frozen under my covers. I didn't dare look to see if my brother was awake. On nights like these, I fought for sleep and hoped for better moods in the morning.

It would take me years to understand the craziness of Dad's logic. Dad's approach kept Mom with her apron on at home, a role and place where she was more comfortable than the new world into which her husband was growing.

Even by day, Mom knew how to smear salt into Dad's vices. Over one family meal, she jokingly said, "Your daddy doesn't love me anymore." Another time she angrily told him in front of us, "You never rush home to us as you rush to your fancy clubs and whore friends." Her tongue could sting like hot paprika, and it grated on all of us. It took me a long time to realize this was the only way she knew how to express her mounting frustration as she watched her husband and marriage slip away.

In her most hurtful and lonely moments, Mom cried to my brother and me. "I love your father more than anything. But he doesn't show that he loves us more than his company and his business friends."

The more that Mom tried to hold onto Dad, the longer he stayed out at night and was away "working" on weekends.

An hour before the end of one of Dad's Tokay birthday celebration, Mom turned to Dad. "Johnny, you've had a lot to drink. Please don't have more."

He looked at her with rage in his eyes but said nothing. He stood up, walked away, and happily engaged with his guests, albeit a little shaky on his feet. She later came up to him and tried to pull him away gently, asking him to come back and sit down at our table. He forcefully said, *"Hagyj békén!* [Leave me alone!]" He then avoided her for the rest of the evening.

He later confronted her in the parking lot as we were getting into our car. Wobbly on his feet, he didn't pay attention to which language he was using. He went up to her, pointed his finger at her chest, and yelled in English, "You think you know everything. You know nothing! Mind your own goddamn business and stop involving yourself in things you know nothing about."

Mom's face became tense, her lips pursed. It looked as if she were going to speak. Instead, she glanced at my brother and me. Seeing us standing frozen on the other side of the car, she held back her reactions.

When Dad realized Steve and I were listening, their confrontation ended in its typical troubling stalemate. None of us said anything, though I prayed Mom wouldn't prod Dad with more of her words. I hoped we could pretend Dad's blowup never happened.

Usually, Steve and I sat up front with Dad. This time, Mom gestured for us to get into the backseat. During the ride home, our parents looked forward, not saying a word. My brother and I sat still behind them. We stared into the headlights of the oncoming cars, each of us, in our way, inextricably caught between Mom and Dad's old and new worlds.

* * * *

10

Separation Pains

Through the window of my private high school's dorm room, I could see it was a dark, wind-blown, snowy evening. It was February 1969; I was fourteen years old and in the middle of my second year of boarding school. My roommate and I were doing homework quietly in our room during evening study time.

I lifted my head from my desk as I heard heavy footsteps coming down the hallway. The housemaster appeared at the door. His voice was quiet. "Harvy, please put on your boots and bring your coat. There's someone here to see you. He's waiting down by the front doors."

The master started to turn to leave, and then he looked back at me. "Please knock on my office door later, before coming back to your room." He gave a slight smile, turned away, and walked back down the hall.

I grabbed my winter boots, coat, and hat. I walked down the hallway quickly and quietly so as not to disturb other students. At the entryway, bundled in his long dark wool coat and felt hat, my father was waiting. I was surprised to see him, but I smiled and kissed him as I usually did. His winter coat smelled thick of cigarette smoke, as it typically did. Thank goodness he didn't smell of alcohol or perfume. "What are you doing here, Dad?" I whispered.

At our boarding school, parents weren't ordinarily permitted to see their kids during weekdays, especially not during evening study time. Parental visits were permissible only on Sunday afternoons, after compulsory morning church services. Our school, situated in the Eastern Townships of Quebec, was a two-hour drive from our home in Montreal. Something serious must be going on for Dad to make this trip on a windswept, snowy weeknight.

"Hi, son," he said. "Can you please come with me for a little while? I need to talk to you for half an hour or so. Your brother is already in the car outside."

"What happened, Dad?"

"I'll tell you in the car. Please put on your warm things and come with me." My father spoke softly, but his tone was serious.

I did as he asked.

His large, black, Oldsmobile 98 was a few meters away from the entrance doors. The engine was running. From the building front porch light, I could see the car's thick exhaust fumes mix with the cold air and falling snow before it dissipated quickly into the night air. The car windows were fogged and frosty. In the thin light, I could tell that there were others in the vehicle. I opened the back door and climbed in.

Even with the car's overhead light on, the car's interior was dark. The only sound was the windshield wipers going back and forth. Steve was sitting in the backseat. He nodded to me, said nothing, and avoided looking at my eyes. In the dimness, I couldn't read his face.

A man I didn't recognize was in the front passenger seat. When Dad opened his door, the car's interior light turned on again. I could tell that the other guy was years younger than my father. Unlike Dad, the top of his head was almost hairless. The long grey-black hair from one side of his head was combed over neatly to cover his baldness. The man turned back to look at me and grinned. "Hello, Harvy," he offered. There wasn't much warmth on his face or in his tone.

I nodded. "Hello." I didn't look into his eyes that seemed to be glaring at me.

After Dad had shut his door, the only light came from the car's instrument panel and a campus street lamp situated a few meters in front of the vehicle. The car reeked of cigarette smoke.

Dad switched on the car's interior lights and looked back at me. "Harvy, do you remember Mr. Mack, my lawyer?" I nodded again. "He came out here with me for the drive, both to keep me company and to help me talk to you guys."

I wondered why Dad needed his lawyer to talk to us. I looked at my father. "What happened, Dad?" I repeated. "Did something happen to Mom?"

Dad reached for the cigarette that was burning in the ashtray. He took a puff, glanced at Steve, and then looked back at me. "I told your brother just a few minutes ago, and I now want to tell you, Harvy. I'm sorry to let you know this way, but I left your mother. I took my things and moved out last weekend."

Steve said nothing. I, too, sat in silence, not knowing what to say or how I should feel. Mom and Dad's troubles were well known to us.

Months earlier in our Dorval home, while I cowered under my covers once more, woken by their shouts, she yelled at him in all three of their languages in common. I could make out some words. She screamed, "Why are you out all the time with your gypsies friends and never here at home with us?"

Dad shouted back, "I'm out there for our family. How I do my business is not your concern. I don't tell you how to manage the children, so stay out of how I run my affairs."

Their back and forth had gone on for what was an eternity but may have been only a few minutes. It ended when something banged and then smashed on a table or counter. Dad screamed, "Leave me alone and go to bed! Otherwise, I'm leaving right now!"

Mom rushed up the stairs and into their bedroom. She shut the door, but I could hear her sobbing. Later, I could hear Dad snoring on the couch, as he often did after such altercations. This one had been far from their first.

For what seemed forever, I held myself still in my bed after their fight. Like times before, I shook with fright under my covers. I kept my eyes closed as I tried to numb myself from my angst and get back to sleep. I told myself, *I'm dreaming.* I then pleaded with God. *Can't they just get along?* Later, *Please let me sleep; I want to get sleep.*

God had never arrived to put an end to Dad's shouting or Mom's crying. I wondered if I had done something wrong, causing Him to abandon me. *Was my parents' fighting a test for me from The Almighty?*

Sitting in the back of Dad's car, I felt as if I had been naïve. I never suspected he would leave Mom, at least not before Steve and I were grown. But there had been other warning signs that went back over a year.

At home, during one of my parents' fights before my brother and I entered boarding school, I heard Dad threaten our mother. "One day I'm going to disappear," he yelled.

I never thought it would be this soon.

Perhaps Dad wanted to shield Steve and me from the fallout of his and Mom's fighting; thus, he placed us away from home for our high school years. Or maybe he wanted to have us at a distance from our mother in preparation for his pending departure.

On the last day of our first year of boarding school, on our drive home from school, I could tell that Mom was poking Dad as they sat together in the front seat. Dad kept glancing at her, his face looking annoyed.

Eventually, he turned his head toward Steve and me. "Boys, you've now had a year in private school. Do you want to go back to public school, or do you want to remain in boarding school?"

Both Steve and I answered, "We like boarding school better." It could be we both wanted to be out of the blast zone of our parents' battles. Might we have had an inkling of Dad's imminent departure?

Now, half-way through our second boarding school year, Dad announced his departure from Mom with his lawyer looking on. The air stood still for what seemed an eternity in his now snow-covered car. After about ten seconds, Mack entered the conversation. "Your mother is threatening to take you two out of this school. I'm here to tell you that she has no right to do that."

I listened but still wondered why Dad needed his lawyer involved in our family's business. Both Mom and Dad had several times told us, "Don't tell your friends or anybody about our private affairs here at home." I suspect they had meant for our not talking about their yelling and screaming. Now, this lawyer guy was here and in the know.

The previous Sunday evening, during a regular weekly call with Mom, she had told me, as she always did, how much she missed us. I knew she had very little life outside of her husband and two children. This time she added, "I gave up being a seamstress to have and raise you and your brother. It's not right that your father is always out doing business and never at home with us."

Mom also meant that she never got the opportunity to have a dressmaking and alteration shop as she had had in Košice after the war. Instead, she raised my brother and me almost single-handedly while Dad spent six days a week at his factory and many late evenings with his colleagues and friends. Most nights, he didn't return home until Steve and I were a long-time asleep in our beds. Many nights, he came home long after Mom was sleeping too.

What will my mother do now without us at home and with Dad gone? She had no one else for which to cook, clean, or sew. Mom might be crying this instant, not knowing what she should or could do to ease her loneliness. But would she pull us out of private school? Dad wouldn't have brought his lawyer with him this evening if he had thought otherwise. I wasn't sure of anything.

I glanced at Steve in the dim light of our backseat. I couldn't read any expression on his face. He and I continued to stay silent. Mack continued. "If your mother tries to come out here to get you, you don't have to leave with her. She has no legal claim to take you out of this school."

Dad raised an open palm. "I want you to stay here and not be concerned about your mother and me. Don't get yourselves involved in our matters; we will work it out ourselves."

Mack agreed. "You need to stick to your studies," he offered. "You are in a good school, and you should focus your attention here." He raised a finger. "When you are old enough, you will be more on your own and will have appreciated the education you received."

My brother spoke up. "Are we allowed to talk to her?"

Dead air filled the car for another eternity. My sides trembled as I waited for Dad's reply. He nodded and spoke softly. "Sure, like always. Call her collect on Sunday like you usually do."

"But try to stay out of being in the middle of your parent's affairs," Mack added, his voice a few decibels louder. "It's best you don't become a messenger for either of your parents or to try to negotiate any arrangements between them."

I looked at my brother and then back at my father. Steve said, "Okay, Dad." I repeated the same. I imagined the "I can't believe I'm alone!" crying, and "What am I going to do now?" sobbing I would get from Mom the next time I talked to her.

Though I felt empty in my chest, I looked back at my father. I was going to do my best to follow both his and his lawyer's instructions. Wouldn't they know what was best for Steve and me?

Before I headed back to my dorm room, I stopped in front of the housemaster's office door. I tried to quell my shaking from the outside cold— or was it from my father's declaration? I knocked as the housemaster had requested.

Within seconds, he opened his door and motioned toward a small chair in front of his desk. "Come in, Harvy. Please have a seat."

He looked at me as I sat down. A soft expression was on his face. "Your father told me a bit about your mother's and his situation. If you ever want to talk, you're welcome to come and find me."

I avoided his eyes; they seemed to be looking through me. "Thanks, but I'm okay." I lied. I buried any feelings I had. *When I'm old enough, I'll get far away from my parents.* I figured if I held myself together, focused on being a good student, then in time, I could distance myself from Mom and Dad's troubles.

"Are you sure?" the housemaster asked as he eyed me carefully.

"Yes, I'm fine." I didn't want to dwell on what I was or wasn't feeling. It was easier to pretend nothing was wrong.

He looked doubtful. "Okay, but let me know if there's anything I can do. I'm here anytime you want to talk."

"Yes, okay," I said quietly. "Can I go back to my room now?"

A couple of moments later, I entered my dorm room, sat down on my bed, and grabbed a textbook. My roommate looked up from his studies. "What was that about, Harvy?"

"Nothing important," I said.

I kept my eyes glued to my book, but nothing on the page became captured in my mind.

For the rest of the school year, I carried on as if my parents' separation hadn't happened. Dad came to visit us every few weeks, on Sundays, without Mom. Having no car and not able to drive, Mom talked to us every Sunday night. She told me how lonely she felt at home without us.

At spring break, Dad drove us home. He said little about his and Mom's situation. He asked us about our studies and talked about his summer plans for us. When Steve asked him where he was living, he said, "For now, I'm using the spare bedroom in the home of our good friends, the Meyers." When he later dropped us off in front of our home, he told us, "I'll pick you guys up next Sunday and drive you back to school."

Mom's eyes were teary when she saw us at the front door. Throughout that vacation week, in front of us, she pretended as if Dad were away on a business trip. After she had thought we were asleep in our beds, I could hear her cry and talk over the phone in Slovak or Hungarian to a friend or relative. She did that for what seemed like hours.

* * *

That summer, after a short stay with Mom at home, Dad had already arranged for Steve and me to go back to our private school for a month of French summer classes. My brother and I hardly saw each other that month because we were in different class grades and sports activities. When we did see each other, we never talked about Mom and Dad.

For the remainder of that summer, we remained at home with Mom. We biked to our town pool, where we hung out separately with our old public school friends. We played tennis at the town courts, arguing the whole time whether my brother's brawn or my brains was the more critical capability for our contest. We biked around town, with Steve sometimes leaving me in the dust as he rode off to visit his friends—I had to ride home alone.

At night, we watched hours of television. It was a good thing we had more than one TV in the house so that both Steve and I could see our favourite shows. I preferred *Star Trek, Outer Limits,* and *Twilight Zone* reruns that sent my mind to other places and planets, or they projected me into bizarre realities other than the one I had at home. Other programs like *Sky King* and *Lassie* offered stories of boyhood and adult adventure, albeit in a more secure family setting.

Steve was more a *Gunsmoke* and *Hawaii Five-O* fan. We both enjoyed *The Prisoner,* and I wondered how the former *Secret Agent Man* star was going to escape his open captivity in a coastal village of crazy characters. Maybe Steve, like I, felt as if we were prisoners in our parents' drama.

Steve and I spent most of our summer Sundays with our father. Dad would come early in the morning to take us to church. Other times we went on drives to the countryside, or to the local golf driving range to hit a few balls, or to the latest movies. He rarely talked about Mom.

Mom, on the other hand, cried to us in her loneliest moments. She repeated what she had told us times before, "I love your father more than anything. I want him home, and I would have him back anytime." Maybe she wanted Steve and me to repeat to our father what she had said to us, but we never did.

Like my parents, I too began to feel as if I lived separated lives, one inside and one outside of myself. I felt tightness in my stomach as Mom unhappily sent us off with Dad—her face looking down and her eyes heavy with sadness.

After we had returned home from being with our father, she peppered us with questions: "What did you do with your daddy? Where did you go? Who did you see?" Her relentlessness wrenched my mind and twisted my gut.

Steve and I worked on following Dad's lawyer's advice. I tried to ignore Mom's interrogations, walking away to get away from her constant questioning. I turned to my favourite television shows. I pretended to be like *Star Trek's* emotionless Mr. Spock—to separate myself from Mom's anguish and my pain.

One Sunday evening over supper, after Steve and I arrived home after a long day with Dad, Mom was worked up. Perhaps she had been particularly lonely that day. Over her Hungarian goulash, she went through her litany.

My brother and I gave her short answers: "We did nothing special, Mom." . . . "We just drove up north to the Laurentian Mountains for dinner at a friend of Dad's, and then we took a walk." . . . "We saw nobody in particular." We didn't lie, but we didn't reveal. Dad had asked us not to mention details to our mother about having visited his friends for a garden party.

Mom continued peppering us with questions. "Was there another woman there? How is your father with her? Does he love her?"

Steve and I offered that there were other men and women around, some we knew and some we didn't, and Dad had spoken with everyone. I didn't know if my father was seeing another woman; perhaps I didn't want to know. My brother begged, "Please leave us alone about it, Mom. There's nothing to talk about."

Her voice elevated. "But I need to know if your father loves her and will marry her. If not, then I have hope he will come back to me."

Steve stood suddenly and walked out of the kitchen. When he reached the dining room, he turned toward a wall, made a fist, and smashed it through a small oil painting. His blow tore through the canvas and dented the wall behind it. Without saying another word, he went downstairs to the den and turned on the television.

Mom stood from her chair, took in a big gulp of air, and froze in place for what seemed like forever. One hand covered her mouth in shock while the other grabbed the back of a chair for support. She then sat down again and placed her elbows on the table and her head in her hands.

For a minute or two, she wiped away tears from her eyes while I sat frozen in my seat, not saying a word. She then stood again and went to her bedroom, not another word emanating from her.

I finished my supper alone in silence, not fully understanding what had triggered my brother's physical outburst. When I finished my meal, I put my dishes in the sink and headed for the living room television, pretending again that nothing terrible had happened.

By the next morning, Mom had hung a different painting over the damaged wall. None of us said more about it.

Steve and I never talked about our parents' troubles. Having left me stranded across town during our bike excursions, and continually poking and prodding me from as far back as I could remember, he didn't seem like someone in whom I could confide or from whom I could gain comfort.

The only solace I felt by having my big brother around was that I was less of a solo target of our mother's disquieting questions, incessant ire, and inconsolable sorrow regarding Dad.

* * *

It was hard to tell what was worse: to live through my parents' fighting when they were together or to live a double life in their separation.

I don't know how it happened, but Mom and Dad reconciled after eight months of being apart, again while Steve and I were at boarding school. I surmised that Dad might have gotten tired of the other woman and came back to what he knew he had with Mom. Who else would cook Dad's favourite Hungarian meals for him, iron his work shirts and slacks each day, and go shopping for his underwear and socks?

After Dad had moved back, Mom and he came to take my brother and me out of school for what was supposed to be a relaxing Sunday family dinner during our October Thanksgiving weekend. We were also celebrating my turning 15. Dad took us to a fancy resort restaurant close to our school. The restaurant overlooked a pristine Quebec finger lake that was surrounded by rolling hills. Bright autumn leaves were on the ground.

After we had ordered our meals, Mom looked at me with a warm smile. She reached across the table and put her hand on mine. "Son, your daddy came back home to me as a present for your birthday."

I bristled at her words. I looked away and didn't respond. I wished she wouldn't put me in the middle of anything having to do with her and Dad's marriage, even the good news of his returning home. Dad and Steve also may have felt a sting from her unexpected comment. I prayed that Dad wouldn't get angry on my birthday.

Mom pulled her hand away from mine and dropped the topic. Neither Dad nor Steve said anything. We went on with the meal, pretending that no one had said anything out of the ordinary.

* * * *

11

Snowbird Bon Voyage

Dad's good friend Aras leaned forward and spoke in his heavy Lithuanian accent. "We've come a long way and done a lot since we met twenty years ago, haven't we Johnny?"

I watched as the short, mustached man looked around the posh restaurant. The smell of flowery perfume and fancy aftershave filled the air. Women in colourful cocktail dresses and men in light suits sipped wine and champagne. Our table, covered with a white linen cloth, had silverware set for a five-course meal.

"Yes, Aras," my father replied. He glanced at the menu card on the table. "Ah! Garlic steak and herb stuffed scampi for supper; very nice!" He looked keenly at his long-time pal. "It's hard to believe that I had only fifty U.S. dollars in my pocket when Anna and I had come off the boat from Europe." He looked at Steve and me. "And the first thing I did in Canada with that money was to put it into the bank to earn interest."

Dad took another breath and looked again at Aras. "We've worked hard and have had fun together along the way. Here's to the next twenty years." Dad lifted his glass of Stoli to toast his good friend.

In contrast to my Dad, who had a growing-midriff, Aras was svelte. His face had lines showing his age, a decade more than Dad's. He raised his glass of Cutty Sark and followed my father's lead. Their glasses clinked, and they exclaimed in unison, "*Na zdorovye!* [To your health!]" Each of them took healthy swigs.

Aras pinched the end of his small moustache before turning toward the rest of us. "I made a *beeeg* mistake in '53 when I loaned Johnny money to start his business." He glanced and winked at my brother across the table. "Your mother was just pregnant with you back then, Stevie." He chuckled. "Instead of giving your father a loan, I should have become his partner. Over these years, your dad has done much better in business than I have."

He pointed his finger at himself. "Not that I have anything to complain about." He then pointed upward and shook his finger slightly. "Who would have imagined your father would become so successful after he and your lovely mother arrived in Canada almost naked after the war?"

I had heard the same account from Aras before, and I never tired of it. Dad was a big shot in his business. My chest swelled with pride to be his son.

Dad allowed me to sit right next to him at this large, circular restaurant table. Steve sat on the other side of me. It had been this way for as far back as I could remember, and I liked it.

Aras lifted his drink again and nodded at my mother. She, with her pretty blue eyes and bleach-blond coif crafted from hours of colouring and curling, sat on the other side of Dad. She gently grabbed Dad's arm and smiled at Aras, the man who often competed with her for her husband's time and attention. When my father came home late from a night of business entertaining, the Lithuanian was often in the mix. Mom didn't say anything off-key as she looked at Aras; all was now well in her world (and ours too) after Dad had come back home.

My feet felt the restaurant's floor vibrate slightly from the low rumble of the engines deep below us. Otherwise, I couldn't tell that we were sailing south at a steady twenty knots.

Dad looked at his friend. "And who would have thought even ten years ago that we'd be sailing the ocean for two weeks on a big fancy ship like this?"

Aras looked back at my father. "I'll drink to that, my friend." He saluted with his glass. "*Skol*, Johnny."

They took another sip of their libations and beamed at each other. I grinned too, for I enjoyed being in my father's company when he was relaxed.

It would take years, maybe even decades, for me to realize that travelling on family vacations and having fancy restaurant meals was one way we connected and endured as a family. It was also the way I survived during my turbulent upbringing.

* * *

Having been accustomed to milder winters in his homeland, Dad often joked, "Canada has only two seasons: July and winter."

Our father announced our surprise southerly trip during a Sunday family dinner in the fall of '69, soon after he had come back home to Mom. I was fifteen, and my brother was sixteen. Dad declared, "Aras and his wife had planned a holiday cruise vacation with other friends. Because those friends couldn't go, I was able to get their tickets for peanuts." Excitement filled his voice, and his eyes opened wide. "We're going with Aras and his wife on a two-week Christmas and New Year's cruise to the West Indies. We will depart out of the port of New York City."

I counted the calendar days until our departure. I looked in the world atlas for our pending destinations. In the days before our voyage, I opened that atlas every evening. I examined the varied colors and jigsaw-puzzle shapes of the small bits of land we were going to visit.

I thought about how far those tropical isles were from Canada's gigantic frozen mass. I measured 1400 to 1900 nautical miles of ocean travel that we were to navigate to our closest and farthest island destinations. I counted not only the days but also the hours until we would step onto the ocean liner. I was excited about having my dad virtually at arm's distance for the whole time.

On the day of departure, we woke at five o'clock in the morning to drive the seven hours from Montreal to New York City. I was the first one down to the car to take a seat up front next to Dad.

In NYC, we boarded the Incres Line's MS *Victoria* at the Manhattan docks. The small 575-foot luxury cruise liner would carry us, and 600 other lucky passengers, to seven ports of call. Along the way, MS *Victoria* would make "saintly" stops: St. Maarten, St. Lucia, St. Thomas, and San Juan. It was a commendable Christian excursion for the Christmas holidays.

On the evening of our cast-off, on a cold and cloudy late-December day, our family stood on the ship's Promenade Deck, five stories above the docks. In our bulky winter coats, we waved farewell to the people on the pier, though we knew no one.

As people on the dock waived to the other passengers on our deck, I stood at the rail and swung my arms from side to side. I threw big kisses into the air with both my hands and yelled, "Goodbye, New York! Bye, everybody! Wish us snowbirds a *bon voyage.*"

After the ship had left the dock, my brother and I went inside to explore our home for the next thirteen days. My parents stayed outside in the chilly weather to watch the New York skyline as our ship left the harbour.

That evening, at our first supper on board, Dad shared, "Standing on the deck and looking at the city reminded us of when we crossed the Atlantic twenty years ago from Cuxhaven, Germany to Quebec City." His mood was pensive. "The last time we were on an ocean-going ship like this, we had no idea what was in our future."

* * *

MS *Victoria*'s six interior floors were a teen's delight. That first afternoon, Steve and I ran through the ship, chasing each other down the hallways. We passed the Galleon Bar, the Gallery, and the Library. We played catch-me-if-you-can through the narrow corridors and stairs of the stateroom decks.

We stopped running when an Italian cabin steward blocked our path, lifted a finger at us, and sternly said in his broken English and Italian accent, *"Bois! Dont maka da trauble!"* We turned our eyes downward and said, "Sorry, sir." When we were out of eyesight, we bettered our behavior by trotting instead of galloping along hallways and down stairs.

Located on the ship's Sapphire Deck was the dimly lit Bamboo Club. On its ceiling were lights that flashed for late-night rock-and-roll dancing. After supper that first evening, we spent a few minutes checking out the older teen crowd. Steve and I were too shy to partake, and our waltzing and fox-trotting parents didn't gyrate to what Dad called "that boogie-woogie music."

As the *Victoria* sailed south to warmer waters, we spent afternoons in the El Patio Lounge on the Rendezvous Deck. There we bet money on cruise-style horse racing. A steward rolled out a track of sheet plastic on the floor. Another one rolled six dice to determine how far each of six, different coloured, paper-mâché horses would advance down the track. Dad spotted Mom, Steve, and me for a few rounds, but anymore had to come out of our winnings or wallets.

Tingles went through my body as my horse advanced in the field. A loud, arms-up "Hurrah!" came from my father whenever any one of our horses won, even if his horse was dead last. For our first night onboard, Aras and his wife joined us. Other days, they snuck away to the adult-only, smoky Galleon Bar for a cocktail before supper.

On the ship's outdoor Lido Deck were double saltwater pools. There, on warm sunny ocean days, we basked like seals on lounge chairs. If the weather was warm enough and the ocean breeze not too windy, we ate up to three of the ship's seven daily meals on that deck. Besides breakfast, dinner, and supper, there were large snacking buffets—before, after, and in between—of soups, finger sandwiches, and pastries.

One morning, a combination of too much tropical sun and rich breakfast pastries caused my mother and brother to hug the head in my parent's cabin for a couple of hours. Dad told them, "It's a long cruise. Remember that your stomach is not as big as your eyes. You don't need to eat everything in front of you."

During the seafood dinner buffets, I didn't see my father struggle with the mussel-laden bouillabaisse, or the creamy clam chowder, or the steamed, smoked, and seared salmon dishes, or the stuffed scampi and skewered shrimp.

After every meal, both he and Mom patted their stomachs and exclaimed in Hungarian, *"Én jól laktam.* [I lived well.]" I, too, ate my fill and felt like a beached adolescent orca. I was proud that, like my father, I never heaved a meal into the head or over the side.

For supper every night at the Coral Deck restaurant, men dressed in jackets and ties while women wore long dresses. On a Saturday afternoon before our Montreal departure, Dad had taken Steve and me to a fancy Montreal menswear store. He bought each of us a new black suit, a white dress shirt, and a thin black tie.

As per the ship's dress code, we were to wear those spiffy outfits to the Captain's and the New Year's Eve suppers on board. Thankfully, Dad let us take off our stiff jackets and tight ties after we sat down and ordered our meals.

During suppers, Dad permitted my brother and me to have Dubonnet cocktails, also our mom's favourite drink. He allowed us to drink the champagne at the New Year's celebrations. Pointing his cigarette at us, he provided his drinking instructions. "Sip it slowly, and don't use a straw, for it makes the alcohol go faster to your head." He added, "And be sure to eat something when you drink, so you don't get loaded."

Steve and I nodded our understanding. I felt warm inside not only from the Dubonnet but also from Dad preparing us for when we would turn eighteen, Quebec's legal drinking age.

At night, Dad and Aras turned into boys themselves as they downed their evening Stolichnaya, Cutty Sark, and their after-supper Remy Martin. Aras showed us magic tricks that made Mom and Dad laugh, and my brother and I giggle. He made coins disappear from his hands and reappear from behind our ears. He broke a toothpick and mysteriously made it reemerge whole.

One night, I was in awe as Aras miraculously placed a filled water glass upside down on a side plate without spilling a drop. He said, "You first need to smear the plate with a pat of butter. Then you turn the plate over and place it on top of a filled water glass."

As Aras held the buttered plate with one hand against the glass in his other, he slowly turned the whole thing over until the full glass sat upside-down on the plate. Not a drop of water spilled or escaped onto the plate. He added, "You can only do this if the china and glassware are first-rate." He placed his construction in the middle of the table, looked around the room, and said quietly, "Let's see how the busboy deals with this."

"I bet you five bucks that he'll spill and make a mess," Dad declared.

I was disappointed when we didn't find out who won that bet. The perplexed busboy left Aras's water puzzle on the table until we had left the dining room.

Unlike my father, alcohol made Mom drowsy. To stay awake after supper, she ordered a cup of strong Brazilian coffee, laced with hot cocoa, whipped cream, and "Just one small finger of rum." She showed the waiter her pinky sticking out from her raised fist.

My brother and I stayed up with our parents for the evening variety show performed in the dark, spotlight-lit El Patio Lounge. The revue included sharply dressed male and female singers, as well as a slender couple who performed modern dances. The passionate duo held each other close.

The swanky, sexy woman later switched into a long, tight black dress with open slits down the side. My adolescent eyes opened wide, and tingles filled my body as I watched the woman lift her legs high, and the man touch her side gracefully.

Their routines aroused me, but I was falling asleep in my chair by the end of the program. I couldn't make it to the ten o'clock buffet or the midnight pizza party at the Bamboo Club. I could hardly wait to be like my dad, able to stay up for everything.

* * *

Over one supper during our voyage, after starting a second scotch and second cigarette, Aras told us his story. "Before the onset of World War II, when times became hard for the Jews in Lithuania," he began, "my uncle, my aunt, my mother, and I escaped our country together. We travelled by train across China to Shanghai, and eventually immigrated across the Pacific to Vancouver."

He took in a long drag of his smoke. "When we got to Canada, my uncle Chasen tried to start an appliance distributorship, but the Vancouver market wasn't big enough." He shook his head. "Within a couple of years, we uprooted again and came to Montreal, where my uncle felt business would be better, and it was."

Aras shook his hand above the table, the burning cigarette between his fingers. "Since my uncle had no sons, only two daughters who were born in Canada, he took me under his wing. I learned the appliance business from him, and it's been feeding me well ever since." He looked at Dad as he pointed his cigarette. "But we were never as successful as Johnny and his Montreal Phono."

My father, also puffing away on his smoke, looked at Steve and me. "Aras and I met in 1951, soon after your mother and I came to Montreal. We met through the city's Eastern European business community. Aras' uncle helped me a lot in business, even lending me money when my bank refused to give me a loan."

He took a long breath. "Chasen was like a second father to me, and he gave me lots of good advice." He pointed to Aras." Right from the onset, Aras and I became good friends."

There hardly was a Hungarian, Russian, or Slavic establishment in Montreal that those two compadres hadn't frequented, especially places that had lively gypsy or Cossack music. When I went with Dad and Mom to Dad's big birthday parties at the Tokay, Aras was among the guests.

After having a couple of drinks, Aras would grab a mic and stand in front of the band to sing his favourite Russian songs. He gave renditions of the uplifting "Kalinka," or the passionate "*Ochi Chiornye* [Black Eyes]" or the somber "Moscow Nights." He closed his eyes as he performed, waving his arms above his head as he gyrated to the music.

Dad happily sang along at our table. For an encore, Aras followed with "If I Were a Rich Man" from *Fiddler on the Roof*—perhaps coyly displaying his envy of Johnny—and he did more hand waving. His deliveries were followed by lively applause from Dad and his guests, though I occasionally found the Lithuanian a little off-key.

At those celebrations, Dad and Aras tested their manhood by competing to see who could down a 6-oz glass of vodka the fastest, without spilling a drop, to shouts of *"Pij do dna!"* from their Slavic companions. Having escaped the Soviet takeovers of their countries, they worked hard to remember where they had come from. They worked even harder to forget what they had gone through.

For decades after my father returned Mr. Chasen's loan, he continued to repay Aras with drinks, suppers, and companionship. During our cruise, Dad never let his good friend pick up the tab for drinks or smokes—the cruise included the food.

If the waiter ever moved toward Aras with a bill, my father wagged his finger and firmly exclaimed to the server, "Don't dare give him the tab!" Dad pointed to himself. "If you do, you won't get a tip from me the next time I pay."

If the bill wound up on his friend's side of the table, my father reached over and tugged the slip out of Aras's grasp, saying, "Please, Aras, let me take care of it."

Aras sighed, "Ay! Johnny, Johnny, Johnny," and let his comrade win the tussle. I understood that it had been this way for the longest time between these two. I was glad that Aras was able to return my father's favours by helping him secure our bargain-priced cruise vacation.

* * *

On the morning of our third day at sea, my father woke me before sunrise. We left my snoozing mother and brother in their beds.

On the Promenade Deck, Dad grabbed a hot coffee, prepared for early risers. I took hot chocolate. We picked out powdered sugar sprinkled breakfast biscuits and croissants that had been arranged neatly on silver trays covered with linen napkins. Carrying our pre-breakfast snacks, we strolled outside onto the forward deck. It was our first morning on board the ship without jackets.

We watched the Caribbean awaken. Unlike our first three days of gently rolling ocean travel, the ship now sliced through the water like a canoe through a tranquil pond. We could see dolphins riding the front wake, and seagulls flew overhead chasing the boat. The sky above was clear, with scattered crimson clouds along the horizon.

Even before the warming orange-yellow sun rose out of the ocean, my father and I could make out a landmass toward the south. I felt like Christopher Columbus's first mate as Dad pointed in the distance to a dark patch along the horizon. A dark, mountainous mass was ever so slowly rising out of the sea and into the brightening blue sky.

Dad put his coffee cup down on a bench. He lit his first cigarette of the day between cupped hands and took a big puff. My father then placed his foot upon a railing as he looked out over the Caribbean. As my dad exhaled, the smoke was whisked away by the wind. He pointed. "Look, son. There's St. Maarten, our first port of call. We'll be in Philipsburg, on the Dutch side, in a couple of hours."

I was tall enough to stand shoulder to shoulder with my father, though his shoulders were much thicker and rounder than mine. "It's amazing!" I said. "The island looks like a volcano growing out of the ocean, yet there's no smoke coming from it." I felt excited as if I were among the first European explorers.

Dad added, "We'll spend the day at one of the beautiful bay beaches near the town."

He and I stood side-by-side in silence. We sipped our hot drinks and nibbled on our baked goods, our hair blowing in the wind. We watched the dark mass of St. Maarten grow more massive and brighter each minute as we gazed into the expanse. I wished the moment wouldn't end.

A couple of hours later, after a full breakfast, we said goodbye for the day to Aras and his wife and headed for an island beach. Dad's friends were not beachgoers; they preferred to tan and mingle by the ship's pool.

As our family disembarked the dinghy that brought us to shore, the crew members handed out box lunches. We walked a kilometer to a white sandy beach and resort in Great Bay. There, we lay for hours on complimentary lounge chairs. Dad, Steve, and I played tag and threw around a ball in the warm salt water. Mom blissfully baked her oil-covered body in the blazing sun.

Mom and Dad allowed my brother and me to sip their piña colada and yellow bird drinks, served by scurrying waiters dressed in short-sleeved white shirts and matching shorts. The sweet taste of those drinks made them go down smoothly.

After putting down our filling box lunch of hearty ham and turkey sandwiches on thick white bread, it didn't take long for me to doze off in my chair. In my daze, I could hear both Mom and Dad snore like beached walruses in their lounge chairs behind me.

At the end of the afternoon, my parents had to throw half the Caribbean on Steve and me to wake us. We ran in our flip-flops to the transport dingy, beach bags flying, our skin inflamed from the burning sun. We reached the last dinghy moments before it departed the dock.

* * *

Aras had recently married Celia. It was the second marriage for both of them. She was a gray-haired, square-faced, big-boned Lithuanian American with a protruding chin. Having lived most of her life in North America, she was college-educated.

Unlike my mother, a professional seamstress turned housewife, Celia was a learned and sophisticated woman. She had travelled to Eastern and Western Europe, frequenting theatres, museums, and art galleries across the continent. Unlike Aras and my dad, Celia called my mom "Anne" instead of "Anna."

Celia knew which silverware and glasses to employ with every course. When my brother and I fumbled with the extensive set of dinnerware, she offered, "Start with the outside fork and knife and work your way in." After Dad and Aras had finished their Stoli and Cutty, she chose the wine for her and Aras.

Mom had not gone to high school. Instead, she had moved to Budapest from Košice at the start of WWII to attend a dressmaking trade school. Celia and my mother spoke politely to each other. They talked about the mineral bathhouses of Budapest and the famous Erzsébet Dom in Košice.

After they had exhausted Mom's knowledge of Vienna and Salzburg, where my parents had lived as refugees in '49, Mom and Celia found little else about which to talk. They recounted what they ate at the many meals on board, or the island purchases they made, or the excursions we took offshore.

Celia and Aras went off the ship only when island shopping was involved. Celia offered, "We've been on cruises before. These day trips become the same after a while." She raised a hand. "But you go ahead and enjoy yourselves."

Mom seemed content to focus on eating what she liked, especially the potatoes that were boiled, baked, mashed, stuffed, and fried. They were dressed each night differently, covered with mounds of butter, sour cream, chives, parsley, and salt and pepper. She smiled as she glanced at Dad. "I'm happy not to have to cook." Her only food concern was to remind Steve and me to eat our vegetables.

Over many suppers, Celia worked on eating as much black Beluga caviar appetizer as she could. After evenings of multiple caviar orders, our waiter tried to curb her appetite. When Celia saw nothing else on the menu card that interested her, she kept asking for more of that fishy stuff.

Each time she requested more, the waiter gave her progressively less. Undeterred, she sent the waiter back to the kitchen five or six times for another portion. My brother turned to me and whispered, "I don't know why the server doesn't just give her a couple of cans of that black gooey stuff, along with a bag of crackers, and let her go at it."

As if she had heard Steve, Celia raised her head and declared to everyone, "Why not indulge in what you like!" She delicately placed the fish eggs on a cut of cucumber, laid them gently on a cracker, and took a bite. "I'm on vacation, and I love this *cauviar*." She said that word as TV's Julia Child might say it. She added, "It reminds me of when I visited Saint Petersburg."

My mother stayed away from the foods she hadn't been accustomed to. When she chose the shrimp cocktail appetizer, Dad jested, "After we had come to Canada, I had to teach your mother how to eat shrimp." He grinned. "I had to take the heads and tails off for her before she touched them."

Mom laughed as she poked her index fingers at us. "I couldn't eat those ugly little things while they had their two little black eyes staring at me."

We all chuckled.

My more adventurous brother spooned a small taste from Dad's caviar appetizer. A glum smirk came to his face, and he shook his head.

My father turned to me. "Want to give it a try, son?" He placed some on a cracker and passed it to me.

I nearly gagged on its salty taste and squishy texture. I almost retched from its fishy smell. "How could anyone eat this yucky stuff?" I said a bit too loudly.

Celia came back, "A small can of 'this stuff' costs $25 or more."

Steve leaned into me. "I would rather have the $25," he whispered.

Some minutes later, Celia looked at us. "It's important that you boys know about the world, its geography, and its history. For example, do you know the capital of Turkey?"

I thought for a moment then asked, "Constantinople?"

Celia responded, her face straight, "The Greeks, Romans, Byzantines, and Ottomans would have agreed with you, but it was moved to Ankara after World War I. I'll give you half marks on that one."

She peppered us the rest of the evening with more questions. She kept us occupied and on our toes until we excused ourselves after dessert.

To keep Celia at bay during subsequent suppers, whenever caviar was on our menu, Steve and I ordered that appetizer and then handed our portions to her to feed her habit. In return, we received a reprieve from her school-teacher questioning.

* * *

The next morning was warm and sunny again. Before breakfast, we reached Antigua. Its main harbour was not deep enough for our small cruise ship to dock in town. Instead, we weighed anchor about 1,000 meters offshore in a pristine blue bay on the leeward side of the island. A peninsula and smaller juts of land kept the bay sheltered from ocean waves.

An hour before we would ride the ship's dinghies to Antigua's capital, St. John, we heard splashing and yelling in the water by the liner. Looking over the Promenade Deck's railing, Dad and I saw about a dozen island boys splashing in the water. Dad said, "They swam out to our ship to do business with the passengers."

Treading water ten to twenty meters away from the ship's hull, many boys raised their arms and shouted, "Throw a coin! Throw me a coin!"

I didn't understand what the boys' calls were about, but I soon found out. From every outdoor deck, passengers threw loose change into the warm, clear bay water. The closest boy then dove after a coin. He surfaced a moment later with the shiny bit in his hand and a sparkling white toothy smile on his face.

My dad pointed at the furthest kid and yelled, "Hey, you! Get this one." He took a step back from the railing, wound up, and threw a quarter a meter or two beyond the boy. The kid saw it coming, turned in the water quickly, and dove after it. The light skin on the bottom of his feet was the last thing we saw before he disappeared under the surface.

After I had lost the boy in the sun-reflecting sea surface, I started to get worried. He was underwater for nearly a minute. My heart pounded but became relieved when I saw the kid resurface. A big grin was on his face as he held Dad's coin in his outstretched hand.

Dad raised an arm and shouted, "Hurrah!" The boy motioned for Dad to do it again. My father complied with the silver coins he had left. He weeded out the pennies saying, "Throwing those things would be an insult." My dad worked to chuck each silver piece a bit further. The boy retrieved it every time.

Dad gave me coins to throw, and I fished more from my wallet. I tried to get my Canadian coins as close to the kid as I could, hoping he wouldn't feel slighted by my non-U.S. currency. He accepted my bay deposits with a big wave.

When we were out of change, Dad put out his arms and open hands to show the boy he had nothing left. The kid grinned again with his big teeth, saluted us, and moved on to seek other customers. Dad turned and put his arm around me and said with a grin, "We made that kid work for our money."

"I was a bit worried about him," I confessed.

"They know their business, son. They know you don't get something for nothing."

* * *

That evening, while the wives headed to the ladies' room after coffee and dessert, my dad and Aras lit cigars and blew the smoke toward the ceiling. Dad leaned towards his friend and quizzed him quietly. "Aras, why did you really marry Celia?"

Celia was a head taller and at least fifty pounds heavier than the short, thin Aras. She couldn't hold a candle to my blond, blue-eyed mother.

Aras took a puff of his stogie and responded with a straight face. "You can see that she's intelligent and interesting. I can talk to her in my language, and we can discuss anything. She keeps my attention."

"Is that all there is to it?"

A grin came to Aras's face. "Johnny, you know that Eastern European women are strong, like bulls. They can live a long time and take good care of their men."

Dad smirked. "With her expensive tastes, she's going to eat through your money."

"That's okay." He gestured toward my brother and me. "We have no children like you and Anna. Celia has money too, saved from working for many years, and from her divorce settlement."

He took a puff of his cigar. "We figure we should spend what we have while we can. You can't put it into the casket and take it with you, you know. You have to live a little before the lights go out!"

"I'll drink to that," my father said. He lifted his glass to his friend. "You never know what tomorrow could bring."

Dad turned to Steve and me. He leaned forward on his elbows and held his cigar close to his mouth. "Like when I flew over the Russian front for the Hungarian military in World War II," he reminded us. "I ditched my plane on the Soviet side to get away from the Germans and defect to the other side. The Soviets placed me into a POW camp, and I expected the war would be over for me."

He lifted his hand that held his cigar and pointed it our way. "I never imagined that, six months later, the Soviets would take all Czechoslovak citizens out of their camps and make us fight against the Nazis."

Steve and I nodded. I put my hand on my belly that was protruding from another gargantuan shipboard supper. Whenever Dad talked about his Eastern European past, I wondered if I could have survived his trials.

Dad looked at his longtime friend and raised his glass. "*Egészségedre!* [To your health!]" he offered in Hungarian. He might have said the similar, "*Egész seggedre!* [To your ass!]" to his multilingual friend, for they chuckled together.

A glint in his eye, and finishing his third drink of the evening, Dad continued. "Celia is so much bigger than you, Aras. Is there enough room for you and her in your bed at home?"

Aras replied, "We sleep in separate beds at home as we do here on this ship." He laughed as he knocked back his drink. "Otherwise, with one wrong turn, and she could crush me to death." He slapped his hands together sideways to demonstrate.

Dad laughed too.

Perhaps having drunk a bit too much, my father asked another. "Does Celia excite you, or do you have to keep your eyes closed when in bed together?"

Aras responded with a belly laugh. "What's the difference, Johnny? After a few drinks, don't all women look about the same?"

He and Aras looked at each other and burst out laughing. Dad seemed to have no qualms talking about manly things in front of his maturing sons. My brother looked away as if he hadn't paid attention. Though I felt a twinge in my lower gut from their banter, I kept my eyes away from Aras and Dad. I placed a linen napkin over my face and held back my snickers.

Dad continued to chuckle as he looked at me. "You liked that one, huh, Harvy?"

At 15-year-old, I did find Aras's comment amusing. I continued to look away as I giggled into my napkin. Perhaps I had had a bit too much dessert.

* * *

On the ship's Sapphire Deck was the Grand Auditorium. There we received disembarkation instructions and tour information for our respective island visits.

The night before we disembarked for a day trip to St. Lucia, the ship's host offered a lengthy warning. "We emphatically recommend that you don't buy any products from the dock vendors who will be waiting onshore in the morning."

He raised a hand. "Even though their wares might look good, like this watch on my wrist, you'll be disappointed with the quality of what they sell you. Their purses, perfume, wallets, and watches are cheap knock-offs." He pointed upward. "Instead of Omega, they'll show you an Omeca; instead of Chanel, it'll be Channel; instead of Christian Dior, you'll see Christen Doer."

He continued. "After you leave the docks to head into town, those vendors will disperse quickly; you'll end up stuck with whatever you bought. There is no way to return anything." He eyed the audience. "We very much recommend that you stick to the reputable stores in town where you can get a replacement or refund—even by mail—if you want to return what you buy."

The next morning, my mother didn't heed the host's warning. A force overtook her. Within minutes of setting foot on the dock, Mom went into bargaining mode with a tall, well-built, black man dressed in a white shirt and slacks.

The St. Lucian displayed dozens of cheap watches in a portable viewing box sitting on a collapsible stand. Dad, my brother, and I walked around, perusing the wares of adjacent vendors, but we avoided buying anything. Aras and Celia departed the dock area and headed into town.

Pointing to a shiny timepiece, my mother asked the vendor, "How much for this one?"

"Fifty dollar U.S. for you, ma'am," the giant man said.

My short, stout mother was a head or two smaller than the man. She countered, "That's too much; I'll give you ten."

The two of them went back and forth for twenty minutes. Their tones became progressively louder, and their hand movements increasingly energetic. The man lowered his price to $40, then $30, then $25, then $20. My mother argued, "No; this is all I have," and she shook a U.S. $10 bill under his nose. She walked away from him a couple of times while saying, "You have to do better than that." The handsome black man waved her back. "Okay, okay, lady; I give you a special price." Their price duel continued.

Dad became irritated about Mom's wheeling and dealing. He said, *"Szóval vegyél, vagy ne vegye meg, Nusi. Menjünk!* [So buy it or don't buy it, Anna. Let's go!]"

Mom snapped back. *"Nem, anélkül, hogy az árat!* [Not without getting my price!]" I think she wanted to show us that she was as much a smart businesswoman as Dad was a shrewd businessman.

Not wanting to stand around, my father, brother, and I walked away to follow Aras and Celia. As the dock emptied of passengers, my mother caught up to us. Her purse hung from her left elbow. She waved the watch in her closed right fist. "You see! He took my $10. That's how you need to bargain with these *fekete* [black] people."

Dad countered in Hungarian. "Yah, we'll see! Bargaining is one thing, Anna, but buying cheap junk is another."

At breakfast onboard the next morning, Mom's face was glum. She showed us her new Omeca watch once more. It had stopped ticking, and one of the straps had fallen off.

Dad didn't want to examine it. Steve looked at the watch briefly and said he couldn't fix it. I looked closely and then shrugged. "The holes that hold the watch-band pin to the watch are only small depressions and not real holes. The band won't stay attached."

Not wanting to be embarrassed at American customs when we got back to New York City, Mom left the broken, new watch in her cabin before we disembarked. We knew not to ask her about it.

* * *

Our dining room stewards, dressed in black and white, were Italian. Their uniforms well matched the recent redesign of the ship, including the dining room's vaulted Roman ceiling. These handsome, svelte men spoke quickly and energetically, their hands in continual motion.

Three dedicated servers, dressed in black and white, were assigned to two tables of eight guests each. A middle-aged waiter took the meal orders, a younger assistant waiter served the meals, and an even younger busboy poured the water and took away our dinnerware at the end of each course.

Dad liked to get friendly with the people who served him. One night, he conversed with our waiter. "Is everybody who works on this ship Italian?" he inquired.

The Italian responded matter-of-factly. "No signore; we are an international crew."

"So, where are the rest? All I've seen so far are the Italians."

The waiter leaned over slightly. With a straight face, he confided, "We keep the Bulgarians busy in the engine room."

Dad laughed loudly. He pointed to Aras, Celia, my mother, and himself, and then asked. "At this table, we are Slovak, Hungarian, and Lithuanian. Where do you keep people like us?"

The waiter gave a wink and a slight smile. "Anywhere they want to be, signore."

Everyone at our table chuckled. Dad added, "I like you. Can my friend and I buy you a drink at the bar after you finish work tonight?"

The waiter swept his arm to his chest, and he gave a slight bow at the waist, and he responded, "Signore; that is only for our guests. I am here to serve you, which is my pleasure."

During suppers, two red-jacketed wine stewards scurried around the tables, collecting drink orders. They impressed me because they never touched a glass and seldom poured a drink—the assistant waiter did that. Those heads-up and chests-out stewards opened and poured the Italian wine and French champagne, and they smelled the cork of every bottle. They taste-tested every Rothschild and newly opened Portuguese port wine using the small silver cup that hung from a silver chain around their neck. I wondered if these guys ever got tipsy from those bottles they tasted, but I was too shy to ask.

Celia once asked our steward, "Do you ever reject a bottle?"

The man answered, "It happens, but not too often. We have a fine stock."

As I watched the steward concentrate on his taste testing, my father looked at me. "Son, would you like to have a job like that one day?"

"It looks really important," I said.

He grinned. "Yes, but I couldn't do it. It would drive me crazy only to smell the corks and to test the goods."

Everyone laughed, and so did I. Mom laughed too, yet I notice her eyes were intense and lips pursed. Maybe she didn't like Dad alluding to his drinking. I was glad she said nothing about it.

Mom mentioned Dad's drinking habits only once during our trip. As we walked off the ship at Trinidad, it felt as if we were still at sea. For a few moments, it was funny to watch us not able to walk a straight line as we embarked onto dry land. As we stepped off the gangway on this sunny but breezy day, Mom joked, "Now you know what your father feels like after he had one too many."

Dad overheard her and countered. "Yah, what do you know?" I could hear his annoyance. "I hold my alcohol a lot better than you do."

I felt uncomfortable by their bickering but said nothing. Steve stayed quiet too. I was glad that Mom and Dad let their terse exchange fly off with the pelicans.

Dad had no desire to walk around Port-of-Spain. He preferred to travel the island by car. Not liking to be "herded like sheep" on the bus tour arranged by the ship, he hired a cab off the docks for a half-day excursion.

The deep black, round-faced, Trinidadian cabby drove as fast as he talked, recounting the isle's sights. Dad sat up front in the cramped stick-shift car while Mom, my brother, and I squished into the back.

From the car's rearview mirror hung gold pendants of Mother Mary and St. Christopher. My father showed the cabby the small, gold St. Christopher pendant that hung from his neck. It was a gift he cherished, given to him by his parents when he reached eighteen and was heading into the Czechoslovak military. He offered, "We have something in common." He pointed. "Both of us are Catholic."

The driver looked at Dad's pendant and responded, "You must be a good man." He reached under his shirt and revealed a large gold pendant that hung from his neck. It showed the baby Jesus in Mother Mary's arms. He presented a toothy grin. "I must be an even better man than you." He gave a gargantuan guffaw, and Dad laughed too.

Every time the driver stopped at a stop sign or traffic light, he spoke to a man standing on the sidewalk or shouted jovially to a woman across the street. He talked to them in what seemed like a foreign tongue. After he had finished one conversation, my father looked at him. "You seem to know a lot of people here."

The deep-voiced guy responded, "Port-of-Spain is a small town."

Dad reached his hand out toward the fellow and asked a question that probably was on all our minds. "Do you mind me asking what language you are speaking?"

With a puzzled look, the cabby responded with a heavy British accent, *"H'english, sir! Caun't yu tell?"* He displayed his big white teeth again. He explained. "We speak it so fast here that you Americans don't understand. Like when you say, 'Where are you going, my friend?' we say, *'Whe yu go, mon?'*"

My startled parents later confided to each other that they couldn't understand a word of the Trinidadian's English. Except for an occasional phrase, my brother and I, too, were stymied. Dad later likened their tongue to rural Quebec French, where the proper *"J'ne sais pas* [I don't know]" became *"Ch'ez pa."*

Our island guide took us for short visits to Christopher Columbus and Independence Squares, Gothic Rosary Church, Royal Botanical Gardens, and various ocean and city lookouts on the hillside behind Port-of-Spain. Beautiful flowers—bright red ones that looked like a bird's head and others that looked like red tubes—bloomed everywhere, giving the air a sweet smell.

I took in the warmth and beauty. I thanked my lucky stars for not being in icy and snowbound Montreal. I asked my father, "Can we do more vacations like this one?"

Dad put his hand on my shoulder. "We'll see, son; we'll see."

The driver overheard us and said, "If you come back to Trinidad for a longer stay, I will show you the whole island. You will be *veeerrry* impressed."

"Sure, give me your card," Dad replied. "And here's mine. If you are ever in Canada, come to see me. I'll show you Montreal and its *real* nightlife."

The cabby nodded as he examined Dad's card. "Thank you, Mister John." He pointed to Dad then himself. "We are friends now."

Though I enjoyed the cabbie's wit, I silently wished the man wouldn't come to Canada. Dad didn't need another reason to be away from us for another late night on the town.

* * *

I became particularly fond of our assistant waiter, Roberto. He served me as if I were a young aristocrat. He greeted me at meals saying, "How is the young Master Simkovits today?" He opened the meal menu card and placed it before me. He suggested dishes I might like. He made sure I never got too much ice in my evening Dubonnet. Like my mother, I didn't like to have lots of ice.

Roberto jiggled, never spooned, extra foam out of the small, silver, steamed-milk pitcher for my daily double dose of cappuccino, with chocolate and cinnamon sprinkled on top. He held the pitcher delicately with white gloves and a folded linen napkin, offering a big grin as he poured. In return, I smiled shyly at him and said, "Thank you, Roberto." Dad smiled and nodded, pleased that the Italian was taking good care of me.

I sipped my hot cappuccino slowly while Aras and my father sipped their after-supper cognac and coffee. They sucked on Cuban cigars they had bought onboard. Aras asked, "Johnny, you once told me that your mother died when you were young. What was that like?"

Dad took a puff of his stogie. "Outside of her pictures, I don't remember my mother. She contracted tuberculosis when I was two and went to the sanatorium in Budapest." He took a long breath. "I never saw her again. She died some months later, before I turned three." He looked down at the table. "My father buried her in Budapest. I wasn't at her funeral."

He took another sip of his drink. "My father couldn't take care of me by himself, so he placed me with his brother's family. My cousin and I were the same age." He shook his head. "But after a year, his parents didn't want me with them anymore."

"Why, what happened, Dad?" my brother blurted out. We both knew that my father's natural mother had died when he was a toddler. Relatives then raised him for some years, but we never heard more details. Until now, Dad had never offered them.

Our dad looked with kind eyes toward Steve. "My cousin got very sick with a fever that year. He and I shared things, even our utensils at meals." Dad lifted his coffee spoon. "My uncle told my father that I made my cousin sick because we had shared a spoon." He sighed. "From then on, my aunt and uncle didn't want me to live with them. They asked my father to place me elsewhere."

"So, where did you go?" I asked. It must have been horrible not to be wanted.

Dad puffed his stogie, looked at me with his big blue eyes, and answered matter-of-factly. "My father next arranged to move me to my mother's extended family. I lived with the Tabody family and their younger son, Gabby, for several years, until my father got remarried." He smiled. "Gabby was named after my mother's father, Gabor."

Dad's eyes shifted between Steve and me. "You boys remember Gabby Tabody, don't you? I helped him immigrate to Canada in '68, during the Prague Spring, in the time of Alexander Dubček." He pointed his cigar into the air. "I even loaned Gabby money to help him start his garage business in Montreal. I sometimes take my Mercedes to him for service. He's a good mechanic and knows a lot about German cars."

My brother and I nodded. "Yes, Dad." We had many times visited Mr. Tabody's dingy and overcrowded garage while Dad had his car serviced. Steve added, "Unlike your factory, Dad, Gabby's place is small and smelly. It stinks of oil."

Dad looked at Steve, his eyes turning a little intense. "You have to start somewhere, son. If Gabby does alright, he'll get a bigger and better place next time. When I started my business, my first place was an apartment above a tavern in Old Montreal." He pointed downward. "You could smell the grease from the kitchen coming through the cracks in the floor. Luckily, we were there only a couple of years before I bought my first Montreal Phono factory building."

Aras looked at my brother and me. He leaned forward and raised an index finger. "Gabby couldn't have even opened his first place if it hadn't been for your father."

He took a swig of his drink. "Your dad is generous to the people and families who had helped him. Even though it was Gabby's parents who took your dad in as a kid, Gabby had been like a younger brother to your father, and your father is helping him now." He pointed his cigar toward Dad as he continued to look at us. "And, your dad has helped many other Slovaks to come to Canada and resettle here."

Our father sat quietly, a proud look in his eyes. Aras turned to him. "But your father eventually got remarried, right?"

Dad took another puff and then tapped the ashes into an ashtray. "I went back to live with him after he married my stepmother." He shook his head. "But she didn't show me much attention or affection. After my half-brother Edo was born, when I was 11, she favoured him."

Dad took a fork and pretended to push food off his plate. "Once during supper, she got mad at my father for giving me an extra piece of meat from his plate after she had served us."

Dad's voice became strained. "My stepmother complained that I was a rascal." He looked away and then back at Aras, a bit of a smirk on his face. "She may have had a good reason." He smirked. "On warm spring and fall days, my friends and I played hooky from school. We would go swim in the Hornád River that flowed near our home in Košice."

Dad turned to my brother and me. He pointed his cigar and said firmly, "Don't you boys get any ideas. You keep your attention on your school studies!"

Aras and Celia grinned. Mom, Steve, and I said nothing. I lowered my eyes to my cappuccino, wondering why my dad thought I'd consider playing hooky from high school. It had never crossed my mind. I wanted to please my father by being a good student.

Celia spoke. "Johnny, did you do other things to upset your stepmother?"

Dad's grin widened as he sat back in his chair and took in another long puff of his cigar. "We sometimes played tricks on our school teachers. When I was in a middle grade, a few friends and I gave our new teacher a present for Christmas. Because she was young and very good looking, we wanted to get her something special."

A rambunctious boyish grin filled his face. "We put our money together and bought and nicely wrapped an unusual gift for that teacher. We gave it to her in front of the whole class."

Dad's eyes widened. "When she opened the box, her face turned beet red. Inside was a sexy silk bra and small panties." He grinned. "When the whole class saw it, the boys couldn't stop laughing, and the girls giggled and covered their faces." Dad laughed heartily. "It was so much fun."

Aras burst forth with a howl. Celia smiled and said, "Your stepmother was right, Johnny. You were a rascally boy."

I didn't lift my eyes from my cappuccino. Though I probably was as old as my father had been when he plotted that prank, I felt a little young for the thought of skimpy panties.

Though my father's youthful forays intrigued me, I never considered doing what he had done. I was his good boy and never got in trouble at school. I did my homework studiously and hung out with the bookish kids.

Only once in elementary school had I gotten in trouble for not completing all my homework. It was an absentminded oversight rather than a deliberate intent, yet the teacher sent me to the principal's office. I felt so ashamed after having received an earful from the stern-faced male principal that I never again forgot to do my homework.

Dad continued talking through his chuckles. "But my parents were not happy about my behavior with the teacher. My father spanked me good when he learned from the school principal about our gift." He glanced at my brother and me but said nothing this time.

Mom took a sip of her Brazilian coffee and spooned the drink's whipped cream into her mouth. "You boys would never do such things. You're not as foolish as your father was."

I glanced at Steve. His face was blank. We both stayed silent. I knew my father had a proclivity to engage a loud howl—not only directed at us kids but also at our mother—whenever Steve and I didn't follow his instruction. I never wanted to be the cause of Dad's ire. I worked to please my school teachers as I tried to please my father.

Dad looked at Aras and Celia. "My parents got mad at me for other things too. For example, my father wanted me to learn to play the violin."

Dad tapped his cigar ash into the ashtray and then pointed his stogie toward his friends. "On a nice spring day after school, before I had to go to my music class, my school chums wanted to play soccer. My team needed goalposts, so we used my violin case for one of them."

He raised a flat hand shoulder high. "As we were ending our game, my friend scored a goal against my team." His hand started to come down. "The kid fell—*BOOM*—on my violin." Dad's palm hit the table hard. "The case got broken, and the violin cracked. It was unplayable. I skipped my music class that day and was afraid to say anything to my parents." Dad took another puff and blew the smoke toward the ceiling.

Celia's was wide-eyed, and so was I. "So what happened, Johnny?" she asked, her eyes full of anticipation.

Dad looked at her wryly. "Two weeks later, the violin teacher called on my father to find out why I hadn't shown for my lessons. When my father confronted me, I told him honestly how the violin got broken. He got angry, but this time he didn't spank me. Instead, for the next few weeks, he didn't let me play with my friends after school."

Dad's elbows sat on the table; his hands were close together. The corners of his lips curled upward as he twirled the cigar between his fingers. "But I was happy that I didn't have to play the violin anymore."

His face hardened. "Yet, for the following school years, at my stepmother's urging, my father sent me to a private Hungarian *gymnázium*." He looked at Steve and me. "It's like your private high school." He looked back at Celia. "My mother felt I needed to be more controlled." He took another puff. "The teachers at that *gymnázium* were a lot stricter; I couldn't fool around or play hooky anymore."

Maybe that was why Dad sent Steve and me to boarding school. During our earlier school years, my brother and I had bugged each other with fingers, sticks, and fists. Things escalated until I, the smaller kid, went crying to Mom. She then screamed at the two of us, especially if our rambunctiousness distracted her from her cooking, sewing, or telephone talking. While at our private school, Steve and I hardly saw each other, so our wrangling subsided.

Celia came back. "I can't believe your stepmother was all bad. Was there anything you liked about her?"

My father's face softened. "I learned to cook by watching her in the kitchen." He pointed his cigar upward. "When I was old enough, I rose early on Sunday morning to go to the first church Mass. Then I got back home in

221

time to see my parents and kid brother leave for the next service. While they were out, I cooked a nice dinner for everyone, having it ready for when they got back."

A small grin came to his face. "They enjoyed my good Hungarian cooking. I was especially good at adding just the right amount of spices."

The military component to Steve's and my boarding school education contributed to our stopping our rambunctiousness with each other. May 1968.

"You should cook for us in Montreal, Johnny," Celia exclaimed.

Mom motioned a hand toward Dad. "Johnny's a good cook. He even taught me how, after we had come to Canada." Her tone altered slightly. "But other than making steaks on the grill during summer weekends, he's too busy with his business to cook at home."

I couldn't tell if her comment was mocking or not. Dad glared at her but said nothing.

I looked down and took a sip of my cappuccino. For a moment, I didn't dare look at anyone. There always seemed to be something ominous lingering between my parents. Mom's snide comments could later escalate into yelling and screaming matches between her and Dad. The smallest provocation could get one or both of them angry. Their words would turn terse, and their voices would elevate to shake the walls and my insides.

Since Dad returned to Mom months earlier, those two had somehow extinguished previous roaring fires. But something continually smoldered between them. It was hard to predict when the next blaze would ignite. Thank goodness we were together with Aras and Celia on this posh vacation, and thank heavens that there were no other pretty women in our group to distract Dad.

I stayed quiet, my brother too. I hoped that whatever bothered my parents would jump ship and drown in the sea. I was pleased that Dad's friends were here to keep us in good spirits. I guessed Mom felt happy because Dad was by her side, and he couldn't go running off all day to play golf or all night to party with his colleagues. She didn't have to cook or clean for a whole two weeks.

When my parents felt good, I felt good. This cruise was undoubtedly one of our family's best vacations. I hoped that our family life would continue with such good feelings when we returned home.

* * *

Puerto Rico was our last and only late-night port of call. There, the black suits my father had bought for both Steve and me came in handy once more.

After we had dressed as well-to-do gentlemen, Dad eyed my brother and me. "Aras, Celia, Mom, and I will surround you tonight as we enter the El San Juan Casino. We'll time it so that we'll go in with a big group." He put his thick hands on our shoulders. "Just act as if you belong there."

An hour later, we walked in tandem through the casino's big double-doors. We were lucky that no one asked about my or Steve's age. If they had, Dad would have said he had forgotten our passports. We would have then turned around and walked away, perhaps trying again later.

Watched over by Mom, my brother and I played roulette with fifty-cent bets while Dad and Aras took a seat at a $5 blackjack table not far away. Celia went looking for the slot machines. My father and Aras ordered their regular drinks and lit cigars. They blew thick fumes into the air as they concentrated on the cards.

Dad had given $10USD each to my brother, my mother, and me with which to play. I had another ten in my wallet. Dressed like a gentleman in this formal casino atmosphere, I sat straight at the roulette table, hoping to look as if I were a regular. After I had played several losing rounds, I noticed a woman at our table; she had chips piled high. I started copying her betting pattern. For every bet, I spread my chips across a similar array of numbers on the board, only veering from that pattern occasionally, as the woman did.

My brother sat on the other side of me. He placed his chips randomly across different numbers each time he bet. He said, "It doesn't matter where you place your bets; the odds are the same no matter what numbers you pick."

I said nothing but continued to concentrate my bets across the same block of numbers. I put chips on edges and corners of spaces so that they covered two or four different numbers simultaneously, though the payouts were that much less.

I avoided the eyes of the tuxedo dressed croupier and held in my teen exuberance. I didn't chat with my brother, mother, or anyone, focusing instead on the action at the table. I continued to watch the woman near me. I pretended I was an undercover operative and kept my cool, like James Bond.

I felt tingles of anticipation as the little white ball rolled around the roulette wheel before it bounced and dropped onto a number. I kept my eyes down, and my face stayed expressionless. I lost some bets but pulled in a few dollars with others. I watched chips being moved about the table at lightning speed as everyone staked their positions, or as the croupier made payouts and gathered people's losses.

My mother played only a few rounds with a few chips, preferring to keep her allowance secure in her purse. Instead, she watched the men and women in the casino, examining the clothes and accessories they wore.

In less than an hour, I more than doubled my $10 while my brother gradually lost his. I smirked at him when he walked away to watch our father play. In the distance, I could hear my enthusiastic dad shout "hurrah" when he or Aras beat the dealer on a big hand. I couldn't wait to be all grown up like them.

Dad won a few hundred bucks playing blackjack that night. Over our last days of ocean travel back to New York City, he spotted my brother and me for shipboard horse racing and bingo. There was not much else to do during those three days at sea, with the deck lounge chairs put away and the swimming pool closed as the outside air slowly crept down to freezing.

At bingo, I won another fifty American bucks. Greenbacks were more prized than our Canadian dollars, which we mocked as "Canadian Monopoly money" because of their different coloured bills of lesser value.

I kept my $60USD roulette and bingo winnings, plus the ten Dad had originally staked me, secure in the new leather wallet my father had given me at Christmas. I was going to save the cash for the next time our family went on a U.S. vacation. Or I was going to put my winnings in the bank and watch it grow—Dad would applaud that.

One afternoon, drained of cash donations from Dad, my brother asked me if he could borrow a buck for a horse race. I said, "You spent or lost yours, Steve. You *ain't* going to lose any of mine."

* * *

The night after saying farewell to Puerto Rico, my brother and I stayed in our cabin below deck. We didn't attend supper. We felt woozy from our ship rocking in the open ocean swells of the Bermuda Triangle.

Our cabin had a buzzer with which to summon the steward. My brother had pushed it a couple of times that evening to get club soda, ginger ale, and Alka Seltzer to calm our stomachs.

Before lights out, Mom checked on us once more. We told her we still had bellyaches. For a third time, she pushed the steward button to ask if we could get hot water bottles.

A moment later, the Italian steward knocked then opened our door. Not seeing my mother, he stared at Steve and me. He spoke quickly and energetically. "What! You *keeds pusha da* button again. *Yu maka da trauble fo me?*"

Steve and I sat frozen, like kid deer in this Italian's headlights. Seemingly startled by the tall, thin, and squeaky-voiced man, Mom said nothing about her having pushed the button. She looked at the steward. "Can my boys get hot water bottles for their upset stomachs?"

The steward gathered himself. "*Sì, signora,*" he said. He nodded his head as if he were serving royalty, and he then immediately left to fetch the bottles. As our cabin door slowly closed behind him, we could hear the man mutter, "*Deese keeds just maka da trauble.*"

After our cabin door closed entirely, and a few seconds elapsed to give the steward a chance to get out of earshot, Mom grabbed herself and burst out laughing. She then wagged her finger and loudly mimicked, "*Dont pusha da button! Dont maka da trauble!*" Those phrases would become her favourite bedtime lines with us for many months to come.

On the last night of our voyage, Dad gave big tips to our restaurant and cabin stewards. Aras told him, "You have to remember that we were on board for two weeks, and these people have worked for us every day." He spoke assuredly. "Most of these fellows spend up to six months on the ship before they get time off to see their families. They deserve our generosity."

My father sealed many $20 American bills, totaling hundreds of dollars, into the white envelopes that the room stewards had conveniently left in our cabins. Aras added, "You only need to give one envelope to the waiter; he will divide the tips fairly with his colleagues. They use a preset formula, with the waiter getting the largest share and smaller portions going to everyone else. The smallest portion goes to the wine stewards."

"Doesn't that cheat those guys?" I asked, looking at my father.

Aras answered. "Not at all! Each of the wine stewards gets a portion from half of the tables in the restaurant, not just from the two tables that each waiter and server have to cover. They make out very well."

I was glad to hear that, for the restaurant's wine stewards had put on many kilometers scurrying around the dining room during dinners and suppers.

I was glad again when Dad discretely slipped our waiter's assistant, Roberto, extra cash. The polite and proper Italian accepted the envelope with a nod, smile, and *"Grazie."* He quickly tucked it away in his jacket.

Seeing his big, affectionate grin made me feel content as our ship listed and rolled gently in the cold waters and frigid air of the North Atlantic.

In the wee hours of the coming morning, we docked in New York City. After our last breakfast on board, the crew shepherded us off the ship for good. After another seven-hour drive through New York State's snowbound North Country, we returned to our Montreal igloo home.

It felt special to be my father's son during this grand holiday, especially with Mom and Dad having no severe upsets. I hoped we would have many more *bon voyages* together.

* * * *

12

Secreting of a Son

On a grey summer day in 1972, Dad drove our rental car into the no man's land between Germany and Czechoslovakia. It was a few months before my eighteenth birthday and a month past my graduation from high school. Our family was again heading to my parents' homeland.

We were to spend a couple of days in Prague, visiting Mom's brother Geza. After that, we were to head to Košice for a few days to reunite with my parents' family. I was excited about traveling once more to Eastern Europe with my family intact. I looked forward to seeing our kin again.

Our drawn-out border crossing dampened my mood. As it had been four years earlier, barbed wire fences and high lookout towers lined the Austrian-Bohemian border. Military uniformed personnel carried a sidearm or a machine-gun.

The concrete grey border station seemed starker than what I remembered. The border guards were gloomy, too, with no brightness emanated from anyone. Heads turned as Dad drove our Mercedes sedan into the parking area, but faces stayed glum. It was as if the Prague Spring of '68 had never happened.

It took over three hours to go through the Iron Curtain rigmarole. We waited in long lines at the border station and then stood alongside our car while a contingent of sullen border officials checked our passports and stamped our visas. They opened and searched our luggage and handbags, climbed in and looked through our vehicle, examined the unwrapped gifts we brought for our relatives to determine that they weren't contraband, and obligated my father to buy the country's currency at the official state rate. The 10 Czechoslovak korunas per U.S. dollar that Dad received at the border station were thirty percent of the exchange he could get on the streets of Košice.

After the guards had completed their checks and inspections, and we repacked our luggage into the trunk, my mother and brother returned to our car's backseat. Dad and I remained standing a few paces in front of our vehicle. We waited for the final stamping of our papers by the border officer standing in his nondescript grey-metal guard shack. He was all that stood between us and the gates leading into the Czechoslovak province of Bohemian.

The clean-shaven thirtysomething officer wore a dark khaki uniform that sported a single gold star on each epaulette. He eyed our papers slowly and carefully, ticking things off on the documents. When he finished, he raised his head and looked directly at my father. He was so tall and buff that, if he had lived in the West, he might have played center on a basketball team.

The blank-faced fellow motioned with his right hand as if he wanted my father to give him something. Though he spoke in Czech, which I couldn't understand, his tone sounded like an order.

My stout Dad, who was a full head shorter than the guard, didn't hesitate to obey. He reached into his back pockets and took out both of his wallets—a black leather money wallet and a brown leather credit card wallet. He placed them into the guard's outstretched hand.

The situation struck me as an affront to Dad's privacy, but here at the Czechoslovak frontier, it came across as the standard operating procedure. I guess Dad didn't want to raise any suspicions by not complying; otherwise, we might be hours more in this border limbo.

I looked over my dad's shoulder—I was several centimeters taller than he was but not even close to the height of the guard. The officer opened my father's wallets, pulled out the contents, and spread them across the small desk in his guard post. He perused the cash, traveller's cheques, and many business and credit cards. He said nothing as he scanned the contents, picking up and examining each item.

The guard unfolded a slip of paper that came from an inside pocket in my father's money wallet. The officer's eyebrow rose. Seeing the item for the first time myself, I, too, was curious. The guard eyed the small document that was a Canadian cheque or bank draft. I was close enough to see that it was a cheque made out to my father for the amount of $72,000.

My eyes widened. I held my breath and kept silent. Had I asked about the draft, it might interrupt the delicate conversation Dad was having with the border official.

During a pit stop before the frontier, Dad had told us in a stern tone, "Don't say anything when we are at the border; let me do the talking." He cautioned, "It took months for Montreal's Czechoslovak consulate to get visas for our trip this time." He had pointed a finger. "Entry into Czechoslovakia has become harder since the clampdown on the Dubček era. The border guards could scrutinize anything. The smallest thing could be a reason to reject our entry because I escaped the country in '49."

Dad's face had been deadly serious. "It's a different matter to deal with the officials here at the frontier than the people in the Montreal Czechoslovak consulate. There are no computers here. Paper records at this crossing may not match the records in the Slovak capital where they issued our visas." He looked with intense eyes at my brother and me, "I don't want any confusion or trouble, so I want your mouths closed; *kapish*?"

Steve and I had nodded our agreement.

The border guard now turned Dad's creased cheque over a couple of times. He raised it closer to his face, eying it keenly. He turned to my father and asked him several questions. My father had said nothing about the cheque until the guard made his inquiry.

Dad coolly and calmly answered the questions, pointing to the cheque and then to himself. I couldn't understand what they said, but I did hear my father say "*Zürich*" and "*banka*" in their common language. Maybe he told the guard that the cheque was for important business he had in Switzerland.

Dad leaned toward the guard but didn't touch him. He directed the fellow's attention to a business card sitting on his desk that had come from the same wallet. Dad read "*Banka Ženevě* [Czech for *Banque de Genève* or Bank of Geneva]" as he continued his conversation with the young, stone-faced fellow. Standing behind my father, I stayed motionless and expressionless so as not to divert attention from their serious but, so far, peaceful exchange.

After another moment of scrutinizing my father's face, the guard ended his inquiry. He gathered the wallets and their contents that had been strewn across his desk and put them into my father's hands. He turned to the papers and made a notation in my dad's visa. He then gave the permit back to my father along with his passport.

Dad turned to me, "Son, please hold our travel papers while I put everything back into my wallets."

I complied while my father reinserted everything carefully.

We turned and ambled toward the car. I couldn't hold back my curiosity. Keeping my voice low, I asked in English, a language no guard here understood, "What was that about, Dad, with that bank draft?"

Matching my low tone, my father responded, "That draft is for banking business I have in Zurich." He pointed to the papers in my hands. "The guard put a note into my visa. I will need to show the same draft to the customs officials on our way out of the country."

"So Czechoslovakia doesn't want your money?" I quipped.

Dad's tone remained somber and steady. "They don't want anybody involved in any black market business here." He looked at me. "*Lassen* to me, son. Be a good boy, not saying anything to Mom and Stevie about what you saw or heard. Just keep that draft between us." He pointed to himself and me.

If I asked my father too many questions, I knew he'd respond, "Don't be nosy, son." He might tell me that with a smile or with a stern look and a pointed finger. This time his face was blank, and his fingers remained occupied with his wallets.

I acknowledged my father's request. "Okay, Dad. No problem." Though I continued to be curious about the cheque, I knew not to ask more about it. I said nothing to Mom or Steve. Having Dad trust me with his business affairs made me feel special and closer to him. Over the years, situations like this became our secret.

* * *

As we did four summers earlier, our family spent only three days in Košice. We were again "up to our growing waistlines" in gargantuan meals at Aunt Irén's home. Dad's relatives also invited us over, providing unending midday snacks. One morning, on the last day of our stay, Mom and Steve went shopping with Mom's sister.

Mom and Irén had a little international trade venture going. Though Czechoslovakia was a poor country, Irén had good connections and could obtain quality linens, laced doilies, handkerchiefs, and Bohemia lead crystal glassware. Dad had said that these were vital Czechoslovak exports, controlled by the state to obtain western currency.

Aunt Irén had a knack for ferreting out Czechoslovak treasures from both underground and legitimate vendors. Some friends and family, even Irén herself, referred to her as *bolond Irén* (crazy Irene) for the way she talked fast and laughed with a high-pitched shrill, and for the way she moved her arms and hands frenetically when she spoke.

Mom knew that the Czechoslovakia customs officials were less thorough when people exited the country than when they had entered. Border guards might glance into our trunk, and they would have Dad open only a bag or two. Mom might show them a few crystals and linens and tell them that they were gifts from her relatives. The rest of us knew she was going to sell those items in Canada and return the proceeds to her sister.

What we didn't take across the border, Irén would package and ship to Canada in a few months. Mom received large "care packages" from her sister roughly every six months, at the limit of what was permitted to leave Czechoslovakia.

Mom might drag my brother and me to Canada Customs in downtown Montreal to retrieve Aunt Irén's large packages. She told the customs officials that the contents were gifts; that way, she wouldn't face Canadian import fees. Sometimes she won those arguments. Sometimes she lost, and she'd have to pay duties before she could have the package.

In her preparations to exit Czechoslovakia on this trip, she had stuffed our luggage with her sister's wares until Dad remarked angrily, "That's enough already! Our suitcases are over the airline weight limit. Have your sister ship the rest."

Mom retorted, "The kids will help me. Each of them will carry an extra handbag onto the plane."

Steve and I kept our mouths shut while Mom and Dad hashed it out. Usually, Mom won these skirmishes having to do with her family's livelihood.

While Mom and Irén busied themselves with their shopping excursion, Dad and I walked around the city's main street. He showed me the location of his post-WWII radio store and repair shop, *Prima Rádió.* I was excited to see where my father had had his business beginnings. He offered, "The store looks just like it did twenty-three years ago, but it has a different name. The sign said *Rádia a Elektronika* (Radios & Electronics).

In addition to radios in small wood boxes, the store sold small TVs and vacuum cleaners. Products sat in the storefront affixed with price tags marked with big, black, block numbers. No prominent or colourful signs were displayed to attract people's attention.

Dad continued. "The government hires the store manager and sets the prices. There's no competition. There's only one brand of everything, typically made in Russia. The prices are rarely discounted and are pretty much the same all over the country."

Across the narrow street, I noticed a man looking at us. He seemed to be my father's age. After a few moments, the guy walked across the street toward us. As he approached, I saw deep lines and pits on his face. Dad now noticed him too. When the man reached us, he pointed at Dad and asked a question in Slovak. It sounded like, "*Prosim* [Please], are you *Janosh Shimkovich?*"

Dad responded in their native tongue. The man broke a smile, revealing yellowed teeth and gaps where some had been. For the next few minutes, the man and Dad seemed to have a pleasant exchange.

I heard my father mention "Montreal" and "*Kanada,*" and he pointed to me and said, "*Mój syn* [My son]." The rest I didn't understand. When they ended their exchange, Dad politely shook hands with the fellow and said, "*Dovidenia* [Goodbye]," and we walked away.

I looked at my father. "Who was that guy?"

Dad pawed his hand into the air. "Just someone I knew when I lived in Košice after the war." He left it at that. I was surprised that Dad had met and recognized an old acquaintance on the streets of his hometown after being away for twenty-three years. I wondered if my dad would have looked as old and worn as his comrade if my father hadn't escaped from Slovakia in '49.

Some weeks later, after our return to Canada, Dad showed me a letter he had received from his stepmother's brother. "My uncle Jaro says that the police knocked on his door the day after we left the city. An officer was looking for me."

My father's face projected concern. "Jaro told them that we already left Košice and that he didn't know where we were heading." He raised a hand. "He asked the policeman what they wanted, but the guy told him that it was none of his business."

By now, my parents' Soviet paranoia had become seated deep in me. My father's words, "You can't trust the government; they can take your freedom away in a minute," had become etched into my psyche. I looked at my father and asked, "Do you think that man we met near your old Košice shop may have had anything to do with the police showing up?"

Dad gazed at the floor. Was he wondering if he would be a marked man in Czechoslovakia for the rest of his life? Might he think that he had been only one step ahead of being thrown back into a communist jail cell that day, accused of escaping his country illegally in '49?

My father looked at me. "I'm not sure, son," he said. "God only knows what would have happened if we had stayed another day in Košice."

* * *

While we were still in my parents' hometown, my uncle Geza and his son Jirka came from Prague for a visit. Uncle Geza and his wife had divorced over a decade earlier. When I asked my mother why Geza and Marta had separated, she told me, "They didn't have enough in common. Geza liked to stay home at night while Marta liked to go out dancing."

In my uncle and aunt's divorce settlement, their older son Jirka went to live with his father while his younger brother Tomas remained with their mother. I wondered if such a division of kids would happen to Steve and me if our parents ever divorced. I wondered as to which parent I'd live with. I hoped my parents would stay together, at least until I was on my own.

While my aunt Irén and her husband were in the kitchen, putting things away after supper, Geza glanced out an open window to make sure no one outside might be listening. He then looked at Dad and Mom, and he spoke quietly in Hungarian, "I'm worried about my son. I don't know what future Jirka will have here in Czechoslovakia." My cousin, in his mid-twenties, was a journeyman printer in a print shop in Prague.

Dad looked at Geza and responded quietly in Hungarian. "He can't go far in his profession here. There would be a better future for him in the West." He raised a hand off the table. "If Jirka can escape to Canada, I can help him find better employment. There would be many more opportunities for him there."

Everyone stayed quiet as Geza spoke again. This time, angst was in his voice. "But how can Jirka get out of Czechoslovakia?" There was deep concern in his voice. "Because he is young, the government won't let him out on a visitor's visa, and it's too dangerous to escape. If the border guards catch him, they will put him in prison or send him far away."

Mom looked at Dad and offered in Hungarian. "Jani, don't put crazy ideas into Jirka's head. He can't escape as we did in '49, or like your brother did in '68. Geza is right; it's too dangerous these days."

Dad pointed to his temple. "I have an idea," he said in English. He then nodded toward me and spoke quietly. "We can give Harvy's passport to Jirka, and Jirka can exit with us when we leave the country. He and Harvy look enough alike; they wear similar glasses."

Oh, my God! Does my father want to see me stranded in Czechoslovakia? Shivers went through my body at the thought. I wondered how my father could make such an offer without asking me first. I glanced at Jirka and saw that he was also looking at me. *Did he and I look that much alike?*

Mom raised her voice and responded in English. "Jani, then how could Harvy get out of the country? We can't leave him here." I was glad she was speaking on my behalf. I stayed silent, along with everyone else at the table.

Dad looked and pointed at me again, and he said matter-of-factly, "Harvy can go to the Canadian consulate in Bratislava and tell them he lost his passport. He recently got his driver's licence, and he can use it to prove his identity. They will give him a new passport. He'll have it in no time, and we'll give him enough money to fly back to Montreal." Dad was making it sound like it was no big deal.

Mom said, "Jani, that's crazy."

Geza understood English, but he responded in Hungarian. "I can't ask Harvy to give his passport to Jirka." He turned to his son and put his hand on the young man's arm. "I agree that it would be too risky." Maybe he also didn't want his son to leave him.

Jirka, who probably got the gist of the English portion of the conversation, put his hand on his father's and said nothing.

I said nothing too and felt relief when the conversation turned to other things.

* * *

After completing our visit to my parent's hometown, Dad drove our family back to Switzerland. The plan was for our spending two nights and one full day in the Swiss capital before flying back to Montreal.

During breakfast on our first morning in Zurich, Mom mentioned the purchases she had made in Košice and the consignment items she had received from her sister. Among the treasures, she had a few of Uncle Bus's oil landscape paintings rolled up in a big cardboard tube. She said, "I'm going to have the paintings framed back in Canada and sell them to our Eastern European Canadian friends," she glanced at Dad, "and maybe to the wives of Daddy's Canadian customers. I'll then send the money back to Auntie Irén."

Dad said nothing to Mom's statement. He might get annoyed at her for using him as a sales agent, but he often put himself out for her family.

Steve asked, "How does that work? How do you send money back to your relatives?"

Finishing the last bite of his breakfast, Dad looked at my brother and me. "Czechoslovakia permits foreigners to buy what is called Tuzex currency at certain North American travel agencies that specialize in travel to Eastern Europe." He took a sip of his remaining coffee. "Your mother can send the Tuzex to her sister back home. Using those money vouchers, Irén can buy imported goods at Tuzex stores in Košice or any other major city in Czechoslovakia. She can even sell the Tuzex to her friends either for American dollars—if they have them—or for Czechoslovak koruna."

He grinned a bit. "It's as if Czechoslovakia made a *legal* black market for foreign money and goods. Without it, the *illegal* black market would take over."

His face turned glum. "It's also a way for the Communists to drain hard currency that's held by its people—like the U.S. and Canadian dollars I gave my relatives when we visited them." He lit a post-breakfast cigarette. "By people using their hard currency in Tuzex stores, they won't be tempted to give or sell western cash to someone who wants to escape to the West."

How sneaky those communists are! They were holding their people hostage. I was once again appreciative that Dad and Mom had escaped to a free country. I was once more impressed with what my father knew and understood.

Dad took another puff and turned to Mom. He said unexpectedly, "I have to go to a bank here in downtown Zurich for business. It shouldn't take more than an hour."

We knew that Dad had travelled to Europe many times to source and buy electronic components for his Canadian manufacturing company. His need to do local banking was not out of the ordinary.

Though Mom frequently became peeved about Dad's attention taken away from us, she didn't raise her voice against it this time. She could make use of the time to repack the items she had gotten in Košice.

After breakfast, we went back to our room. Dad collected a thin, leather briefcase from his suitcase. As he was ready to leave, he turned to me. "Harvy, do you want to come to the bank with me?"

I was surprised but honoured to be a part of Dad's private business. I responded without hesitation. "Sure, Dad!"

My father turned to my brother. "Stevie, stay with Mom and help her finish packing. Then go and find pamphlets in the lobby regarding the tourist things you and she want us to do this afternoon. Harvy and I will be back soon."

"Okay, Dad," my brother said. "I'll get on it right away." He stood to follow us out of the room. I suspected he preferred the tourist research assignment rather than to help Mom repack.

Before my brother moved too far, Mom spoke up. "Wait a minute, Stevie. Help me with these things; we can then go down to the lobby together."

Walking toward the door, I turned my head to see a displeased look on my brother's face. I said nothing except to offer him a smirk as I quickly headed out the door, right behind Dad.

My father and I grabbed a cab in front of the hotel. Within ten minutes, we were at the Zurich branch of the *Banque de Genève.*

The building seemed centuries old. It had large Roman columns and steep exterior steps that led to the main floor entrance. I was taken aback by both the vaulted ceiling in the lobby and only a few patrons in the bank. I wondered if it was too early in the morning for most of the Swiss to do their banking. Maybe only well-to-do businessmen like Dad were its customers.

My father pulled the *Banque de Genève* card from his wallet, the one I had seen during our Czechoslovak border crossing. He approached the receptionist and asked to see the person named on the business card. The expressionless woman picked up her phone receiver and dialed.

Within a few minutes, an assistant ushered Dad and me down a wood-paneled hallway and into a large, high-ceiling, wood-paneled office. She guided us to a dark-suited man who sat in front of a big, cherrywood desk.

The man shook my father's hand. "Welcome, Mr. Simkovits." He spoke slowly and with a Swiss-German accent. "I am Mr. Aeschbacher, the manager you spoke with over the phone from Montreal. I trust you are having a pleasant stay in our country."

"Good to meet you, sir," my father responded with a slight nod. "We drove in yesterday via Austria from my home country of Czechoslovakia. Your Swiss countryside is beautiful, and your city is immaculate."

"Yes, we are proud of our Swiss appearance and heritage," the manager said. He turned toward me. "I see you have brought your son," his voice half-remarked and half-questioned.

"Yes, this is my son, Harvy," Dad offered. He didn't mention my brother.

I shook the manager's hand. His grip was firm, but not overpowering like that of our Slavic male relatives. Those Slovaks gripped hard enough to squeeze the blood out of one's whole arm.

The manager looked at my father. "How long will you be staying in Switzerland?"

"Just another day before we fly back home."

Mr. Aeschbacher showed a small smile. "Hopefully, you will have more time to see our high mountains and glacial valleys the next time you visit."

The Swiss bank manager motioned with his hand to two chairs in front of his desk. "Please sit down." He then got down to business.

He pulled out forms from his desk and put them in front of my father. "Please take your time to fill these out. While you are doing that, I will see to it that you get coffee," he glanced at me, "and a cold drink for your son." He smiled again. "I will send in my assistant, and I will return shortly."

He pointed to the papers. "As you complete these documents, please leave the signature areas blank for now. I will show you where to sign when I return."

Dad nodded. The tall gentleman nodded too and left the room.

I sat still as I watched Dad fill out several forms. During our Czechoslovakia border crossing, he had asked me for help with our entry and customs forms. He completed these Swiss banking documents on his own. I asked no questions because I felt privileged to be here with my father.

My eyes scanned the big room. Its ambiance was rich and immaculate, with wood paneling going from floor to ceiling. Oil paintings of mountain and valley scenes hung on the walls. Sturdy leather covered the thickly cushioned wood chairs.

I thought this manager must be an important person to have such an office. I wondered if one day, when I was old enough, whether I too might work in a beautiful space like this. It was very different from the veneer paneling, simple wood molding, and boxy furniture in my father's factory offices.

A woman entered. She brought coffee for Dad and an Orangina for me. Minutes later, the manager returned. Dad handed Mr. Aeschbacher the completed papers, and he eyed the documents one-by-one. "Everything looks in order," he said. He pointed. "Please initial here, sign here, and here."

Dad complied, applying his customary unintelligible squiggles.

The manager added, "What do you plan as your initial deposit?"

Dad pulled out his black wallet and retrieved the neatly folded $72,000 bank draft.

The blank-faced Aeschbacher took Dad's cheque, perused it for a few seconds, attached it to the completed documents, and made notations on the paperwork. He then gave my father a slip of paper. "This is the number for your new account."

I sat still while the manager and my father spoke. They conducted what seemed like an everyday bank transaction. As the two men conversed, a hot flash went through my body. I felt as if some higher force had thrust me into a

James Bond 007 movie, with Dad an aspiring Goldfinger and me his trusty Oddjob—though I wasn't a hefty Asian and hadn't a hat that could kill.

Another moment passed. My father asked the manager, "What are your interest rates and fees?"

From a desk drawer, the manager fetched and handed Dad a sheet of paper. "These are our current rates and account fee schedules." He pointed. "Of course, the interest rates change weekly as the market changes, yet the bank fixes its fees for the year." He pointed. "Our current term deposit rates are there on your sheet."

"I'll call you next week from Montreal and let you know how I want the money invested," my father said coolly. "Keep it at your daily interest rate for now."

"At your leisure, Mr. Simkovits."

Dad put the sheet of paper in his wallet and returned the wallet to his back pocket. We all stood. He and the manager shook hands and said goodbye. I received a departing nod from the banker as Dad said, "C'mon, son. Let's go."

Keeping up with Dad's pace, I followed him out of the room, through the office suite and bank lobby, then through the building's front doors. I felt like a puppy with a tight collar and short leash. When we reached the street, Dad hailed a cab to take us back to our hotel.

I wasn't sure when it dawned on me as to what had gone on during Dad's seemingly professional banking exchange. Between Mr. Aeschbacher having said, "Mr. Simkovits, you could access your money with this account number and passcode," and a moment later adding, "You must not lose these numbers for it's the only way to access your funds," I felt thrust into that James Bond movie. It then occurred to me that my father was making a sizable deposit into a private, hidden Swiss bank account.

More than once, Dad had told me, "No government can be completely trusted to protect you and your money. You need to learn to protect yourself." I remembered how his former Czechoslovak business was summarily nationalized by the communists, becoming the property of the state. He had told us, "All I got for it was a piece of shit government paper."

241

Ever since I had been a young teen, my father spoke about the Quebec separation movement. Some years ago, Quebec had seen the birth of *Le Parti Québécois* (PQ). Since then, Dad grew more apprehensive and sarcastic about what he called "*les* bloody Quebec separatists."

When I had once visited his office after the PQ came into existence, Dad told me angrily, "Those separatists are growing in strength and one day might rule our provincial government." He huffed. "If the socialist PQ ever became the majority government in the province, they'd split Quebec from Canada. If that would happen, then every Quebec business could be nationalized as the communists did to me in '48."

He banged his fist on his desk. "The money in our Quebec banks might even become worthless outside the province. It's like what happened to Czechoslovak currency when the communists took over my country."

I was young, impressionable, and surrounded by the growing fear of Quebec separation. My apprehensions were fueled not only by my father's views but also by Canadian news programs.

I had been shocked and amazed as I watched TV news while at school, seeing the unfolding of the October Crisis of 1970. A radical cell of the FLQ (*Front de libération du Québec)* had kidnapped two government officials and murdered one of them.

Our prime minister, Pierre Elliott Trudeau, invoked Canada's first peacetime use of Canada's War Measures Act, declaring martial law in our province. Canadian armed forces were deployed across Quebec, detaining hundreds of people associated with the Quebec sovereignty movement.

My father railed over what might happen to Quebec, echoing "those bloody militant separatists" at every opportunity. I wondered how these things could be happening in Canada.

Over the years, Dad also complained about how much the Canadian federal and provincial governments were taxing him. He said he was in the top tax bracket that reached as high as 70% in some years.

During our recent trip behind the Iron Curtain, Dad once explained capitalism to his extended family. He told them in Hungarian, "Unlike here in Czechoslovakia, where the state owns everything, the Canadian and Quebec government acts as your silent business partner. It's as if they owned half of everything you have built in your lifetime."

He pointed a finger. "You work hard for your company profit, and then they take 50% of it away every year in taxes. They give you little in return, except for the privilege of running your company. And what they do give you, like universal healthcare and the construction of roads and bridges, is corrupted by unions and crooked politicians who suck away the money for themselves."

He took a long breath and continued his rant. "And then, when you try to take your hard-earned money out of your business or try to sell your property, they tax you again," he bellowed. "Who needs communism with that kind of capitalism?" His relatives' wide eyes and bent ears had remained with him in amazement.

As we left the Swiss bank, I felt my father was justified to hide his money here. He had earned it, and no one should take it from him. And by being his trusted son, I might obtain access to his stash one day.

Though today, I no longer agree with my father's views; back then, I not only walked by Dad's side but also stood with him firmly.

While we waited for a cab in front of the *Banque de Genève* in the warm sun and fresh Swiss air, Dad reached his hand out toward me. "*Lassen* to me, son. Please keep what we did today just between you and me."

"Okay, Dad; no problem," I responded.

My father's request to keep his new bank account secret was unnecessary. I didn't feel that I needed to share any of what I knew with my mother or brother. Keeping our father's financial confidence would be my way of fighting back smartly against my poking and prodding brother. Steve was always bugging me with his fists and fingers, but I would best him by using my bean, and by being closer to our father.

Steve was more inclined to stand up for our mother whenever she and Dad quarreled. Once, Mom complained to my brother and me about not getting enough money for her household expenses. Steve then went to our father and asked him why he couldn't give her more. The next thing I knew, Mom and Dad had a big argument. Dad came home high late one night and blasted her. "Why do you use your son as a go-between? You don't have the guts to talk to me directly?"

Over the years, Steve had made bonafide attempts to be a mediator between our continually quarreling parents. One night, during a family vacation in Portugal, when I had been 16, my parents argued in our hotel room. It was about Dad drinking too much at supper or sleeping our vacation days away while Mom wanted to go out and sightsee. Steve calmly asked, "Why do the two of you fight so much?"

I said nothing. Resigned to my parents' eternal bickering, I saw my brother's efforts as useless. I hoped the issue would go away if I ignored it. To my surprise, the three of them talked calmly about what was happening.

After a few minutes of what had seemed like my parents pointing fingers at each other, Dad said with resignation, "Just forget about it." Mom and Dad turned away from each other and dropped the subject. Steve dropped it too.

I felt so exasperated by their lack of consideration that it crossed my mind to run away. *That would make my parents pay attention!* I even considered jumping off our hotel balcony. *That would certainly show them!* Their bickering made me angry, scared, and depressed. I held in the emotions that wanted to burst out of me. Though I imagined jumping off a building whenever my parents fought, I never attempted it.

A couple of days later, during that Portugal vacation, my parents were at each other again. Dad was overtaking cars too fast while driving on a narrow country road. Mom yelled at Dad, but her words didn't deter his driving. Between my parents, there was always something about which to argue. I wanted to jump out of the car and run away again, but I didn't know where I would go.

Mom was as much a perpetrator as a recipient of their recurrent quarrels. She prodded Dad about his repeated late work nights and weekend business gatherings. One night at home, she had pleaded harshly, "Why are you away so much? We need you at home."

He came back strongly, jabbing his finger toward the floor. "I'm working hard for us. I don't complain about your job here at home, so don't complain about mine out there."

Mom's ill-timed, biting tongue was her biggest downfall. One Sunday after church, when my brother and I had been young teens, Dad took us out for dinner in Montreal's Chinatown. In the middle of eating sweet and sour chicken, fried rice, and gooey spare ribs, my mother muttered unexpectedly, "Your father stopped loving me after five years of marriage."

I held my breath and looked down at my food as an eerie silence engulfed our table and family. I could imagine Dad ready to blast her, but he said nothing. I froze, my gut turning to rock.

After a moment that felt like an eternity, Mom came back, "Are you boys eating enough?" She pushed meal dishes toward us. "Have more fried rice and spare ribs."

The more my mother said such abrasive things, the more my parents bickered, and the later my father would come home at night. He'd arrive after everyone was asleep, long enough to have a snooze on the living room couch, change into a clean business shirt and suit, and then head back to his factory before anyone else was awake. I knew because I sometimes woke as dawn broke to hear our noisy electronic garage opener signal my father's very late arrival or very early departure.

Now, at seventeen, I admired my father. I liked the way he followed his drumbeat, even in the way he went to see movies. He never let a published start time dictate when we were going to see a film. He could enter in the middle of the screening. At the end of the film, we'd sit in the theatre until the next presentation started, to catch what we had missed.

Dad was always good to me. We played cards, chess, or other games when he was home on the weekends. He and I had nice times during our family holidays and winter vacations. I never wanted to draw his ire.

During my elementary school years, I had sat next to my father on many Saturday nights while he and Mom played gin rummy with their Hungarian friends. They gambled a nickel or dime per card. I watched Dad play his hands while Steve went to watch television in the den or to do something in the basement.

Dad offered me a nickel or dime for my moral support every time he took in a big haul of a dollar or more. He grinned and called me his "lucky charm," as he rubbed his freshly dealt cards on my head. He had me fake-spit on his playing cards for luck before he revealed his hand slowly to see the cards he had received.

On Saturday afternoons during those years, Dad, Steve, and I often played soccer in our backyard with other neighbourhood kids. I was the smallest kid, so I played with my father. It was my dad and me against the world. I played goalie and watched my father's back. Dad laughed as he pushed the ball past kids half his size. Three kids might grab him, trying to push him away or take him to the ground. While he played solo offense, I stayed back and low, near to our makeshift goals marked by a couple of old running shoes. Knowing that Dad was on my side encouraged me to stop shots and rush out fearlessly to grab loose balls. I reveled in taking goals away from my brother and his friends. Dad and I won most of those matches.

Because of that early soccer training, I became an accomplished goalie on my high school junior varsity and varsity teams. I lost only three games in thirty-three starts. Dad came to my weekend school games, later bragging to his friends about his "great goalie son" and how he had started my career in our backyard. I felt good to make him proud.

Dad and I now shared a solemn pact that confirmed my having his favour. For better or worse, I chose to put my fortunes with him. My future felt more secure by being both on and near Dad's side.

I knew deep down I was abandoning my mother and felt painful pangs in my chest whenever she pined for Dad. But I felt greater pleasure and esteem in being my father's favourite. Siding with Dad also meant I was siding against my brother. Allying with Dad would be my way of getting back at what felt like Steve's continual disregard of me.

While we waited for a cab at the curb outside of the *Banque de Genève*, and while we rode it back to the hotel where Steve and Mom were waiting, neither Dad nor I ever said the words "hidden offshore money." I understood and accepted the safeguarding of my father's secret. I wondered if he might be testing me for even bigger money endeavours.

* * * *

13

Making of a Chosen One

On a warm, summer afternoon, when I was ten years old, my father came home early from his usual Saturday half-day at the office. It was rare to see him home before 1:30, but today he was in time for Mom's dinner of crispy Wiener schnitzel, buttered mashed potatoes, and sweet and sour cucumber salad. Food covered every corner of our plates.

During the meal, Dad turned to me. "Harvy, do you want to come this afternoon to see my new building? I have a crew working there to clean the place. I want to see what they're doing. It's not far away; we won't be long."

He offered a small smile. "It's close to Dorval Airport. Afterward, we can go to watch the planes land, as we sometimes do."

I looked at my father, my heart beating faster. "Sure, Daddy!"

My dad knew of a secluded road that was parallel to one of Montreal airport's long runways. For an hour or more, he and I'd watch the MacDonald Douglas DC-3s, Vickers Viscount and Vanguard prop planes, and the newer MD DC-8 and Boeing 707 jets, as they came in for engine-roaring landings.

The planes passed only a few hundred meters away from where Dad parked. As he and I leaned against his car hood, we pointed into the sky as we saw each plane expand as it came closer from the horizon. Grey-black engine smoke trailed behind the jet aircraft.

My heart pounded, and I felt tingles as these big birds gracefully glided in for a touchdown. Their rear wheels hit the ground with a burst of tire smoke before the front wheels drifted onto the tarmac seconds later.

We covered our ears and screamed our lungs out as the jet engines roared when the pilot reversed them to slow the aircraft. The power and cry of those powerful Pratt & Whitney and GE engines overwhelm all other sounds, including our shrieks. It was thrilling to be there, especially with my father.

Dad knew the tail markings. We imagined travelling the world and back on Trans Canada, Lufthansa, Air France, TWA, Alitalia, Pan-Am, and others.

Steve was less interested in doing such things with our dad. Perhaps he found such things not appealing to an older kid. Maybe he liked to stay at home with Mom, or maybe his plastic construction models were more interesting. Either way, I was pleased to get my father to myself for an hour or two, our chance to have fun together.

Dad and I left home after Mom's dinner. In the car, he pulled out a quarter from his pocket and held it between his right thumb and index finger. "So tell me, Harvy, what is eight times twelve?"

I knew this game. If I got the answer right, I'd have the quarter. "Ninety-six," I said with a giggle and grabbed for the coin.

He held the quarter tightly between his fingers. "Okay, that was too easy. Do one more; what is 17 times 14?"

I thought for a moment. *10 times 17 is 170; 2 times 17 is thirty-four, so 4 times 17 is 68; 170 plus 68 is . . .* "238!" I shouted.

He released the coin into my fingers. "Good boy, Harvy, the quarter is yours."

Dad played the game a few times more. Each question was a little harder, but I got the answers right. "Can we keep doing it, Dad?" I asked.

"Maybe later, son." He smirked. "You'll take all my money if I give you a chance."

We turned from the main boulevard onto a street where there were many factory buildings. My father pointed. "My building is halfway down the street, on the right. It was a warehouse. The previous owner sold it to me as is, so it has a lot of junk and garbage in it. I hired a Polish crew to clean up the place and repair the offices." He took a big breath. "I hope to rent it as a warehouse or a factory, depending on who I can find as a tenant."

Though I was young, I noticed that many of the people my father hired were of one Eastern European ethnicity or another. He especially liked to give work to his fellow Slavic, Hungarian, and even Russian immigrants who had escaped Soviet Communism. They spoke languages in which my father was versed.

"Okay, Daddy. But why do you need to go see your building today?" I wondered why my father had to work on Saturday and not stay at home with us.

He glanced my way and patted my lap. "I want to be sure that the guy I hired is doing his job properly. You have to check on people who work for you; otherwise, they tend to take shortcuts and not do things right."

I nodded my understanding but wondered why hired people wouldn't do their jobs the way they were supposed to. Couldn't my dad find workers on which he didn't have to check?

Dad parked his car in front of the building, and we walked to the entrance. Someone had pasted a "Sold" sticker over a tattered "For Sale" sign. Dad had a key to enter the front office through double doors with cracked glass.

The room was dusty; the windows were dingy; the aluminum frames were dull and pitted; wallpaper was peeling all over; the linoleum floor was yellowed and deeply scuffed. The room had no furniture. It looked as if robbers had stolen everything that wasn't attached to a floor or wall.

I was accustomed to Mom taking Spic 'n Span to every linoleum floor in our house and using Comet on every metal cupboard and Formica countertop in our kitchen. I recoiled from what I saw and held myself back from touching anything.

My father spent a moment looking around. "We have a lot of cleaning to do here in the office before I can rent the place. But that's for another day. Let's go into the warehouse where the people are working."

He must have seen my look of surprise and disgust. He added, "I don't mind the mess for now because I got the place for an excellent price."

I followed my father through the office's back door and into the vast expanse of the warehouse. The long building seemed to be half the size of a Canadian football field (longer and broader than its USA counterpart). The cavern-like space was dim and smelled of dust and grime.

Broken wooden pallets, dirt, and chipped concrete pieces lay on a cracked concrete floor. The concrete-block walls sported stained, shattered, and smoky windows. *What a mess!* I followed my father into the grey void. I considered that my Mom would die of a heart attack if she ever had to clean this place by herself.

Dad looked sternly at me. "Don't get yourself messy in here, and don't touch anything. Mom will get angry if we come home dirty."

I looked at my father. "Okay, Daddy. I'll be careful." But I didn't need the warning. I wasn't about to put my fingers anywhere. I wondered why anyone would leave a place this filthy.

There were men doing work in the back of the building, by a garage door. One of them spotted us and started walking our way. Dad looked and pointed. "I need to speak to this foreman a few minutes. Don't run away anywhere. Stay close to me and stay clean, okay?"

He winked at me. I nodded back.

The foreman approached. He hailed a greeting in his Polish tongue, similar to Slovak, with a "Mr. Simkovits" tacked on. Dad greeted him similarly, but only offered the man's first name.

The fellow was shorter and more rotund than my father. He wore dirty and tattered coveralls compared to Dad's white shirt and black slacks. The two men talked in their common language.

I didn't know what they said. Dad seemed to ask questions as he pointed to various places in the building. The foreman also gestured with his answers.

Getting bored, I sauntered a few paces to one side. On the floor were broken pieces from wooden pallets. I started to kick them. I watched as thick plumes of dust rose off the floor as my short kicks moved random pieces of broken wood into a pile. I worked to keep my pant legs away from the small clouds I created.

Suddenly, an angry scream rose from behind me. Electricity went through my body as I turned around to see Dad punch the foreman in the arms and then the chest. My father was yelling at the top of his lungs, again in their language.

The other guy raised his arms to defend himself, and he backed away. After landing a punch or three, my father stopped his blows. He continued to scream at the man, leaning forward and towering over the shorter guy.

I had seen my father's quick anger before, when he yelled at my brother for not doing what he was supposed to do, and when he shouted at my mother for saying something that riled him. My body trembled those times too. In those moments, I remained motionless, hoping my father's furor would dissipate if I stayed silent and still.

I had heard his yelling at his factory employees too, but never this loud, and I had never seen him punch anybody. My foot didn't dare kick another board or speck of dust. I didn't know what else to do but to remain frozen.

After a moment of sound reverberating between concrete block walls, Dad calmed down. His hands and arms stopped flying around, except for a pointed finger wielded at the Pole. He and the guy continued to talk vigorously.

I stared at them from about five meters away, which I hoped was a safe distance. My insides were shaking as if Dad had yelled at me. I wanted to disappear behind one of the building's support beams, but I stayed still.

After a few more minutes of loud back-and-forth chatter, Dad's voice calmed to his normal tone. The other guy also talked normally. My father pulled out his cigarette pack and offered one to the foreman. He retrieved his lighter to light their smokes. My dad then chuckled and patted the guy on the shoulder. They spoke nicely to each other again, like best pals. Dumbfounded, I remained frozen. My head ached, wondering what had created the commotion.

In a couple of moments, they ended their conversation. Dad dropped his cigarette on the ground, stubbed it out with his foot, turned to me, and calmly said, "Okay, Harvy; let's go."

We walked back toward where we had come. The foreman went the other way toward his crew. I asked quietly, "Daddy, what were you yelling about with that man?"

He looked at me seriously. "The guy wasn't doing the job I wanted him to do. Like I told you, you've got to watch people working for you, so they don't take shortcuts." He winked. "Everything is okay now. He is going to do things the way I want him to."

Dad grinned, showing me his stubby cigarette-yellowed teeth. He put his hand on my shoulder. "Now, let's go over to the airport and look at those planes land."

I nodded and followed closely behind. I couldn't wait to get out of that dingy place. Like a jet airplane reversing its engines upon touchdown, the power and roar of my father's furor had overtaken me. I might pass out, or maybe even die of a failed heart, if he ever wielded that kind of ferocity toward me.

* * *

It was the spring of 1970; I was fifteen, and my brother was sixteen. Steve and I were home from boarding school during spring break. Over supper, with Mom looking on, Dad turned to us. "I want to send you boys to France this summer to a French immersion school." My father was on his French-language kick again.

My head rose from devouring Mom's Hungarian stuffed cabbage—infinitely more delicious than my boarding school's drab shepherd's pie and tasteless grilled cheese sandwiches. Kids might faint on the school's sports fields, or crash dead-tired afterward on their dorm beds, after our cafeteria's less than nourishing meals.

Two years earlier, Dad had sent my brother and me to a Swiss French summer camp for three weeks while Mom stayed with her relatives in Slovakia. The next year—the year he had left my mother for eight months—we had had a month of French camp at our boarding school. Now, he thought of another way to continue our foreign language learning.

He reiterated, "Becoming fluent in French is important here in Quebec." He looked straight at us. "If you two are going to be good at it, then you'll need to be immersed in the language. You are not getting that here at home or in your private school."

Our father didn't say what I suspected he believed: that my brother and I had been stymied in our French studies in *La Belle Province de Quebec*. Mom spoke Hungarian with us, our school friends were English-speaking, and we regularly tuned to the English channels on the television.

My brother and I glanced at each other after our dad's proclamation, but we didn't say a word. We understood our father's message. He continued. "I've heard that the best French is spoken in Tours, France, and taught at the Institute of Tours. This time I'm placing the two of you into French summer school there for eight weeks." His face was stern. "I'm putting you in separate boarding houses near the school. If the two of you are in one place together, then you'll speak only English with each other. I want both of you to graduate high school speaking good French."

Dad wasn't wrong. When we had been in French-language school in Switzerland, Steve and I probably taught more English to the French teachers and camp counselors than they were able to improve our French. The following summer, after a month of foreign language studies at our private school, our French language skills had improved only marginally.

I was a top student in math and sciences, but languages didn't come to me as readily. Unlike my father, who could converse in English, Hungarian, Russian, and four different Slavic dialects, I eked through my English and French courses at school. Dad had decided that if he was going to get French into us, he had to immerse Steve and me for the whole summer and have us reside separately. For me, at fifteen, two months of dull French classes a continent away from home was going to be grueling.

Mom normally spoke up when the family conversation had to do with her boys. I suspected she was going to have a hard time with us away. This time she said nothing during Dad's spiel. I could see a worried look on her face, but she kept her lips pressed together. Dad had probably talked to her earlier, not wanting her to contradict his plans for his sons.

That June, Dad accompanied my brother and me from Montreal to Paris. After our overnight flight, the three of us emerged bleary-eyed into the early morning sun. Steve and I lugged heavy, mother-packed valises with enough clothes for perhaps three summers in France.

My father stopped when we got to the taxi stand. He looked at the faces of the cab drivers and quickly scanned the cars parked along the curb. He picked out a short, thin guy standing by his compact Fiat. The man was enjoying a cigarette. "Do you speak English?" Dad asked the guy.

The cabbie looked at my father, quickly took the cigarette out of his mouth, and responded in a heavy French accent. "Yes, *monsieur.*"

"Can you take us to Tours?"

The cabbie looked perplexed. "Tours? *Dat* city is about 275 kilometers and three *ours* from *ere. Dat* will be expensive, *monsieur.*"

Dad continued. "Are you able to take us there today and then bring me back to the airport tomorrow?" He pointed to my brother and me. "I'm taking my kids to the Institute of Tours for summer school, and I'm flying back to Canada tomorrow afternoon. You can help us find a place to stay there and spend the night with us before driving me back here tomorrow."

The driver raised his eyebrows.

"Don't worry," my father said with a small grin and open hand. "I'll pay for your room."

Steve and I were quiet as Dad negotiated matter-of-factly with the cabbie. We knew that he didn't like to be interrupted when he was doing important business. "And forget about your meter," our father added. "Give me a fixed price to take us there now and to bring me back here tomorrow."

The cabbie put his hand to his chin and thought for a minute. He looked straight at my father. Both of their faces were blank. "That will cost you 550 French francs, *monsieur*, plus the *otel*, of course."

Dad paused for a long moment, and I could see his eyes shifting back and forth. I was also making the foreign exchange conversion in my head. I figured the cabbie was asking for a little more than 150 Canadian dollars. Dad looked intently at the guy. "Okay, let's do it."

The driver responded, "You give me *alf* now, and *alf* when I bring you back *ere* tomorrow. Also, I will need to stop by my *ouse* to pick up some *tings* and to tell my wife *dat* I will be away for *de* night." His voice stayed composed. "It will not take long; my *ouse* is not far away."

"Okay, *pas de problem*," Dad said in his limited French. He dug out his wallet, removed three crisp 100-franc bills, and presented them to the fellow.

The cabbie took a pace forward, broke a smile, took the cash, and gathered 25 francs to return to our father. Dad gently batted his open palm to indicate that the cabbie could keep the extra francs. The man said, "*Plaisir de faire votre connaissance. I puts* your luggage into the trunk. Your boys can *puts* their rucksacks in the car." He nodded at Steve and me.

One by one, the short, svelte Frenchman grabbed our suitcases and configured them into the taxi's tiny trunk. My brother and I packed ourselves and our bulky backpacks into the sardine-can cab. Dad plopped into the small front passenger seat and looked back at us. "Boys, rest as much as you can back there. We'll be in Tours in a few hours."

Within a few moments, the driver returned to his seat. He looked at our father. "*Mon nom...*, my name is *Jean*."

My father put out his hand, "Hello Jean. I'm Johnny." They shook hands. Dad pointed to my brother and me. "These are my boys, Stevie and Harvy."

Jean looked at us over his shoulder. *Bonjour à vous, mes amis."* He offered a big grin of yellowed teeth. I figured he smoked stinky cigarettes and drank black coffee as much as our father did.

Steve and I nodded and showed small smiles. I didn't cozy up to new people the way my father did. Dad and Mom told us to be wary of strangers. I wasn't old enough to distinguish when strangers were okay to encounter.

Within fifteen minutes, we stopped by Jean's home in a suburban area of low-rise, attached stucco buildings. Unlike at our Dorval home, there was no grass or park on this street. The three of us waited in Jean's car while he walked quickly into one of the buildings.

In twenty minutes, the Frenchman returned with a satchel that he stuffed into the trunk. He brought into the car a brown paper bag, which he placed on the floor near his feet. "My wife; she makes me a lunch for today and a supper for tonight."

Dad batted his hand at the driver. "Save your wife's supper for tomorrow." He pointed to the rest of us. "Tonight, you will eat with us."

For the next three hours, Dad and the cabbie tried out each other's cigarettes and chatted in English with a few French words mixed in. They spoke about the weather, the cabbie's history and family, as well as French and Quebec politics.

Dad said, "I don't know about you, Jean, but I'm glad Charles de Gaulle is gone. He made a lot of trouble in Quebec with his *'vivre Quebec libre'* speech two years ago. Now every Frenchman there wants separation from Canada."

While holding the steering wheel with his left hand, Jean put together the thumb and first two fingers of his other hand, and then raised and shook that hand in the air. "I agree *wit* you, *Monsieur* Johnny. De Gaulle was a—I don't know *dis* word—he had *des grandes rêves."* He threw his hand into the air and opened his fingers as if he were jettisoning them.

Dad offered, "Yes, he was a big dreamer."

"*C'est ça;* that is it!" Jean proclaimed. He took a breath. "Our President Pompidou is much more practical. He was our prime minister many years before. He will do more for France."

My brother and I had listened awhile before we caught needed sleep. The car's motion and the warm weather lulled us into a summer slumber. We employed our backpacks as makeshift pillows.

Approaching Tours, Jean crossed the Loire River Bridge that led into the center of the city. Dad said, "Drop us off at the Bank Nationale branch that is downtown." Dad showed Jean a slip of paper with the bank's address. Jean nodded. "*Certainement,*" he said.

Dad continued. "Here are another 100 francs and my business card." My father put the money into the cabbie's hand. "Find us a nice *penzion* right here in town, something clean and not expensive. Get a couple of rooms; one of them big enough for the kids and me. Give the place this as a deposit, and they can use my name as it is on my card. I'll take care of the rest when we go there later." He placed his hand gently on Jean's arm. "Then go and have your lunch, and meet us at the front of the bank in ninety minutes."

Jean nodded. "*Oui, une heure et demi.*"

When we arrived at the lobby of the Bank Nationale, my father asked for the person named on the slip of paper he had shown Jean. Within the hour, our father had opened bank accounts for both my brother and me, and he deposited 8,500 French francs into each account.

It took Dad fifteen minutes to sign his name to nearly fifty $100 Canadian travellers cheques, stopping for a drag of his cigarette—and maybe to rest his hand—every one to two dozen cheques. The money was to pay for our French courses at the Institute, as well as boarding house rooms, meals, and incidental expenses over the next two months. Our living expenses, meals included, would be about 90 francs per day.

Our father had scheduled that my brother and I arrive at our respective boarding houses the next day, and we start our classes the following morning. Dad would be back in Canada by then.

Never before had Dad put this much money into our names. It felt special that he would trust us with such amounts this far from home. Instead of paying our boarding costs ahead of time, maybe our father was testing how Steve and I would manage that money. Or perhaps he was hedging his bet, for Steve or I might detest the school and want to come home early.

After we had completed our banking, the three of us sat on a park bench across the street, waiting for Jean to arrive. Dad raised his hand. "Boys, be careful when you carry cash to pay for your school studies and your landladies. Take from the bank only what you need for a couple of weeks. Pay for your courses and your landlady right away, this way you won't have too much cash to handle."

He placed his hand on his lap. "Always keep your wallets in your front pocket; it's safer that way. And never walk alone at night or down an empty street during the day."

"Okay, Dad," we both said. "We'll be careful."

Jean soon found us. He had located a small hotel a couple of blocks away, checked us in, and brought our luggage to the rooms. Before walking there, we grabbed a quick dinner at a restaurant next to the bank.

Dad asked Jean to join us for the meal. The Frenchman only had a beer and a cigarette because he had finished his wife's bag lunch before he came to fetch us.

After Dad, Steve, and I had devoured *croque monsieur* sandwiches, we walked to our hotel. Jean had found a quaint and inexpensive guesthouse on the wide main boulevard of Tours. Along that boulevard were open-air cafes with umbrella-covered tables. Jean said, "This place is a very good location and price."

Dad looked at him. "Good work, Jean."

Next door, a few steps below ground level, was a French restaurant. Dad pointed. "We'll have supper here tonight and breakfast at one of these cafes early in the morning before we drop you boys off. Then, I'll head back to Paris."

My father yawned. "Boys, I think we all are still tired. Let's take a nap and get up around six o'clock for supper. We can eat by six-thirty, which is like dinnertime back in Canada."

Because I still felt the sting in my eyes from the time change, I agreed right away with Dad; so did Steve.

That evening, Dad treated Jean to supper, drinks, and more Canadian cigarettes. Dad put the wine menu into our cabbie's hands. "Pick out a good wine, Jean." He grinned. "I'm here only one night and want to know what France is really like." My father didn't ask for his customary scotch or vodka on ice. He probably figured, *While in France, do as the French do.*

A smiling Jean picked out a Pinot Noir. He and our father polished off the bottle before the restaurant served our main course. Dad encouraged our driver to pick out another. He chose a Pouilly-Fumé from the Loire Valley area where we were.

Being minors, Steve and I stuck with *orange et citron pressé*—like Orangina and a lemony version of the same. Dad asked the waiter for a couple of extra wine glasses. He then poured small tastes of that blood-grape drink for my brother and me. Our father cautioned, "Sip it slowly, boys; you don't want to get loaded."

Steve and I drank our samples gradually. I found the strong oaky tastes and pungent fruity fragrances not to my liking. Little did I know that I would become acclimated to French wine by the end of the summer. My boarding house matron would serve her patrons a bottle or two of five-franc ($1USD) bottles of red table wine at every supper.

During our meal with Dad and Jean, Steve and I stayed quiet, or we wrote in puzzle books we had brought with us. Jean attempted to speak to us in French, as he did during our taxi ride to Tours. We offered a few French words in response but soon shrugged at our inability or unwillingness to go further.

Our tipsy Dad said, "Jean, you now see why I need to send them here to France to learn your language. They speak too much English in Quebec, and they're too shy to speak French. But it is important that they learn."

Jean nodded. "*Je suis comme vous, Monsieur Johnny.* I want my children to speak your *anglais* like you want yours to speak our *français*. We live in an international world!"

Our father raised his glass to his new friend. "*Bien sûr, Monsieur Jean.*"

At the end of our supper, my father and brother had to help our wobbling, rubber-legged taxi driver to his room. Dad and Steve fell into their beds too.

Before retiring, I went for a walk to help digest my coq au vin entrée and Napoleon custard dessert. I walked along the busy main boulevard filled with people and cars. It was well past nine o'clock, but the sky was still light.

I pondered what the rest of the summer would be like in this small French city. Would I learn enough French to graduate high school? Would I act responsibly with the money Dad had placed in my name? I didn't want to come home with little to show for my father's investment.

During the next two months in Tours, I was serious about my French studies. I went to class every day and did my reading and homework assignments.

I was the youngest person in my class section. Dad had lied on both my brother's and my application to get us into the program. To meet the minimum age requirement for admission, he wrote that I was a year older than I really was, and he did the same for Steve. I felt shy talking with others in my class, but I did try to please the teacher by raising my hand when I thought I knew the answer.

I was in a different class and proficiency level than my brother. Because he and I walked to the Institute from different directions, we didn't see much of each other during the weekdays.

When I wasn't studying, I hung out at parks with the young American, British, and Belgian students who were staying at my boarding house. I was the only Canadian. We spoke English outdoors, but our matron insisted we spoke French when we were in her boarding house, especially when attending meals.

One evening during supper, a funny thing happened with the French table wine that our matron served. Though I, like most of the other boarders, diluted the blood grape drink 50/50 with still water, the wine loosened me up. During the middle of one supper, the matron asked a newly arrived, young American woman student, "*Veux-tu plus des patates?* [Would you like more potatoes?]"

The student responded politely, "*Merci,*" then sat there quietly, no telling expression on her face.

The matron paused for a few seconds. A perplexed look came over her face. She waited for the young woman to say more or pass her plate forward if she wanted more potatoes.

The woman student said nothing and sat still in her chair, perhaps expecting the matron to serve her, but her intentions weren't clear. Everyone else froze in their seats for those few long seconds, waiting to see what the matron would do. Finally, the matron said, *"Dis-tu 'merci oui' ou 'non merci'?* [Are you saying 'Thank you yes' or 'No thank you'?]"

The student jumped in her seat as if she had been startled from a dream. *"Oui, oui, oui! J'aimerais avoir les pommes de terre un peu plus.* [Yes, yes, yes! I would like to have more potatoes.]" She then picked up her plate and held it close to the serving dish.

The matron dished out a serving and said, *"C'est bon de savoir si elle est 'merci oui' ou 'non merci.'* [It's good to know if it is 'Thank you yes' or 'No thank you.']"

I had been through similar situations over the weeks with different American teens in our boarding house. While I still held wine in my mouth, I started to giggle at the momentary stalemate that had happened in the conversation between the French matron and the young woman. I coughed the oaky drink into my nasal passages. I then couldn't stop giggling, coughing, and snorting at the same time.

The whole American side of the table burst out laughing at my reaction. The matron's face looked perplexed, and so did the British and Belgium students. It was as if the latter had no idea what was funny about what the American woman had said, or what had caused my little fit.

After supper was over, one of the British students asked me about what happened. I tried to explain that the American student thought she had been clear in her wish for more potatoes, but then sat back as if she were expecting the matron to serve her. She didn't realize the matron was puzzled about her initial response of only *"Merci,"* which was the typical affirmative response in America but not in Europe or Canada.

The Brit shook her head, not understanding what had been funny. Maybe, as a Canadian, I had been the only one to see the dilemma that had stymied the matron and bewildered the American student. Both the Brit and I shrugged and left it there.

All that summer, I was prudent with Dad's money. Sanctioned by him, my brother and I took Saturday bus tours to the French chateaus, some having dramatic evening sound-and-light performances. Coloured spotlights flashed as giant speakers boomed out Napoleonic battles. My brother and I munched on brie and baguettes, washed down with bottles of Orangina.

On Sundays, we went to see French comedy movies starring the Spaniard, Louis de Funès, one of France's favourite actors. His funny facial expressions and snappy impatience made it easier to follow what was going on in the film. As my parents had done when they learned English in Canada, Steve and I stayed in the theatre after a performance to see the movie again. No one came to ask for another entrance fee.

During those passing weeks, I didn't spend more money than seemed reasonable. The one thing I did splurge on was a long-weekend trip with my brother between our two summer-school semesters.

Steve suggested we head to the French coast for a few days. Our rucksacks packed, we took the train to La Baule, a beach resort town near the mouth of the Loire River. There we found a small hotel and restaurant that was within walking distance from both the train station and the beach. The place wasn't more expensive than the combined costs of our boarding house back in Tours, for which my brother and I received credits for not being there for those few days.

In La Baule, I noticed that my brother and I had different spending habits. Steve wanted to latch onto the first decent hotel or restaurant we spotted. I held out not only for cleanliness but also for a reasonable price before committing to a place to stay or eat. He wanted to try new and expensive things on restaurant menus, while I usually went for the less elaborate courses. I only splurged on *les Napoleons* or *les croissants au chocolat et le chocolat chaud*.

During the day, Steve preferred hanging out on the stony ocean beach. I found shade by the sidewalk and tried to read a French *Tintin* comic book or a magazine with lots of pictures. Though Steve and I probably got on each other's nerves during our time together, we managed to get through our beach holiday without an altercation.

Two weeks before the end of our second semester, my brother looked for me after class. His tone was matter-of-fact. "Harvy, I'm going away for a long weekend to Paris with a few of my house friends." He volunteered, "One of them has a car; four of us are going." He didn't ask me if I wanted to come along. Even if there were room, I wouldn't go on an excursion that hadn't been sanctioned by our father.

I became peeved. "I don't think Dad would be happy about your going to Paris when we are supposed to be here in Tours."

Steve didn't look fazed. He ignored my comment and offered a quick wave of his hand. "See you next week," my brother said. He then turned and walked away.

It seemed as if Steve had spent most of his remaining cash in Paris. On our last day in France, he and I headed back to Paris on an early train to catch our afternoon flight to Montreal. Steve hardly had a *sou français* left. I paid for our food on the train, plus the cab ride from Paris to the airport. My brother had just assumed that I would have enough money for those expenses.

When we arrived in Montreal, Dad was waiting at the airport. After a round of happy hugs and hellos, I placed a wad of four or five crisp 100-French-franc bills into my father's hand. I smiled. "Here, Dad; thanks, but I didn't need this." I didn't say that I could have returned more if Steve hadn't spent all of his.

I saw a surprised look and then a small smile on my father's face for what I had returned to him. I knew I had impressed him with my money management. I didn't look at Steve, but I could imagine him rolling his eyes.

Steve had nothing tangible to offer our father, other than having sent him a postcard from Paris. In the car, Dad said, "Stevie, I never said you could skip out of your French studies and piss away your money on a separate trip."

Steve looked shyly at our father and said nothing. I said nothing too, and I knew I had won my father's appreciation. I imagined my brother was irritated by my giving the money back to Dad, but my father's quiet recognition was worth it.

Years later, I suspected that Steve's rambunctiousness in going to Paris paralleled my father's childhood deeds. Dad had told us he had played hooky from school to go swimming with his friends in the Hornád River that ran through Košice. Steve's Paris trip could have been a mimic of our father's behavior, yet I doubt that my father would have advertised such a misdeed to his parents. Part of me envied my brother's nerve. But if Steve was going to be dumb enough to send Dad a glossy postcard from his hooky-playing, then he received the scolding he deserved.

I was proud that I had learned enough French in Tours to get a solid B grade in my French oral and written exams the following spring in school, and a noteworthy 80% grade on my Quebec high school French matriculation exams. (Interestingly, I did worse in my English exams.)

It felt good to have my father know that his expensive investment in my language ability had paid off and that he had gotten a few francs back for his trouble. I hoped he saw me as a frugal spender, a worthy follower in his money footsteps, even years before he took me to his offshore bank in the summer of '72.

* * * *

14

Legacy Burdens

October 1999, continued.

Twenty-seven years had passed since I witnessed Dad hand a $72,000 bank draft to a *Banque de Genève* banker for deposit into a secret Swiss account.

As a kid, teen, and young adult, I had been deeply attracted to my father's fire but deathly afraid of his ire. I had aspired to be a good student, a frugal spender and money saver like him, and a devoted and loyal son. I longed for Dad's anointment as his preferred offspring. But the 45-year old in me was now disgusted by my dad's devious money scheming, his domineering anger, and his deceitful tax-avoiding ways.

All my adult life, Dad had coaxed me into his offshore underworld. I had kept his secrets, attracted by his fatherly charm and accumulated money. Had I been afraid of his abandonment? Here at Elliot Trudell, and for the last number of years, I was aching to release myself from his grasp and to redeem my conscience.

My stomach was still in knots after spending the last half hour with André in this dark-wood-paneled conference room. He had helped me to deal with the shady annuity agreement that Dad had signed eight years earlier at a Lux bank with the Independent University of Luxembourg.

When André had said that the annuity wouldn't be legally binding unless my father had written it into his will, I became half-relieved. I still didn't know how I would tell my brother about Dad's crooked commitment to that university. I hoped my confrere wouldn't insist that the agreement was morally binding. What might I say to him if he asserted that claim?

I had a second offshore bank document to show André. I pulled out the thick wad of folded papers from my suit pocket. André stayed quiet as I fumbled with the papers and handed the jumble to him.

The pages were severely creased. They had been in-and-out of my father's hands in the last month and in-and-out of my jacket pocket for the last couple of days. As with the Luxembourg university agreement, I had borrowed these papers from my father's hiding place above a loose ceiling panel in his private office.

André took the documents and carefully unraveled the many folded sheets. They were statements of several bank accounts. Listed on the pages were security names, purchase dates, share amounts, original costs, and current values. Totals were well into the seven figures.

After perusing the papers for a moment, my friend looked at me. "Okay, Harvy, now tell me about this." His tone was low and serious.

My face grew warm, and my insides started to shake once more. The secrets on those pages pitted my commitment to my father against my loyalty to my country and kin. I hoped my nervousness wasn't showing.

I took a deep breath and said, "Those pages represent a set of hidden offshore accounts my father has owned for some decades."

I didn't mention the name of the bank, and there was no indication of its name on the statements. Even Dad's name wasn't on the papers; the only evidence of ownership was a nine-digit number placed in the corner of each page.

I could feel my heart pound as I uttered the words "hidden offshore accounts." I was afraid to tell André how long that money had been hidden, imagining that he would think lesser of me for what I had known for so long.

Now that I had placed the documents into his hands, a previously locked door swung wide open. That door had guarded my father's furtive finances and tax-avoidance sins for half my lifetime. Those transgressions were now, for the first time, in the view of an outsider.

I didn't know what kind of state condemnation and public penance lay beyond that threshold. Will my name be exposed in the newspapers, like when Revenue Canada, twenty-three years earlier, had caught and prosecuted my father and his company for corporate tax fraud? Will I have to face criminal charges for what I knew, and pay the price in jailhouse stripes behind a penitentiary door? My mind was running away from me.

Even worse, my father would raise the roof with his boisterous anger if he ever found out where I was today and what I was revealing. I remembered his heavy-handed outbursts decades ago with a Pole who had tried to skirt his duty to my dad. He was the same if one ever tried to get one over on him. He became chummy only when he got his way.

If Dad knew I was here with André, revealing his decades of money secrets, risking the loss of his accumulated money legacy, would he ever shake my hand or slap my back again? Indeed, he'd be deeply disappointed and bare-faced angry with me. Could my father accept that the money he had promised me for decades would soon be mine to do with as I wanted? Could my dad understand that what I was doing now was because I didn't want to own the money mess he was leaving behind for me?

I wanted to be here at Elliot Trudell today. I desired André's help to guide me through my father's money maze. Whatever lay beyond this open doorway into Dad's hidden world had to be a better place than where I had been all these self-conflicted years.

I now knew that I didn't have the stomach for my father's decades of illicit offshore deceits. I no longer wanted the pangs in my gut for his illegal tax-skirting games—even if it meant that I would no longer be his favoured son.

I cleared my throat and looked at my lawyer friend. "These pages represent a set of connected offshore accounts, each with its *raison d'etre.*"

I pointed to one side of a page. "The items you see here are bond, mutual fund, and other fixed investments." I gestured to the far side of the page. "The security values you see are in different currencies. This particular section is in U.S. dollars; other sections are in Canadian dollars and euros."

André's eyebrows lifted. "Euros?" he asked.

"Yes," I responded. "Though euros are not yet available to the public, one can hold them in European investment accounts like these."

André put the papers down on his lap, and he eyed me carefully. My friend spoke slowly. "Harvy, I think I understand what you are talking about and showing me here."

He paused for a moment, looked down at the floor and then back at me. "Unfortunately, this is not a specific area of my expertise," he said. "I cannot effectively advise you on this one."

My heart skipped; my breath stopped; my legs shook. Had I come this far for naught? Had my U.S. attorney, Jay Henry, pointed me to the wrong Canadian counterpart?

André stayed calm, but he must have noticed my anxiousness. He added quietly, "Harvy, we do have an attorney in our firm who has growing experience in this area." He pointed to the documents and looked at me with strong and caring eyes. "Would you be willing to talk to my colleague about this? I can arrange that if you wish."

My spirits lifted, and I slowly nodded. "Yes, okay." I saw no other avenue for my cause, or was it my curse?

André reached for the conference room phone. He called to arrange a meeting for me with a person named Bernard. Bernard and I would meet in a month, on my next trip to Montreal.

André handed me the wad of bank statements. I folded them and tucked them back into my jacket pocket. By tonight, they would be hidden again in the ceiling of my father's private office.

We stood and turned toward the conference room door. André assured me. "Harvy, your father's situation is not unique among wealthy Canadians. There are well-established procedures with the government about how to deal with such matters effectively. Bernard would be able to fill you in on that better than I can."

I looked attentively at my friend. "Thanks for your thoughts and referral on this, André. I very much appreciate it."

I felt relief to know my father wasn't the only tax-skirting crook in the country. I had no idea of what monetary penalties, criminal record, or personal shame lay ahead. I was ready to hear from André's colleague as to what punishment would be in store for me. I'd have to prepare myself for the penance I'd have to perform for the sins of my father, and for my years of having been knowledgeable—arguably even complicit—to Dad's clandestine dealings.

André looked at me again with a soft expression in his eyes. "I'll keep what I know just between us. You can share as much or as little as you like with Bernard. And I'm not going to charge for the time we spent together, but Bernard will expect compensation."

"What's Bernard's rate?" I asked.

"Probably similar to mine: $325 Canadian per hour. But you will be better off with Bernard, for this is his area of expertise. And I may not be around here much longer."

I gulped at the big-city lawyer rate, which was 50% higher than my corporate consulting rate. At least it was in cheaper Canadian dollars. I knew that I had been lucky to have had a free legal ride until now with both André and Jay.

André and I had spent less than an hour together in this elegant Elliot Trudell conference room. But it felt as if half a lifetime had gone by regarding my family's history. Our conversation, and the steps I was taking, marked a defining moment in my father's Canadian chronicle and legacy, and mine too.

I was finding relief from a twenty-seven-year burden hidden behind an office ceiling panel. That weight was firmly on the ground in front of me, its malice ready to be terminated. It had haunted me since that summer of 1972 when I had gone with my father to open his first hidden offshore account.

Though I had been excited by the prospect of being heir to my father's concealed stash, the possibility of stiffing my brother and Revenue Canada now troubled me profoundly. I needed the know-how to get this burden off my head and shoulders. I needed to extinguish its hold on me.

André and I said goodbye at the living-room-sized reception area where I had walked into his firm. He shook my hand firmly and caringly. I strode out of the Elliot Trudell offices with greater confidence that I was on a clearer course to clean up what my father had crafted and what he had cajoled me into.

As I walked through the Elliot Trudell's all-glass entrance doors, I wondered if I would have another conversation or meeting or phone call with either André or Jay. When I returned to Boston, I sent each of them an e-mail saying, "Thank you so much for your help."

But would I reach out to them again, or might they contact me? Their light-beacon jobs were now complete. André was placing me in the hands of a yet unseen guiding light, Bernard.

I walked out of the Canadian Imperial Bank of Commerce building into the nippy, windblown, prewinter day. I pulled my coat tightly around me. I wondered what future lay in front of me and my father's financial skeletons.

I thought of my long-deceased mother and the trauma and suffering she had been through, not only with my father but also in her life before she married him. I prayed that she knew that I was trying to do the right thing, not just for me but for both of her sons.

* * * *

Part IV:

Oy Vey Mama!

15

1 First Avenue

After my brother was born in 1953, Dad moved our family from an apartment on Montreal's upper Crescent St. to a townhouse in Montreal's predominantly French East End. Dad had said to Mom that he wanted his kids to go to a French school to better fit into our Québécois environs.

A happy time in our family; c. 1957.

In 1959, nearly five years after I was born, Dad changed his mind. That summer, he moved our family again, this time to the West Island of Montreal. In that part of Montreal, speaking English was more predominant, and my brother and I could attend English Catholic School.

Dad told us, "By moving to Dorval, Harvy can get into school one year behind you, Stevie. He doesn't have to wait another year, considering his birthday is in October. Because you two are only thirteen-and-a-half months apart, you should stay close to each other in your school grade."

I didn't know if that was good advice, yet I trusted my father's opinion.

Eight years later, when Steve and I were about to enter boarding school for our high school years, I found out Dad's other motive for having moved us to Dorval. He said, "Back in '59, a French Quebec civil court judge called me a 'bloody immigrant' when he ruled against Montreal Phono in a labour relations case. Because of that, I changed my attitude toward the French. I no longer wanted to send you guys to their schools."

Though I was one of the youngest in my elementary school class, I was a top student, especially in math, geography, and science. I struggled with English and French, and boring Canadian history too. Maybe my language challenges were because Mom always talked to Steve and me in her native Hungarian. At some point during our early school years, our teachers told her, "Please, Mrs. Simkovits; talk to your kids in English. They need to learn that language first."

Though Mom tried to stick to English, she reverted to Hungarian whenever her new language failed her, or when she wanted only our understanding of what she was saying, or if she got mad at us for spilling our milk or staying up past our bedtime.

When Dad sent my brother and me to summer camp—from the time I was nine years old—Mom tried to write us letters in English. Because she never got the gist of English grammar, very different from Hungarian grammar, I laughed or scratched my head at what she had tried to say.

Because of my mixed-language upbringing, I barely passed my English and French language exams each year in both public elementary and private high schools. I was both astonished and relieved that those schools never held me back for my lack of language skills. Perhaps it was because the rest of my grades were good, maybe even great.

Because of my mixed language learning, and being young for my school grade, I felt awkward among the other kids in my public school, especially the girls.

My first crush was on Eva Deshinsky in sixth grade. Her last name was as long and as weird as mine. Other kids had surnames like Wilson and McFarlane.

Eva was the only girl in my class who I could talk to without blushing. I kept a safe distance from the blossoming young females who suddenly sprouted bumps on their chests over summer vacation. Eva was a late bloomer, cute but flat, so my eyes didn't wander below her neckline.

That year, Eva sat right behind me in class. She wore a cheerful smile whenever she looked at me. I turned around to show her things I had doodled, or I quipped about what we were working on in class.

During one math lesson on right-angle triangles, I passed her a note: "The square hippopotamus is equal to the sum of the other two square guys." We chuckled until our teacher, Mrs. Burns, looked sternly at us. Her lips tightened, and her face smirked when she said, "Stop giggling you two, and pay attention."

Eva, like I, was a good student in most everything but languages. We raised our hands often to answer the teacher's questions. Sitting in front of her, I tried to block Eva's thin outstretched arm with mine so that Mrs. Burn's would pick me. We almost always got the answers right. Mrs. Burns let us chat quietly under her radar—at least that was what I thought.

Eva lived a half-dozen blocks west of our school. I lived a half-dozen blocks east, so we couldn't walk together to or from class. During school recess, she went to skip rope and chat with the other girls while I kicked a soccer ball with my chums. She and I never sat together during lunch because "What would our classmates say?"

I was too shy or thought it not right to ask her to my house to play after school. She never asked me to come to hers. The time that was ours was the minutes we had at our desks: before class started, at the beginning or end of lunch, right after the last school buzzer of the day, and during our class-time glances and giggles. For those moments, Eva was my girl and my friend. I was charmed by her wide toothy grin, deep blue eyes, and a cute button nose. Her appealing short hair fell straight to the middle of her ears, making her look boyish. She was a sweet Peppermint Patty to my awkward Charlie Brown.

Eva and I talked about anything and everything, like our favourite superhero comic characters and how both of us rose early on Saturdays to watch *The Adventures of Superman*. We shared stories about where our immigrant families had come from, and when and how they come to Canada. We shared daydreams of how we would visit our European homelands and the high and snowy Swiss Alps.

I told Eva how my mom cooked awesome Hungarian stuffed cabbage. She told me how her mother baked yummy Dutch apple cobbler. We both said that we hardly saw our dads because of their busy jobs. We shared how much our mean older brothers bugged us, and how we sometimes hid their stuff to get back at them.

I'm not sure what Eva liked about me. Was it my tall height, my chubby cheeks, or my big grin like hers? It didn't matter; we cackled and chattered on in the moments we had.

When I came back to class after the Christmas holidays that year, Eva wasn't sitting in her chair behind me. A kid I hardly knew was in her place. I gazed quickly around the classroom to see if I could find her. I wondered if she had left school and moved away, or if she had suddenly died and gone to kiddy heaven. My voice shook as I turned to the new kid in my girlfriend's spot. "What happened to Eva?"

He pointed kilometers away to the other side of the classroom. Eva was settled at another desk, surrounded by a group of girls. She chatted away, wore her Eva smile, and didn't look my way.

Eva and I never got back what I thought we had had. Eighteen months later, Dad transferred my brother and me to a private all-boys school. Though I never saw Eva again, I never forgot that first crush.

* * *

The address of our West Island home was 1 First Avenue. Though it had only three bedrooms and one-and-a-half baths, our split-level house was the largest on our short avenue, located between two parallel streets.

Weedy fields surrounded this post-WWII development. There, young boys chased each other on their bikes. Some might hide in the tall grass and pounce on an unsuspecting kid—not that I was doing the pouncing.

Because Mom didn't drive, she brought her groceries home by taxi from an outdoor strip-mall less than a kilometer away. In the mall was a deli that made great Montreal smoked meat sandwiches. Mom took us there for lunch on the days we were off from school—her way to get us to go shopping with her.

Nearby were a bowling alley, movie theatre, outdoor swimming pools for summer bathing, public tennis courts, and a Chinese restaurant—things we could do if Dad weren't around to drive us places, which was most of the time. He was busy at his factory, even on Saturday. Six days a week, Mom single-handedly raised my brother and me.

The houses in our development were packed close together, no more than six meters apart. They faced each other neatly across our short avenue. There were small yards in the front with shrubs and trees. In the back were bigger yards for outdoor play and parties.

Because of the closeness between homes, it made snowball throwing easy from kid-built snow forts that lined the road in winter. A passing car could get stealthily pelted with snowballs—from both sides of the street—as it turned onto our avenue after our 4:30 winter sundown. Kids then scurried inside for hot cocoa and homework.

This layout of houses repeated for five more blocks, up to Sixth Avenue. Every house on the southeast corner of those six blocks looked the same as our home. This repeating pattern was not acceptable to Mom. She wanted our house to be different and more beautiful, for when her relatives and Dad's city friends visited.

Dad spent what seemed like wheelbarrows of money, probably doubling the $5000 original cost of our home, and months of construction work, to refurbish the house in the way Mom wanted. I told myself he was doing it to make us feel special in our new neighbourhood.

To make our home stand out, and have better insulation from winter cold and summer heat, Dad added a layer of fancy orange bricks to the existing wood and red-brick exterior walls. He had the outdoor staircases completely rebuilt in that orange brick and Canadian granite.

I wondered if the extra layer of brick and stone was necessary for insulating sound rather than heat. Though Mom and Dad's nighttime yelling seemed to make the walls shake, the brick mortar never crumbled.

During those months of reconstruction, early every workday morning, Dad and the contractor—usually an Eastern European immigrant like him—walked around our home to examine the work progress.

Dressed in a suit and tie to be ready for his seven o'clock office start, Dad inspected the work and talked about the next steps. He might bring along an extra cup of Mom's coffee for the foreman, or he might offer him a cigarette if there were construction favours to ask.

Through my open bedroom window, I could hear Dad make crude jokes to lighten the mood. He pointed to something that didn't seem right and said in Hungarian, "We need to straighten that board (or nail or whatever). It looks crooked like my dick."

On another occasion, while Dad spoke to a Russian foreman, I overheard him chuckle and say in English. "No matter what you do, you can never satisfy your wife."

"*Da, da.*" snickered the Russian.

"*Vimen*! Who can understand them?!" rolled off Dad's tongue. "You know what I mean," he said with another chuckle. "Yesterday, they wanted it this way. Today they want it that way."

The Russian chuckled. "My wife like *dat* too!" he offered.

When I became an adult, I knew that my father and his contractor were disparaging women. As a boy, I smiled mindlessly at their off-colour humour.

While my father talked with the contractor, I recalled his teachings about watching the people who work for you, or else they would take shortcuts. Dad could hit the roof between sips of coffee if he felt he was getting the short end of a two-by-four.

On this day, under my open bedroom window, Dad didn't shout at the crew boss about something not being right; he only asked the Russian to do something extra. I was relieved there were no backyard outbursts.

* * *

Mom was afraid of dogs and cats. Whenever one came toward her, no matter how small it was, she placed her purse between herself and the animal and backed away slowly. She told us she had been frightened by a stray dog when she was a child.

On the other hand, Dad loved dogs. At our previous Montreal east-end townhouse, he had once brought home a jet black puppy that he said he had found abandoned on the street. (Maybe he mentioned that so Mom would feel sympathy for the dog.) The creature was so tiny that it had fit into the breast pocket of Dad's shirt.

When Steve and I saw the pup, my brother and I jumped up and down in delight. We fell over ourselves as we tried to pet the cute thing as it jumped and yelped among our toddler's legs.

Mom said, "If we keep it, it has to stay outside when it no longer is a baby."

Our backyard was fenced and had a small shed in the back. Dad said, "Blackie can stay in the shed. You two boys will have to feed the dog every day."

My joyful brother and I agreed.

Under Mom's supervision, Steve and I fed and played with Blackie every day, but our mother kept her distance. When home, Dad showed us how to play fetch with it, how to pet him and rub its tummy gently, how to say "Good dog" or give it a dog treat every time it did what we asked. The three of us loved that puppy.

Blackie loved Dad more than his dog food. One morning, when Dad left for work, Blackie was running around loose in the backyard. The dog dug into the earth at the corner of our picket fence. In minutes, it was under that fence and ran after Dad's car.

Steve and I cried after our escaped dog. Mom called Dad at work, and he came home right away. He drove up and down the adjacent streets calling out Blackie's name, but the dog didn't come. Steve and I cried once more. We never saw our pooch again.

After a week or two of Dad, Steve, and I feeling gloomy, Dad fixed the hole in the fence and came home with another puppy. We called our second dog Brownie, like the colour of his coat.

Within a month, again one early morning, Brownie too dug under the same place in that fence and ran after Dad's car. We never saw our pooch again. For days, I whimpered in my bed for the loss of another companion.

After those losses, Mom put her foot down. She said she didn't want to have another animal living with us. We never did.

As a special Christmas present for my brother and me, after we had moved into our First Avenue home, Dad got two, large, black-and-white, stuffed RCA mascot dogs. The mascots were named Nipper. "His Master's Voice" was written on the collar. Dad said, "I got those dogs from the folks at RCA, my customer."

My brother and I cherished our two stuffed pups as much as we enjoyed the real ones. Unlike Blackie or Brownie, Mom wasn't afraid of our Nippers. We could take them to bed with us, which we did for years.

My father enjoyed the scent of Canadian spruce trees. Soon after the contractors had completed refurbishing our new home, Dad planted a 2-meter high blue spruce in the middle of our front lawn. Its fragrance was sweet.

For many years, Dad made that spruce into an outdoor Christmas tree, placing multi-coloured bulbs around it like a glowing winter blanket. Those lights stimulated warm feelings in anticipation of Christmas Eve when we ate Mom's Canadian turkey and stuffing along with deli rye bread and a side of Hungarian cucumber salad.

Right after Christmas supper, my brother and I raced to open presents. One year, Dad gifted Steve and me multi-band shortwave radios. At bedtime, I listened to it under my covers, its volume on low and speaker close to my ear. I sought faraway broadcasts until I fell asleep.

Within a decade, our spruce tree reached beyond the roof of the house, and its width occupied most of the front yard. The tree became too big to wrap in lights each Christmas, so Dad strung lights on the outdoor staircase handrails and around the house's big kitchen window. When those large bulbs glowed through centimeters of freshly fallen snow, I had a warm feeling of having a normal family life.

In the ensuing decades, our blue spruce grew to become the tallest tree on our block. It was a symbol of not only the specialness of our house but also our making our mark on our little avenue. It showed that we, the Simkovitses, liked to do things in a big way.

*Dad at 47, with his pipe and black Oldsmobile 98,
in front of our renovated Montreal suburban house, 1967*

*Dad, sons, and blue spruce tree at Dorval house. Spring 1967.
The tree is less than half the height it grew into over the ensuing decades.*

All of Dad's upgrades made our #1 First Avenue home live up to its address. But its outside appeal masked the inside angst and anger that regularly rose between Mom and Dad.

My mother kept her electric sewing machine in our small den that exited to the backyard. She, a skilled seamstress and a penny saver, made many of her skirts and dresses on that Singer. While wearing a simple housedress with two large front pockets, she spent many weekday afternoons and evenings whizzing away at her machine.

Mom tailored pants and shorts for my brother and me. She stitched many a patch on those things as fast as my brother and I could rip holes in them from our outdoor playing. She scolded us with a shaking fist, saying, "I told you not to dirty and damage your new things!"

Outside of the den lay our backyard patio. On it stood an aluminum and wood picnic table with matching benches and chairs, and a big shade umbrella. There, Dad and Mom hosted many weekend barbeques. My father's "RCA gang" came *chez nous* several times each summer. Many of those RCAers lived on Montreal's West Island, and that may have been another reason why Dad wanted to live in Dorval.

RCA was Dad's first and foremost customer. Each year, Montreal Phono built thousands of record players and stereo consoles for them. The RCA logo was present on many items in our home, including clocks, pens, and several television consoles. Not only did it feel special that Dad had a close connection with a big company, but also it was a reminder as to whom our family was beholden.

Our weekend backyard barbeques were fun. Mom enjoyed combining Hungarian and Canadian cuisine. She cooked appetizers of deviled eggs and Hungarian *körözött* (a cheese spread with lots of paprika) accompanied by sliced deli rye bread. My brother's and I gobbled down that appetizer in no time.

As soon as guests arrived, Dad got them their favourite drinks. He served stiff gin and tonics, rye whiskey with 7-Up, and other adult concoctions. Steve and I poured the soft drinks, though mostly for ourselves.

The men swigged their drinks while the women sipped theirs. Everyone puffed on British Rothmans or Canadian Du Mauriers.

I watched as those gents, both English and French, laughed as much as Dad's Slovak relatives had back in Košice. But I was thankful that they were not as loud. Dad kept the alcohol and extra carton of smokes close by, stashed on a drink cart inside the den. He made sure everyone had their fill. As the evening wore on, the volume of people's voices rose as the grins on their faces widened. I enjoyed being around the happy hubbub and my cheerful father.

Dad got around to every guest, making sure all were having a good time. He never talked business at such gatherings; instead, he chatted about football and national politics with the men. (He knew to stay away from the more contentious Quebec politics while entertaining both Anglophone and Francophone guests.) He complimented women on their summer outfits and talked with them about good restaurants and prime vacation destinations.

Dad was full of big grins, hearty laughs, and knew everyone's favourite libation. No one went without. He was the center of everyone's attention. I couldn't wait to be all grown like him.

At one barbeque, my father wore a new white chef's hat and apron. He was in charge of his long chef's fork and knife that held tags of the RCA logo. They had been given to him by the head buyer at RCA's Montreal branch.

Dad was a barbeque expert. To start the charcoal grill, he utilized a full can of lighter fluid to soak the coals before striking and throwing a match onto the bricks. I stood next to him as he threw the lit match. I watched from a meter away as the coals burst into flames.

While the flames died down and the coals became white-hot, Dad engaged his RCA fork to stab his steaks repeatedly as they sat on a platter next to the grill. He told me, "You have to tenderize the meat before you put it on the fire."

He showed me how to sprinkle special spices onto the meat. He had bought those spices at a Montreal steak restaurant. They were a mix of garlic, onion, salt, peppers, and other secret herbs, adding a *je ne sais quoi* to the beef. Dad generously sprinkled both sides of the steak with those seasonings. Everyone, including me, loved the spicy smell and the tasty result.

I watched the meat drippings sizzle on the hot coals. Dad pointed his fork my way. "Son, the trick to a good steak is being liberal with the spices and then making sure you turn the meat only once when it's on the grill." He pointed to the steaks with his chef's fork. "The best time to turn your steaks is when you see blood oozing from the top of the meat. Turning it then will lock in the juices." He then cautioned, "Turning your steaks many times, as some people do, dries out the meat and makes it tough as rubber."

I listened carefully and nodded my understanding.

After the steaks had turned dark brown outside, he looked at me again. "You can tell when the meat is close to being done by cutting into your thickest steak first. When the meat inside has turned reddish pink, then you know the rest are ready. More red makes the meat rare, and less pink makes it well-done." He pointed with his RCA fork. "You don't want to wait until the meat is brown inside before you remove it from the fire. That will kill the steak, for it still cooks for some minutes after you remove it from the heat."

I watched Dad's work and nodded my understanding. I felt my father could teach me a lot in life if I paid attention.

Before serving his main course, Dad served the hot dog and liver appetizers he had prepared earlier on the grill. He had gotten the idea from Schwartz's, a famed steakhouse and deli in Montreal's Jewish district. He didn't want only to copy Schwartz's menu but to exceed it. He told me, "Son, I get the best meats from a Hungarian butcher who I know in the city." Dad obtained bigger and tastier hot dogs, the freshest beef liver, and thick T-bones instead of ribeyes.

While Dad served the meat on large, wooden serving plates, one RCA guy said half-seriously, "Johnny, I'm not sure you did those things right."

Voices quieted, and Dad looked puzzled as if to imply, *What are you talking about?*

The guy grinned. "By the way, can I have a second one to take home?"

Everyone laughed, including Dad and me.

While Dad continued to serve, my teeth ached in anticipation as I took in the spicy aroma and watched meat juices ooze onto the wooden plates. I sank my chops into my T-bone that was tenderized, turned, and prepared to perfection.

Everyone exclaimed, "Great steak, Johnny!"

"It's my pleasure," he said with a smile.

Dad certainly knew what he was doing in the barbequing department.

To add to Dad's flair, Mom baked pans of *rakott krumpli* (layered potatoes, salami, and hardboiled eggs) and a barrel full of her sweet-and-sour cucumber salad. Her Hungarian cooking was unusual for native Canadians, and she got "Great dishes, Anna!" from both the men and women.

Mom enjoyed entertaining as much as Dad did. Unlike him, she had only one drink and a couple of cigarettes to be social—more than that would make her woozy. She chatted with guests and never complained about the long hours she spent preparing food and cleaning the kitchen afterward.

Before she took leftovers away, she turned to Steve and me, "Did you boys eat enough?"

I tried not to disappoint her. The scrumptious food certainly helped to enlarge her boys' waistlines, which kept Mom busy letting out our clothes on her Singer.

During dessert time, Mom came out with Hungarian store-bought *dobos torta* (a 7-layer sponge cake with creamy chocolate filling) and her homemade brownies. She traded alcohol glasses for cups of strong coffee so that guests were awake as they left for home.

The way some folks teetered to their cars, they seemed more wide-awake drunk than sober. But I never heard about a mishap while anyone drove home. Maybe it was because the wives were driving.

I was impressed by how Dad and Mom worked together like synchronized swimmers when they entertained. While Dad got things ready for the outdoor grill, Mom prepared her hot and cold side dishes in her kitchen. As Dad got the ice ready and served the hard drinks, Mom delegated the soft-drink pouring to my brother and me so she could spend more time in the kitchen. As Dad brought in the dirty dishes and neatly piled them next to the sink, Mom washed them, from big trays to wooden plates to small dishes. Her two hands were her dishwasher. Together, she and Dad put everything away. Neither of them retired until their jobs were complete.

Mom was the last to get into bed, Dad already there and snoring. Steve and I lay peacefully in our beds too, feeling like Canadian kid walruses on a sunny subarctic shore after feeding on endless schools of fish.

Our family looked forward to these summer get-togethers, especially in having Dad around. We were happiest when he was in a jovial mood and when we ate until our bellies nearly burst.

* * *

Mom's kitchen was post-war modern. It had a linoleum floor, Formica countertops, and painted metal cabinets. A GE refrigerator and stove—coaxed by generations of GE repairmen to last thirty years—filled out the picture.

During weekdays, after the cooking and cleaning were complete, Mom remained at the kitchen table past Steve's and my bedtime. She wrote long letters to her family back in Czechoslovakia while she waited for Dad to come home from his evening business meetings.

The kitchen overlooked our front yard. By day, Mom could see my brother and me arrive home from school. By night, she watched out for Dad's car headlights, hoping he'd arrive home before she retired for the evening.

Mom and Dad did have their loving moments. She read him family letters from home as they sat together in their favourite living room spots. After a hearty home-cooked meal that she had happily prepared for him, he might tell her, "*Jóllaktam, cicám.* [I'm full, my kitten.]" After another successful backyard barbeque, he complimented, "It was a very nice party," and Mom smiled with pride.

But anger could flare up between them at a moment's notice, causing my stomach to knot and body to freeze. Any abrupt slamming of a door or accidental drop of a pot or plate sent a shock through my gut, my thinking that Mom and Dad were at it again. It felt as if I were living in a WWII enemy minefield. I was never sure of when the next exploding verbal-abuse charge would be triggered.

Mom often started the altercation by mentioning Dad's absences or inattentiveness to her. I kept looking over my shoulder to sense their mood. I vowed to be a cooperative kid and serious student, never wanting to be the cause of their Hungarian-Slovak anger—almost fiery enough to make the paint melt off the ceiling.

The smallest things could set off Mom. The wallpaper in our kitchen had slightly-raised paisley designs. Over the years, those paisleys were scratched, peeled, or rubbed off by my brother or me as we waited for Mom to serve our meals. Or we might damage those paisleys when we didn't quite like what she had put in front of us or when we daydreamed instead of ate our supper.

Once, noticing the scratched wallpaper, she pointed and blurted out crossly, *"Isten örizz!* [God forbid!] What are you boys doing, ruining my kitchen?!" I suspected my brother had peeled some paisleys sneakily right next to where I sat so that I would be the one to get an earful from our mother.

Dad finished our basement with dark wood veneer paneling and another linoleum floor. At one end, he had a quarter-circle bar built in the corner. Next to the bar was a sitting area that came in handy for Dad's parties whenever the weather wasn't conducive for being outside, which was most of the year. Dad called the colder Canada's seasons "almost winter," "winter," and "still winter." He called the warm months "road construction season."

Behind the bar was a large mirror that covered the wall above a back cabinet. Mounted on chrome rails that hung snugly between mirror sections were shelves of clear glass. On those almost invisible shelves, Dad displayed a variety of expensive spirits in decorative bottles: the fanciest rye, whiskey, gin, vodka, scotch, aperitifs, and digestifs he could find.

After houseguests had consumed the liquor, Mom didn't throw away the fancy bottles. She filled them with tea. Depending on how dark she made the tea, bottles looked like dark whiskey or light-brown rum. I only figured out Mom's ploy when, during my early adolescence, I choked on a quick swig from one of those elegant bottles. I hadn't realized Dad kept the real stuff hidden in the locked cabinet behind the bar.

Dad permitted my brother and me to have our first Dubonnet at a fancy restaurant when I turned fourteen. During a subsequent New Year's Eve party at our home with Dad's RCA gang and other family friends, I had my first glass of champagne. It tasted so fizzy and sweet that I quickly consumed a few glasses of that stuff. The alcohol soon hit me, causing my world to spin and my eyes to close as I sat in our cushy living room chair.

I don't remember how I got to bed that night. The next morning, my father was mad, saying, "Harvy was sneaking swigs while no one was looking."

I replied, "I drank that stuff from a glass, and it was in front of everybody. No one said anything."

Mom came to my aid, but her face stayed serious. "At least you were a cooperative boy when you were drunk. You let me take you straight to bed."

She might have been commenting on Dad's lack of cooperation when he got loaded.

Between the bar at one end of our basement, and the study area that Dad's factory people built for Steve and me at the other end, stood an RCA television console in a solid wood cabinet.

That unit, lasting for decades, provided music for our parents' parties. Dad stacked a set of American and Eastern European LPs that played for hours. He had the unit wired so that people could hear it through speakers installed upstairs in the living room and outside in the backyard.

Watching TV on that basement console provided a good distraction for my brother and me. Once, Dad came home late on a summer Saturday afternoon after playing a round of golf with his RCA buddies, followed by a couple of rounds of beer shandies. Mom picked a fight the minute he walked into the house—it was the typical complaint about his not being home.

It was rare for Steve or me to talk about our parents' fighting. This time, while my brother and I sat watching that basement television as loud voices emanated from upstairs, Steve turned to me and said, "Mom and Dad sound like a broken RCA record." I offered nothing in return and kept my eyes glued to the screen.

Though Dad had had his people build our basement study area, I preferred to do my homework on the living room coffee table upstairs. That locale was closer to Mom's kitchen, where I could grab a snack or sweet before or after dinner. I sat on the floor between the coffee table and Dad's couch. That couch was the place where my father liked to watch television and to take long weekend naps after a tiring work week.

When he was home, it seemed Dad lived on that Chesterfield more than he lived anywhere else in the house, including his and Mom's bedroom. While he was awake, my father enjoyed watching sports events and movies. He especially liked movies where the Nazi's or Japanese got outmaneuvered or defeated by the British or Americans.

Our living room television was yet another big RCA console. It stood as another testament to Dad's favoured customer who helped to put food on our table and presents under our Christmas tree.

On lazy Sunday afternoons, Mom, my brother, and I gathered around the television with Dad. We took cat naps on the furniture, or my brother and I rested on the shaggy carpeted floor. Those were warm and tender times of our being together as a family.

Our cozy Sunday scene lasted into the evening as we ate Mom's home-cooked supper on the coffee table. She swept in and out of her kitchen with our favourites. It was as if our RCA TV had become the center of our family's home life, just as RCA was the center of Dad's business life.

Dad had had a central AC system installed in our home for Montreal's hot days and muggy nights—needed for no more than a few weeks out of the year. But that AC system never seemed to create enough coolness on the hottest days and humid nights. During those sticky times, Mom bickered with Dad. "It's so hot upstairs that nobody can sleep."

He countered. "You just don't know how to use the system properly." He pointed upstairs. "Close all the windows in the house, and open only the small one in the top floor bathroom to let out the hot air."

Mom initially gave in to Dad's know-how on such matters. But his method never worked. Hot outside air poured into the house through that bathroom window. He never accepted that he had undersized the AC unit. Heck if he was going to spend more money on a bigger AC or an additional window unit for his and Mom's bedroom.

On oppressive nights, Mom slept on the couch in the living room or den while my brother and I sweated in our top floor beds. I didn't mind the heat and humidity as long as Mom and Dad weren't at loggerheads about it.

* * *

Occupying every room in our house were Bohemian cut lead crystal vases, bowls, trays, and crystal ashtrays for Dad's use. Cut glass serving bowls, plates, trays, fancy decanters, and an assortment of wine, champagne, port, and water glasses filled Mom's dining room buffet and hutch. Every horizontal surface in our house mushroomed with pieces of that clear or coloured crystal.

Mom adored her crystal. Once, a semi-annual package arrived from Aunt Irén with several broken pieces. When Mom saw the damage, she put her hand to her mouth and shouted, "*Yoy!*" She almost cried. She didn't dare write to her sister about the broken items for fear Irén would blame herself for the insufficient packaging.

On another occasion, Mom went into a high-pitched angry shrill when my brother and I broke a crystal platter. We hit it while playing pitch-and-catch mindlessly in the dining room.

Over the years, Mom turned our home into a showplace for Czechoslovak art. My parents' friends were envious of her varied and growing collections of Czechoslovak crystal and linens, and scenes of Slovakia painted by Irén's husband, Bus.

When a guest asked her how she got such beautiful things, Mom spoke about her dear sister and brother-in-law. She mentioned how they had only the bare necessities back home. She then took her guest's eyes to the oil paintings on the walls or to the linens that covered the dining room table. If the guest, now turned customer, was interested in seeing more, Mom brought out a few of Bus's canvas rolls and Irén's crystal and linens that were available for sale.

Besides sending Mom her husband's paintings and perhaps a half-ton of crystal over the years, Irén sent boxes of white handkerchiefs to Dad, Steve, and me. Decades later, on a visit to her Košice home a year or two before her death, I thanked her (albeit tongue in cheek) for gifting me a lifetime supply of those hankies. She touched her chest with her palm and became teary with the knowledge she had had a lasting impact on my life with her gifts. I made use of her handkerchiefs for decades.

Through the 1960s, every one of Mom's Czechoslovak sisters and brothers came to visit us in Montreal for a six-month stint. Dad's stepmother and half-brother also came for such extended stays. Our relatives came to visit one-at-a-time—the only way communist Czechoslovakia allowed family members out of the country. The communist authorities wanted to ensure that travellers returned home to their families before their 6-month visa expired.

During my early school years, it felt as if we continually had a relative living with us. Each stayed in our third bedroom—well decorated with Bus's paintings and Irén's Bohemian crystal sitting on Czechoslovak laced doilies.

My brother or I rarely brought a school friend over to our house during our relatives' extended visits. I felt awkward having my Canadian cohorts exposed to my extended family's foreign accents, odd language, and drab clothes from their not as prosperous country. None of our kin was up to date with the latest toys, games, or music. They had never even seen a deck of 52 playing cards; their Eastern European decks containing only 32.

Even the smells in our home were different, mustier, and oilier than the Mr. Clean and Dial Soap odors of my friends' houses. Mom was a Spic 'n' Span housewife, and she believed in the power of lemon, vinegar, and Ivory Soap. But those cleaning agents never fully masked the stuffy smells of my parents' homeland.

Other than Bus, who painted oil portraits in our den, Dad put his brother and brothers-in-law to work as clerks, administrators, or factory workers in his factory's office. There they could earn hard currency (cash of course, because they didn't have work visas) and learn English. During their time with us, Dad encouraged each man, even his half-brother Edo, to stay in Canada as a refugee from communism.

"*Lassen* to me!" he proclaimed to any relative who'd listen. "Why go back to Czechoslovakia? There is nothing for you there. Stay and build a life here in Canada." He pointed to himself. "You could work for me as long as you want, or until you get yourself settled in something else."

Though Dad was generous, he was always selling. Even though he offered his help and the benefit of what he knew, most of our relatives responded, "I have to go back home. My life and family are in Czechoslovakia."

There were exceptions. One was Mom's brother, Gyuszi (Hungarian for Viktor). My uncle accepted my father's proposal; he didn't return to his communist homeland after his six-month visa expired, risking incarceration if he ever stepped foot again into Czechoslovakia. He left behind a wife and stepdaughter in Košice for the sake of a better life in Canada.

Edo basci (Uncle Edo) working in Montreal Phono's messy electronics testing area. 1967.

Uncle Viktor soon enrolled in a Montreal college to study music, eventually getting a master's degree. He became a high school music teacher, but a series of strokes later in life caused my uncle to curtail his career. He lived in our home for over a year to recover from his second attack.

After being in Canada for twenty years, and after the Iron Curtain came down in Eastern Europe in 1989, Uncle Gyuszi retired. He obtained his pensions from Canada and Quebec, which those governments were willing to send him in Czechoslovakia. He departed for his homeland and reunited with his wife and stepchild; they were ready and happy to have him back.

Before he left Canada, my uncle told me, "I'd rather be a richer man in a poor country than a poorer man in a rich country." I didn't know if he had been better or worse off by having followed my father's advice to stay in Canada.

When it was my Košice aunts' turns to visit us in Canada, Mom put each of them to work to help her cook, house clean, and sew. She and her sisters could fill the days with constant chatter and continual housework. They stopped only to sit and watch daytime soaps like *As the World Turns*, which my brother liked to call *As the Stomach Churns*.

Translating for her sisters, Mom filled them in on the recent happenings of strained, failing, and adulterous TV relationships as if those scenes were realistic slices of North American life. I stayed away from those conversations because I didn't want to know about other people's problems. We had enough drama within our family.

As a kid, I felt anxious around my mother. An *"Isten őrizz!"* could emanate from her in a heartbeat if Steve or I dirtied our new or freshly clean clothes. My fear of spilling my juice or cereal at breakfast caused me to spill. Mom's voice immediately cried out, *"Istenem! Mit csináltál!* [Oh my God! What have you done!]" and then *"Vigyázz! Vigye el onnan!* [Watch out! Move from there!]" Within seconds, she pulled me away from the table and cleaned the mess swiftly with a cloth or sponge.

After he had lived with us for an extended period, my uncle Viktor once told me, "I love my sister, your mother, dearly, but it's sometimes hard to live with her." I said nothing to his remark, but his statement sent reverberations of familiarity through my bones.

When I got older, I understood my mother's character better. I imagined she, the youngest of six, was told what to do, where to be, and how to behave by her five elder siblings. Maybe she was unconsciously reciprocating as an adult by doing the same to her kin, including us, her children. Then again, I had heard my other Czechoslovak relatives scream at their kids too, so maybe her behaviour was normal for a parent of her nationality.

Though she had a temper, Mom went out of her way for her kin, doing for them in any way she could. More than once, Dad became irritated with her, saying, "You involve yourself and worry too much about your family."

That didn't deter Mom from asking Dad for favours on their behalf. He gave jobs to her relatives. He sold Bus's paintings and Irén's linens and crystals to his customers and colleagues. He brought our relatives on family trips to Niagara Falls in the spring, the Laurentian Mountains in the summer and fall, and Florida for the Christmas holidays. I suspected Dad wanted them to think of him as generous and successful. In my youth, I saw my father that way.

There was a Hungarian expression that Mom and Dad employed. It went something like, "You don't want your family to hang from your neck." But that's what my parents seemed to want to do with their kin.

The presence of Mom's relations *chez nous* did keep her happily occupied, and she complained less about Dad's absences from home. I don't know about my brother, but I was more pleased than not about having our extended family live, travel, and hang around our family. I just didn't bring any of my Canadian school chums over to our house.

* * *

My brother and I shared a bedroom. There, Dad engaged his factory people again, this time to build a headboard and shelving behind our twin beds. When I was old enough to understand such things, I admired Dad for his little business tricks of having his company pay for our home projects.

In our teens, my brother and I wheeled into our bedroom the portable RCA TV that my parents kept on a movable stand in their bedroom. Pretending as if we were electrical engineers like Dad, my brother and I wired the unit to our roof antenna by way of a 30' makeshift antenna wire that ran through the hallways and down the stairs to the antenna outlet in the den.

Mom was not happy about having that wire running through the house. She said, "I'm afraid to get a shock. That wire could cause a fire and burn down the house."

Mom at 48-years-old in our living room, dressed in a gown she made herself. She had done her hair and was ready, with her fur coat on, for a rare night out with Dad. She is bookended by the RCA console television (right) and her Czechoslovak crystal on the piano (left); c. 1968.

So she wouldn't scream at us, we agreed to connect the wire only when she went out for an occasional Saturday evening party with Dad, or for her regular Thursday night bowling club at the local alley. We had to make sure we disconnected the wire and put everything away before we went to sleep; otherwise, we'd face a shaking fist and reverberating voice in the morning.

Mom abandoned her career as a seamstress after my brother and I were born. She received a weekly stipend from Dad (he called it her "salary") to buy food, clothing, and other necessities. She rarely had extra money to buy anything on her own.

If my mother needed a new appliance, like a vacuum cleaner, she had to get permission from Dad and then present the bill to him for reimbursement. He granted his consent for a new machine only after he or his Montreal Phono factory tech couldn't fix the old one.

Mom didn't seem to mind her husband trying to save. Having been raised through The Great Depression, she saved her pennies too. She collected every thread and piece of cloth from her sewing at home, turning excess fabric into cleaning rags. She ate the over-ripe fruit that had stood on the kitchen counter too long. She told Steve and me, "My father had owned a small grocery store in Košice near to where we lived. He saved the best fruit and vegetables for the customers; my brothers, sisters, and I ate the things that got old." Mom never treated her two sons that way. She fed us fresh foods and never brought home a damaged can good.

As in a Hans Christian Anderson story, Mom's fastidiousness was second to none. Everything we owned was stored tidily in closets, drawers, or on cabinet shelves. She ironed and folded the laundry neatly and put everything away the same day. She never went to bed until her housework was complete, even if it took into the evening.

My mother said she had learned to clean from her eldest sister, Ilonka. When their mother died—Mom had been only twelve years old—her big sister took care of her young siblings. Ilonka told her little sister, "Never clean just where the priest walks," and Mom lived by that philosophy.

She took Spic 'n Span to every centimeter of every horizontal surface in her kitchen. She carefully scoured not only open areas but behind and under the toaster, bread box, and any container that stood on the counter. Once a month, she tackled the refrigerator and kitchen cabinets, moving things out, in, and around until every corner was spotless.

Dad never found fault with Mom's cleaning. He liked coming home to a tidy house, though he might leave crumbs behind when he cut bread in the kitchen. Or my father might leave glass watermarks on the living room coffee table when he ate a late supper in front of the TV. Mom was not far behind with a damp rag—never wasting money on paper towels.

Mom made us put away our toys neatly after playing—otherwise, her angry voice was not far behind. If she found our stuff lying around after we left for school or went to bed, she put those things away herself. I never worried about not finding my things, for Mom returned them to their proper place.

Dad didn't go into the kitchen when Mom was cooking or cleaning. She saw herself reigning in her place of bread cutting as Dad reigned in his place of breadwinning. She didn't like any of us to mess with the things in her domain, especially her kitchen utensils.

She once became irritated at Dad for borrowing and then partially dulling her good serrated knife. She had bought that prized utensil in the city and had it for years. She employed it every day to slice Dad's favourite rye bread for his breakfast and supper. Without thinking, or Mom knowing, he took that knife from the drawer and used it to cut the weeds in and around the outdoor walkway and backyard patio.

When Mom saw the tip of her serrated knife dulled, her face turned long. She put her hand over her mouth. She quickly sucked in air, uttering a big "Huh!" in a tone that sounded as if the sky was falling. Her voice was dejected. "Oh my God!" she blurted. Half angry and half sad, she turned to Dad and pointed to the damaged edge. "Jani, look what you did!"

Dad batted his hand at her. "It's not a problem; the knife is still good." He turned and walked out of the kitchen.

After another heavy sigh, she looked at the utensil as if a loved one had died. She said nothing more. I thanked my stars that she placed the knife carefully back into the drawer.

Mom stashed assorted cookies, chocolates, biscuits, and candies in the cupboard under the counter next to the refrigerator. She declared that cabinet hands-off to protect her sweets for guests. Her warning rarely stopped my brother or me (or Dad) from making off with portions of the sugary stash while we did our homework or watched TV.

Mom, too, loved sweets. Instead of having dinner and supper, she could eat a box of cookies or a tin of chocolates throughout the day. She allowed our taking of the lesser sweets but maintained her "hands-off" policy on the fancier stuff she reserved for visitors.

Our family's affection for confections contributed to Steve's and my becoming chubby ("husky," as Mom called it) throughout most of our childhood. Sweets brought our family together, with smiles emanating from our faces and "Yum" from our mouths. Dad got a kick out of our chubbiness, happily pinching and poking our spongy thighs and bellies. As youths, my brother and I relished his tickling attention and his calling us, "My two fatso boys."

As a treat, Mom made a whole supper of delicious Hungarian *palacsinta* (crepes) filled with chocolate syrup or apricot jam. As an alternative, she rolled, boiled, and then fried *turosh ez silvash gombotz* (baseball-sized dumplings of sweetened dough stuffed with sweet cheese or a pitted plum). A half dozen of those could make a whole meal, including dessert.

Mom enjoyed cooking, cleaning up after, and clothing her two growing boys. We didn't even have to put our dishes in the sink. She did everything for us—except for our homework. She saw her work and sacrifices as perpetual gifts to the boys in her life, including her husband. From her "Good morning sunshine!" when she woke us in the morning, to her "Hello my loves!" when we arrived home from school, and to her "Good night my sons" when we retired to bed, Mom enjoyed doing for her children.

When Steve and I became old enough to leave home and live elsewhere in Montreal, we continued to go back to Mom's First Avenue kitchen every week for our Hungarian favourites. Preparing her stuffed cabbage, chicken paprikash, plum balls, crepes, and anything else richly Hungarian, continued to be her way to have her boys back home and to herself.

* * * *

16

More Snowbird Travels

Preparation and Departure

Ka-chunk! Ka-chunk! The sound echoed in Dad's 2-door black Oldsmobile Toronado as he and I slammed our doors shut on this dark and early December 25th morning. It was 1971, and I was 17 years old. Our family of four was bundled tightly in our winter coats.

Dad and I sat in the front seat while my brother and Mom crowded into the back. Though I wore my wool winter coat, hat, and gloves, I couldn't stop shivering inside our cold auto awoken from its night slumber.

Dressed in his grey flannel slacks and flannel coat, Dad pressed the garage remote under the driver's visor. The paneled door rose until we heard the familiar *click*. He looked into the rearview mirror to check that his black hair, combed straight back, was not disturbed by his car packing effort. He had a lit cigarette in his mouth, his second of this young morning. I disliked its stinky smell, yet Dad was calmer when he took in the stick's warm glow.

He put the car in reverse, twisted his 5'8" frame—complete with round shoulders and growing midriff that nearly touched the steering wheel—and looked back through the partially ice-fogged rear window. He lifted his foot off the brake and gently tapped the car's accelerator. The rest of us sat silently as our car exited from our garage into the Canadian winter.

The time on the car's analog clock read 4:35. We waited a moment in our short suburban driveway until the garage door closed to seal our brick igloo home from the elements. Dad cracked open his side window to flick his cigarette stub into the shimmering snowbank.

The outside air was quiet and still, except for the low rumble of the car's engine and the squeak of the newly-fallen snow under the car's tires. Small snowflakes fell gently, looking like a shower of silver flecks in our beaming headlights. The city's plows had not yet cleared the freshly fallen snow that blanketed our street.

We were the first to make tire tracks this morning. Not another soul was out at this God-forsaken hour of Christmas Day. Santa had completed his work, and all the elves and their beneficiaries were asleep—except for us.

It was the morning we had been anticipating for weeks, one that had put my brother and me to bed at nine o'clock on Christmas Eve. We had feasted on Mom's supper of turkey and stuffing. Steve and I had ripped through our holiday cards and presents that lay under a 3'-high tinsel tree. (Mom feared that a real tree could catch fire when covered in holiday lights.) We had then squeezed in an hour of Christmas Eve specials on television before we headed to bed.

I felt excitement for our trip as I privately said goodbye to our darkened, snow-bound home. Our car voyage would take us far away from what my Eastern European parents called "our cold country of Canada." As we started our journey south, I thought back to my parents' preparations for this long-anticipated day.

* * *

Our mother had had our pre-departure packing ritual down pat. The previous weekend, Dad had reminded her, "Don't take more than one big suitcase for each of us."

Over the next days, she set out our bags on the guestroom floor and our summer clothes on the futon. After supper one night, she called in her three men, one by one, and showed us what she thought we should pack.

When it was Dad's turn, he told her what she should pack for him. During my turn, I worked to be as agreeable as I could with Mom's clothing choices for me. I wanted to avoid a last-minute trip to the department store with her for an extra shirt or pair of shorts.

Mom tended to overpack. The night before our departure, Dad walked into the guestroom and spied many unpacked items. "Anna," he said with frustration, "why are we taking all this baloney?"

She retorted, "Johnny, we need these things down there. I packed only one suitcase for each of us." She made no mention of the extra things she had stashed in the closet, biding their time for our migration.

Despite Dad's chiding, my undeterred Mom snuck in several handbags filled with extra sneakers, balls and paddles, lotions, towels, and an extra bag to carry those things. The more time we spent relaxing where we were going, and not have to shop at an air-conditioned mall, the happier she would be.

Up with Mom at 3:30 on the morning of our exodus, Dad washed and dressed quickly and then rushed downstairs. Waiting for him were a cup of strong instant black coffee and a slice of buttered, garlic-rubbed, rye toast. Mom had prepared those for him while in her flannel nightgown, curlers still in her hair. He probably ate standing so as not to linger.

Dad then hurried to our upstairs guest bedroom to grab the luggage that Mom had finished preparing late the night before. She had made it into bed who knows when, and only after packing our suitcases with a mother's care. She had performed her duties without complaint.

He carried the luggage and extra bags to the garage. He arranged them in the trunk of his Toronado as if he were solving a jigsaw puzzle.

Precisely at 4 o'clock, fully dressed but her hair and face not entirely done, Mom walked into our bedroom. She turned on the light and caressed our shoulders while standing between my brother's and my beds. "Wake up my *son-shines*; it's time to get ready to go." She pointed. "Your travel clothes are ready for you. Leave your pyjamas here; I packed other ones for you."

She looked around the room to ensure nothing had been forgotten or not put away. "Come down right away for breakfast. We're leaving in half an hour."

It didn't take prodding to get me out of slumber; rising excitement banished sleepiness from my eyes. I grabbed my dark corduroys, black turtleneck, and wool sweater Mom had placed at the foot of my bed. I threw them on as quickly as my waking body could manage.

I glanced behind the room's window shade. Frost coated the edges of the aluminum-framed double window. Outside, the snow was falling gently but steadily. It created an eerie, hypnotic halo around a street lamp. It looked as if five to ten centimeters of the fresh stuff had fallen. *Oh, shoot! It looks frigging freezing outside., and the driving will be slow.* I turned to rush out of our small bedroom, almost knocking over my barefoot brother as he stood to zip his pants.

I ran down to the kitchen and sat in my usual spot. I grabbed the Corn Flakes and the cold milk that Mom had put out.

My mother's hair was now neatly combed. She had made up her face with a light powder and rose lipstick. She wore her long grey flannel slacks and a loose grey tunic held together in the center with a broad, red, plastic belt. The belt matched her lipstick. They went well with her blond hair that she had spent an hour bleaching the previous day.

The house was cold. Mom had the kitchen stove's door cracked open with the heating elements on low. Dad had turned down the central thermostat, and my mother knew he would become riled if she touched it.

My brother walked in as I started to chow down. "Ah!" he said. "Corn Flakes and orange juice; those are my favourites for four o'clock in the morning, especially on Christmas day."

I kept my head down and said nothing. I had a purpose in mind that kept me consuming my cereal.

Mom sputtered, "Hurry and eat, boys, then go to the bathroom quickly. Your father wants to get going."

She grabbed groceries off the kitchen counter and packed them into already bulging shopping bags. She pointed. "After you finish breakfast, Steve, take this bag to the car and put it on the floor next to where I'll be sitting."

I could hear my brother grumble about his duty, but I didn't care.

It was 4:20, and tiredness still stung my eyes as I laced my shoes by the front door. I heard my father's gruff voice yell from downstairs. "Okay, everybody, let's go!" He wanted to make it through and past the city limits and onto the border before the roads became crowded with holiday travellers.

I rushed to put on my coat while my brother tied his shoes both neatly and snugly. Mom would follow after she checked the stove, light switches, and lamp timer for the second time. She looked around to collect any straggling items. My coat open and laces loose, I flew down the staircase that led to the garage, holding my rucksack over one shoulder. I jumped two and three steps at a time to get to our car before Steve did.

I threw my pack, full of new science fiction books, onto the front seat before my brother got his chance. I looked to see if I could help my father with any stray luggage. In a minute or two, I'd tell my one-year-older, yet now slightly shorter brother, "Steve, since you'll probably be driving more than I'll be on this trip, let me sit up front first." By helping Dad with our bags, I wanted my father on my side.

Dad stood behind the car in our freezing garage. A cardigan was the only thing keeping him warm. He was staring into the car's trunk compartment. He had bought his new two-door Toronado the previous spring. It had a smaller trunk than the Olds 98 he usually purchased every three years.

With a cigarette hanging from the corner of his mouth, his face showed exasperation. He slammed down the trunk lid with both his hands, pleading "Hesus Maria!" which seemed almost appropriate for Christmas Day. The trunk didn't stay shut.

I looked his way. "Dad, what if we put a couple of the small bags between Mom and Steve in the back seat? And we can put another one between you and me on the front. You can use it for an armrest."

304

"Okay, take these." He lobbed me a couple of bags. I caught them with my secure goalie grip—I was a varsity soccer goalkeeper in high school—and placed the bags into the car.

When Steve entered the garage a moment later, grocery bag in hand, I said my prepared line. A pained look formed on his face. He glanced at Dad then looked back at me. "Okay, Harvy, you can sit in the front seat to start."

My brother squeezed himself and his bag through the passenger door and onto the car's compact backseat. My mother followed right behind him with more grocery bags, one in each hand.

Steve and she were now surrounded by luggage between them and groceries at their feet. They shifted things around to find comfortable positions. *Those two might now know what it's like to be in a Gemini space capsule.*

My father got behind the wheel and started the engine. He pushed the door's remote control, and then he backed out of the garage slowly as he looked through the partially fogged rear window. Still peeved about our excess luggage, he energetically delivered Slovak phrases in Mom's direction, phrases my brother and I didn't understand.

My mother's makeup compact was already out. She checked the blond coif she had washed and set the day before and combed out earlier this morning. Squeezing through the forward-slanted front seat to get to the back had altered her hairdo. Mom parried Dad's thrust, snapping at him in Slovak. Given her tone, she might have told him to buy a car with a bigger trunk and maybe a bigger backseat too. She might even have scolded, "If you gave me more money, I'd be happy to buy what we need when we get to where we are going and then leave it there, so your trunk won't get overcrowded."

Dad said nothing more. His stern face and tight lips told me he remained peeved.

Squished like Canadian herrings, barely enough room for their arms and legs to move around, Mom and Steve sat quietly. When he was on the avenue, Dad shifted his laden Toronado into forward. He turned onto the adjacent street and headed for the highway.

I kept my eyes forward. *What a way to start a family vacation! I can't believe we've made it this far.*

* * *

Dad clicked on the radio. "Let's hear the weather report."

Within a moment, the weatherman came on. *It's cold outside this Christmas day; thirteen degrees Fahrenheit at Dorval airport. The snow will continue to fall lightly for the rest of the morning. We're expecting a few more centimeters on top of the already seven centimeters on the ground.*

"I bet the going will be slow for a while," Dad said. "It's good we are out early."

I sat quietly, with my whole body still shivered. Moisture from my eyes fogged my thick black-rimmed glasses. I pressed my legs together firmly and fisted my gloved hands within my coat pockets. I could see my breath in front of me. *I sure as heck hope the car's heater gets going and puts an end to my shaking.*

Dad had put the heater fan on high. It was blasting cold air toward the windshield. Behind me, Mom yelled in Hungarian, *"A fütés az, Jani?* [Is the heater on, Johnny?]"

My father growled back in their first language, "Wait a minute! The engine isn't warm yet."

I told myself the cold was temporary. In about thirty-two hours, we'd be sitting by the pool in the warm southern breeze, soaking up the sun, and wearing nothing but bathing suits and a healthy coat of Coppertone Oil. And, for most of the car ride there, I would have my dad by my side.

"Can you believe it!?" he said. "This is our eleventh time in twelve years that we are going south like the Snowbirds."

"Yah, Dad," I responded, "but they were a lot smarter to leave in October."

"Did you know that Snowbirds only migrate at night," my brother chirped, "just like we are doing?"

"Don't worry, boys; we'll be in Florida in no time, faster than those little pipsqueaks could ever get there."

Not able to stop myself from shaking, I wished I could be as optimistic as my father.

Dad entered the highway. Mom said in Hungarian, "Jani, are you sure you want the boys to be driving during our trip? The roads could be dangerous."

Her voice was edgy. "Wouldn't it be better if we stop for a night so you can drive most of the way yourself like we used to do when the kids were small?"

Mom had learned to drive only recently, in her early 50s, and not with confidence or much success. She once told us, "It's your father's fault I don't drive. He never takes me to practise my driving around the shopping centre on Sunday afternoons."

That was the only day of the week when the mall's parking lots were empty. I had once gone out with her and experienced her form. With her 5'4" frame, she needed a cushion so she could see above the steering wheel. Her head protruded over the wheel like a stork reaching for its prey. When she stopped at an intersection, she looked both ways many times before initiating a turn or crossing the street.

The next time she asked us to go out driving with her, Steve and I dodged her request. I think all of us were glad that she didn't want to sit behind the steering wheel on our trip to sunny Florida.

When my brother and I were in our single-digit years, Dad had been the sole driver to take us the 2800 kilometers (1,750 road miles) south. He sat behind the wheel for twelve hours each day. It had taken two-and-a-half days to make the trip to our oceanfront hotel in Miami Beach or Hollywood. Dad stopped every four hours for gas and bathroom breaks. He drove from before dawn until dusk, when he pulled into a nondescript roadside motel with its "vacancy" sign lit.

In response to Mom's concern about Steve's and my driving, Dad assured her. "I want to get there and not waste time stopping on the road. I'm going to drive past New York City myself. There the roads are highways and should be clear of snow." He pointed to my brother behind him. "Stevie can take over and drive late into the evening. I'll get some sleep while he drives, and then take over the driving again through the night. Harvy can drive early the next morning until we get to our hotel at midday."

Yes! My newly minted driver's license was in my wallet. I had turned 17 a couple of months earlier. I couldn't wait for my turn on the open road. And the speed limit on Florida's Sunshine State Parkway was 70. *Awesome!*

"Are you sure it will be okay?" Mom asked.

"I'll be watching them the whole time," Dad replied. I didn't know how he'd accomplish that while snoozing as my brother or I drove.

Mom looked out of the window at the still falling snow. "It's too bad we don't have Ned or Edo anymore."

After our first few years of multi-day Florida migrations, Dad no longer wanted to waste extra days travelling during our two-week vacation. He arranged with a business colleague and friend, Ned Meyer, to be our second driver.

Ned, a Romanian immigrant, was a professional road salesman, thus an expert driver. For a few years before we joined Ned in Florida, he had already driven there for the winter holidays. He took his wife, Mimi, and their young son, Tony. When our family first joined them, Dad drove our car right behind Ned's as we wound down the eastern seaboard. Then, for a few vacations south, Ned came with us in our car and left his family at home. I didn't know why he did that for those winters; I never asked.

When Ned was with us, he and Dad switched off driving every four hours (about 400 kilometers, or three-quarters of a gas tank) as they maneuvered us to a warmer climate. The two drivers, plus an American interstate highway system that provided more divided highways each year, allowed us to make the trip in 32 to 34 hours.

Being the smaller kid, I sat between Dad and Ned on the front bench seat of Dad's Olds 98. Ned, ten years Dad's elder, was shorter than my father, and he sported an even more rotund belly and a rounder face. He had almost no hair on his head and spoke in a thick accent. I felt a bit squished between the two paunchy men, but it was good to be sitting up in the front with them and to listen to them talk about anything and everything.

On one trip, Dad said, "Can you believe how much money the Canadian government is spending on Expo 67? It's nice to celebrate Canada's 100th birthday, but the government is going crazy with the money they're pissing away."

Ned regularly travelled across Quebec for business and pleasure. He spoke French fluently and understood provincial politics. His voice rose. "The federal government spends money in Quebec to appease the French.

Quebecois nationalism is growing." He raised a finger. "The French are rising against the Catholic Church and Anglophone businessmen that have controlled Quebec politics for decades." He pointed that finger forward. "Our federal Liberal government is finally permitting French to be an official language of Canada."

Dad came back. "Yes, and appeasing the French will lead to Quebec separating from Canada. Every big Montreal business and English Quebecer will move to Ontario."

Ned continued the sparring. "A new francophone Prime Minister will help keep Canada together. It's time for our English Pearson to step down and make way for a younger and bilingual PM, like that Justice Minister Pierre Elliott Trudeau."

"That Trudeau's a good dresser," Mom shouted from the back seat.

"Yah!" Dad cut Mom off, hitting the steering wheel with his hand. "Pearson was an idiot to let France's De Gaulle into Canada and let him give that *'Vive le Quebec libre'* speech. Pearson is no Diefenbaker [Canada's previous, long-standing, conservative PM]. It's time for him to go."

Mom leaned forward from the back, "And doesn't new Canadian flag look stupid with its big red maple leaf? It almost looks communist."

"Yes, Anna," Ned responded politely. "Pearson knows Canada has to get rid of that old Union Jack flag and our British ties; otherwise, the French will stay resentful."

He turned his head to grin and wink at my mother. "And Canada does have a lot of beautiful sugar maple trees. And red in Canada represents democracy."

Dad switched gears in the conversation. "I like that Trudeau guy. He's a flamboyant bachelor, but he also has spooky ideas. He's for homosexuals and easy contraception, divorce, and abortions."

"That stuff happens anyway, so why not legalize it?" Ned said that with a manly laugh as he slapped his hand on his thigh. I smiled but stayed out of the manly conversation.

Given a chance, Ned could go on and on about the latest car upgrades, like the new ABS braking systems and front-wheel drives that "will change the way everyone drives." He spoke about turbo diesel engines that would offer more engine power and gas savings, and he went on and on about catalytic (I first thought he said *Catholic*) converters that will have cars give off fewer emissions.

In *Flor-I-da* (as he put it), Ned came with us to the Monkey Jungle, Flamingo Gardens, and Seaquarium. Being an avid photographer, he carried both movie and still cameras around his neck as we partook of those tourist places. At every opportunity, he took shots of our family and the animals from different angles. He made funny faces to get us to smile or laugh.

I enjoyed having Ned around. He loved French tongue twisters. Once he had me repeat one about the price of sausages:

Bonjour madame de les saucisses.	(Good day sausage lady.)
Combien coûte les saucissons ici?	(How much do these sausages cost?)
Les saucissons ici coûte soixante six sous.	(These sausages cost 66 cents.)
Si les saucisses ici coûte soixante six sous	(If these sausages cost 66 cents,)
C'est trop madame, merci madame	(That's too much mam, thank you, mam.)

Ned was into Big Time Wrestling on TV. "You should see what they do to each other!" he exclaimed when Dad once mentioned the subject. Ned covered his face with both hands as if he were the schmuck being lifted high into the air and thrown on the mat by one of those massive, ugly, sweaty guys.

Dad said, "That's crazy, fake stuff." I felt the same, never able to watch more than two minutes of that baloney on TV. Ned insisted, "Those moves are the real deal."

My father and Ned could complain about each other's driving as if they were two cowboys trying to ride one horse. One time, sweat poured down Ned's face while Dad was maneuvering the car on a congested primary road. "*Pleeeze*, Johnny!" he pleaded, "Drive more smoothly with the accelerator!"

Dad was jerking his foot on and off the pedal rather than applying pressure gradually. His poor technique prevented Ned from sleeping on his off shift. "There's nothing wrong with my driving!" Dad retorted.

"Johnny, the accelerator is not a switch you turn on and off with your foot," Ned bellowed. "Driving is my business; I drive over 40,000 kilometers a year over Quebec and Eastern Ontario. It's a problem for your passengers when you drive the way you are doing."

Nobody else said anything as these two Eastern Europeans duked it out. Dad grumbled something and continued his driving style. Ned threw up his hands, "Johnny, this is not a good way to drive!" and did his best to get rest.

After several winters of travelling with us, Ned no longer came as our second driver. Instead, a few days before our departure, he headed to Florida, again with his wife and son. They were probably thinking about us right now as they sat outside their beach apartment while we were still in ice-and-snow country. Part of me missed Ned's company, but our best driving times together may have faded into the rearview mirror.

After Ned had departed our ranks, our *Edo bácsi* (Uncle Edo) became Dad's alternate driver for the next couple of years. Dad's late-thirties, bachelor half-brother, a refugee from Soviet communism, had immigrated to Canada in the fall of '68.

Uncle Edo, age 37, with his nephews soon after he had immigrated to Canada. Fall of 1968

A year earlier, in 1967, Edo had been in Canada on a six-month visitor visa. During that visit, Dad had urged his brother, "*Lassen* to me, Edo! You'll have a better life in Canada than in Czechoslovakia; do stay here."

At the time, Edo didn't listen to his big brother; he went back home to live with his mother. As the Soviets were closing the doors on the 1968 Prague Spring, Edo changed his mind.

He and a few hometown friends escaped to the West. The friends had been members of the Czechoslovak water polo team that was participating in a tournament in Yugoslavia. Rather than return to Czechoslovakia after their match, they—with Edo in toe—abandoned the team and escaped the country. They sought asylum in Austria until they got Dad's help to come to Canada.

As kids, my brother and I had seen Edo several times when Mom took us to visit our relatives in Košice in '60 and '64. Edo called me his "pick-me-up boy" for the innumerable times I asked him to exercise his strong arms by lifting and carrying me. He was a quiet, handsome, svelte Slovak who was physically fit and athletically agile.

"Brazil Edo" on the beach while holidaying in Hollywood, FL, in 1967.
It was the winter before he escaped Czechoslovakia and sought refuge in Canada.

When we went to Florida together, Edo brought a soccer ball or volleyball, which we kicked or threw around in the Florida sunshine. He could keep the ball in the air almost indefinitely, bouncing it off of his feet, chest, knees, and head, simultaneously shouting "Pelé, Pelé, Pelé!" (a reference to the famed Brazilian soccer player). He liked to work on darkening his skin to a deep bronze tan such that his Slovak Canadian friends called him "Brazil."

Though Edo was a fun guy with whom to play soccer, his driving scared me at times. Once, we were travelling on a two-lane North Carolina road, heading south on a dark rainy night. Only the car tail lights ahead of us, and the headlights come toward us, showed the way. A drowsy Edo was behind the wheel. I sat between him and my snoring father.

Edo's eyes glazed over, and he drifted into the oncoming traffic lane. I kept my eyes on my uncle, with my hand ready to grab the steering wheel if he dozed off. Mom and Steve slept in the back. I felt as if I were the only one who could protect us from a head-on collision or landing in a ditch.

There were a couple of scary moments when an oncoming car blinked its headlights at us. I came close to grabbing the wheel as Edo drifted once more into the opposing lane. To my relief, he guided the car back into the southbound lane just in time.

When we reached our next gas stop, I said nothing to my father about Edo's driving. I didn't want to get him in trouble. I would have felt awful if Dad yelled at my "pick-me-up" uncle. But I was thankful when Dad returned behind the wheel so I could get shut-eye after my hard work of watching my *Edo bácsi*.

We could see the city lights glowing diffusely through the falling and blowing snow as Dad drove close to downtown Montreal. The car's clock read a few minutes past five o'clock. Mom spoke from her capsule seat. "It's too bad your *nagy fasz* [big dick] brother had that big car accident earlier this year."

She was referring to a severe fender-bender Edo had had in the city. He totaled Dad's company station wagon, put a pedestrian into the hospital, and got arrested for drunk driving.

313

"Yes, and it cost me dearly," my father grumbled. Dad had bailed out Edo from lock-up on the night of the accident. He paid for a pricey lawyer to keep his brother out of the pen. Later, Dad had to deal with the auto insurance company raising his insurance rates as a result of his brother's offense. "Edo was lucky to stay out of jail," he added. "By pleading guilty, he lost his licence only for a year."

I didn't say a word. I felt thankful that Edo wasn't driving south with us this Christmas. We had no place to put him in Dad's Toronado, and my uncle's presence might have robbed me of my turn at the wheel.

Dad looked at Mom via his rearview mirror. "Did you give the keys to the Brissons?"

Mr. and Mrs. Brisson were our neighbours. Eleven years earlier, during our second trip to Florida, our home heating system had given out. The water pipes froze and broke in many places. Our basement accumulated water higher than our ankles by the time we got home. We had to vacate our house for several days until the water was pumped out and furnace repaired. It took weeks more for the plumbers and carpenters to fix the house's busted plumbing and water-damaged walls and floors.

Since then, Mom enlisted the Brissons to check on our house while we were away on vacation. Though Mom and Dad disliked having strangers, even friendly neighbours, come into our home while we were away, the risk of another malfunctioning furnace made it a necessity. Mom replied, "Don't worry, Jani. I took the keys over to them yesterday."

"Good," he said.

* * *

Talking and Feeding

We crossed the three-kilometer-long Champlain Bridge over the St. Lawrence River then turned south on Quebec Autoroute 15 toward the U.S. border. The snow was still falling steadily, and the river was pitch-black. Past the bridge, work crews had plowed the highway partially. In places, the only exposed pavement was two tire tracks in the right lane. There were only a few cars on the road, and most of them drove fifteen km/h below the speed limit.

Dad followed a faster car in the passing lane. "It's a good thing most Quebecers know how to drive in bad weather," he said.

"And winter tires help too," I offered.

"Yes, son," Dad added. "Without good snow tires in Canada, you might as well be driving on a skating rink."

When Dad passed a slower car, he explained. "You can't be shy when you pull out into a snowy lane. You need to keep your foot steady on the gas and move the car firmly into the passing lane; otherwise, the snow there can push you back into the right lane." He demonstrated as he switched lanes, and then continued. "You can't pass too fast; otherwise, you'll risk getting out of control and hitting the other guy. Also, it's good to follow somebody else's tracks into and out of the passing lane so that the car's wheels don't have to work so hard in the snow."

Because I was a new driver, Dad showed me a neat trick for driving in the white stuff. He oscillated the steering wheel back and forth gently but rapidly. "If you jiggle the wheel slightly, like this, with your right hand near the top of the wheel, and your other hand lightly on the side, you'll keep better control of the car when there is snow on the road." His voice stayed as steady as his driving. "If you hold the wheel too tight, then you risk overcorrecting when you lose your track. You can then wind up in the ditch."

As we headed toward the U.S. border, Dad explained how to pump the car's brakes to stop safely in slippery conditions (no ABS yet in 1970s cars). "If you slam the brakes, your wheels will lock, and you'll skid out of control." Dad demonstrated the pumping technique. "You see how that works. You get better traction this way because your wheels keep turning."

I listened to my father and watched his motions. I was glad he was driving in these snowy conditions. He had never had an accident, had never gotten stuck in the snow, and had never slid off the road.

Only once did Dad have a car mishap. He had left his Olds 98 running by the side of a Montreal street on a cold, early December evening. It was when he crossed the street to drop letters into the postbox. He was gone only a minute, yet a stranger jumped into his car and stole it right from in front of him. Dad wondered if we would make it to Florida that winter.

After a week of searching, the police found his vehicle. The thieves had abandoned it and put it on blocks in a Montreal back alley. Dad had his car back from the dealer within two more weeks, complete with a new radio, new tires, and fresh upholstery. He offered, "Thank goodness I have good auto insurance. We can now go to Florida on schedule."

We continued to drive south. The only light came from the auras of car headlamps and the occasional rural road streetlamp off the highway. As we neared the Canada-USA border, the crusty snow-covered farmland of the St. Lawrence River Valley turned to thick forests. It was nearly six o'clock when we arrived at Champlain, NY, the start of I-87 South, which would take us to New York City. We were among a handful of cars waiting in line.

"Good that we left early," Dad reminded us.

We had been through the U.S. border many times before. The rest of us knew to stay quiet while Dad did the talking with the border official.

The U.S. officer wore a big parka and was leaning out of his border cabana. He and Dad exchanged smileless hellos as my father handed the man our Canadian passports. The officer examined the papers and looked at our pictures. He looked at my father, "I see you and your wife were born in Czechoslovakia. How long have you been living in Canada?"

"We immigrated in 1949 and became citizens five years later," Dad responded. "And our two sons were born here." He motioned to us in the car.

The officer nodded. He asked a series of questions about the purpose of our trip, how long we would be in the U.S., and if there was anything we had to declare. It was the same to-do whenever we crossed into the USA.

To the guard's prescribed laundry list, my father gave his preconceived answers. "We are going to Florida for two weeks for the holidays," . . . "I'm bringing a carton of Canadian cigarettes and a couple of pouches of tobacco for my personal use," . . . "We have no alcohol with us; it's cheaper in your country." He said the last comment with a bit of a grin, adding, "We have nothing we'll leave in the U.S."

Except for our money, I figured he was thinking.

The officer's face remained expressionless. Before their short, scripted salsa ended, the bundled-up official looked at each of us through the car's open front and frosty rear windows. We were lucky that he didn't ask us to open our bulging trunk. He handed Dad our papers and said in an upbeat tone, "Welcome to the USA. Have a good trip."

Dad put our car in gear, and we were on our way. As we departed our home and native land, I sat straight and felt excited about having crossed the frontier without a hitch. I was again happy that we lived in Canada rather than behind the Iron Curtain. Crossing into the U.S. was a lot easier to do than getting into Czechoslovakia.

I smiled inside. *Look out U.S. of A.; the Simkovitses are here.*

America was less than an hour's drive from downtown Montreal, but it felt like another world. Dad accelerated down the interstate. "See how the highways here are wider, better plowed, and have less cracking and buckling than our roads in Quebec. In our *la belle province,* we don't have the kind of money that the U.S. spends on its interstates. And, like in France, the Quebec unions are so powerful that they close down the construction industry for two weeks in the summer—in the middle of their prime season—so that the crews can take a vacation."

I jumped in. "And there are a lot more billboards here too."

Marlboro cowboys, Camel humps, and Captain Morgan pirates showed up along the highway. Those giant posters allowed me to daydream about things other than what was in my sci-fi books.

I opened a map of New York State not only to keep myself occupied but also to help Dad if he asked for directions or distances. "Just a little more than 30 hours of driving left," I said with a smirk.

"Yah! We're almost there," came from the back. Steve said that as he looked out from his sardine can of a back seat at the lightly falling snow.

A moment later, the snowfall subsided unexpectedly. "Funny how it stops snowing south of the border," I said. "I bet that's how the Americans decided where the border should be when they defeated the British in the American Revolution."

Steve chimed in again. "Had the rebels held onto Montreal when they raided and occupied it early in the revolution, and then made it to Quebec City, then Canada wouldn't exist. I don't think the British would have retreated to Chicoutimi."

I said nothing. Chicoutimi was even more like the North Pole than our Montreal. Though I rarely agreed with my brother, this time, I did.

Morning light formed toward the east over Lake Champlain. Dad looked to his left. "It will soon be daytime." I was the only one who heard him because Mom and Steve had fallen asleep. Content to provide Dad company, I kept myself awake while he drove.

Dad powered down the highway at a steady 75 mph (120 km/h) as the dawn light grew. He grabbed his pipe and tobacco pouch and handed it to me. "Please clean and fill this for me, son?"

My chest swelled as I followed his instructions of scraping the bowl with a pipe tool he carried in his cardigan pocket. "Just pour the burnt tobacco into the *arsh*-tray," he quipped with a grin. "Then blow into the mouthpiece to make sure nothing is stuck in there."

After cleaning and blowing, I opened Dad's leather tobacco pouch and placed a few pinches of the moist brown fibers into the bowl.

"Don't pack it too tightly; otherwise, I'll have to suck too hard," he said with a wink. He handed me his gold-plated Dunhill lighter from his vest pocket. "Here, son, can you light it for me?"

It felt good to be Dad's assistant. He couldn't light his pipe without taking both hands off the steering wheel. He might light up while guiding the wheel with one knee. This morning's snowy road conditions were not the time to perform such a trick.

I struck Dad's Dunhill and placed the flame over the pipe bowl as I had watched my father do many times before. Thick fumes filled my mouth and throat as I inhaled the growing red glow of the tobacco. I let out a few coughs but kept them quiet. I didn't want to disturb Mom or Steve. The only consolation to my gagging was the sweet scent of the tobacco smoke—much better than my father's putrid cigarettes that smelled like something rotten burning on a stick.

Dad cracked open his window to let out the thickening smoke. He took the pipe from me. He was half smiling and half-serious as he said, "You know, if I ever catch you smoking, I'll punch your nose."

I had heard his line before. "Yes, Dad," I responded shyly.

Dad and I talked in low tones, yet he did more of the talking while I did more listening. Mom and Steve continued to sleep.

"It was crazy busy in the company before the holidays," he started. "Every customer needed their holiday orders out before Christmas. We had to hire extra people off the street, and that resulted in big headaches."

He took a puff from his pipe. "I had to fire the troublemakers, which made things even crazier in the factory. Luckily, we managed to get almost everything out in time."

He took a couple more puffs. "The bloody union tried to get into the company again, but I showed them." He grinned. "Some of the people we hired turned out to be union organizers. They walked around the plant during lunchtime to talk to the employees about joining their union."

"How did you find out?" I asked.

"Some of my long-time employees came to tell me. And can you believe that it was the frigging French pipefitters union? Those people have nothing to do with the electronic goods we produce."

"So, what happened?"

Dad explained. "The union reps try to sign up as many of the company's employees they could, and then they'd take a vote in an open meeting of everyone." He tapped his pipe-holding hand on the steering wheel. "If more than 50% of the people voted for the union, then the union would become the middleman between the employees and me."

His face turned serious, and his voice rose. "Once those people get their hooks into you, you can't get rid of them. You'll then need 100% of the employees voting against them to get them out."

He shook the pipe in the air. "Some radical bastard even sent me a threatening letter saying there would be sabotage in the plant if I didn't give in to their demands." His voice was terse. "We never figured out who that was, and I couldn't tie the letter directly to the union. Otherwise, I could have put the bum in jail."

While Dad continued to suck on his pipe, I thought about the French vs. English altercations I had experienced during my one year in public junior high.

Across the divide of my school cafeteria came a French-accented call, "Hey, *youse H'inglish* bloke!"

A belligerent response bellowed from a kid on my side. "Yah, *ya* French frog!"

My 1000-student high school in Montreal's West Island was attended equally by English and French students. French kids took their classes mostly in their language, except for mandatory English language courses. English kids learned in their language, except for the required studies of oral and written French.

Though we all were Catholic, the two cultures were segregated and never commingled in the concrete behemoth of our high school building that housed five grades. During school hours, English and French kids saw each other only during staggered lunch periods.

French kids sat on one side of the school cafeteria while the English kids sat on the other. A serving area separated the two language blocs, each group having its separate food lines. The two factions could see each other across the way, but it was unusual for anyone to engage across the divide.

One day, a student from my English side yelled to the other side. "Hey, go home to frigging France, you dumb *Frenchie*." A French kid replied tersely, "Go back to your *H'ingland*, you *stupeed* bloke."

I knew this refrain well. On Canada Day the previous summer, my brother and I had gotten into a firecracker war with a French kid living across our avenue. There was no real risk, for brick banisters protected us as we huddled on our respective front landings. We also couldn't throw those crackers far enough to do any harm.

In our euphoria, our kid neighbour, along with my brother and I, shouted *H'inglish* and *Frenchie* phrases at each other as we chucked firecrackers across our street. Though we laughed, it felt as if we were reliving the French-English wars of two hundred years earlier, that animosity seeming infused into our Canadian tap water. The fun ended when the police arrived to shut down our firecracker throwing.

Dad didn't punish us for our youthful disturbance. The inner kid in him had been a part of the action just ten minutes before the cop arrived. Our father did apologize to the policeman for his "children's recklessness" and took the rest of our crackers away.

At our school cafeteria, teacher monitors were on duty at the French-English boundary. They would stop any physical engagements or retaliation, though the verbal ones got through.

During the year that I spent at that school, I had heard about some English versus French student skirmishes. They had taken place outside the building after class. It was mostly a war of words about the relative intelligence levels of our differing cultures, plus perhaps bloodless pushing and shoving.

Two hundred years had passed since the Treaty of Paris brought New France under Great Britain's control after the Battle of Quebec. The Anglo-Franco animosity was still alive and brewing slowly but steadily into a Quebec French separatist movement. Through the 1960s and into the early 1970s—through my elementary and high school years—we had seen the rise of the FLQ (*Front de Libération du Québec*).

Though our *allophone* (of ethnicity that was neither English nor French) family was as Catholic as the French, it made little difference. Many times, Dad came home from his factory with the words "those bloody separatists" blaring from his lips. He told us, "I made a mistake in hiring too many French labourers during our busiest times in the factory." His voice grew loud. "Most of those bums act as if I owed them a job." He was almost spitting. "I hate them!"

I had prayed to God that my dad would have no further trouble with the French people working at his company. I couldn't understand why we Catholics couldn't get along.

Dad paused for another puff of his pipe as he looked down the interstate. I was glad he had sent my brother and me to boarding school, not only to buffer us from the growing English-French altercations in our province but also to distance us from his and Mom's fighting at home.

I glanced at him and saw his grin come back. "But I showed those union bosses this time when they tried to unionize us," he repeated.

"How so, Dad?"

His grin widened. "I took some of my long-time, loyal employees off hourly wages and put them on a weekly salary. This way, when the union rep came to count the employee punch cards—you know, the cards that hang on the wall in the factory lobby entrance."

"Yes! I remember," I said.

"The rep counted those cards against the names of the people who had signed the union membership. At some point, the union thought they had 50% of the employees favouring unionization. But when they took the actual vote in a meeting, they got only a third of the employees voting for the union."

Dad took a long breath and smiled. "Now, they have to go away and leave Montreal Phono alone for at least a year, or they might never come back." He let out a hopeful sigh. "I have to be smarter than them and stick with hiring only recent immigrants."

His voice rose once more. "It doesn't matter to me what their religion is or where they come from, as long as they aren't Quebec French!" His voice stayed edgy. "Immigrants know better how to work, and they don't cause trouble. The fucking union bosses don't care about the employees but only about supporting their bloody union."

Smoke billowed from my father's mouth and maybe his ears too. "And the troublemakers I fired are going to take me to the labour court, with the union paying their way." He was trying to control his tone, yet his anger came through. "But I would rather have that, and pay a fine, than have those bastards tell me how to run my business."

Though Dad's biases and crudeness were getting under my skin, his shrewdness impressed me. He was one for plotting with his business advisors and colleagues over drinks at the Tokay or Troika. He'd also have visions in his dreams about how to turn a tough business situation to his favour.

How could those union people think they could get away with causing trouble for my dad and his company?!

Years later, as an adult, I reconsidered my views. My father had been damn lucky to have gotten away with his blatantly unethical business trickeries. The government could have prosecuted him for illegal interference in unionizing activities.

Dad continued to puff his pipe as he glanced at me. "How's your last year at boarding school going? What subject do you like and who are your best friends?"

I responded, "School's good; I got top marks again in math, physics, chemistry, and geography, as well as great SAT math scores—I'm in the top percentile across North America." Before he could ask about my weaker subjects of English, French, and history, I named a few of my classmates he might recognize.

"You know," Dad interrupted, "languages have been essential in my life. My father put me into a private school in Košice for my high school years, as I did with you and Stevie here in Canada. Though it was a Hungarian school, I also learned to speak Slovak. Without knowing Slovak, which is distantly related to Russian, I could have been killed as a spy by the Soviets when I defected from the German air force in '43."

He continued. "Later, in a POW camp near Odessa, I learned Ukrainian and Russian. When I came to Canada, I also had to learn English to be able to start my business."

He put his right hand gently on my left arm. "You are fortunate that here in Canada, you only need English and French. Please do your best to be good in those two languages."

He pointed my way. "You and your brother were fortunate that I was able to send you to France last summer to learn good *française* French, not the patois that the farmers speak. So please don't lose what you have learned."

"Yes, Dad; I'm trying."

I looked out at the oncoming traffic. Languages didn't come to me as quickly as they did to my father. Even high school English was a struggle, considering I had hardly spoken that language when I entered elementary school.

I was hoping to attend college outside of Quebec. Most of my high school chums were leaving the province, heading to Ontario, Nova Scotia, or the U.S. after graduating. Later in life, I'd become disappointed in myself for not having maintained my language abilities. Still, as a young adult, I looked forward to living where a second language would be less important.

My father took a few more puffs of his pipe, opened his window a tad more, and asked me to turn up the car's heater a bit. He then offered, "I hope you stay in touch with your good high school friends after your graduation. It's just as important *who* you know as *what* you know."

He raised his pipe. "I knew Mr. Dumouchel, the head buyer at RCA, from the consumer electronics shows I attended in the early 1950s. If I hadn't known him, I might not be working for myself today."

He took a long breath. "In 1953, I showed up at RCA looking for a job." Dad pointed his pipe toward the backseat. "It was the year your brother was born."

He lowered his hand that held his pipe and tapped my thigh with the bottom of that hand. "Doumie [what close friends called him] saw me there and brought me to his office. Instead of giving me a job at RCA, he gave me a purchase order. He helped me start Montreal Phono and to make products for RCA."

Dad lifted the pipe and took another drag. "Doumie liked my character, and I looked up to him as a second father." He tapped his hand on my arm. "That's how our Montreal Phono got started, you know."

"Yes, I know," I said quietly.

I stared down the highway at cars that were turning off their headlights in the waking morn. I wondered whether I could become a well-respected entrepreneur as my father had become, but I didn't share my concerns with him. I hoped he thought I could.

Dad asked me to switch on the radio. "Find a station with Christmas music, but keep it at a low volume so Mom and Steve can still sleep."

I complied. Nat King Cole sang a rendition of a Christmas song. The melody seemed in sync with the car's windshield wipers going back and forth. The wipers pushed away leftover precipitation and road spray to the beat of:

> *Chestnuts roasting over an open fire . . . swish swish*
> *Jack Frost nipping at your nose . . . swish swish*

I watched the luckier cars, like ours, heading to a warmer south, and the less fortunate ones heading toward a colder north. I anticipated the outside air becoming warmer each time we stopped for gas. While Dad saw an open road and no cop cars in either direction, I watched the world go by at 75 or even 80 mph.

* * *

The sky remained cloudy but was brightening. Mom shouted from her backseat cavern, "Anybody hungry?" She leaned forward and showed a motherly smile. "I made lots of good things for us."

Dad wanted us to waste little time and expense in reaching Florida. Stopping for meals wasn't an option, nor was it a problem when Mom was in charge of food.

She rummaged through her shopping bags, poking her hands into sacks around her and my brother. One container or plastic-wrapped package at a time, she unwrapped the food she had spent hours preparing the previous days. She passed things around to the rest of us and took the last for herself.

For breakfast, Mom's car kitchen included shelled hardboiled eggs with fresh cut deli rye bread. Small glass jars of juice helped to wash down her meal. Later, for dinner, she had prepared a stack of buttered (mayonnaise and mustard were only for Americans!) salami and ham sandwiches on rye bread.

Accompanying the sandwiches was a big slice of green pepper, or a sour pickle, or long carrots she had peeled and cut. In the mix was a meter-long piece of thin, spicy, Debrecen kielbasa Dad had bought from a Hungarian butcher in the city.

For supper, she had prepared a big container of battered fried chicken (like Quebec's *Poulet Frit Kentucky*) that we dug into fervently—along with more carrots or celery as our vegetable. She also brought fried potato pancakes—a family favourite; they were delicious cold anytime.

There was a big container of thick, breaded ground pork, veal, and beef burgers called *fa-sirt* (meaning "the tree wept" in my parents' language). That *fa-sirt* was for our second day's dinner. Not even my parents knew how Hungarians came up with that strange word.

Each of us could put down two or three of those yummy *fa-sirts* in one meal. We never had "food just enough for one tooth," a mocking expression Mom employed for finger sandwiches and canapés.

Nothing could compare to Mom's fare, and it was a good thing that Steve and I had grown out of our childhood chubbiness through active sports programs and boring cafeteria meals at our private high school.

Car meals entailed a lot of reaching over and across our seats for Mom's delicacies. She held onto her one cutting knife. Arms extended every which way; it was amazing that no collisions happened inside our cramped car. We never had a major spill—I would have remembered a loud *"Hesus Maria"* from Dad or a piercing *"Isten orizz"* from Mom.

Dad announced, "Be sure you use a napkin. I don't want greasy food stains inside my new car."

"Yes, Dad," Steve and I responded in unison.

Mom had brought a bag of soft drinks. She gave out a hearty laugh when she said, "I have *Tsotsa-Tsola,"* pronouncing Coca-Cola in Hungarian.

I asked for a Coke, and my brother requested a 7-Up. It was just that way between us. No matter what one of us wanted, the other wanted something different.

Dad said, "Hand me some *wishy* water." That was his name for the French *L'eau de Vichy.* Mom handed him a bottle. He swigged big gulps as he drove.

For dessert, Mom passed out our favourite candy bars, along with the dense chocolate brownies she had baked. She enjoyed baking but could never get those brownies right. Though they shrank to half their thickness as they cooled in the pan, I enjoyed their chewiness. They stuck to the top of my mouth and took ten minutes of tongue work to get off my teeth and gums.

Dad avoided sweets, saying, "You guys can afford that stuff better than me." Instead, he had me refill and re-lite his pipe for him.

In the end, my brother and I held onto our stomachs and begged, "It's enough, Mom; I had enough." Dad said, *"Elég Nusi, jól lactam.* [Enough Anna, I lived well.]"

My mother repackaged our leftovers and repacked them into their rightful shopping bags. Her feeding job done, she resettled into her backseat nook and looked at the world outside her window—until our next car meal.

Dad downed the last bite of the kielbasa he had had for breakfast. He wiped his greasy mouth and fingers on a napkin, and then he handed it back to Mom for later disposal. He took a final swig from his Vichy bottle and passed it back to her. He offered, "Remember when it used to take us up to 34 hours and nearly three days to get to Florida when we first drove down there twelve years ago?" His mood was cheery. "It's about four hours less driving now.

And when the Interstate is complete in a few more years, it will be less again by at least four more hours."

It had been over fifteen years since the start of the Eisenhower Interstate Highway system. Most East Coast sections were now complete. Mom had less to worry about, for there were fewer crowded primary roads for Dad to negotiate through N.Y. State Adirondacks and in the American Southeast.

"I can't wait until they finish the highway," Mom shouted. "The way you and Meyer drive on busy two-lane roads, I could get a heart attack back here."

Ned was a road warrior. He had studied maps to know which turns to take on the main roads and which exits to take off the interstates. Ned knew how fast one could drive over the speed limit in each state, day or night, without getting pulled over by a cop. He had warned Dad, "Be careful not to drive more than 10 kilometers (or 5 miles) per hour above the limit in South Carolina and Georgia. Those poorer states need money and have speed traps all over. The cops there have quotas and will catch you if they can."

My father was good at spotting and avoiding the traps that caught unsuspecting travellers. A cop with a Smokey-the-Bear hat once stopped him in Georgia. Dad had been pushing past the speed limit during a pelting rainstorm. The officer gave him an earful about driving fast in the dark on a rainy night and windswept road.

Dad did his usual, "Gosh, I'm sorry, sir," and "Yes, thank you, officer," and got off with a warning. After we had gotten back on the road, Dad said, "I guess these smokeys have nothing better to do than stop people like us. We wasted twenty minutes with that guy."

Ned taught Dad driving tricks to apply on busy, two-way roads—where drivers slowed to below the speed limit as long caravans of cars followed a local yokel Sunday driver or an old fogey, fuddy-duddy, slowpoke. To complement my father's car passing on straight roads, where one could see far ahead, Ned told him to watch a half-dozen cars ahead as we approached long bends.

Ned explained, "Johnny, if you see a car, up way ahead, jumping out to pass on the far side of the bend, it means that no one is coming the other way.

You can follow that passer even though you can't see around the curve." He pointed down the road. "Then, when you see that car jump back into our southbound lane, you must come back into that lane as soon as you can, for you know a car is coming the other way."

Meyer was a master at this maneuver. He floored the car's accelerator as he followed a passer up ahead—his five mph rule flying out of the window during these "passing" moments. Determination in his eyes, Ned might leave only a few seconds to spare before an oncoming car or truck zoomed past us in the opposite direction—luckily, they slowed down a little when they saw Ned coming. He drove like a cowboy riding a mighty metal steed, and it gave me a rush as I sat next to him. I watched with my eyes open wide as we overtook two, three, or more cars, or a big tractor-trailer, at one time.

I relished Dad making those moves too; my heart pounded as he pulled out of traffic into the oncoming lane. *"Yes! Okay!"* raced through my mind as we left another fogey driver behind.

To Dad's passing, Mom pleaded in Hungarian, *"Isten orizz, Jani,* please don't drive so fast. Don't be crazy like that Meyer fool."

Dad shouted, "Anne, I know what I'm doing. I don't want to get stuck behind these old ladies."

My brother and I said nothing. Steve kept his nose in a *Popular Science* magazine. I concentrated on the cars ahead as if the force of my mind could help Dad avoid any potential disaster. I wished Mom wouldn't bother him when he was working so hard. I could see the satisfaction on his face as he won an edge over the slow drivers who followed a snaking row of snail-pace vehicles that meandered south.

I worked to subdue Mom's fears about Dad's driving by becoming his co-pilot. Ned had taught me to read road maps. I located parallel secondary roads that allowed us to bypass traffic on the main routes. Speeding down a nearly deserted byway I had come across on a Carolinas map, Dad said, "Good boy, Harvy! Find another shortcut like that one!" My backseat brother could never one-up my front seat navigation.

Mom settled into her seat after our morning breakfast. She placed her purse on her lap and reached in to retrieve a couple of recent, hand-written letters from her family overseas. With Dad well satisfied by Mom's meal, it was a good time to tell him the latest goings-on from their homeland.

Dad listened as she read and summarized family happenings in their native tongues. She switched from Hungarian to Slovak when she didn't want my brother and me to understand.

A letter from Aunt Irén talked about how difficult it was to buy western goods in Czechoslovakia. Mom said, "Without having dollars or German marks, they have a hard time getting things like radios, TVs, watches, even good tobacco. The government doesn't bring enough of those things in from Russia, and Russian products are like 'made in Japan' [a reference to their poor quality]. The only way to get even a decent toaster or blender is with hard currency on the black market or in Tuzex stores."

"Yah!" Dad said with a hint of annoyance. "The communist government is hungry for western currency. They hope that people like us here send dollars or Tuzex back to our relatives over there to spend at those stores."

Mom continued. "Irén is asking if Buš can come to Canada to stay with us for a few months next year. He wants to make some dollars by painting portraits for our friends and us."

There was no answer from Dad. I said nothing, hoping that their conversation would stay civil. Steve stayed quiet too.

My mother took a breath into the frozen silence, offered a few words in Slovak, and then added, *"Mit gondolsz, Jani?* [What do you think, Johnny?]"

He glanced at her in his rearview mirror. "Didn't Irén just finish being here for six months this past year?"

She quickly responded, "That was only for a visit. Buš wants to work!" She took another breath. "They could use the money. One Canadian dollar to them for food and clothes is like ten dollars to us here."

"So, do I have to find customers for him?" my father asked with a hint of displeasure.

"Irén says that Buš will make a free portrait of you and me first, to hang in your Montreal Phono office. All you need to do is let your friends see it when they come to do business with you. You can then ask them if they wanted one for themselves. Buš only wants 100 dollars Canadian for each, and he'll do one for us for free."

Dad's eyebrows and mouth tightened; his eyes shifted back and forth. After a moment, he responded, "Maybe he should do one for each of us."

I wonder if my father was signaling that he wanted only a portrait of himself in his private business domain, or that Mom should extort a second one for free for herself from her brother-in-law. He said, *"Beszéljünk inkább erről később.* [We can talk more about this later.]" He kept his eyes focused on the road and cars ahead.

Mom said nothing more for now about her brother-in-law's pending visit, but she was sure to bring it up again. She worked hard for her family. If she had to, she would pay Buš herself for the second portrait, and allow Dad to obtain the free one for his referral services.

I was relieved that no harsh words had emanated from this car conversation.

Portrait of Dad, painted by Max Bus. The image came from a black and white 1960s photograph.
Dad liked the portrait so much that he gave Buš a crisp Canadian $100 bill for it.
Dad then had Buš paint another one from a photograph of his father (right).

We were a couple of hours south of the Canadian border. The snowfall had subsided. The morning sky was cloudy but brightening each passing U.S. mile. The roads were dry through the rugged and frigid New York Adirondacks.

The pine trees along the highway were laden with white this Christmas Day. Walls of ice hung down sheer cliffs where waterfalls flowed in the other seasons of the year. The snow had been plowed off the highway and sat in high banks along the edge.

Dad was pushing 80 mph on the interstate. I was reminded of his speed every so often because he had set the car's speed control beeper to 81. It buzzed almost every time we went downhill, interrupting my reverie in the snowy, tree-filled mountains.

I turned around and said to my brother, "How about we count license plates?" It was a game we played to see how many different state and provincial plates we could identify on passing cars. A point was given to the first to spot a different state plate.

"There's New Your State," Steve said. He looked out the side window at a car that whipped past us, starting the game off to his advantage. "And we have Quebec on our car," he added with an annoying smirk. "I have two points."

Our game lasted for our entire trip, or for as long as my brother and I stayed interested. We had to remain vigilant for different plates on cars both on the road and at gas station stops.

Dad sometimes helped me. With a casual nod or a pointed finger, he indicated a different car plate before my brother spotted it. "There's Vermont on that truck up ahead," I chimed with a grin. "A point for me."

My brother said nothing as he looked forward and back out his side window, his eyes alert.

The mountains, rolling hills, and snow-covered forests soon gave way to the flatter lands and small towns of the Hudson River Valley. South of Albany, we turned off the interstate and into a gas station. The time was nine o'clock.

As she always did at our first stop, Mom said, "Okay, everybody; go to the bathroom and don't touch anything. Put toilet paper down on the seat, and make sure you wash your hands. These places are always dirty."

Mom was a bit of a clean freak, but we abided by her hygiene and housekeeping rules; otherwise, she might get annoyed. Though she was a caring mother, her *Isten orizz* could rupture an eardrum if she became riled.

My father pointed to the gas station's price sign. "Gas is so much cheaper here, even though our Canadian gallon is 15% bigger. Look! It's less than 40 cents U.S. for a gallon of high-test." He looked at me, his eyes wide. "Harvy, it's time to get out your paper and pencil."

To pass the time on our voyage, Dad asked me to compute our gas mileage and to keep tabs on our gasoline costs. Ned had instructed Dad to fill the car's tank the night before we left Montreal; this way, we would know how many gallons we had utilized when we next filled-up.

I liked numbers as much as Dad, and I worked on calculating our mileage and fuel costs along with him. I employed a pad and pencil while he figured in his head. We competed to see which of us could arrive at the answer first. Most often, he won our arithmetic duels.

When I was younger, Dad liked to tease me with silly math riddles to pass the time on long drives: He once asked, "If you have two coins that added to 55 cents. If one is not a nickel, then what are the two coins?"

Seeing a confused look on my kid's face, he offered with a chuckle, "Son, if one is not a nickel, the other one is."

My father had hard puzzlers too, and they kept us occupied awhile. At some point, his tone turned serious as he continued to speed down the highway. "I hope you apply to MIT and pursue electrical engineering. I got my Masters in electronics when I was 19 years old, you know."

"Yes, Dad, I'll apply there, but it's a hard place to get accepted. Most of my school friends who are going into engineering will be applying to Queens in Kingston."

Queens University was where my brother was studying electrical engineering. Many of my English-speaking Quebec friends were going there to get away from the growing separatist mood in Quebec.

"So apply to both places, and we'll see what happens," he suggested.

"Okay, Dad."

I applied and got into MIT that spring. Dad encouraged, "Son, MIT's the best engineering school in the world. You'll make new friends there."

Because he wanted me to go there, and because my high school teachers and classmates congratulated me on my accomplishment, I couldn't back out.

Five years later, after I graduated MIT with my bachelor's degree, and I was in the midst of my master's degree program, Mom told me that Dad wasn't a recipient of an electrical engineer master's. "He was just a Master Electrician," she said.

I was surprised. But by that time, I understood my father's tendency to exaggerate to his friends, colleagues, and associates. It took me a lot longer to understand why he did the same with me.

* * *

Recollections and Attractions

The car's clock was nearing noon as we passed through Newark and Jersey City along the New Jersey Turnpike. The stench and smoke of industrial plants along the highway reminded me of my father's stinky cigarettes. In the distance, toward the east, we could see the tops of New York City's skyscrapers.

We had spent a night in the Big Apple a couple of times during previous migrations south. In addition to seeing a Broadway show and going to the top of the Empire State Building, Mom and Dad liked to shop for bargain wallets, purses, and key chains from street vendors in the city's Garment District. Dad found inexpensive souvenirs for his key people at Montreal Phono; Mom found the same for her relatives.

Walking down one street, we spied unkempt black men wheeling racks of clothing. Under her breath, my mother said something to my father about *piszkos fekete* (dirty blacks) and "*Boldog vagyok nincs azokat az embereket Kanadában* [I'm happy we don't have such people in Canada]." She had similar sentiments about her home country's *cigányok* (gypsies).

I cringed at my mother's comments and wondered why she felt that way about people different from us. Wanting to avoid any unpleasant conversations, I neither asked nor said anything about it, and neither did my brother.

On this vacation trip south, NYC held no allure for our Florida-bound Simkovits clan. No one wanted to stop there again to look at the city from the top of tall buildings, or to eat deli chopped liver sandwiches or NY cheesecake. "New York City is too crowded and dirty," Dad said. "It's dangerous for people with Canadian license plates."

I didn't know if he knew that for sure, but he could be right. In Montreal, we never saw as many metal grates, shutters, and padlocks protecting store windows and doorways, or so many parked cars with cracked windows, banged-up bodies, or bald tires. NYC was now an unwanted diversion. Instead, after we passed Newark airport, Mom took us through another round of her backseat kitchen goodies.

After our car lunch, Dad stopped again for gas and bought a Mid-Atlantic States map. Mom threw out the trash, and we made another bathroom run. After eleven years of the same, we had the routine down pat.

Steve took over the driving, and Dad took my front seat position. I relocated to my brother's spot in the backseat, ready for a well-earned nap. My driving-assistant job was over for the next eight hours. I put my head on a car pillow and looked outside until my eyes would shut. I glanced at the billboards we passed and the occasional license plates, but Steve's and my game was fading down the roadway behind us.

I watched the patchy snow-covered farmer's fields pass; their furrows seemed to run alongside our car. My mother's backseat cuisine had satiated me. I gazed out at the world as it went by, white line after white line, car after car, billboard after billboard, mile after mile. I wondered how much warmer it would be and which state we'd be in when I woke.

The sky was getting dark when I opened my eyes again. From the highway markers, I could tell we were in Virginia. I rubbed my eyes and stretched my arms and legs as much as I could in the cramped back seat. "Did I sleep through Delaware, Maryland, and DC?" I asked.

My brother said, "I'm at thirteen different license plates, Harvy; you better get cracking!"

I had seven license-plate points when I fell asleep, and we rarely saw more than twenty-five different state and provincial plates for our whole trip. I acquiesced, "I guess you are going to win this one, Steve."

I was glad DC was behind us. As with New York City, Washington had become a "been there, done that" experience for our family. Dad had taken us there for a few days on an earlier trip to Florida, in 1964, after Steve and I entered our double-digit years.

At that time, Dad's stepmother had been visiting us in Montreal for six months. Since it was the first time Dad had been with her since he escaped from Czechoslovakia in 1949, he wanted to *megmutatni Amerika* (show America) to the woman who raised him and his half-brother.

In Washington, we went on a bus excursion that included the Arlington Cemetery and the John F. Kennedy Memorial, among other sites. I found visiting dead people a bore, as much as my Canadian history classes. Because it was the year after JFK's assassination, both of my parents wanted to visit the former President's final resting spot.

On the day JFK had been killed, kids in Montreal had been let out of school early. Dad, too, had come home from work early—a rarity for him. We stayed glued to Walter Cronkite. (U.S. stations broadcasted into Canada.) Over again, the news anchor took us through what was known about the President's assassination earlier that day and his subsequent death in a Dallas hospital. My teary father couldn't stop saying, "Gosh! It's unbelievable." My mother cried as she repeated, "He was so young; his children are just babies."

The snowy weather of our DC stay, combined with stone buildings and monuments of the city, reminded me of the stone-cold expression of my *nagymama* (grandmother). A tall, heavy-set, rectangular-faced, Slavic woman, she kept her lips tightly pressed together most of the time. Only my father could separate those tight chops by making her smile or laugh.

Nagymama (left) and my mother are standing by the JFK Memorial, Arlington Cemetery. Late December 1964, an unusually snowy day in DC

337

Nagymama spoke only a few words of English. Most days, while staying at our home, she sat in the same living room chair. From there, she watched TV, though she didn't understand a word of what she heard. She mended her clothes and wrote letters or postcards to her siblings back in Czechoslovakia.

When she wasn't sitting, she hovered around my mother while she cooked and cleaned the house. I rarely approached the old woman unless Mom asked, "Go and nicely call your *nagymama* for dinner."

"*Létszives gyere enni, Nagymama* [Please come eat, Grandma]," I said. I led her into the kitchen like a dog leading its master.

More than once, I saw a pained look on my mother's face for not knowing how to get a kind word from her mother-in-law. Dad, too, had his frustration with his stepmother. She continually told him in Hungarian, "Your brother doesn't have what you have here in Canada. The older should help the younger." Dad responded, "If he immigrates to Canada, I can help him more." *Nagymama* then looked at Dad with an even more stern face, as if he had suggested ripping her baby from her arms, but she didn't say anything.

One evening at home, while I was doing my school work in front of my favourite afternoon TV show, *Nagymama* attempted to speak to me in English. She pointed to me, my homework, and then the TV. She asked, "You do school on TV?"

I giggled at her statement. I called Mom from the kitchen and told her what *Nagymama* had said in English. Mom and I chuckled as my mother explained to her mother-in-law what she had said.

Nagymama later complained to my father about how we had made fun of her. When Dad asked Mom about it afterward, my mother said, "She misunderstood us. We were not laughing at her, only at what she said."

He pressed her for more information. She raised her voice, "Why are you and she making such a big deal out of nothing? Your mother always tells me how to cook and clean, and I don't say a word."

Nagymama seemed to have held a grudge. After that incident, she spent more time in her bedroom. Her first visit to North America also became her last.

We started to see SOB billboards sprouting along the roadway. I offered, "Steve, let's forget about counting license plates and spot the SOB signs."

"Good morning, sleepyhead," Dad said. "We'll be at South of the Border around midnight. We'll stop there like we often do." He cracked open his window to take in the fresh and warmer Virginia air, and to light his pipe once more before our in-car supper.

South of the Border (written "SOB" on many billboards) was a southwestern-style resort hotel, golf course, 24-hour restaurant, and retail shopping complex on Rt. 301 (I-95 was not yet complete through the Carolinas). "They built that SOB place just for us," Dad said with a smirk and laugh. "And they even have a small chapel there if you need a fast wedding." He chuckled again as he poked at my brother.

Steve recoiled with a laugh.

One could not miss SOB. A giant, 5-story, neon Pedro (SOB's Mexican mascot) greeted visitors there. Over a hundred billboards, starting from two hundred and fifty miles in either direction, foretold of Pedro's coming.

Steve, Dad, and I vied to see who first noticed the next SOB sign during the hours leading to the place. SOB would provide a welcome respite to our long and tedious drive.

After midnight, we rolled into South Carolina's South of the Border. We exited our car without our winter coats for the first time. We went straight to Pedro's Coffee Casa.

As in previous years, the place was flush with noisy travellers and scurrying waitresses. Dad had us sit at the main counter so we wouldn't have to waste time waiting for a booth.

My tired eyes stung from the restaurant's bright lights. The din of fleeting customers and rushing servers kept me from nodding off. We ordered bowls of chicken soup, milkshakes for Steve and me, and coffees for Dad and Mom.

When he finished, Dad stood and said, "Hurry up, everyone. I'm going to pay the bill and go find a toothpick for my dessert."

Mom added, "Make sure to go to the bathroom, boys. We'll meet at the souvenir shop where we can get *tchotchkes*."

She grabbed a fistful of paper napkins and sugar packs and tucked them into her purse—as she did at every coffee shop and restaurant we stopped at during vacations. Had there been bread or rolls left from our meal, she might have wrapped them in a napkin and taken them too.

Dad said, "We're going to spend only five minutes in that SOB store."

A treasure trove of cheap souvenirs filled the SOB shop. We quickly examined the shot glasses, drinking cups, coffee mugs, and wooden back scratchers—all decorated with colourful images of Pedro or his big sombrero.

Dad bought a few things for his office staff. Mom bought items for her brother's family in Montreal. Dad allowed Steve and me to pick out one cheap item for each of us, for which he paid.

My brother and I obtained yet another back scratcher—previous ones having been broken or lost. Those long, shellacked, wooden sticks came in handy for dueling when we got into a brother-bugging mood.

Back home, our souvenirs would join similar items on our basement bar shelf, or they would become tucked away in a drawer or gifted to my Montreal uncle, aunt, and cousin. (Mom wrapped the items carefully in white tissue paper before gifting them.) A South of the Border souvenir brought a grin, hoot, and kiss from our relatives who never had the opportunity to pass through Pedro country.

As the clock in Dad's car hit 1:00 in the morning, Dad started the engine. Backing out, he glanced up and down the roadway. "We should pass through here during the daytime. We could play mini-golf, or climb Pedro's sombrero tower, or get something at his Ice Cream Fiesta."

We fervently agreed, but we never visited Pedro when the whole resort was open. Our return trip brought us back here in the middle of the night.

The moment we left SOB, we knew Florida wasn't far away.

I was next to Dad again as he drove south the rest of the night on Rt. 301, through the sleepy towns and dark villages of South Carolina and Georgia. He was careful not to drive more than five miles over the speed limit. He was not about to be stopped by a ticket-hungry cop who was short on his tourist-catching quota.

Every hour or so, we passed another one of those buggers. Their cruiser lights flashed while they stopped an overzealous driver, or their vehicle lurked in the darkness by the side of the road. If I saw any of those smokeys before Dad did, I pointed them out quickly so he could take his foot off the gas and slow to no more than the speed limit.

The night-time limit on Rt. 301 was down to 50 mph, even less in the towns and villages. Few travellers were on the road in the wee hours of this morning of Boxing Day. Dad's right hand clenched the top of the steering wheel firmly. His left forearm was on his lap; his left thumb and index finger pinched the side of the wheel. He lifted the palm of his right hand every minute or so to check the speed reading. I sat still next to him, allowing him to concentrate on his driving.

My belly was satisfied with Pedro's cooking. I watched far-off headlights take many minutes to come toward us from a distance. They then zipped by quickly and disappeared behind us as if they had never existed. After what had seemed like an eternity of head bobbing on a car pillow placed against the window, I nodded off for the night.

The sun was rising over the horizon when I woke on the morning of our second travel day. Spanish moss hung from the southern oak and cypress trees. I had tried to stay awake to help my father with map reading, pipe filling, or anything else he might need, but sleep had taken me over before Savannah.

I didn't remember Dad stopping for gas in the middle of the night. Cold outside air no longer rushed through an opening door to spur me awake. Dad was on I-95 again and doing 80.

He touched my arm. "Good afternoon, sleepyhead," he quipped. "Hope you had a good rest." He said that quietly, for Mom and Steve were still snoozing. He pointed to the oak trees that lined the highway. "Did you know that Spanish moss is neither Spanish nor moss?"

"Yes, I know, Dad," I said in a sarcastic kid voice. Years ago, Ned had told us that it was a plant. I looked for a road sign as I yawned. "Where are we? And, how much longer before I can drive?"

Dad grinned. "We're already in Florida, which means we're 'almost there.'"

I knew he was kidding. We had perhaps seven hours of driving left in the Sunshine State. I-95 was not complete along the entire Florida east coast. We had to take I-4 to Orlando and then follow the Florida Turnpike south.

"When do you think I can drive?" I asked again.

"As soon as everybody is up and we have breakfast. We'll then stop for gas, and you can take over."

My waking eyes were still tired. The sun peeking through the clouds made them sting, but the worst of the trip was behind us. I could feel the warmth of the early morning sun on my body as it slowly rose higher in the sky. It beckoned me to bask like a purring cat.

There now was more room to maneuver in our car. We had devoured most of Mom's cuisine; we had removed bags of garbage at our gas station stops; Dad had moved the handbag—that had been between him and me—to the back seat; he had miraculously stuffed our winter coats into our swollen trunk when we left SOB.

Moods lifted as everyone awoke from restless car sleep, peeled off sweaters, and put down the car's visors to block the sun's bright rays. We donned cheap plastic sunglasses that Mom had brought for our trip.

My father kept his promise. I took over the driving after another round of hardboiled eggs on rye and our next gas stop. Dad asked me to adjust the car's speedometer beeper to 75 mph (five miles over the limit) so that I stayed at or under that speed. He grumbled when I surpassed that limit one too many times; the beeping was keeping him from nodding off. I worked to keep the car's speed steady, which—considering Florida's flatness—became easier each passing mile.

Soon Dad was snoring like a bull elephant. He had driven through the entire night. He had stayed awake the whole previous day, keeping his eyes on my brother while he had taken us through the busy sections of I-95. Dad was dead tired. It felt good to know he trusted my driving enough to fall asleep.

Every hour or so, Mom leaned forward and asked, "How are you doing, son? Not too tired?" She took a breath, "Should Daddy or Stevie drive?"

I kept my attention forward, both hands on the wheel, and said, "I'm fine, Mom. I'm doing just fine."

Rumble, rumble, rumble, cha-chunk. Rumble, rumble, rumble, cha-chunk. The Florida Turnpike with its concrete road panels and expansion joints raced below our noisy winter tires. Oak and cypress trees were lush along the highway. Short palm trees stood near the exits. The only time I could see past the forest expanse was at the occasional overpass that crossed a water canal or perpendicular road. In easterly and westerly directions, dark green treetops, brownish bogs, and light blue sky were the colours of the day.

After hours of snorts and groans, his head bobbing like a bobble-head doll on his pillow resting against the window, Dad opened his eyes. It was a quarter past noon. He asked, "Okay, where are we?"

With the Florida map open on his lap, my brother chirped from the back. "We just passed Palm Beach. We have about 45 minutes before we hit our Lauderdale exit."

Dad rubbed his eyes and looked into the mirror on the back of his visor. He put his fingers through his straight-back hair to get it in place. He shook the sleep from his head and said, "How are we doing on gas, Harvy?"

"We are down to a quarter of a tank."

"That should be enough to get us there," Dad said. "Gas is more expensive on the turnpike. We'll fill up after we get to our hotel."

He turned around to look at Mom. "*Cica, van valami maradt enni?* [Kitten, do you have anything left to eat?]" Dad could be affectionate when his stomach was growling. Thank goodness his belly noises weren't as loud as his snoring.

My mother had anticipated his question. "The kids have eaten, but I saved you a couple of *fa-sirt* and some rye bread. And I still have Vichy left." She pulled out the last bottle to show him.

"Ah! Warm square-bubbles," Dad said. "I bet it tastes like piss." He didn't smile.

After eating a *fa-sirt*-on-rye, and taking a few swigs from the bottle, Dad let out a big belch. "*Yoy!* That was good piss."

We knew it was futile to fight against Dad's crudeness. If we did, he might respond, "Excuse my French," and then he'd forget he had ever apologized.

After Dad had his fill, Mom asked, "So what are the things we want to do during our days here?"

"First, I want to get more rest," Dad retorted.

My brother came in behind him. "Can we go to Miami Seaquarium again, and go fishing on the Lauderdale ocean pier next to our hotel?"

There was something about fishing that Steve enjoyed. I never liked the smells of dead fish and live worms. I preferred to hang around the pool or beach with my paperback, work on my tan to impress friends back home, play shuffleboard and paddleball, or kick around the soccer ball with Dad and Steve.

Mom leaned forward and touched Dad lightly on the shoulder. "And let's go to Black Angus Steakhouse. You and Ned like that place."

Mom (left), Dad (center) and Nagymama (right) on the beach next to the Attaché Resort Motel in Hollywood, FL. 1964

I thought of the Black Angus tender, bloody, mouth-watering plank steaks. When served, they hung over the edge of their long, flat wooden plate. I imagined its tender, juicy meat between my teeth, and could taste its succulent spices in my mouth. Those steaks became branded into our family tradition, just like Dad's summer barbeques.

Mom continued. "And maybe we can go out for New Year's Eve again. What do you think the Mosers are doing this year?"

Gillian Moser was Dad's accountant, who first convinced Dad to come to Florida over the Christmas and New Year's holidays. Every winter, the Moser family drove down to the Attaché Motel in Hollywood, a hangout for the Montreal and New York Jewish crowd.

We, too, had stayed there for a couple of years, but Dad found the place too crowded and expensive. He no longer wanted to spring for poolside happy hours or suppers for everyone. But he continued to take Mom there for New Year's Eve parties with the Mosers while Steve and I stayed in our hotel room watching New Year's Eve specials on TV.

Mom and Dad in Hollywood, FL. 1964

After our years at Attaché, Ned found a cheaper place, "Petit's Riviera" in Lauderdale-by-the-Sea. The French name had attracted Ned to the place. The owner, Mr. Petit, was a retired French Quebecer. Ned liked the idea that he could *pratiquer Français en Floride*. The local corner store even carried Montreal English and French newspapers. Every morning, before the rest of us awoke, Ned had a coffee with Mr. Petit and talked about *les nouvelles du Québec*.

Petit's Riviera held small apartments instead of hotel rooms, complete with kitchenette. Dad liked the idea that Mom could make breakfast and lunch every day during our stay, thereby saving money. To give Mom a break, we went out to supper every night to different restaurants, and to Black Angus Steakhouse at least twice during our 12-night stay.

To Mom's request about going to Black Angus, Dad responded. "We can talk about that tonight during supper. Right now, let's get there, get unpacked, and get to the pool where I can get a break from all this travelling."

Soon after we'd arrive, we put on our bathing suits and a good dose of Coppertone Oil. We'd then baked in the sun until we looked like a rare steak, a cheap souvenir of our time in Florida. We could then show everyone in cold, sun-deprived Canada what fabulous weather we had enjoyed.

Year after year, we never tired of doing the same things in Florida.

By 1:00, we exited the turnpike. Dad said, "It took us only thirty-two-and-a-half hours this year."

"I can't wait until they finish all the highways," Mom blurted.

We entered familiar town streets. Mom and Dad looked around to see what changes had occurred from the previous year. "Look at the new sandwich shop there, "Mom said. "Let's try that place for dinner one day."

Perhaps Mom didn't want to prepare all our midday meals, or maybe it was the new women's clothing store next door that interested her.

Dad pointed. "And I see a new tobacco shop there too." That store might be enough to have him take us out for a meal, as Mom suggested.

"They have milkshakes at that sandwich shop," Steve added. "Look! Double chocolate malted Oreo shakes," he read off a window poster.

"Yum," I said. "I'll have two."

An obese man, with a paunch larger than my father's, was walking down the sidewalk. As the guy entered the sandwich shop, Dad smirked and offered, "I feel much better when I see a guy like that."

I bet you can outdo him with your elephant snores.

As we drove into our hotel's parking lot, everyone shouted, "Hurrah! We made it!" We said that with our arms up, touching the car's ceiling—but I kept one hand on the steering wheel. Dad would get angry if he saw me steering the car with my knee as he sometimes did.

"Good driving, son," Dad said. "You and Steve can get the luggage out of the trunk, but leave our winter things there. I'll check in while you guys get everything out of the car." He opened his door. "We'll then find Ned and Mimi. They're probably sitting outside their beach apartment waiting for us."

"And don't rush off to the pool too fast," Mom said. "I have to make a shopping list. I need to know what you want for breakfast and dinner."

"Okay, Mom," Steve and I replied. I wondered why she couldn't have made her list while we had been sitting for hours in the car.

I opened my driver's door and looked up at the palm tree fronds that were waving in the warm Florida breeze, marking our arrival. I stepped out, stretched my stiff legs, and gazed up at our hotel's moniker located on the building. "Petit's Riviera" was written in big cursive letters. I stood next to the car for a moment while Dad's Toronado gave birth to my brother and mother, squeezing them out of the backseat through the car's front doors.

I took in our non-*petit* travel accomplishment. *Here we are, Lauderdale; the Simkovits snowbirds have arrived! Dad and I (with a little help from Steve and Mom) did it! So now, sunny, sandy, and surf-y Florida, what have you got in store for us?*

* * *

Travel Postscript

This driving vacation to Florida was to be our last. In future years, Dad flew our family on package deals to the Bahamas, Cuba, Jamaica, and Cancun for the week surrounding New Year's Eve. For most of those trips, Dad brought an entourage of relatives and family friends. He told me, "When I sign up ten other people on a package, I get my air ticket and a hotel voucher for free."

Our family is lounging at Petit's Riviera right after our long drive to Florida.
Late December 1971

The best thing about those subsequent trips was that we were out of Canada's cold weather, and Dad was with us the whole time. Those Caribbean spots were good trade-offs to our long southerly drives. Though the places where we stayed were a distance away from main tourist areas and attractions, the weather was better than in finicky Florida. We also got a warm turquoise-blue sea instead of a sea-weed grey ocean.

On the other hand, I missed those many hours of sitting by Dad's side as his trusted driving lookout, pupil, assistant, confidant, calculator, navigator, and son.

* * * *

17

More Frigging Separation Pains

It was early 1973, the spring of my freshman year at MIT. I was 18 years old, among the youngest among my classmates. It was Sunday night, and Mom was sobbing over the phone. She cried, "Your father left me again for another woman!"

When they were apart that initial time, he acted as if nothing terrible had happened. But Mom cried continually about being abandoned and alone.

After Dad had come back to her, things between my parents were good for some time. Steve and I heard no yelling or screaming for a year or two. Their troubles eventually returned as if the hostility had never left. Their nighttime arguments escalated until something became broken, or until a boisterous "Stop bothering me or I'm leaving right now!" emanated from my father.

Now, four years later, it was Mom who told me first about Dad's second departure. "Does Steve know?" I asked. I didn't want to know the circumstances of their second separation.

"Yes, I just talked to him at Queens." My brother was in his second year there. "He's coming home this weekend for a day or two."

Steve was closer to our mother than I was. The college where he lived was only a two-and-a-half-hour drive away from home, and he had a car.

Regarding her problems with Dad, he was more supportive of her than I. "I'm sorry that happened, Mom," I offered. I didn't know what else to say.

I guess Dad had seen another opening to *foot-scoff* from Mom, considering that my brother and I were now away at college. *Couldn't he have frigging waited until I was finished with school, had a job, and lived on my own?* "What are you going to do, Mom?" I asked.

"I don't know," she wailed. "I'm sitting at home and crying all day. Harvy, can you tell your father to forget about that other woman and come back to me?"

The last time Dad left Mom, both of them had—for the most part—kept my brother and me out of it. Now, she was dragging us into it.

I felt an ache in my chest for her anguish, but I didn't want to get involved. Both Mom and Dad could yell and spit harsh words at the drop of a non sequitur. I offered, "I don't think Dad will listen to me."

She kept on pressing. "Can you please talk to your daddy, son? I don't know what I'm going to do without him. He'll listen to you and your brother if both of you tell him to come back to me."

"I don't know, Mom. Let me think about it."

"Please, son," she pleaded. "Steve is going to talk to him when he comes home from school this weekend." She sighed. "I love your father more than anything. I want him home with me."

I wasn't sure Dad would give Mom the love and attention she wanted. I said, "Okay, okay, Mom; I'll talk to him when he calls me." I wasn't prepared to leave my college studies and fly back to Montreal to get stuck between my parents.

Dad called that evening. "Son, I don't know if you know, but I left your mother." He didn't say "again."

I had been thinking about it all day, but I still didn't know what to say. I spoke sheepishly, "Yes, Mom called to tell me." Then I said something that I hadn't expected. "Why did you leave her again for someone else?"

There might have been a judgmental tone in my voice. Dad's voice elevated. "So what if I'm with another woman? I can't live with your mother; she's too controlling."

There's a Slovak pot calling a Hungarian kettle black!

His tone rose in defiance. "What's happening between your mother and me is not your concern, so please stay out of it." He spoke intensely but didn't yell. "Your attention should be on your school studies."

I was taken aback by his harshness, and I said nothing more.

The air became still for a few seconds. Dad's voice then turned quiet. "*Lassen* to me, son. I'm 53 years old and have no intention of getting married again or having more children. First and foremost, I care about you and your brother, and I've told Stevie the same." He took a long breath. "Please don't worry about me ever abandoning you. It would be like me cutting off my right arm; I couldn't do it."

I had heard Dad say similar words to Mom when Steve and I had been kids, but he still walked out on her. Would he want to stay unmarried for the rest of his life? Might he one day leave Steve and me for another—*gulp!*—family? That thought scared me into my bones. *How would I survive without him?* Or was I mimicking my mother's fears?

Dad's voice turned soft as a pussycat. "When are you coming home next time, son? We can talk more then."

I called my mother at our regular Sunday evening time. When she asked if I had spoken to Dad, I told her, "I'm sorry, Mom. Dad doesn't want me involved in what's going on between you two."

Part of me wanted to scream at both my parents and to run far away from them forever. Another part of me yearned for them to be together and for us to be a happy family again. I didn't say those things to either of them; I hadn't the courage.

There was a pause at the other end of the phone. I could hear Mom take a long breath. "So, when are you coming home?"

I said, "I'll be there next month, during my spring break."

I didn't want to go home and spend time with either of them, but I felt little choice. I didn't want to be cruel. Besides, I didn't know where else I would go.

I still didn't know what was better: to have Mom and Dad together and continually fighting about Dad's late-night whereabouts, or to see them separated and Mom being inconsolable about being alone and lonely. I felt dependent on my father for my college education. I shied away from confronting him about his other woman without the risk of losing his support and favour. I worked to ignore my mother's crying. Thinking about their never-ending drama gave me stomach quivers and nighttime shivers.

I didn't know who I could talk to, or if I should speak to anyone at all. Both of my parents had told my brother and me not to confide in anyone about our family problems. They wanted us "to keep it within the family." If I shared my concerns with a doctor, psychologist, social worker, or my student advisor about what was going on at home, I might feel and look fragile. I had to maintain an aura of being my father's special son, having him see as a worthy man, not weak. I made believe that nothing terrible was happening.

My only plan was to do as Dad wanted: to stay focused on my college studies. I had to tolerate the time I spent with my parents, though I didn't want to be involved with them. I hoped they would work out something on their own.

Perhaps I was naïve, but I looked forward to the day of being totally on my own, no longer tied to either one of them. *When I'm old enough, I'll get away as far as I can from my mother's whining and my father's womanizing.*

I don't know what Mom did to keep herself busy at home while Dad was out of the house. Without her "three boys," she had no one else for whom to cook, clean, shop, or sew. I'm sure she must have written long letters to her Czechoslovak family and spoken weekly to her brother and sister-in-law in Montreal.

I talked to her every Sunday night. She said, "I'm lonely here alone. You and Stevie are off in college, and your father is gone." Her words oscillated between, "I love him so much and want him to come back home," and "I can't believe he brought me way out here to Dorval, far away from the city, and now left me stranded for a *piszkos kurva* [dirty whore]."

I once told her, "You need to find other things to do, Mom."

She responded harshly. "What do I have that somebody would want? I can't work anymore. My hands are not the same as they used to be; I can't sew like I used to. My job for the last twenty years has been to be a mother to you and your brother. That's all I know how to do."

"You need to try to do something new, Mom."

She stayed with her entrenched lines. I found it hard to listen to her words of hopelessness. Part of me didn't even want to talk to her. But if I didn't call her every Sunday, she'd get worried and later pelt me with questions about why I wasn't calling home.

When I talked to Dad, he never mentioned Mom or his mistress—a woman I hadn't yet met. On one Sunday call, he offered, "I purchased a chalet in the Laurentian mountains. It's a big A-frame with three bedrooms. It's next to a pond that has a little beach."

He was as excited as a little kid with a new toy. He added, "A paddleboat came with the place. You and Steve can come there on the weekends when you are home for the summer." I could sense him smiling through the phone. "You can bring a friend if you want to."

I winced inside. I didn't have a girlfriend or even a woman friend at the time. My MIT class was 90% male, and some MIT women I saw in the institute's hallways looked like men with long hair. If I found a nice girl, I wouldn't want to bring her into the middle of my parents' separated life.

I suspected my father was going to use his chalet as a place for my brother and me to meet his mistress. I didn't want to do that, but I had no idea how I was going to avoid her without upsetting my father. I loathed the thought of being immersed in my parents' craziness. Once again, I felt as if my gut were in a tight knot that I couldn't untangle.

* * *

During the following summer, my brother lived at home with Mom and went to work every day at Dad's Montreal Phono. I don't know how he managed that kind of back-and-forth existence; my angst would have eaten my insides.

I decided to remain at MIT for two months out of the university's three-month summer break. I took extra courses to advance in my studies. Cocooning in MIT's lecture halls and libraries both distanced and distracted me from my mother's pining for Dad, and my father's pretending nothing was out of the ordinary.

Dad maintained Mom's monthly "salary." Though by the end of the month, when her bills were due, she complained, "That *fasz* [dick] father of yours spends like crazy on his friends and whore, but he doesn't give me a penny more. I have to save on my stomach while he throws money around like there's no tomorrow."

It might have been easier on Mom had Dad opened his wallet to her, his wife of 25 years. "What if you find a lawyer and sue him?" I was afraid to add the words "for divorce."

She came back quickly and harshly. "I still want your father to come back when he gets that other woman out of his system."

I joined my brother in working for our father during some summer weeks. I wanted extra cash and to show Dad that I wasn't slacking off. I wanted to spend time with him without having to see his other woman.

Living a home life with Mom and working days with Dad was undoubtedly awkward. The atmosphere was a little better at work because Dad never talked about Mom unless Steve or I broached the subject. I don't know about my brother, but I rarely mentioned her to Dad.

At home, questions and comments oozed out of Mom about Dad. She continually prodded, "How is your father doing? What did he say to you today? Anybody special come to see him? Did he say anything about me?" Hardly a breath came between her questions.

Steve and I responded: "Same as always, Mom; nothing new. Do we need to talk about this now? Thanks for supper; I'm going to watch TV."

Dad enticed my brother and me to do things with him on weekends, like play golf or see a professional football game. He took us out for Sunday suppers at the upscale Carlos Italian Restaurant at the posh Windsor Hotel in downtown Montreal. We travelled to the Laurentian Mountains to spend the day at his new country chalet.

I met Dad's mistress once or twice at his chalet. It felt as if she were mostly in the background, like a nondescript painting on a back wall. Maybe I hung her there, not wanting to get to know her close up. I vaguely remember how she looked. I did remember her blond hair and what kind of European accent she had. I didn't remember her name or face; perhaps I didn't want to.

My mother didn't allow Steve or me to forget about her abandonment. Late one Sunday, after my brother and I had spent the whole day with our father, Mom barely waited until we had taken off our shoes before she rattled off her questions. "How does your father look? Did you see that other woman? Did he take you to visit her? Did she go out with you or come over to your father's country house? Did your father say anything to you about their relationship?"

Not wanting to feel in the middle, my brother and I gave the brief answers we had learned during my parents' first separation. "I don't know, Mom. We didn't see her. We had dinner at Dad's chalet and then we went go-cart racing. We're home late because the traffic coming back was bad."

Dad had asked us to say nothing to Mom about having seen his mistress. "Your mother won't understand if you tell her that my girlfriend had come over. It would just get her upset."

When we sat down in the kitchen, Mom pushed us further. "Does that other woman wash and iron his clothes the way I did?"

I was getting frustrated. "Mom, can you *please* not bother us with those things." I wanted to run away from her ceaseless tongue that cut like a carving knife. I could hardly imagine the sharpness of the pain that must have been inside her.

She looked at me with a deflated and then defiant face. She hit her left palm repeatedly with the back of her right hand. "Tell your father to leave that other woman and come back to me." She shook her fist. "What does he see in her anyway? Nobody else can ever love him, take care of him, and be faithful to him as I can."

I didn't say a word.

My brother was known for smashing a cup or a plate when Mom's prodding and pleading tipped his patience. This time he stood from the kitchen table and headed for the dining-room door. His face was tight and lips pursed.

After he had walked out of the kitchen, he turned around and smacked the dining room wall hard with his open palm. It was near to where he had previously smashed his fist through a small painting. He then headed to the den or basement where he could be alone. My back had been to him and the kitchen doorway, so I had no idea what he looked like when his palm smacked the wall.

Mom suddenly stopped her jabbering. She looked at me, but her face divulged nothing. She said, "Did you get enough to eat, Harvy?"

I don't know how my brother lived at home with Mom for that entire summer. I couldn't wait to get the hell out of Dodge.

* * *

I never asked or said anything to Steve about our parents' problems, and he rarely said anything about them. I believed that if I ignored their ongoing troubles and my gnawing gut, then the turmoil would dissipate on its own. I was very naïve about that.

Perhaps Steve found solace by turning to the Catholic Church. He attended Mass every Sunday and participated in meetings and gatherings after service.

My brother later took on horseback riding. He went to the stables several evenings each week and all day on Saturday. No doubt, his horse was always excited to see him and never interrogated him about his life outside the barn and corral. Steve made friends with horsey people and stayed out late with them, though he was home before eleven o'clock at night.

Steve and I slept only an arm's length from each other in our shared bedroom, but there could have been a western horse ranch between us. I found no comfort in confiding in him. Perhaps I couldn't forgive him for things he had done to me during our early childhood. He had perpetually nagged me, even after I yelled at him to leave me alone. During those years, when I was smaller than my brother, only our mother's scream would get him to stop poking or prodding me.

One Sunday afternoon in our youth, Steve and I had been playing soccer in our backyard with Dad. I bent down to grab the loose ball that had lodged in the hedges. Inexplicably, Steve pushed me into the recently-pruned branches.

Had I not been wearing my thick, wide-framed eyeglasses, the force of his push might have damaged my eye on a sharp stem. I rubbed my forehead and slightly bloodied cheek from the scratches I had obtained. I yelled at Steve, "Why did you do that?" Perhaps I had taunted my brother as I recovered the ball, but I had no recollection.

Dad lashed out too. "Steve, how could you do something so irresponsible? You could have hurt your brother badly. You're the older one and should know better."

My brother didn't look at Dad but stared at me with a blank face. Our soccer game concluded there, and perhaps our weekend soccer matches with Dad ended too. My shock and distress at my brother's senseless actions lasted a lifetime. Maybe he saw me as "Daddy's little suck-up boy," and I might have been just that. Perhaps he wanted his baby brother to disappear off the face of the earth. His underlying message was clear: *Don't look to me to protect you from anything.*

When I was a kid, I had a recurring dream of being Superman. I wanted to fly down the street and away from home, but I wasn't able to get higher than a meter off the ground. I then woke with a start as I was ready to crash into a fence or house in my dream.

As a teen, I thought of the intelligent and rational Vulcan Science Officer, Mr. Spock, on *Star Trek*. In dealing with hostile life forms and Klingon archenemies, he engaged his cool-headed logic to guide himself and his starship's captain.

Like Spock, I wanted to shut out my emotions and put my logical mind to work on my studies. In time, I would latch myself to a leader, like Captain Kirk, who was more to my liking. That would become my way to survive my family and thrive in life.

I carried my Mr. Spock notion into my university years. In my off hours, I affixed my eyes on *Star Trek* reruns that whisked me away to other planets and civilizations. Whatever was going on between my parents, I imagined their strife parsecs away.

Outside of my short stays at home and brief stints at Dad's Montreal Phono, my time at college was my escape. I couldn't wait to get into the work world and no longer be dependent on my father.

I did look for summer internships in the Boston area, but it was hard for this non-American to find a U.S. internship. It was also hard to turn Dad down when he said he needed me in his factory, but that may have only been his excuse to see more of me.

* * *

The summer after my junior year, I went on a three-week adventure with my high school chum. John and I drove across western Canada and back to Montreal in his standard-shift Ford Pinto. He taught me how to drive a stick shift. He showed me how to shift gears without using the clutch—in case the clutch cable ever broke.

John had female friends and acquaintances in many major cities—the advantage of having gone to a Canadian college—and those girls had sisters and girlfriends. John and I were 19, old enough to drink beer in any province. We racked them up in Calgary with John's former girlfriend and her three (yes, three!) sisters, though a couple of them had boyfriends. We went to a western bar, ordered a bunch of 6-oz glasses of brew which were slung onto the table for $1.20 a dozen by a pretty cowgirl. We jigged to cowboy music for half the night.

In beautiful middle-of-nowhere British Columbia, John and I joined the girls' family at their lakeside country home. Their father taught me to waterski behind the family's boat. I got up my first try.

In Vancouver, John and I took the ferry to Vancouver Island and picnicked with two other women. His older brother had arranged that date for us—he was the kind of big brother I would have loved to have had.

On our drive back to Montreal, we met more of John's women friends in Thunder Bay. We made a bonfire and roasted hot dogs on the shores of Lake Superior. Though I still was awkward with the opposite sex, it was a relief to get away from my parents and brother and to be with young folks who were like fresh Canadian air.

But being a distance away from my parents didn't always provide relief. There still were Sunday phone calls from Mom, her saying, "Your father is gone. Your brother is with his horse. When will you be home again, son?"

I tried to ignore the gnawing feeling inside me about my family, but my body wouldn't cooperate. During the following school year, I suffered unexplained ailments. Pounding headaches kept me from my books. Constipation kept me sitting unproductively on the toilet for hours. Lackluster moods kept me in bed until noon on weekends. Bad dreams caused me to bolt upright from bed with my heart pounding. I did what I could to ignore those symptoms, going to class no matter how I felt. I was desperate to get my MIT-degree meal ticket and find my own life.

I studied diligently in my dorm room or hopped between libraries on weekends. I played junior varsity soccer to keep myself fit—though I could gain ten pounds or more in the offseason on New England fried clams and chocolate frappes. In the winter, I went downhill skiing during vacations, even if I had to go by myself. I maintained a near-perfect GPA in my engineering studies. I felt lucky to have a sound mind, but I couldn't feel the same way about my aching heart and my troubled gut.

I felt terrible for my mother's feeling helpless and hopeless, but I wasn't going to fight her battle with Dad. I was determined to finish my degree, never again work summer jobs for my father, never be around my brother, and never again live at home with my mother. I counted the months and days that I had left with my hell of a family. I couldn't wait to leave them for good.

It's surprising that I didn't get into illegal drugs, or even into smoking and boozing the way my father did. Most years at my boarding school, cigarette smoking was forbidden, though students went behind the outbuildings to light up after bedtime. Once, on a French study trip to Quebec City, I stole out late one evening with a friend to try a Du Maurier. Before we finished half that cigarette, I was coughing and choking, my mouth tasting like dry manure, and my stomach turning upside down. I never again touched one of those things. I couldn't fathom consuming packs of cigarettes each day as my father did.

At MIT dorm parties, the soft drinks often went faster than the beer. If I did drink beer, my eyes got heavy soon after my second. I held my liquor as my mother couldn't rather than as my father could.

In my last year of college, a dorm buddy offered me weed when we went out to a party in the city. The unpleasant memory of cigarette smoke in my mouth and lungs made me decline his offer. As we sat together in a car, he lit up and smoked by himself.

Before I graduated with my Master's in Engineering, I met a thirty-year-old woman and went out with her a few times. On Saturday nights, she liked to smoke pot on her house porch with her housemates. Wanting to be social with her gang, I joined in once or twice, taking a drag or two. The crappy taste and my upside-down stomach told me that illicit drugs were not a part of my makeup. My addiction was studying, and maybe the fried clams and chocolate ice cream in my college cafeteria.

I didn't know if I was realistic about finding a good engineering job away from Montreal. When I would, I was going to pack my bags and do to both my parents what Dad had done to Mom, now twice.

My single-minded attention to my coursework helped to mask my anguish about my family. I made it into the top 10% of my MIT junior and senior classes. I was invited into the Tau Beta Pi engineering honour society after my junior year and into the Sigma Xi research society soon after I graduated with my bachelor's degree.

Only the future knew if my engineering degrees would be enough to buy my freedom. I wondered if there might be a life reward or compensation from God for me going through the crap I was experiencing with my frigging family.

* * * *

18

What Am I Again?

What!? reverberated in my mind.

In May of 1973, I had completed my first year at MIT and was home for a couple of weeks before returning to college for summer classes. My brother was there too, returned from his second year at university. Mom was happy to have us with her. I was also glad to be home from school for a week or more of mother pampering, as long as she didn't go on about Dad having left her months earlier, and as long as my brother didn't bug me or break something.

After loads of laundry dutifully attended to by our mother, she cheerfully called out, "My loves, I have your favourites ready for you." She could be sweet when she put aside the pain of her separation from Dad. They had now been apart for nearly half a year.

Waiting in her kitchen was her homemade Hungarian cuisine. It welcomed us back into her fold. Her caring cooking easily trumped the tasteless shepherd's pie served at our boarding school. Though college food was better, especially the fried clams and battered scrod I had discovered in Cambridge, it was no comparison to Mom's cooking.

The homeland creations she meticulously concocted and brewed all afternoon atop the stove filled the air with warm, familiar aromas of onion, garlic, black pepper, and paprika. Those odors tied us to her heritage and returned us faithfully into her domain.

Along with her home-made *húsleves* (meat soup) and *töltött káposzta* (stuffed cabbage) with *édes-savanyú uborkasalátá* (sweet and sour cucumber salad) on the side, Mom offered an unsettling fact about her past. Her eyes looked uneasy as she engaged a hand to wipe the sweat from her brow. I thought it was because she had had a long, hot May afternoon in her kitchen, but there was more.

She stood on the other side of our Formica table, a fixture in her kitchen since we had been kids. "Boys," she said slowly and calmly, "I have something important to tell you."

When she saw our eyes on her and not on our bowls, she continued. "You know, I was born and raised Jewish." She then turned to put her soup pot back on the stove and to get her main course ready.

What!? echoed in my head. I stopped spooning Mom's soup into my mouth. She had made this declaration as if it were nothing. *Could that be?*

Though my heart started to race, I tried not to let my confusion and disbelief show. I held tightly to my soup spoon and lowered my eyes into the beef, vegetable, and noodle-laden broth. I was motionless and speechless as if God himself had come down from heaven and smacked me.

In this redefining moment, my whole being—raised Christian from the moment I exited my mother's womb—felt stunned and numb. Instead of blurting out my uneasiness, I held my tongue. My mind drifted to recall our close Eastern European relations.

There were Mom's four siblings who we had visited several times in Czechoslovakia. And there were Uncle Lali and Aunt Martha, Mom's brother and sister-in-law, who had followed Mom and Dad to Canada in 1950, one year after my parents' arrival. I then saw the faces of the immigrant Montreal families with whom my brother and I had grown up: the Vesely, Freedman, and Meyer families. Similar to Mom and Dad, these Eastern European parents were WWII survivors. They had sought new and better lives outside the Iron Curtain after the Soviets occupied and took over Eastern Europe. It suddenly struck me that all these people were Jewish.

How could I have missed this? No wonder we are so close to these families. Having shared many Sundays, holidays, and vacations with these folks, they had become like kin. Might I have had an inkling that they were Jews? Maybe I didn't want to know or admit that I did.

I swallowed hard. I thought of my seventh-grade religious studies class. Our Catholic priest teacher had come to the classroom one day and asked, "Does anyone know what dope is?" I raised my hand as I thought, *That's easy. It's a 'fool' or an 'idiot.'* When he called on another student, and she answered, "It's drugs," and the Father agreed, I felt stupid. No one, not even my parents, had ever mentioned that dope stuff before.

I had the same feeling of stupidity today. No bell had ever rung in my head about this ethnic possibility in our family, or maybe a part of me never wanted it rung.

I couldn't look at my brother, who sat right next to me. I couldn't fathom why Mom had never said anything about her true faith before. She had allowed us to believe she was Christian like Dad. I wondered why none of our relatives or family friends ever said anything about it. Was there a religious conspiracy going on?

Neither Dad nor Mom had ever spoken about the religious origins of our Eastern European family and friends. But there was something about those folks—their mannerisms, accented voices, last names, and their occasional use of Yiddish terms—that should have been a giveaway.

In my innocence, or deliberate naivety, or instinct to stay away from difficult topics, I never asked questions about their religions. *Boy! We have a boatload of Jewish relatives and friends!* And I never considered my mother could be Jewish. Hadn't she cooked fish on meatless Fridays and come to Sunday church with us?

On the occasions when Mom joined Dad, Steve, and me for Mass in the city, I could tell she wasn't comfortable in the Catholic milieu. She never quite knew when to sit, stand, or kneel. She followed Dad's lead, as Steve and I did.

Because I couldn't follow Latin, Slovak, or French services, I assumed Mom, too, had her translation issues. Taking in another spoonful of her meat soup, I now realized it was the religious translation rather than the language translation that had made her act awkward.

Mom never partook of the sacrament, unlike my brother, who went for those hosts almost every week—as if they held magical powers. Like my mother, I abstained too. I felt I wasn't sin-free enough to swallow Christ's body. Maybe I was angry at Him and his Father for never curtailing my parents' fighting. I saw my mother's host abstinence as her and I sharing something in common. Dad didn't participate in the sacrament every Sunday, perhaps not feeling absolved enough from his sins.

I continued to spoon Mom's soup into my mouth, but it turned tasteless. *Does Mom's declaration mean I'm Jewish too?* A lump formed in my throat, and I was unable to ask my question aloud.

My childhood had been dominated by Catholicism in public elementary school and then Protestantism during my private high school years. My experience of Judaic rituals was limited to one Bar Mitzvah—for the son of my father's accountant. That Jewish rite was very foreign to my Catholic sensibilities of first communion and confirmation. Jews wore a funny skull cap and black suits and ties as if someone had died. I didn't dislike Jewish people, but I didn't want to be like them.

Mom turned toward us from across our kitchen table. For a moment, she stood motionless. Her face was tight. She held her soup ladle and tilted it in our direction. She glanced down at the table and then looked up at us. "Boys, I'm telling you this because of your Daddy having left me again." After a pause that lasted a heartbeat or two, she added, "And I want you to know the truth about your mama."

Holding back her sadness, even bitterness, about her most recent loss of Dad, Mom continued to reveal more morsels of her hidden past. "When Daddy and I came to Canada from Europe in '49, Canada was accepting only Christian couples. I had resigned from my Jewish religion after the war. I wrote in my immigration application that I was Catholic, like your father, so that we could come here."

Mom stopped talking and took a short step toward the stove. She seemed pulled between her concurrent aims of cooking and confessing. She looked back at us and paused for a long second, perhaps wanting to see if we hadn't fallen into our soup bowls from her unexpected news. She then wheeled back to the stove to serve her next course.

In this momentary break, my mind filled again. I wondered why Canada had only accepted Christians back in '49. Wasn't Canada a free and open country that took all immigrants? My notions about my "home and native land" began to turn like my stomach did to Mom's suppertime revelation.

And how had she 'resigned' her Jewish heritage? In Dad's Catholicism, I knew one could get excommunicated for wrongdoings against the church. I didn't know how anyone could officially quit their religion. *Wasn't it bestowed upon you at birth?*

Our public Catholic and private Anglican schools had required my brother and me to have religious education classes and participate in weekly Mass. Those classes left me with troubled feelings about Jews. Didn't the Hebrews command Christ's crucifixion? Hadn't Jews and Christians been religious rivals? *Could this be why Mom and Dad fought so much?* My confused mind was struggling, yet my quivering mouth remained silent. *Though Dad held nothing against them, didn't he sometimes make fun of Jewish people?* I cringed as I bit my lip while chewing hard on a thick strand of meat from my soup.

I glanced at my brother. I could see he was silent but attentive as he chowed down on Mom's meal. We probably didn't want to blurt out any sharp questions that might place more salt onto Mom's marriage wounds.

Perhaps she was so upset about our father's latest departure that she no longer wanted to hide her real history from us. But concealing her heritage was what she had deliberately done both during her and Dad's twenty-four years in Canada and with Steve and me for the last eighteen.

Mom glanced over her shoulder toward us. She may have caught Steve's and my hesitating briefly, momentarily suspending our spoons above our bowls. After she had neither seen nor heard any hostile reactions to her pronouncement, she continued her tale. "When your Daddy later started his business in Canada, he still wanted me to pretend I was Catholic like him, because of his Christian customers."

She took a long breath. "Only my relatives and Jewish friends know I'm Jewish. But most of us don't practise anyway; it was never a big part of our lives."

She turned to look directly at us. "Do you boys want any more soup?"

Knowing what was ahead of us, at least in the food department, my brother and I responded, "No thanks, Mom. The soup was good!"

Mom readied the table for the next course and possibly more verbal discourse. She spooned out her Hungarian stuffed cabbage, complete with buttery boiled new potatoes and a side of sweet and sour cucumber salad.

Seeing what was in front of me, I was glad to have declined an extra helping of her first course. Having been, like my brother, husky as a child, I had worked hard through high school and college sports to keep my physique trim.

Mom returned her pans of food to the stove and turned down the heat. She came back to stand by the table. "You know boys," she said slowly, "my maiden name, Anna Tatransky, wasn't my original name."

I chewed and swallowed a mouthful of hot cabbage roll too quickly, its heat almost burning my tongue and throat. Though I cringed from the pain, I prepared my eyes and ears for what our mother was ready to reveal next.

She went on. "I was born Hannah Friedmann." After a reflective pause, she added, "I was named after my great-auntie, Hannah." She looked at us. "My Hungarian name, Nusi, is the Hungarian form of Hannah. Those names translate to 'Grace' in Hebrew. The name I use in Canada, Anna, is the English version of Hannah."

Oh my Gosh! A second supper shocker! "Hannah" was a lot more to swallow than "Anna."

She further explained. "Yet Hannah was only used by my friends when I was young and part of a socialist Zionist movement; it was a youth guard, called the Hashomer Hatzair." She batted her hand. "It's like the Scouts you boys did here in Canada."

Gosh again! Our mother was part of a Jewish movement too! I wasn't sure if I could handle her admissions that she dished out with her stuffed cabbage. *What happened to our trying to be a regular Canadian family?*

Mom kept her eyes on us, and her voice remained steady. "Our Friedmann family was never very religious; we rarely went to synagogue services. Instead, I worked on the weekends with my brothers and sisters in my father's grocery store on the main street of Košice." She pointed to herself. "We survived that way as a family."

Okay! I tried not to show any outward anxiety about Mom's hidden history. Hannah Friedmann certainly sounded Jewish. I got that she may not have had a religious upbringing, but could I digest her newly revealed heritage?

Steve raised his hand. "Why did your family change your last name from Friedmann to Tatransky?" He and I had known our aunts and uncles only as "Tatransky."

Mom took a breath. "After the war, my whole family decided to change our name. We didn't want to be considered Jewish in Košice. We weren't a religious family anyway; we felt it would be better if we had a Christian last name. Many Hungarian Jewish people were doing that after the war, and my family agreed to do the same."

Mom sat down to eat with us. For a moment, the air in the room was still. My brother spoke again, his voice calm. He pointed to both of us. "Mom, are we now Jewish too?" Steve was better than I at raising piquant questions that were also on my mind.

Mom seemed to have been ready for his query. She robustly responded, "You boys are very much Catholic, like your Daddy. Both of you were *seriously* raised that way, and you will always be that way."

Both the room and our supper forks became still for a few seconds. My brother then asked more questions about our Jewish relatives and friends. During the moments he and Mom talked, I couldn't help but wonder what she considered our "serious" Catholic upbringing in Quebec.

* * *

The all-boy boarding school in which Dad had placed my brother and me was Protestant, though some students were Catholic. The school stood in the rural farmlands of Quebec's Eastern Townships. After Dad had broken the news to Steve and me about our going there, he reminded us, "My father sent me to a Hungarian private school in Košice, you know."

He took a breath and added, "In private school, you boys won't stay tied to your mother's skirt." He looked directly at us, his eyes penetrating and voice firm. "You two need to learn to do more for yourselves."

Dad said that in front of Mom. Her tight face and pursed lips told me she didn't like his remark, but she said nothing. Deep down, she probably realized that her sons were too reliant upon her; we needed to become more self-sufficient.

Dad was wise to put his sons into boarding school. He probably wanted us at a distance from the growing English-French troubles in the province and to the brewing marital troubles between Mom and him. But his investment in our private school education had its unintended religious consequences.

During the fall and spring, the townships around our school reeked of pungent pig manure that fertilized the cornfields. Because our school was Anglican, a group of us Catholic boarders walked the one-and-a-half kilometers *en masse* each Sunday morning to go to services in the local village of only 4000 inhabitants. We made that pilgrimage in the pouring rain or falling snow.

To reach the church in the center of town, we had to walk across a polluted river, its brown foaming water flowing even in the cold winter months. In those days, a pulp and paper plant thirty kilometers upriver infused the water with odorous chemicals. In the thickening air of spring, on top of the smells of the fertilized crop fields, the river had a reeking stench. The combined acrid smell nearly caused me—and perhaps other students too—to spew up our Sunday breakfast over the side of the bridge, but I never did.

Church services in town were in Latin and French. Though I had been learning Latin and Parisian French in school, I had a hard time understanding the rustic Quebec French spoken in this rural parish. I also couldn't comprehend the convoluted Latin that put complicated verb conjugations at the end of contorted sentences.

I became bored with Catholic services. Making the pilgrimage across the contaminated St. Francis River each Sunday morning began to feel like a slow calcification of my spirit. After two years of trudging through the tedium, I relinquished my father's religion.

No matter how much Dad had been devoted to Catholicism and had frequented church, he and Mom still had late-night screaming matches while my brother and I tried to sleep in our beds. Though I had prayed to God from under my covers for my parents to stop their bickering, He never came to put a stop to it.

At the start of my third year in private school, at age 15, I joined the school's choir and sang my way through the next three years of Anglican Mass. Because Mom and Dad wanted me to do something musical, they accepted my choir membership along with my now Protestant direction. This adjustment also got me out of piano lessons with our friendly but less-than-inspiring school organist and piano teacher, Mistress Bertha Boxley. Her name well matched her enormous physique, humongous laugh, and unlimited verbosity.

Singing in our school choir got me more engaged in church, though our Reverend spoke in a low, rhythmic monotone that could tax anyone's state of alertness. Then again, the services did have their amusing moments.

Because the choir's pews were on either side of our raised chancel, choir members could view the whole congregation. One Sunday morning, I saw my brother sitting at the end of a pew near the back of the church. He was right in front of the school Masters who sat in their reserved seats in the back row.

Steve must have dozed off during our Reverend's slow-motion sermon. Near the end of the minister's talk, Steve stood suddenly and turned to exit the pew. (He told me later that he had thought the Reverend had finished his address.)

Steve then realized the minister hadn't finished, and he quickly sat back down. But his movement started a chain reaction in the church. Everyone next to Steve, even the Masters sitting behind him, began to stand as if they were ready to leave.

The Reverend raised his voice in indignation. "Please sit down; I'm not quite done!"

I guessed that many of the church-goers were having the minister's monotone words of worship slip in and out of their ears, and any trigger to get up and away would do.

Singing in the school choir and participating in the English-language service lifted my spirit and kept me a bit more interested in church. I stayed close to my school chums and, most importantly, warm and dry on those damp and dreary Sunday mornings in rural Quebec.

* * *

What Am I Again?

My father had accepted my decision to relinquish Catholicism and partake in Protestantism—my staying Christian was perhaps good enough for him. Mom never commented on my religious change. Now, during her supper after my first year in college, I knew why.

Because of her Jewish background and deference to Dad, she had left it to him to decide our religious education. But nothing during my upbringing and schooling had prepared me for her revealing her true heritage.

Perhaps that's why I was so closed mouth about it during her tell-all meal. I wanted to pretend it wasn't important, in the same way she had said Judaism hadn't been vital in her life. While Steve and Mom continued to talk about our Jewish friends and relatives, I kept consuming her stuffed cabbage and remained in my religious reverie.

My Catholic or Protestant religious education classes rarely mentioned Judaism. I did remember reading about the trial of Jesus, when the Hebrews of Judea demanded their Roman governor, Pontius Pilot, to condemn Christ to death. In my still young mind, I wondered whether the Christian and Jewish parts of me were friends or enemies.

I shook off my thought. Though I knew that Christians and Jews were very different, none of my priests, nuns, ministers, or teachers at my schools had ever professed a dislike for the Jews.

The heat under my collar rose suddenly. I recalled one perplexing situation at my boarding school that exemplified how my Christian classmates sometimes treated Jewish kids.

A handful of minority students went to our English Protestant private school of roughly 275 students spread across six grades. Some English Canadian students treated minority kids with disdain or derogatory terms. They referred to French Canadians as "workies." Asians were called "chinks." Kids from the local farming community were "stupid hicks." Jews were disparagingly labeled "Heebs" or "kikes."

Sometimes a student said those latter terms in jest, like "Burns, you Heeb." The student wielding the insult offered it with a grin, an air of humour and respect. It was as if he had proclaimed that he didn't know Jews could be quick and coordinated on the sports playing field or smart in class.

We knew who the committed athletes were. They put their whole bodies into fall football or soccer. They ran with their hearts out on the track field in the spring. We also knew who the smart kids were because, at the end of every semester, the masters posted students' grades and class rankings onto the school's academic bulletin board.

Some Jewish students got the most grief from the English kids. They were continually targeted by their classmates, even across grades. Even the most religious Protestant student could float insults in Jewish-accented statements about big noses or tight wallets. Those derogatory statements were ignored by most. The insult dissipated quickly into the air, but not before doing damage to the recipient's face and leaving a cocky smirk on the face of the wielder.

Some boys knew how to fight back whenever accosted by another's cheeky remarks. I once saw a student look at a Jewish kid and proclaim, "Cohen, you dumb kike!"

In retaliation, Cohen, a respected athlete, immediately wielded cutting statements in a tone that was decibels higher. "Andrews, you're a stupid and inane Gentile!"

Though I cringed at and kept my distance from such interactions, I admired and respected Cohen for his feistiness. Cocky classmates stopped their verbal attacks after a tangle with him.

Then there was Stein, another continually accosted Jewish student. He wasn't as adept at sports. His walk was clumsy, perhaps even comical. His body bounced as he rose on his toes when he strode down the hallways or when he ran—if one could call it running—on the track. This behavior didn't win him friends among the jocks in our school where athletics was as important as academics.

To his detriment, Stein conveyed an air of coldness that spurred classmates' ire. Out of nowhere, he complained, "So-and-so did such-and-such only because they want to suck up to a schoolmaster." At the oddest time, he might say, "I hate this place and the mean kids here that hate Jews," or "I need to look out for myself because no one here cares about kids like me." With his supercilious attitude, Stein had the uncanny ability to fill other boys with contempt whenever he opened his mouth.

Stein once grumbled to a schoolmaster about other students abusing him. But reporting a kid was considered dishonourable among classmates. It worked to escalate the tensions around Stein and isolate him from the rest.

Stein's actions were considered a student crime punishable by "rap"—fist punches to the body or verbal lashings to the psyche. Mean classmates—there indeed were a few—ganged up on a "deserving" kid. They wrestled him to the ground, bestowed a pink belly or a few body bruises, and hurled derisive words like "You master suck-ass." . . . "You heap of nothing!" . . . "You nobody!"

Students never carried out rap in the sight of a schoolmaster. That could lead to a punishment of running laps around the school ground at sunup. Repeat offenders might receive a backside caning from a master who believed in the benefits of such, or in the worst case, have the perpetrator expelled from school.

Thus student rap was bestowed privately and stealthily in a dorm room, an empty classroom, a corner of the sports field, the shower room, or at night when all good boys should be sleeping. Some targeted students believed that the schoolmasters knew about the rap but didn't intervene to stop it—I saw no evidence either way.

Years later, I heard that what I had experienced at my school had been no different from what happened at many other English boarding schools in the province. Some believed that it was this English arrogance and bigotry towards minorities that precipitated the Quebec separatist movement and FLQ uprising in Quebec.

I understood Stein's predicament. I, too, received my share of rap in my early boarding school years. My childhood chubbiness attracted it. Just change the word "Jew" or "kike" in those insults to "tub" or "lard," and you know what I mean.

One evening after study hall, the housemaster made the kids in my junior dorm jog around the school campus to dissipate pent-up energy. During the run, a couple of the bigger kids pushed me around, wrestled me to the ground, and winded me.

I whined a little too loudly about being accosted. For several years hence, out of any master's hearing, a cheeky classmate would declare in a meagre and sarcastic voice, "Harvy got winded!" I heard that disparagement from time to time until my last high school year when I became a school Prefect (student officer). I believed I received more than my fair share of abuse, mainly because I never fought back skillfully with my words or fists.

I was astonished and dumbfounded about the senseless rap that permeated the school, especially in my earlier years there. I didn't know how to stop it without having cutting remarks or bruising fists wielded upon me.

Part of me sympathized with the school's Jewish and other minority students, and I wanted to be their friend. I talked to them about school work and tried not to brandish any rap their way. Conversely, another part of me stayed away from them for fear of being lumped in with them by my English peers.

Once, from an adjacent classroom, I overheard a classmate punch Stein hard in the chest and shoulder while repeatedly screaming, "Stein, you hateful Jew!" I don't even know what the altercation was about, but it seemed par for the course for this peculiar kid who carried a magnetic attraction for such things. No student, including me, came to his rescue.

For a lifetime, I carried shame for never coming to Stein's aid. Ironically, it was the same shame I felt those times when my father shouted obscenities at my mother. I never went to her rescue. I wondered if I was a terrible person. Perhaps I shunned such skirmishes was the only way I knew how to survive my perplexing circumstances.

Similar to my irritation toward my mother for provoking my father's ire, I felt the same way toward Stein. One day Stein told me, "Simkovits, you are such a mother's boy." At the time, I had no sense of what he was referring to, but I couldn't let him get away with what he had said. I retorted, "Stein, you're such a Jew!" and I walked away.

I wasn't sure what I was referring to in him, but my response mimicked my classmates'. I grabbed the most convenient handle that Stein provided. I again felt ashamed that I reacted to him no better than my brethren, but I never apologized. Had I been drinking from the same cup as my peers?

At the time, I couldn't understand what being Jewish had to do with Stein attracting so much disdain. I wondered if there was something in our school's Sunday holy hosts and wine that intoxicated Christians to treat or think of Jews with such contempt.

It later became clear that Stein's Jewishness was only the handgrip with which students could smack him with continual contempt. His presence put bitter herbs onto his peers' palates. It got so bad that Stein didn't return to our school for 12th Grade. He never joined in on any class reunions.

Through school athletics and my growth as a teen, I lost my big belly and thick thighs after a few rap-receiving years. I tried to blend in with the other kids. I didn't want to stick out in anything besides my studies, my success as a soccer goalie, and my growing ability at individual sports like skiing and tennis. I worked to hang around the more respected students, to say nothing stupid, and to keep a safe distance from the kids for whom my classmates had disdain. I neither asked questions nor sought answers to my puzzling observations about the mistreatment of minorities; I was struggling to fit in and be respected.

Though I was not able to defend myself well at boarding school, I did prefer to spend five years there rather than at home with my dueling parents. I received a better education at that private school than I would have had at a public school.

The schoolmasters respected my Grade 12 peer group for our academic achievements and capability on the sports field. Because of that respect, we accomplished more in one year to liberalize the treatment of new boys and younger kids than the school had instituted during the previous decade. I'm sorry that Stein never got to see that transformation.

Led by our Head Prefect, we worked to stop the physical and verbal rap whenever we saw or heard it. We demanded that students speak respectfully to each other instead of lashing out. We encouraged the curtailing of caning—though I once overheard an "old school" master say under his breath, "That one could use something to his backside."

Being the good kid and the don't-make-any-trouble student that I strove to be, I said nothing to that master about his caustic comment. I looked away and was relieved that he hadn't directed his remark at me. I hadn't developed the courage to push back against authority figures in the same way I hadn't the courage to push back against my father.

Forty-six years after leaving boarding school, as I was finishing writing this story, I still felt unsettled about what happened to Stein. I reached out to my former classmate. We reconnected via e-mail, and I told him about my memoir.

I offered, "I want to tell you how sorry I've felt all these years for your persecution at school. Though I felt you had exhibited behaviour that caused rap bestowed upon you, it was no justification for what some students put you through." I then told him about the rap I, too, had received at school, though it had not been anywhere near what he had experienced.

I went on to say, "I wanted to personally apologize to you for my part in never having defended you during the atrocities afflicted on you." I didn't say that I also had felt shame in never having stood up for myself.

In return, Stein offered, "Very kind of you to think of me and to take the time to reach out and apologize. It's not necessary but much appreciated." He went on to say, "Though our high school days had been some of the worst in my life, I have moved on successfully." He then asked me not to write more than that in my memoir, and I agreed to his terms.

In those long-ago school days, our schoolmasters had been white male Christians. Most of the students were sons of Quebec's English elite. We obtained no education regarding our religious, ethnic, or other differences, and I felt less prepared for my life because of it. Our divinity class only offered our deep-voiced, slow-paced, monotone minister who put kids like me into a spiritual stupor.

My public Catholic and private Protestant schools didn't give me ways to come to terms with who I was. My parents provided no support; perhaps they didn't know how.

Then again, I hadn't done much to seek out ways of better understanding myself until much later in my life. I felt a big loss for my youth because of that shortcoming, especially regarding my mother's supper admissions and revelations about her Jewish heritage.

* * *

I shook off my school reflections and continued to spoon Mom's stuffed cabbage into my mouth. *Oh, my God!* I said to myself as I nearly coughed up a mouthful. It suddenly occurred to me: *What if my high school classmates had known I too was a Jew?*

I shuddered. Could I have handled being called a "Heeb" and a "tub" in the same breath? Would I have had to hide my Jewishness from my Christian cohorts the way my mother had hidden her Jewishness from Dad's Christian friends and customers?

This grave possibility sent another jolt into my ribs. I thought of my Bible studies. During my youth, I compared myself to Abraham's second son, Isaac. I wondered if he and his elder sibling, Ishmael, have to take on being chastised for their religious beliefs to obtain the blessings of their father and their one God.

Although I couldn't consider myself as spiritual as Isaac, I identified with his story. I had an older brother with whom I didn't get along, and I saw myself—albeit naively at the time—as my father's chosen son.

I revered my father. He worked to educate me about what he felt was important in life. "*Lassen* to me, son," he told me, pointing his finger at me. "Get all the education you can. Get smart and make good connections so that you can become a 'somebody.' And don't depend on anyone else but yourself."

Dad drew a long breath. He looked away and then back at me, his finger pointing at himself and then at me. "I made a lot of mistakes by depending on people who steered me the wrong way. I want you to be smarter than I was and not let people take advantage of you."

Like Abraham did with Isaac, I felt as if my father were preparing me for something big in my life. I prayed I wouldn't let him down. I admired him for having overcome many ordeals in his past, and for working hard to become somebody in Canada. He confided his secrets to me, especially the knowledge of his offshore money. *Could I become a big man like him? Would I be worthy of his legacy?*

If it hadn't been for my father, I wouldn't have applied to MIT. "It's the best engineering school in the world," he declared. He then added, "And after engineering, you should go to business school too." His eyes were intense. "Then you can become a 'big shot somebody' instead of a 'bloody immigrant' like me."

I continued to chew on Mom's meal. I wondered if her sudden suppertime sharing was a part of the load I had to carry to become somebody in this world. Did all big men have to survive weighty ordeals? Look at Moses; he didn't learn he was Hebrew until his birth mother told him when he was an adult. Then again, was I foolish to compare myself to Moses?

My hand tightened around my supper fork, and my face flushed. *The Jews had done nothing to the Christians.* Couldn't my boarding school chums have left Stein alone about his Jewishness and not harassed me about my fatness? It was unfair and unfathomable that Stein suffered in being a fall guy for centuries of religious struggles, and I for being a fall guy for over-indulgent mothers.

Sunday televangelists had been of no help. They professed Jesus as the only path to eternal light and everlasting salvation. They proclaimed endless fire and damnation if one turned away from Him and God.

I wondered if some of my Anglo-Saxon chums were echoing over a millennium of disdain toward their one-God predecessors. Did newer religions profess to be better than the rest, thus putting down what had come before them? Had Israelites suffered the most because they were the first to worship a single God and then couldn't or wouldn't fight back against other religions that followed?

After I had completed high school, my unsettled religious confusion made me turn agnostic. My skepticism about God kept me from any organized religion. I was never comfortable with Dad's Catholicism or my high school Anglicanism, and now I had Mom's Judaism with which to contend. Religion never did anything to calm my unsettled stomach concerning my mother's crying about Dad's alleged infidelities and his continual absences from home.

When I entered college, I stopped going to any house of worship. I felt God never came to protect me from my parents' fighting or to rescue our family. He had never done anything for me, so I chose to abandon Him.

Looking back at that time, I had been raised by my Catholic and Anglican religions to believe that God lived outside of me and us. The priests and nuns said that He looked down upon us from heaven, judged us to be good or bad, and decided as to whether we went to heaven or hell.

Though Dad professed to be a good Catholic, he was attracted to the devil's vices. His belligerent ire could make the house walls shake, and my body too.

No one taught me to understand that God's eternal spirit was housed in me too. I didn't know that I had the capacity and wherewithal to rise and protect my mother from my father or help rescue us from ourselves. I sensed my only choice had been to run away from religion, the way Dad had run away from Mom, and the way I wanted to run away from my family.

As I neared nineteen years on this earth, I planned to expel from my life both my parents' religion and their culture. I wanted to be a vanilla Canadian instead of a tutti-frutti Catholic 'n Jewish Hungarian-Slovak.

I was going to make college my salvation, focusing on getting educated and putting my sound mind to work. I wanted not only to get ahead in my studies but also to maintain distance from my family, which had now gotten even screwier over Mom's meal.

I shook my head as I finished my mother's stuffed cabbage. It was as good as ever, but I could barely taste it. I wondered why God—if He existed—couldn't have given me a normal family. Hearing about Mom's Judaism certainly stirred my unsettled stomach. I said nothing about it to my mother or brother. I just wanted to get the hell away from my befuddled childhood.

Be strong, Harvy! Stick it out at school. You're probably going through this family crap to be prepared, like Isaac or Moses had been, for something greater.

* * *

While I tried to focus on my meal rather than my thoughts, Steve continued to press Mom for answers about her background. I was glad he was talking because I still couldn't reconcile my conflicted feelings. Steve leaned forward toward her, "Can I claim to be Jewish in Israel, or would I be thought of as Catholic there too?"

Mom showed angst on her face, possibly because she was on the edge of defying Dad's decades of desires for his brood. After a moment, she replied, "Because the Jewish heritage officially passes down through the mother, Israelis would consider you as Jewish—if you wanted to be. All you need is proof that you were born to me, a Jew."

Our mother looked as if she had wanted to say more. Instead, she stopped there and offered, "How did you like your mama's supper?"

Both of us offered a big "Great, Mom!" which seemed to cool down any mounting religious tension in her hot kitchen.

My mind continued to wander. *Was it because Mom was Jewish that my brother and I went to Camp Crusoe?*

For three whole summers before my brother and I went to private school, when I was 11 to 13 years old, Dad sent us to a Jewish camp in the Laurentian Mountains north of Montreal. The camp was owned and operated by Mr. and Mrs. Robbs. Mom said the Robbs had been WWII survivors in Hungary, as both she and Dad had been.

Mrs. Robbs was a mother figure to the kids at camp. She was ready with a Band-Aid, candy, and a pat on the head if a camper hurt a finger or scraped a knee.

She also carried a pair of mini-scissors in her apron pocket. With those intimidating shears, she unceremoniously and publically cut lengthy toe and fingernails if a kid didn't attend to those things appropriately. I had that privilege bestowed on me one day at the camp's waterfront playground. Fortunately, my bunkmates were swimming and didn't see me squirm between Mrs. Robbs' legs, walled in by her thick arms and big hands.

Mr. Robbs was even more peculiar. During our arrival at camp, in front of my parents, he wagged his finger at my brother and me. He spoke firmly, "Boys, you cannot speak your parents' language while here at the camp."

I suspected he feared we might swear like young Hungarian soldiers. I glanced at my father, but he said nothing to Mr. Robb's statement. I felt Mr. Robbs should have directed his remarks to him. My dad had no qualms about swearing openly in any language, though he did cover his mouth with his hand when a woman was present.

Like my father, Mr. Robbs had a deep, accented voice. On grey, wet mornings, he started our camp day by blaring out on the camp's intercom, *"Vake up campers! Vake up! Shine an' rize! Shine an' rize! Tis a boutiful day, except for de rain. ...Vear ur shorts and short sleeves, and de raincoat and rain bouts."*

As much as I could, I kept my distance from that odd guy. I couldn't understand why my parents sent my brother and me to this weird camp.

Dad had arranged with the Robbs to treat Steve and me as Christian campers. Instead of going to Friday Oneg Shabbat services, Steve and I passed those evenings playing board games in the camp's main office. For three years, it felt strange for my brother and me to have been the only Christians in a Jewish camp.

I stared at my empty supper plate in Mom's kitchen. I now understood why Steve and I had gone to Camp Crusoe. *Why didn't Mom say she was Jewish?* Heck, it would have made that crazy camp a lot more understandable!

I stopped myself from blurting out the question; I didn't want to upset her meal. Or maybe I didn't want to upset myself.

Mom removed our dirty dishes from the table and placed them by the sink. She put her apple strudel on the table and fetched vanilla ice cream from the fridge. Though my stomach felt stuffed, I still found room for sweets.

My inquisitive brother pointed at himself and then me. "So why did you have to hide your Jewish background from us?"

My eyes fixed on Mom. She stood motionless in her dessert fetching tracks. Her eyes shifted back and forth; her mind seemed to cross decades of thoughts, searching for a sensible answer to my brother's essential question.

She took in a big breath and responded, "Again, son, it was due to your Dad and his Christian business customers. Because he liked to entertain them often, not only in restaurants in the city but also here for Saturday barbeques, he wanted me to pretend I was Catholic like him."

She looked down at the table and then back at us. "Of course, we couldn't tell you kids about it because you might say something during one of your Daddy's parties." She paused and then continued. "It wasn't a problem for me to pretend to be Catholic. My family didn't care so much about being Jewish. Back home, we rarely went to the synagogue and hardly ever celebrated the Jewish holidays."

She raised the serving spatula in her right hand. "Even your uncle Lali and auntie Martha claimed to be Christians when they followed us to Canada after they had escaped, like us, from the Soviet takeover of our country. Lali and Martha baptized their daughter and put her into a Catholic school here, as we did with you two boys."

She hesitated, and then added, "But sometime after their daughter, Janet, completed elementary school, Lali saw her act badly toward a Jewish man."

Mom looked away and then back at us. "She and her father were walking through the Jewish district of Montreal. They passed an outdoor coffee shop where Hasidic men—you know, the ones who dress in black from head to toe—were sitting and reading their Jewish newspapers. Your cousin suddenly stopped next to one fellow and spat on his paper."

Wow! I couldn't see myself ever doing such a thing. I wondered what school lessons had caused her to act that way.

Mom continued. "Of course, Lali and Martha were shocked about what their daughter had done. They thought the Catholic nuns and priests were teaching Janet to hate Jews. So they sat her down and told her she was Jewish.

"Then, the next year, they moved her to a Protestant school for junior high school. But in the summer, she still went to a Jewish camp as you boys did." Mom spoke as if such a summer camp were typical for children like us.

Boy! Cousin Janet had a mixed-up childhood as Steve and I did.

I felt some solace for my brother and me. We hadn't been the only kids shielded from our true heritage. I filled again with the urge to run away from this religious craziness. I couldn't wait to get back to MIT, where I trusted that logic and sanity prevailed.

Part of me wondered if my cousin wanted to run away from her confounding family like I did mine. Another part of me didn't want to know what she thought—better that we keep such things under wraps. It was easier to deny our heritage than to delve into it.

Mom looked directly at us. There was firmness in her voice and a willful intensity in her eyes as she held her serving spatula tightly in her fist. She proclaimed, "Now that your father has left again, I don't want to pretend to be Catholic for him anymore."

After years of anguish with her Catholic spouse, bending and twisting her history to fit him, Mom now took a stand with her heritage. She ended her story there, with no inquiry, apology, or curiosity for how our confounding religious upbringing affected my brother and me. Steve completed his questioning; maybe he thought that we had consumed enough family heritage at one meal.

Mom rose from the table for the last time that evening. She turned toward her sink, the last of the dishes in her hand. Her face was expressionless. She focused on her motherly chores, leaving her history at the table, a history that couldn't be washed away like the crumbs from her dishes.

As she changed the subject to other things, I could sense calm in her voice and lightness on her shoulders while she tackled her motherly chore and said we could watch TV. I guessed she was relieved the earth hadn't opened and devoured her two kids during her story sharing supper.

My back and bottom were sore from sitting for so long. I was feeling stuffed in both my gut and my mind. I rose quietly and took a stray cup to the sink. "Thank you for supper, Mom." I followed Steve into the living room.

My brother and I didn't mention Mom's history; we acted as if it were nothing. I worked to put it out of my mind. While Mom put away the leftovers and tidied her domain, my brother and I went into TV land.

Mom liked to clean up until her kitchen was spotless, so she didn't join us for a show until later in the evening. When she sat in her favourite living room chair, *Dragnet* and *Twilight Zone* did their job of diverting attention both from Mom's past and the confusing leftovers in my mind.

For many years, I continued to consider: *What does all this make me again?*

* * *

In the years to follow, I never asked Mom if she experienced hate or bigotry in Canada for being a Jew. I had no idea how she felt about Jewish jokes said in bad taste, or about derogatory things said about her faith. She never again shared her thoughts on the matter with us.

It seemed she wanted to continue to downplay her Jewish background, revealing her heritage only to other Jews. Perhaps she wanted to maintain her Christian ruse with everyone else to distance herself from any derogatory word or unpleasant deed.

Hannah (Mom) relaxing after a successful supper at her Montreal home; c. 1985

For me, the less we lingered on my mother's buried secrets and hidden past, the fewer upsets there would be in my perplexed young adult mind. In the years to come, I, too, worked to keep a distance from my Jewish background. I didn't reveal my Hebrew heritage to my friends and colleagues, even if they were Jewish. I didn't talk to my Jewish relatives about their faith.

I wanted to be a typical white-bread Canadian kid and adult, unencumbered by my family's nationality, religion, language, or anything. I wanted people to judge me only by my capabilities and not my background.

I continued to wonder if it was my fear and inability to deal with my buried emotions about our family's history that led to my perpetual muteness on this confusing topic. I wondered how my mother's Jewish history and heritage might affect who I was to become in my life.

* * * *

19

Suppertime Survivor Tale

Mom rarely talked about her family's wartime and post-war history. But this night, over another homemade Hungarian meal of chicken soup, stuffed green peppers in tomato sauce, buttered mashed potatoes, and a side of her staple cucumber salad, she was again in a talking mood.

During such suppers, she usually stood between the table and the stove, minding her pots, pans, and dishes, while my brother and I ate. This time she sat with us.

Earlier that summer, Mom had told us about her Jewish heritage. She still pined for her estranged husband, oscillating between "I hope he gets what he deserves with that whore woman" and "What am I now going to do all by myself?" Sometimes there was only a breath in between. Tonight she put her marriage woes with Dad aside to share more about her family's WWII survival.

My brother and I began to chow down as she started to speak. "I remember that day like it was yesterday," she offered. "I was 17 when the 1938 Munich Agreement was signed. Soon afterward, the day before my eighteenth birthday, the Hungarian army marched through our city. I remember it being a wet and chilly November day."

Mom's hands were flat on the table, her back pressed against the chair. "Our new Hungarian rulers now renamed Košice to Kassa, as it had been when Hungary controlled Slovakia before and during World War I. Near our home, crowds lined the main street of Kassa. Our Hungarian leader, Regent Admiral Miklós Horthy, rode a big white horse ahead of a parade of soldiers. I was watching with my relatives from a neighbour's balcony. Everyone was cheering, including us. People were on their knees, so happy to be reunited with Hungary." She gestured outward. "They were throwing bouquets onto the street."

Her face turned concerned. "Yet, as time passed, my family became not so sure about our future in Kassa." Apprehension rose in her voice, and fear came to her eyes. She touched her chin and continued. "Because Hungary was a German ally, my family expected some Jewish persecution. Months before, thousands of German Jews of Polish origin had been thrown out of Germany and were left to starve at the Polish border."

Regent Horthy, riding through Košice (renamed Kassa) after the annexation of southeast Slovakia to Hungary. November 11, 1938

"Unbelievable!" said my brother. I nodded my accord.

I later learned that most of those Polish Jews had become stuck at the German-Polish border because Germany wanted them out of their country, but Poland refused to let them in.

The Kristallnacht riots soon followed, when thousands of Jews were beaten and killed, their stores and synagogues damaged or destroyed by Nazi sympathizers in both Germany and Austria. Many more German Jews would be arrested and taken away by train to work camps; their property became seized by the state or confiscated by their Christian neighbours.

Mom kept her voice calm and collected. "From my eldest brother, your uncle Geza, we learned in '39 how Jews in Prague were being assaulted and arrested by the Czech fascist police. Geza told us that many Jewish people just disappeared overnight and were never heard from again."

Steve jumped in. "How did Uncle Geza know about that?" His voice was curious but composed.

She stopped for a moment. Her eyes went from side to side as she searched her memory. "Geza lived in Prague," she said. "He had moved there from Košice in 1936 to take a job in an insurance company."

She raised a hand and pointed her soup spoon our way. "In 1938, Geza met his wife, Marta, who was from there. They got married in '39, soon after Hitler's Third Reich took control of the Protectorate of Bohemia and Moravia that was established by the 1938 Munich Agreement."

Steve and I stayed silent as Mom held her spoon firmly. "With things getting worse for Jews in Prague, Geza and Marta tried to get out of the country by immigrating to Palestine. There they hoped to find refuge and see the establishment of a homeland for the Jews."

She lowered her spoon. "But, on their way out of the country, in Bratislava, Marta got a stomach sickness. She became afraid to travel the rest of the way to Palestine."

My mother shook her head. "Marta may not have even wanted to go to Palestine because she and Geza had heard about the hard life that the people there were having. Instead, they changed direction and came to Kassa. In Kassa, things were not as bad for the Jews under the Hungarians. But many knew about the violence that had happened in Prague, and we were afraid."

Mom continued with the bitter story she had prepared with her sweet peppers. She had a look in her eye that said she preferred not to be interrupted. I listened as she continued. "For the next few years, my family lived a fairly normal life in Kassa. Until 1944, most of the fighting in Eastern

Europe was far away in Russia. Kassa only saw the German army pass through in 1941 as they headed to the eastern front."

Years from now, I'd learn from Mom's cousin in Hungary that my parents' hometown had played a critical role in Hitler's alliance with Hungary. When the Germans had passed through Kassa in June of '41, bombs went off in the city. Some alleged that the Soviets had exploded them, but it may have been enacted clandestinely by Fascist Hungarians or Nazi Germans.

Marta and Geza's wedding photo. Prague, 1939.

That bombing led to the Hungarian government declaring war on the Soviet Union. Until then, Hungary's Regent Horthy had avoided getting into the escalating conflict that was orchestrated by Hitler. Because of the bombing, Horthy was compelled to join Germany's eastern campaign.

I later learned that during the early years of the war, things were not as rosy for Hungarian Jews as Mom had let on. The Hungarian authorities removed Jews from their government jobs. They forced Jewish entrepreneurs to close or relinquish their businesses. The fascists sent all able Jewish men to work in labour camps across the countryside to support the war effort. Their wives, sisters, and mothers could only do odd jobs at home or work as domestics for other families.

As my brother and I chowed down on Mom's meal, she continued her story. "After Geza and Marta came back to Kassa, they lived with my eldest sister, Ilonka, and her older husband, Old Geza Klein, in their city apartment on the city's main street." (Mom's family called Ilonka's husband "Old Geza," to tell him apart from Mom's eldest brother.) She added, "As a capable man, your uncle Geza might have been taken away by the army or to a forced labour camp."

She pointed to a wall in her kitchen. "Geza hid in a secret alcove in the Klein's apartment." She opened her hand into a flat palm positioned vertically. "The door of that little room was flush with the wall." She raised her other hand. "My sister and I moved a big dresser to hide the door so no one would know that anybody was in there."

She brought her hand down and looked at us. "Geza hardly went outside for a year. Luckily, no one ever realized he was there."

I wondered what it would have been like to have lived day and night in a cramped closet. I glanced at my brother and imaged us relegated to our room for days, weeks, or months at a time. Out of boredom, we might have bugged each other to our deaths.

Mom put her spoon down and held her hands together in front of her. She continued. "Luckily, my other brother, your uncle Lali, and I were able to leave for Budapest a couple of years after Hungary annexed southern Slovakia. We went there to go to a garment trade school. I was going to become a seamstress and Lali a hat maker."

She pointed to her leg. "Lali had a bad limp from a childhood accident, so he didn't have to serve in the military. In Budapest, it would be easy for us to pretend to be Hungarians, not Slovaks, and to find work. We had spoken Hungarian at home; it was our first language."

Mom's voice turned somber. "But Lali had another big idea and plan. Because we heard from Geza how badly the fascists in Prague were treating the Jews, we feared the worst."

She looked at us, her eyes penetrating. I observed her mouth and avoided the intensity in her eyes. "Lali and I set the way for the rest of our immediate family to follow us to Budapest." She took a big breath. "In Budapest, no one there would know that we were Jews."

She took in another long breath. "One or two at a time, my brother Geza and his wife Marta, my two sisters, Ilonka and Irén, and their husbands, Old Geza and Max, my nephew Ivan, and my father Izidor packed our things and moved from Kassa to Budapest." She blinked a few times. "As you know, my mother, Malvina, had died in 1931."

She raised a hand. "In Budapest, Lali and I arranged separate apartments for everyone. If one group got caught and persecuted or killed, the rest could still survive."

I didn't utter a word, and neither did my brother. I couldn't fathom what it had been like for my kin to have to leave their homes and hide in another city to protect their lives.

Mom put a hand to her forehead. "Unlike my two older brothers, my youngest brother, Gyuszi, had been conscripted into the Hungarian army." She looked away and then back at us. "After a while," she said, her voice elevating, "we stopped hearing from Gyuszi. We couldn't find out where he was or what happened to him."

She looked right at Steve and me. "We suspected he was in a Hungarian labour camp, but we didn't know where or for certain. We worried so much about him; we didn't hear a word from him for years."

Except for Mom's father, who died soon after the war, I knew the people about whom Mom was talking. I had met them during our summer vacation trips to Czechoslovakia. We had lived with them in their apartments, ate meals together, travelled to out-of-town lakes and ponds that had beaches, swam in public swimming pools, rode on the streetcars of Košice (Kassa), and spent days together in a countryside resort spa.

Other than seeing Mom's relatives as a close-knit family who enjoyed being together, I had no clue as to their frightening experiences at the onset of and during WWII. I had never heard them talk about those things. I now found it hard to absorb Mom's family tales. My throat felt dry, and it became hard to swallow my supper.

After a long sigh, Mom went on. "In preparation for my family's move to Budapest, we were able to find or borrow Christian names. Some of us, like me, Lali, my father, my nephew, and even my cousin Joli, got the last name of 'Gurcik.' The Gurciks were domestic helpers who worked for our family in Kassa."

She took another long breath and reached out her arms as if she were going to embrace someone. "Because they were close friends who loved us, they just gave us their identity papers. Members of my family were roughly the same ages as them, so their papers worked okay for us."

My brother interrupted. "So how did the Gurciks get around without papers?" His voice continued to be calm and collected.

I, too, was curious and looked at Mom for a reply.

She looked at Steve and responded calmly. "With some papers, we could make copies or create new false ones. With others, the Gurciks could go to the city hall to get new ones, saying they lost their old ones." She raised her eyebrows. "Fortunately, because Geza had been an administrator in his former job, he was good at reworking what papers he could get."

Mom recounted, "Through his insurance company position in Prague, Geza had learned special skills. With those skills, he was able to create fake official documents."

She stared past my brother and me. "Fearing the worst for us, Lali instructed Geza to make new Christian identity cards and birth certificates for everyone in our immediate family. Geza agreed, and he kept himself busy with that project while he hid in our sister's apartment in Kassa."

She explained. "Geza knew how to use special chemicals to wash the black type out of papers. He then retyped or wrote in new information that matched the characteristics of our family. He added our photos, forged official government signatures, and stamped the documents with fake Interior Ministry or Police Department stamps he made."

I sat still and speechless as I listened to my mother's chilling story while downing her hot meal. Having been born in Canada, where there had never been a war, and where the government worked for the people, I could hardly imagine what Mom's family must have experienced. Might I have mustered the courage and creativity to do what they had done?

Mom's eyes looked away and then back at us. Her voice quieted. "One day, Geza took a chance and went out to visit my sister, Irén, who lived only a few blocks away. When he arrived in her building, he noticed that the door to the apartment next door to Irén's was unlocked. The man who lived there, Radeczky, worked as a teacher at a correctional facility in the town." Mom's eyes went back and forth. "For some reason, Radeczky wasn't home at the time, so Geza went into his apartment and looked around."

She kept her head and voice low. "There, he found a big desk and opened its drawers." She engaged her hands to mimic Geza pulling drawers open. "Soon, he discovered Radeczky's identity papers. Geza 'borrowed' them and quickly left."

Relief came to her voice as she sat a little higher in her chair. "Luckily, none of the neighbours ever saw Geza. He could have been turned in to the police and taken away from us."

She looked again at my brother and me. "Geza got to work on those papers. He changed the picture to his photo. He also made a new Christian identity for Marta, his wife. He soon tested the new documents by travelling by train to Budapest."

She raised a hand. "A day or two after he had left Kassa, Ilonka and Marta got a telegram from Geza. It said just two words: 'Radeczky good.' They then knew he had made it to Budapest without being detained or caught with false documents."

Mom looked down and then back at us. "When Geza returned to Kassa, he and Marta packed up, took their baby son, Jirka, with them, and they left for Budapest under the Radeczky name."

What they had lived through!

I glanced at my brother as I continued to consume my supper quietly. I could see that he too sat still and was rapt.

Tension grew in Mom's voice. "As for Ilonka, Old Geza, and their son Ivan, they were the last of our family to leave Kassa. They got out just before the Nazis sent all Kassa Jews away to Auschwitz."

Decades later, my cousin, Ivan, told me more about that part of the family story. He shared that Hitler and his Nazis had been displeased with Hungary's leniency toward the Jews. The more sympathetic Regent Horthy hadn't readily complied with Hitler's extermination orders for their Hungarian Jewish people. Even though the Hungarian government severely limited many freedoms for the Jews, Horthy hadn't wanted to see them exterminated so quickly. Hungary had been too dependent on its Jewish citizens to keep the country's commerce going.

Cousin Ivan offered, "For the early years of the war, Horthy's greater tolerance won out. But Hitler swiftly deposed Horthy in March of '44, and he began to run Hungary the Nazi way."

By early April 1944, within weeks of seizing power, the Germans had put more restrictions on Hungarian Jews. As it had been in other Nazi-controlled states, Jews had to wear a yellow Star of David on their clothes. They were not permitted to utilize public transportation or visit any public theatres, coffee houses, or spas.

Later the same month, the Nazis created a temporary camp for Jews at a brick factory on the edge of Kassa and sent most of Kassa's Jewish people there. About 10,000 of Kassa's 65,000 people had been Jewish.

My cousin, twenty-three years my elder, said these things matter-of-factly. He acted as if he had only observed and not been a victim of those atrocities. He continued. "Because my father held special military status, my parents and I were exempt at first from wearing the Star of David on our clothes. The Hungarian police also spared people like us from getting relocated to the Kassa brick factory camp or sending us to one of the other smaller Jewish ghettos in town."

He spoke to me slowly and clearly, as if he were talking to his son. "My father, Old Geza, had served in the Hungarian military during The First Great War." He pointed to his leg. "He received a minor injury during the conflict." He smiled a touch. "That service and injury had given him special status as a wounded Hungarian veteran. It exempted him from being treated like the rest of Hungary's Jews."

Ivan took a long breath and let it out slowly. "It was because of this special treatment that my father decided that he, my mother, and I would stay in Kassa into '44, rather than leave earlier to Budapest with the rest of our Friedmann family."

He continued without hesitation. "My father had been a well-to-do garment-material merchant in Kassa, and he had many friends in the community. A few weeks after those Kassa camps were established that spring of '44, a city police detective approached him. The guy, who my father knew, warned my father that the Germans were going to send away all Jews no matter what special status they had."

Part of the Friedmann family in Košice; September 1941. From left to right: Lali, Lenka (a Košice cousin who died in Auschwitz in 1944), Anna (my mother), Marta (Geza's wife), Irén, and Izidor. Geza, an avid photographer, was behind the camera.

There was no emotion in Ivan's voice. It seemed as if any feelings of trepidation or terror had dissipated over the decades. Or maybe they had become locked into an abandoned part of his psyche.

He continued. "My father was prepared for this eventuality. That same day, he had me—I was twelve years old at the time—escorted out of the city by local people who were quietly helping Jews escape to Budapest. I left by train under the name of Charles Gurcik and went to live with your mother and Uncle Lali in Budapest."

His tone stayed steady. "Within another day or two, my father and mother found their way out of Kassa with the false Christian identity of 'Kalina.' They got out of Slovakia just a few days before the Germans took every Kassa Jew, even the previously exempted ones, away to the brick factory camp and then to Auschwitz."

Starting in May of that year, Jews and other "undesirables" (gypsies, criminals, and deserters) were transported by train from the brick factory to that death camp. Over the next two months, the Nazis deported over 13,000 Jews from Kassa and its surrounding villages. Over the ensuing eight months, ninety percent of those Kassa Jews were shot or gassed to their deaths. The killing only stopped when the Russians liberated Auschwitz in January of '45.

Mom pressed on with her family's survival story. Her eyes became wet. "At the time, after Ivan came to live with Lali and me, we didn't know what happened to Old Geza and my sister.

"It was only after the war when we found out that, once they got to Budapest, they split up and went separate ways. If the fascists caught one of them as a Jew, then he or she would not be able to say where the other one was. They didn't want to take a chance to communicate with Ivan or us until the war was over."

Steve and I stayed still as statues in our seats. I don't know about my brother, but I was overwhelmed by the enormity of my mother's story. Though I knew that Old Geza and Aunt Ilonka had survived the war, I had been afraid to ask how they lived through it. Maybe I didn't want to know their horrendous tale. Had I been afraid of my anticipated reactions of horror?

My mother held back tears. Her head was down as she looked at her open hands. "Only after we got back to Košice [after the war, the reinstalled Czechoslovakia government restored the town's Slavic name] did we find out about the Jewish deportation to Auschwitz. No one knew until then what the

Nazis had done. Most of those poor people—and nearly all of our relatives and friends who had stayed in Košice—never came back."

My mouth was open, and my fork hovered in the air, but not a morsel passed through my lips. I continued to wonder what I would have done under those circumstances. As I had considered when my father recounted his dramatic stories of war survival, could I have survived the brutal ordeal through which Mom's family had gone?

My mother's story wasn't complete. She lifted her head and said, "For a while, after Lali and I had arrived in Budapest, there was no war there. We could go out and do things, like going to the public swimming pools, cafés, and parks."

Not wanting my brother to be the only one to ask questions, and because we were now on a less dreadful topic, I broke my silence. "What did you do for money, Mom? How did you eat?"

Lali (center) and Anna (right), at a Budapest outdoor spa with a friend, 1943.
Anna was 22 years old at the time. The identity of the friend is unknown.

She replied calmly. "We had some money saved before we left Kassa. And Lali and I were lucky to find odd jobs, him as a hat maker and me as a seamstress. But when my father and nephew joined us, they couldn't work, so we had to support them."

She raised a hand. "Food was hard to get, especially during the Allied bombings in the last months of the war. We had to share what we had." She looked directly at me, her eyes glaring. "Sometimes, we could buy only a few potatoes."

She took a long breath. "Some people gave away the gold rings from their fingers just to get a loaf of bread." She said this as she touched the only ring on her right hand, one I knew she had worn since before I had been born.

Her voice turned frightened. "Meat became very scarce. In those last months of the war, if a bomb or gun accidentally went off and killed a horse, people would run on the street with their knives. Right away, they cut the poor animal into pieces to bring home. Within half an hour, the whole horse had disappeared."

A small smile came to her face. "We even ate horse meat ourselves, yet Ivan and I didn't know because my brother and father didn't tell us. They spiced it so much that we couldn't tell what it was."

Mom's voice tightened again. "We had to be very careful when we went out on the street, especially after the German army took over Budapest in early '44. During that spring and summer, they took away many Jews."

She placed the back of her hand against her forehead. "From what we found out after the war, the Germans killed or deported all the Jews they could find, over a half-million of them from across the Hungarian countryside. And in Budapest, most of the Jews there were put into ghettos in the city and held until the Germans could send them away. They were the last of the Jews left in the country."

From what I would read years later, the Nazis placed the Budapest Jews into Yellow Star Houses—thousands of mini-ghettos in the city—until they could deport them to concentration camps. There were Jews who resisted and fought back with guns against the killing squads of Hungary's Arrow Cross fascist party.

After Hitler had put the Arrow Cross into power in the fall of 1944, their squads captured many Jewish resisters. They chained Jews, deserters, gypsies, and others they deemed criminals, together in pairs. They escorted them with guns to the banks of the Danube. There they shot them dead with a bullet to the head, letting them fall into the Danube with the chains still attached.

Mom further explained how, one day, her brother-in-law, Max Buš, was stopped in the street by the Arrow Cross police. She pointed to her hand. "A birth deformity in his right arm had given Buš a stump as a hand. That permitted his being exempt from military service. But because of the way he looked," she pointed to her face, "the police accused him of being a Jew."

Mom was laughing and crying at the same time. "To prove his religious identity, Buš had to pull down his pants and show himself." She slapped the table lightly. "Luckily for my sister, Irén, she had married a Catholic man."

Mom didn't say, but I understood. Irén had hidden her Jewish heritage behind her husband's Christian name and uncircumcised penis.

She looked our way once more. "On another occasion, during a quiet evening after supper, Lali, Ivan, Izidor, and I went strolling in the main city park near to where we lived." She quickly looked and pointed behind her, and then she looked back at us. "On the way home, my father got frightened when he noticed a man following us. He thought he recognized the person from Kassa—someone who knew us as Jews."

Mom looked frightened, her eyes shifting. "Thinking quickly, Lali had the four of us split up and swiftly head in three separate directions, with Ivan taking Izidor. We took different ways back to our apartment. Luckily, we made it back to our home without anything bad happening."

An intense look came over her face. "Then the air raids started in the fall of 1944. We spent nearly four months, sometimes day and night, in the basement of our apartment building during those loud sirens and terrible bombings."

Her hands were shaking. "Then came the street fighting, as Soviet troops entered and occupied the city." She covered her mouth with her hand. "Sometimes, we were bombed by the Russian and British planes during the day and then by the Americans at night."

She took another long breath. "During one bad night of bombing, our building shook from the explosions." She pointed ahead of her. "When we came out from the basement after the 'all clear' siren, we saw that the building next door had collapsed entirely. Anybody who had been hiding in that basement never got out."

Mom sighed. "The fighting destroyed nearly half the city. Thousands of people died, and many were badly hurt. There was no electricity. And there were times we had nothing to eat."

Mom glanced upward, her hands clasped and shaking. "During those bombings and the fighting, I prayed every day to my grandmother Matelaye for our safety."

Our mother had previously mentioned a story regarding her mother's mother. Matelaye and her brood were poor, country Jews who often went hungry. Mom had said that Matelaye was a woman of great faith, her husband being a rabbi. It appeared she also had a "higher" connection.

One Friday afternoon in her kitchen, Matelaye started to cook a Shabbat supper for her spouse and three daughters. As she began to boil a pot of water in her kitchen fireplace, she looked around for what food she had.

Finding little for her family's meal, except for a few potatoes, she was overcome with despair and started praying to God. The story goes that, out of nowhere, a fish appeared in the barren fireplace pot, answering her prayers.

Some of Matelaye's offspring believed there might have been a mother stork with a nest on the roof, the bird losing its catch down Matelaye's chimney. Others, like my mother and her eldest sister, Ilonka, were convinced Matelaye had a link to the Divine. When either my mother or her sister was distraught about something, like a sick or distressed relative, they clutched their hands together and called out to Matelaye for help.

Mom's eyes wetted as she offered, "Matelaye's family had been very poor. While on her deathbed, Matelaye promised her daughter—my mother, Malvina—that she would work to help Malvina's children more when she reached the afterlife than she could in her lifetime. She even foretold that 'all would be well' in our coming through a future disaster or ordeal."

Mom raised a hand toward the ceiling. Her eyes followed her hand while she placed the other palm over her mouth. "Matelaye answered our prayers, for we all stayed alive during those terrible Budapest bombings."

Decades later, I uncovered more details from Mom's cousin Joli about what happened to Matelaye's two other daughters and their families. Joli told me that, out of Mom's fifteen aunts, uncles, cousins, in-law spouses, nieces, and nephews who remained in Kassa through the war, only Joli's 14-year-old niece, Magda, survived. Everyone else died in Auschwitz or a forced-labour camp, or they committed suicide just before being sent away to the Košice brick factory. The young Magda had been my mother's only extended family member to have survived the German death camp. Cousin Joli stayed alive by living, like my mother, under the Gurcik name in Budapest.

Mom's clenched her fist while she sat at the table of my childhood. Her voice surged with emotion, like an avalanche breaking free from a mountain top. "What those Nazis did to the Jews, and my relatives, was horrible and unforgivable!" She looked down at the table and repeated, "But we knew nothing about those death camps until after the war was over."

My heart filled with sadness for all the loss. My eyes stared down, hardly able to look at my mother. I could only imagine what the death of most of Mom's extended family had meant for her and her close kin. She was right; the Nazis had been just as she had said: horrible and unforgivable.

After taking a moment to settle down, Mom continued calmly. "After the Germans and Hungarians surrendered in Budapest in February of 1945, our whole family reunited again. We wondered if we should go somewhere else or stay in Budapest. We could have gone to Vienna, which was a free zone, open to all refugees."

She looked away and then back at us. "But Old Geza was homesick. He had spent the last year of the war hiding in a Budapest sanatorium, having paid a doctor he knew there to keep his Jewish identity a secret." She smiled a little. "Ilonka too had been hiding by working as a domestic for a high-up Hungarian government bureaucrat and his family. They never suspected that she was a Jew."

She raised her hand in resignation. "Old Geza wanted us to go back home, and we agreed to stick together. My family decided to return to Košice because we knew that place the best. Only my cousin Joli remained in Budapest because she met her fiancé there during the war. He was a Hungarian Jew who also hid under a fake Christian identity during the war."

"How was he able to do that?" I asked. I didn't want my brother to ask all the questions.

Mom looked at me, the muscles of her face relaxing. "I don't know, son. He never spoke about it, but Cousin Joli did say that he had escaped from a forced labour camp and found his way to Budapest."

Her eyes showed a caring expression. "And my brother Lali, who was a good organizer, made the arrangements for our going back home. He helped not just us but many other Hungarians and Slovaks who wanted to go back to Košice."

A professional photo of Anna at about 20 years old.
Most likely taken for her Catholic Hungarian identity papers during WWII; c. 1941.

She looked at the kitchen table and carefully picked up dirty dishes as if they too were family members. I sat mesmerized by her words, wondering again if I could have survived her family's ordeal.

After placing our dishes in the sink, Mom turned to us once more. "Even returning to Košice had a frightening moment. While we were on the train heading back home, we were stopped in Miskolc [a city in northeastern Hungary] by Russian troops. They were looking for Czechoslovak citizens coming from Hungary, to take them to Soviet camps in Ukraine."

She placed her hand over her heart. "Like many people on the train, your cousin Ivan was showing his patriotism by having a small Czechoslovak flag sewn onto his backpack." Her voice rose. "Luckily, he managed to run into the train's bathroom and rip off the flag only seconds before a Russian soldier could identify him as Czechoslovak. The Russians took many of our countrymen off the train that day—we could see them rounded up outside. Those people were not lucky."

"What happened to them?" my brother asked.

Mom answered matter-of-factly as if her tears had run dry after recollecting her family's story. "They went to a communist indoctrination camp." She stared at the table. "The lucky ones showed up in Košice a year or two later."

I broke in, wanting Mom to continue her original track. "How did you get back home to Košice from Miskolc?"

She looked at me and calmly continued. "The Russians didn't let our train go past Miskolc. We had to take a horse and buggy the rest of the way to Košice, which was over 100 kilometers away."

She grinned again. "Fortunately, when we got back to our city, we saw that the fighting hadn't made much damaged." She pointed to the kitchen wall. "We could see bullet holes in some of the outside walls, but none of the buildings were destroyed as they had been in Budapest."

She took in a few long breaths. "When we arrived at our old apartment by the city's old wall, we found it empty and unusable. The Germans had taken everything out and used that space as a horse stable." She touched her chest again. "But, to our surprise, we did find a box of family pictures in the basement under that stable."

She gestured across the kitchen. "Our family then went to look at the building next door. Because most of the Jews were gone and the fascists had fled, we found empty apartments. My sister and I took a couple of cleaner flats on the second floor. The rest of my family found places a few blocks away.

"We then went around to the neighbors to see what we could borrow—cups, plates, silverware, even a spare mattress and any furniture we could find. Slowly, we put our lives back together."

Excitement rose in her voice, and she put both of her hands on her chest. "And my brother Gyuszi one day showed up from nowhere. We were so happy to see him. He told us he spent the war in a Hungarian labour camp near the Russian front. There, he had dug ditches and looked for buried landmines with fellow workers."

Relief filled her voice. "Gyuszi was so lucky to be alive. My grandma Matelaye again kept her promise to our mother."

The Friedmann family in Kosice. It was before or around the time that everyone changed their names to Christian ones to escape to Budapest. 1942.
Top row: Old Geza, Irén, Helena Gurcik, Lali, Nusi (Anna), Gyuszi.
Bottom row: Ilonka, Izidor, Marta, Geza, Ivan.
In the baby carriage: Jirka, who was Geza and Marta's first son.

Mom lowered her hands. "With help from neighbors, and finding what we could from the people who left belongings behind, we managed to get back on our feet.

Soon Lali opened a new, modern hat store on the main street of Košice. Old Geza was there too with a textile shop. My brother, Geza, and his wife, Marta, returned to Prague. I started my seamstress shop in my apartment, and I had a couple of women working for me. Even my niece Magda, who survived the death camp, worked awhile for me."

She sighed again. "Yet it was so sad to see so few Jews left in our city. Outside of our immediate family, there was hardly anybody left in Košice that we knew."

My brother raised his hand slowly. "It seems you all were fortunate this time."

The Tatransky first cousins reunite in NYC. From left to right: Steve (first son of Anna), Janet (daughter of Lali), Jirka (first son of Geza), Ivan (son of Ilonka), Harry (second son of Anna) and Thomas (second son of Geza), who were born to the Košice Friedmann-Tatransky family. It was the last time that all six cousins came together. Summer of 2007.

"Yes," my mother responded, "Nearly all of Košice's Jews got killed in Auschwitz. While many families lost everybody, it was a miracle that my immediate family remained intact. Our only bad luck was that my father died less than a year after we came back home. He caught pneumonia in the winter of '46 after returning from synagogue on the Sabbath."

The extended Tatransky family of first, second, and third cousins who wouldn't have lived if our forbearers had not survived WWII. Six other descendants (Steve's two children, and Ivan's son and his three children) are not pictured, making the total 22 offspring. The summer of 2007.

After another pause and big breath, she added, "If it weren't for what my brothers Lali and Geza did for us, none of us would have stayed alive during the war. And it was so fortunate that Geza and Marta were able to leave Prague in '39 and come to Kassa to warn us."

Mom was right about that. I later read that, in '41 and '42, nearly every Jew living in the Protectorate of Bohemia and Moravia, and in what remained of Slovakia, was sent to Nazi concentration camps. The fascists then sent all of them to their death.

Struggling to finish Mom's stuffed peppers, I couldn't stop thinking about how remarkable it was that Mom's family survived through such awful times. Over the previous years, Mom had shared snippets of her family's war survival story with my brother and me. I had previously understood they went to Budapest because it was safer for Hungarians to live there—at least until the Allied bombings started—and not because she and her family were Jewish. I now sat stuffed on both another one of Mom's meals and her harrowing experiences.

Maybe I, too, should feel deeply indebted to my great-grandmother, Matelaye.

* * *

Mom put out *mákos* and *diós* (poppy seed and walnut rolls) for dessert. She had trudged, by bus and subway, into the city to get those sweets from a Hungarian bakery. She offered us hot Sankas, adding a big squirt of Reddi-Wip cream on top to make it the way we liked, Viennese style.

She filled her coffee cup and added Reddi-Wip. She offered more about what happened after her family returned to Košice. "When we finally learned about the Holocaust and what the Nazis did to the Jews, we no longer wanted to be connected to Judaism. We were not a religious family anyway." She sipped her Sanka. "Many other Jews were letting go of their Germanic Jewish names and picking new ones. So my family decided to do the same thing." She pointed to herself. "But we wondered what we should call ourselves."

Years later, my cousin Ivan explained to me why Central and Eastern European Jews wanted to change their last names after WWII. He said that, before the late 1700s, the Austrian-Hungarian Empire discriminated against their Jews. Jews lived only in small villages, and they didn't have surnames.

But after the death of Maria Theresa in 1780, her son, Emperor Joseph II, became ruler of the Hapsburg Empire. He soon permitted both Jews and serfs to gain civil rights and become better integrated into Austrian-Hungarian society. The emperor's reforms included having Jews pick German surnames for themselves.

Ivan presented a small smile. "Many Jews chose names connected to a personal characteristic. Some chose 'Friedmann,' meaning 'peace friend,' or 'Schwartz,' meaning 'black,' or 'Weiss,' meaning 'pale,' or 'Gross,' meaning 'big,' or 'Klein' (my father's last name), meaning 'small,' and so on." He glanced away and then back at me. "After WWII, anybody having such Germanic last names identified them as being Jewish, unless they could prove it otherwise."

Mom took a bite of poppy seed roll. She said, "My brother Lali was the one to have another wonderful idea. He thought we should rename our family after our favourite park in the High Tatra Mountains of Slovakia."

I knew this part of the Carpathian Mountains from our family's summer trips to Czechoslovakia. The range carried the nickname "The Slovak Alps." Thick pine forests covered the landscape. Bubbling mountain streams emanated from high glacial lakes. Jagged mountain peaks reached over 3,000 meters above sea level.

Mom continued. "Our family loved to walk, hike, and even ski in the Tatras, near to Štrbské Pleso and Starý Smokovec." She looked intently at Steve and me. "You know those places; we visited there with Daddy in both '68 and '72, on our car trips from Vienna and Munich to Košice."

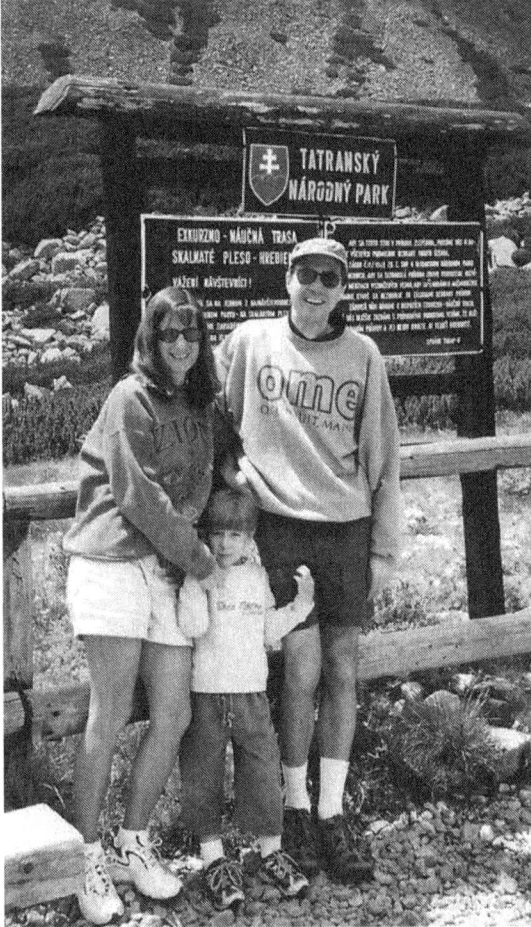

My wife, son, and I are visiting the Tatransky National Park in Slovakia, after which my mother's family named themselves post-WWII. Summer of 2001.

Steve and I nodded. She continued. "Before and after the war, my family often went to the Tatras by train from Košice, just to spend nice times together." She looked our way with pride in her eyes. "My brothers and sisters accepted Lali's idea. We agreed to officially rename ourselves 'Tatransky,' after Tatranský Národný Park."

After the ways the Nazis mistreated the Jews, I could understand why Mom's family wanted to change their last name. And I was puzzled. In my growing understanding of my mother's family background, didn't her family realize that 'Tatransky' sounded about as Jewish as 'Friedmann'? Then again, one might say our Simkovits name seemed Jewish too, but we had heard from Dad that it was a Christian Austrian-Hungarian name meaning "son of Simko."

Chalk up one more last name to Mom's growing list! I could imagine re-introducing her to my friends as Mrs. Hannah Friedmann Gurcik Tatransky Simkovits.

Mom finished her coffee. She seemed relaxed now that she completed the dish stacking and food putting away. She offered, "My Jewish heritage became useful only once in my life."

She looked at us from across the table. "After the Czechoslovak Communist Party took over the government in '48, Jewish refugees were being permitted to leave some Soviet-occupied countries and head to Israel." She pointed to herself. "Your father and I wanted to go there too, with your uncle Lali and his new bride, Martha."

"You wanted to go to Israel?" I blurted out. My voice was raspy from dryness. I couldn't imagine what it would have been like to grow up in a country that was continually at war with its Arab neighbours. I didn't know if my brother had a similar reaction, for I was looking only at my mother.

"Yes," she offered matter-of-factly. The youth group I had been a part of, the Hashomer Hatzair, had a goal of resettling in Palestine. And because Czechoslovakia was then allowing Hungarian Jews to leave the country, it was a legitimate way for me, Lali, and Martha to get out in 1949."

She raised a hand, not allowing me to ask more. "A few Eastern European communist leaders and officials were letting Jews emigrate. They expected that the newly formed State of Israel would become a communist country. Jews from all over Europe were flocking to Palestine to start new lives." Her eyes narrowed. "But later in '49, the Jewish emigration was stopped because Israel didn't turn communist; it became democratic."

I later found out that a higher Russian authority overruled the communist officials who supported and permitted that emigration to Israel. Those officials were then prosecuted and executed for aiding and abetting Jews from Soviet satellite countries to leave Eastern Europe for the new state.

I couldn't believe how cruel the Soviets were to the Jews, even after what the Nazis had done to them. Maybe I also was having trouble grasping what life in Israel would have been like for our family. I sprayed more Reddi-Wip into my coffee in an attempt to counteract my uneasiness.

Mom continued to put her immigration story on the table. "We were fortunate that in early 1949, your uncle Lali, aunt Martha, and I could take a special Aliya [meaning 'ascent' in Hebrew] bus out of the country from Bratislava to Vienna, and then on to Israel. We pretended to be Hungarian Jews, which was easy because Hungarian was our first language."

She gestured towards Steve and me as if she were handing us something. "Lali gave extra money to the bus driver so he wouldn't ask too many questions." She raised her hand to her hair and grinned. "I was bleached blond and had blue eyes. But before I could leave the country, I had to dye my hair back to its original brown colour. Otherwise, no one would have believed I was a Jew."

I considered what my mother might have looked like as a natural brunette. My brother and I had never seen her as other than a blond. I couldn't tell if she would look more Jewish if she had dark hair. She certainly didn't look Jewish as a blond. Maybe light hair been her way to blend in when she lived in Budapest during the war.

She continued. "Before we left the country, your daddy and I were married on April 5th of '49. We had a civil ceremony in Košice and then a weekend honeymoon in Sliač." She looked down at her folded hands. "Lali, Martha, and I left Czechoslovakia soon afterward."

Her voice rose. "At first, my brothers and sisters were against my wanting to marry a Catholic and leave the country with him." Though Mom didn't say it, her father's death in 1946 no longer stood as a barrier for her to marry a Christian or leave her homeland.

She pointed toward a window as she looked at us. "Your daddy had a reputation for having been with other women. So I went and asked my nephew, your cousin Ivan, what he thought about my going away with your father." She took another deep breath. "Ivan told me, 'If you love him, then marry him and go with him.'"

After glancing away, she looked back at us. "I did, so I did," she said. Her tone was confident. "Your dad was charming, nice to me then, and had lots of big ideas about our future. I fell in love with him. I thought he loved me and would never leave me."

A hint of sadness touched her voice, and she looked again at her hands on the table. "I hoped we would live together into our old age."

Anna and Jani on honeymoon in Sliač. Spring 1948.
This photo was the only time I ever saw my parents holding hands.

My brother and I had many times heard from Dad about our parents' marriage and subsequent escape from Czechoslovakia. He had told us, "It was easier for your mother to leave our country by pretending to be Hungarian." Dad never said anything about her being Jewish, and Mom never contradicted or added to his version of the story, until now.

Sometime after this evening, Dad would tell Steve and me, "Your mother was my girlfriend at the time when I wanted to leave Czechoslovakia. I didn't want to leave the country alone. I thought she and I could make a life together." His voice turned cold. "In time, I found out that she was too controlling, always trying to restrict me from my business."

My father didn't explain what he meant, but I suspected he felt she wanted him home every night while he preferred to cavort with his chums and colleagues. Dad might have married Mom because he sensed her unadulterated loyalty to him. I guessed he couldn't show the same to her.

Finishing a piece of poppy seed cake and taking the last sip from her Sanka, Mom again looked at my brother and me. "Lali, Martha, and I reached Vienna by the end of April. We met your father there, soon after he had escaped."

She again looked to one side and then returned her gaze to us. She hesitated for a moment as if she had more to say about our father's departure from his homeland, but then she pressed forward on a related topic. "But your daddy was worried there was still fighting going on between the Jews and Arabs in Israel."

She wiped cake crumbs off her hands and onto a plate. "We heard from others in Vienna that recent immigrants to Israel were writing letters back home telling their relatives not to go there. Those letters told of life still being very hard in the new state." She sighed. "So, your daddy became scared to go."

Our father later explained to Steve and me his reasons for not venturing to Israel. "As it had been for over a thousand years, the region was in constant conflict between Arabs and Jews. In 1948, after Britain had formed Israel into a Jewish homeland, the new country was right away at war with its Palestinian neighbours. The Muslims were claiming the same holy lands and shrines as did the Jews and Christians." Dad took a deep breath. "I felt there would never be peace there!"

For a moment, Mom stared at the kitchen wall. "Something else happened that stopped our going to Israel." She hesitated for a few seconds, her eyes searching, and then she pressed on. "While we were waiting for our Israeli travel papers in Vienna, Daddy and Lali had a big argument. It was about machines and equipment they had sent to Israel from Slovakia to arrive there before we did."

She took a long breath. "Your father and Lali had planned to start a garment factory together. They pooled their money, and your daddy—using his Czechoslovak business connections—bought and collected the materials and equipment. He arranged for the transport of those goods to Martha's brother, who was already in Israel." Mom's lips curled up a little. "Your father knew the customs officials he needed to pay to get a transport container safely out of the country."

Mom looked again at her hands that were clasped together on the table. She seemed nervous, her eyes going back and forth. "Sometime after we arrived in Vienna, we were wired by Lali's brother-in-law. He said that your father's shipment got to him, but the container was empty except for some garbage.

She put a hand to her chest. "We couldn't figure out what happened to the things your father had bought and shipped." She took another long breath. "That message caused much bitterness between your father and Lali.

Mom hunched over, both of her hands now on her face. "Lali speculated your Dad never really intended to go to Israel, but that he took Lali's money and shipped an empty container. Your father, on the other hand, believed Lali's brother-in-law in Israel had something to do with the loss of those things.

"But no one knows the truth," she almost shouted. "Those things could have been stolen anywhere along the way. Lali and your daddy still had a big argument about it, accusing each other of stealing." She gave a big sigh. "After that argument, your father no longer wanted to go to Israel."

I could imagine Mom feeling horrible about being pulled between a husband she loved and a brother who had saved her family's life during the war. She might also have been sad about not making it to Israel, where she might have felt more at home than here in Canada. Instead, Dad compelled her to follow him in a very different direction.

She looked at us. "For a couple of months, your father tried to do business in Vienna, but he just lost money. Then he saw posters in the city saying that Canada and Australia were looking for immigrants. The U.S. was another place we thought we could go, yet Canada was a younger country. Your father felt we could have more opportunity here." She sighed. "But all those countries were accepting only Christian couples. Jews were going to Israel."

Whether her statement was accurate or not, I was grateful that she and Dad had decided to come to Canada. Who knows how I might have felt born and raised in Israel, or even Australia.

Years later, I overheard a Jewish woman friend ask my father, "Why didn't you want to go to Israel when you had the chance?" Dad thought for a moment then respond with a straight face, "I didn't want to get circumcised." I don't know if he was kidding, but I cringed at the thought.

Decades after this supper of family revelations, I discovered that Mom was only partially correct about the ability of Jews to enter Canada after WWII. During the years leading to and throughout the Second World War, Canada had no Jewish refugee program.

Fueled by both the Great Depression and widespread anti-Semitism by Canadian Anglo-Saxon government ministers, Canada had one of the worst prewar records of accepting Jewish refugees from Europe. Only 4000 Jews were allowed into Canada between 1933 and 1939—as opposed to 200,000 permitted into the U.S. during the same period.

The Canada Broadcasting Corporation published an article saying how anti-Semitism was a way of life in English Canada. Many industries did not hire Jews. People in power routinely excluded Jewish professionals from jobs at universities, hospitals, and law firms. Clubs, resorts, and beaches had barred Jewish Canadians. In French Quebec, the situation had been no better.

I was aghast and perplexed that my country had been a closed culture. That wasn't the Canada I felt a part of, though I had experienced anti-Semitic sentiments wielded on my Jewish peers in high school.

Then again, why should things have been different in Canada? Quebec's English-French animosity had existed for hundreds of years. That was short compared to the thousands of years of Anti-Semitism around the world. Religious and cultural hatred can proliferate as quickly as people do.

Mom had not been correct about Canada accepting only Christian couples back in 1949. At the end of WWII, Canada loosened its immigration policy because of their espoused need for increased labour in the booming postwar economy. In the three years between 1947 and 1950, 40,000 Holocaust survivors were accepted into the country, the largest influx of Jews into Canada since the First World War.

I was confounded, and still am, as to why Mom thought and said that Canada didn't allow Jews to enter our country after the war. But I could understand that she and her Jewish family wanted to distance themselves from Judaism because of the WWII atrocities against her people.

She might have been afraid the tide might once again turn against Jews in Canada, or that discrimination would be thrust upon her and Dad if they revealed her true heritage. For his personal and business reasons, Dad may have asked her to divulge nothing about her ethnic background.

Finishing my dessert and coffee, I saw Mom's eyes cast downward again. "From Vienna," she offered, "we wrote our relatives in Košice to ask what they thought we should do, to go to Canada or Australia."

She looked up. "They wrote back saying we should choose Canada because it was closer to Czechoslovakia. In Canada, we could also be closer to our distant Friedmann cousins who lived in Chicago."

Mom explained how, around 1885, her father's much older brother, Jacob, had been sent to Chicago by his parents. "After Jacob had his Bar Mitzvah, at the age of 13, he was encouraged to immigrate to the USA. In Chicago, he learned the fur trade and became a successful furrier until he died in 1943 at 72 years old."

Steve spoke suddenly. "Did your uncle have a family in Chicago? Will we ever meet them?"

Mom looked at my brother, her mood lifting. "Jacob had three children and many grandchildren who now live all over the United States. They know I'm here in Montreal. I get letters from them from time to time. They tell me that they would like to come to visit us."

"That's great," Steve said.

I had a kneejerk reaction. *Oh! Not more Jewish relatives!*

Though I would come to meet and happily embrace members of Mom's extended U.S. family when they came to visit us, I still felt besieged by my newly discovered heritage. I felt as if I had been standing firmly on a dry beach, my back to the ocean, and then an unexpected tidal wave struck me from behind and felled me, stunned, to the ground.

Mom went back to her story. "So because my family said we should go to Canada and not Australia, that's how we decided to immigrate here. I then officially switched my identity to being a Slovak Catholic instead of a Hungarian Jew, so we could apply to come." She lifted a hand. "It was your father's idea to make Maria my middle name. And we changed my first name to Anna, to make my full name sound more Christian."

Anna Maria! How did Mom change her identity just like that? Her change of religion—so she could come to Canada—didn't seem too official to me. It sounded as if it had been a spur of the moment decision, perhaps initiated by a simple pencil stroke or a checkmark on an official immigration application form, plus the adjustment to her name, which made Mom suddenly become a Christian rather than a Jew.

My brother and I remained silent. We didn't ask her more about her change of faith. I suspect we both wanted to show her our acceptance of her now reclaimed Judaism.

Or maybe we were too afraid to confront our Jewishness any further. Part of me felt I needed to chew on and digest what she had told us. Another part wished I hadn't known. And another part wanted to put her revelations into an empty closet and not open it again.

Mom stood and gathered our dessert dishes. "But our problems were still not over," she said. Concern returned to her voice. "From Vienna, your father and I had to reach Salzburg. That was the place where we had to register for the Canada immigration program."

As Dad had once told us, Mom reiterated how, in 1949, the area surrounding Vienna was a Russian-occupied zone. "If the Soviets caught your father and me as we made our way through their zone, they would have sent us back to Czechoslovakia or possibly to a camp in Siberia."

We had known from Dad that, without warning, the communists could make whole families disappear, and they would never be heard from again. Prominent members of the Russian Communist Party then obtained those family's houses and apartments, thus rewarding party members for their loyalty to the state.

As a still young first-generation Canadian son, I found it unfathomable that individuals and families could be uprooted and shipped away at a moment's notice. But I received first-hand experience via my Slovak relatives' apprehensions when we had visited them behind the Iron Curtain.

I remembered Mom's brother-in-law, Max Bus, shushing my brother and me in a Košice park when he and I fooled around in public. My uncle didn't want us to attract attention. We learned from him that anybody could be a communist informant. Those partisans earned points with their higher-up party friends by reporting any suspicious anti-communist talk, behavior, or pursuits.

Mom cleared the kitchen table, except for our coffee cups and a few slices of leftover poppy seed cake in case Steve or I wanted more. She continued to sit with us, saving her dishwashing for afterward. She went on. "In Vienna, we found and paid money to a man who took people through the Russian zone to get to the American zone in Salzburg."

She raised a hand. "We joined one such group. Over a few days, the guide was to take us cross-country both through the woods and on rural roads to get to Salzburg. We would hide in the forest and sleep during the daytime, then travel at night by moonlight."

Her voice grew frustrated. "But halfway through the trip, we woke one evening to find the guide had left us there to fend for ourselves. That bum completely disappeared with the money we had paid. And the shyster never came back."

Mom lifted her palms off the table and then placed them down again. "Our group still wanted to get to Salzburg, and we tried to stick together that night. But after walking for a while, we started arguing about what direction we should go."

She pointed upward. "Your daddy knew how to navigate by the stars from his flight school training. He could tell that our group was heading the wrong way."

She looked away for another moment and then back at us. "But some of the travellers wanted to continue to go the same way we had been going. After arguing more, your father pointed to himself and me. He said, 'We are going to go our way, and anybody who wants to come with us could do so.'" She shook her head. "A few people decided to join us, but the rest went the other way."

Mom clasped her hands together. "A day later, in the early morning, we came across a quiet main road. Soon we saw an older man bicycling slowly down the road and toward us.

"Your daddy quickly told everyone to hide in a ditch alongside the road, and he asked me to go out and talk to the man." She pointed at herself. "He wanted me to go because I was a woman and could speak German, which I had learned in Budapest."

Mom added another surprise. "Your Daddy could speak German too. But because of the way the Germans treated him and his fellow Hungarians during the war, he refused to speak that language ever again."

I had known my father to speak many Eastern European languages, but I had never heard him utter a word in German. Even on our summer trips to Czechoslovakia via Germany, he had Mom speak to German restaurant waitresses and hotel clerks.

I later asked my father if he, indeed, spoke German. He said, "No," matter-of-factly. Though it was a small thing, it made me wonder if my brother and I ever obtained the whole truth from our parents about their past.

I tried not to fidget in my seat at Mom's kitchen table, but my back was getting sore from sitting so long. Steve and I remained quiet, captivated by her tale. She continued. "I went out and nicely stopped the man on the road," she said. "I asked him where I was and where was the American zone." She raised her arm and pointed as if she were the bicyclist. "The guy pointed and said it was down the road, not far away."

There was a sudden lightness in her voice, and she chuckled. "Once our group heard this, everyone grabbed their knapsacks, jumped out of the ditch, and ran like crazy toward the American zone." With a big *Phew!* and fast breath, she added, "We made it!"

Her breathing slowed. "We told the American guards we were Czechoslovak refugees looking for asylum. They helped us reach Salzburg. There, your father immediately registered us with the Canadian consulate."

She batted her hand at us. "And you boys know the rest of the story. From Salzburg, once we got travel papers, a big group of Eastern European emigrants took a train to Cuxhaven on the West German coast. We then travelled by boat across the ocean to Quebec City. By the fifth of October, we were in Canada, and then heading to the refugee camp in Ajax, Ontario, where we started our new life."

I looked at her. "Mom, do you know what happened to the other people you separated from on the way to Saltsburg?"

Into the silence of Steve and my waiting ears, she answered matter-of-factly. "I don't know. We never saw or heard from any of them again."

* * * *

20

Family Mishigas

Mom continued to talk from her chair while Steve and I stayed fixed in our seats. Though stuffed to our ears with her supper and story, we sat still while she served up more. "Some months after we got to Canada," she offered, "I received a letter from my family in Košice that Lali and Martha were coming to Canada too."

Her voice elevated. "I was shocked yet so happy to hear they had decided to follow us to Montreal. They came to Canada on the same immigration program that brought your daddy and me here."

She paused for a moment and then went on. "The last time we saw them was in Vienna. After your daddy and I had left for Salzburg, Lali and Martha planned to take a train to the Mediterranean and then board a ship to Israel."

Mom's tone turned somber as she stared into her near-empty coffee cup held firmly in her two hands. "Martha's family had their war tragedies. The Nazis took most of her family to Auschwitz in the 1944 Košice deportation. Somehow, Martha and her mother managed to survive that Nazi camp, but she had seen two of her brothers killed there." Mom didn't skip a phrase. "A camp guard shot her brothers dead right in front of Martha and her mother."

Oh no! Had Martha's brothers looked too intensely into that guard's eyes? Or were they not hurrying along fast enough? I felt less shaken, even a little numb, to these new tragic accounts. I could better understand why my mother had a detached, matter-of-fact telling of her family's WWII hardships and tragedies.

Mom continued as her face stayed expressionless. "Martha had one other brother, Otto, who found a way to escape from the Nazis and hide somewhere in the woods with other Jews. He managed to stay alive through the war."

"Do you know how he survived, Mom?" I asked. I wanted to hear more about better survivor news.

Steve piped in behind me. "Do you know how Aunt Martha and her mother were able to live through Auschwitz?"

She looked at both of us. "No," she replied calmly. "Martha never liked to talk about what happened to her and the terrible things her family went through." She pointed to her forearm. "All I know is that Martha has a number on her arm from that camp."

She looked past us as she raised an arm off the table and pointed into the distance. "After the war was over, Otto and his mother emigrated from Slovakia to the new state of Israel." Her face softened. "But Martha stayed behind in Košice because she had met Lali, and they fell in love."

Mom's voice stayed steady. "When your father and I left Vienna for Salzburg to get into the Canada immigration program, Lali and Martha were still planning to go to Israel. Before we left Czechoslovakia, Lali had made a promise to Martha that he was going to take her there to join her only remaining family."

Mom looked to one side for a moment and then back at us. "When we reunited with them in Montreal in 1950, Martha told me that she and Lali had packed their bags and gone to the Vienna train station. They were among other refugees who were heading to the Mediterranean coast and then on to Tel Aviv by boat."

She took a long breath. "When they got to the station, they placed their luggage on board and got ready to step onto the train." She put a hand over her mouth, and her voice elevated. "Martha then said that Lali suddenly grabbed her and cried out, 'I can't go to Israel! I have to go to Canada.'"

"Why did he do that?" my brother blurted, beating me to the question.

Mom shook her head. "No one knows for sure why Lali made this sudden change. He never spoke about his real reasons for switching direction, other than that he wanted to be with us in Canada."

New Canadian immigrants and Montreal residents, visiting the Mount Royal lookout that overlooked downtown Montreal. Jani and Anna are on the far left. Martha and Lali are on the far right. The second couple from the left may be Mrs. & Mr. Holy, friends who became my brother's and my godparents. The identity of the other woman and the photographer is unknown. Probably a spring or summer Sunday afternoon after Catholic Church services, 1951

My brother and I stared at our mother. We nodded and said nothing.

I later wondered if Lali felt he needed to protect his kid sister, someone he had looked after throughout WWII. Or maybe my uncle wanted to make sure that my father hadn't secretly absconded with Lali's money from Košice.

Lali and Martha's only child, Janet, was close to my brother and me. During our formative years, our two families gathered on weekends and holidays at each other's homes. Every occasion started with happy hugs and big kisses as we greeted each other on our respective doorsteps. There were many loud *"Ahoys!"* and *"Hogy vagy? Örülök, hogy látlak!* [How are you doing? So happy to see you!]"

The adults and kids then went to respective corners of the house in advance of consuming a Hungarian meal after church on any given Sunday afternoon, or devouring one of Dad's scrumptious barbeque steak suppers on Canada Day, or having a traditional turkey and stuffing midday dinner on Canadian Thanksgiving. Janet, Steve, and I played cards and board games, built mini-brick castles, and watched kids' TV programs in our finished basement.

Once, while we played tag outside, our younger cousin went crying to her mother after Steve or I accidentally tripped her. She skinned her knee and hand. A harsh scolding came forth from my mother. "Play nicely with girls!" she shouted.

I felt shaken by Mom's uproar because neither my brother nor I had done anything to Janet that we wouldn't have done to each other. We did curtail our rough behavior with our only Canadian cousin, but I wondered what it was about girls that required them protection from boys.

While we kids played, Mom and Martha cooked up an Eastern European storm. They talked nonstop about their relatives overseas. Each repeated, "What have you heard about from family over there?"

They shared letters, with many *"Yoy!"* and Hungarian "God forbid!" emanating from them at every account. Mom's family told of staples being hard to get behind the Iron Curtain. Martha's relatives speculated on whether Israel would last as a nation.

Mom once told my brother and me, "Everyone in those countries has a profession or a job. But their salary isn't always enough for a decent living. Good coats, shoes, and appliances are very expensive or impossible to get."

Mom and Martha helped their struggling siblings by sending Canadian care packages of nonperishable food, clothing, and everyday things. They continued to prod each other as to what else they could do for their overseas families.

For their part at these family gatherings, Dad and Lali talked business as spiced T-bone steaks sizzled on the grill in the summer, or as they nursed drinks at our basement bar in the other seasons. My father went for gin and tonics on hot summer days and straight Cutty Sark on cold winter ones. Lali, not a hard drinker like Dad, sipped on refrigerator-cooled Canada Dry.

My mother and her Eastern European relations rarely drank alcohol or put ice into their drinks. Mom told us, "You can save a lot of money at home and restaurants if you don't drink alcohol." Dad certainly didn't follow that rule.

Dad and Lali's chats were all smiles, speaking with arms and hands, no hint of past problems. They took turns talking about business projects and prospects. Lali grabbed paper and pencil to sketch a design.

Lali could engage his creative eye and tailor's touch to craft and produce fancy men's and lady's hats, as he had done in Košice after the war. He later switched to making unusual, multi-coloured lampshades, and then intricate stained-glass tables with images of animals and foliage. Dad bought and placed a couple of Lali's one-of-a-kind lamps and table creations in the lounge area of our basement.

As they jabbered on, my father was as generous with his "*Lassen* to me, Lali!" and "Here's what you should do, my brother," as he was liberal with his deli steak spices.

In turn, Dad sought Lali's reactions to his business plans: "What do you think about this kind of product?" and "Do you think I should buy that property?" Dad once looked at Lali and pointed to himself, "Come to see me if you need help. Maybe we can find something good to do together."

I felt a little thrill hearing them go back and forth with their money-making ideas. I wanted them to be successful so we could have a good life in Canada. Mom had said she was sacrificing by making her clothes and ours, by buying only the things we needed, and by saving pennies on less expensive meats and canned goods. I didn't want her and us to sacrifice more than we had to.

Though I once heard my mother say, "Lali is a hard worker like your father," she added, "But he was never as successful."

My uncle seemed to wander from one product idea to another in search of his pot of Canadian silver. Despite Dad's enthusiasm to do business with his brother-in-law, he later claimed, "That idea costs too much to fund," or "All my money is tied up elsewhere."

After Mom had mentioned the goods Dad had shipped from Czechoslovakia to Israel in '49, which never arrived, I better comprehended why my father didn't do any business with Lali. But I wished Dad would have been straight with his brother-in-law rather than leading him on about them doing something together. Perhaps Lali blamed Dad for his lack of success in a cold country where he never really wanted to come.

I now understood why things flared up between those two from time to time. Their sporadic arguments lead to Steve and me not seeing our cousin Janet for a year or more at a time. I never asked my parents about that family loss, for I never wanted to be the cause of a fight between them.

The air was quiet around Mom's kitchen table. We took sips of our second Sankas. Steve asked calmly, "So what happened between Dad and Lali?"

I avoided such tough topics but could count on my brother to stir the family pot.

I don't know why, but Mom answered him. Looking down and off to one side, she explained what went on between the two most important men in her life. "The bad blood between Dad and Lali had started in Vienna, after the lost Israeli goods situation."

She took another long, deep breath. "In Košice, Lali had been a well-to-do man with his hat-making business. He even owned a Mercedes sports car."

She looked right at us again. "Lali trusted your father. He gave him most of his money to buy those goods and equipment they sent to Israel. Then, in Vienna, after Lali found out that we lost everything, a big argument broke out between him and your daddy in the kitchen of our Vienna apartment."

She put her hand to her forehead. "Lali, like your father, was hotheaded. While your father was cooking supper in our apartment, he turned toward the stove and away from Lali."

Mom turned in her chair and faced our kitchen stove. Her voice started shaking. She put her hand in front of her quivering chin. "I was standing across our small kitchen." She pointed toward the door to our dining room. "From there, I saw Lali grab a big kitchen knife that had been sitting on the counter. He moved toward your father like he was going to stab him."

She stretched out her arm. "When I saw what Lali was doing, I immediately screamed and ran to grab the blade. I put my arm between Lali and your father." She looked down at her hand. "My hand became cut and bloodied by the knife." She looked away. "When your father heard my scream, he turned around just in time to push Lali away."

Mom hung her head in her hands. "Lali ran from our apartment. He and your daddy screamed at each other until Lali was out our front door." There was another pause, sigh, and a shaking of her head. "Your father was very upset. The idea of going to Israel with Lali and Martha was now totally over for him."

I turned my eyes away from Mom as she took a long moment to compose herself. I felt my heart thump fast, and I fought to keep myself collected. I couldn't look at her; I waited silently for what she was to say next. I didn't look at my brother, and he stayed silent too. Part of me wished Mom wouldn't tell us about the troubles between Dad and our uncle. I didn't want the anguish.

When she was ready, Mom continued. "When we all got to Canada, I sent letters to my brothers and sisters back home, telling them what had happened. Lali, it seemed, did the same.

We got letters back from my family, asking us to forgive each other and forget the past. Because Lali was our only family here in Canada, and he was an important brother to me, Martha and I pleaded with him and your daddy to forget about what happened in Vienna. We tried to forgive each other and put what happened behind us."

Mom wiped a wet eye with the back of her hand. "But Lali never completely forgot. For a while, things were good between us, but then something would happen that again got him and your father fighting and not talking to each other."

She looked away and didn't elaborate. Steve and I sat silent and still.

I struggled to picture Lali, Dad, and Mom in that Vienna kitchen. I could tell by Mom's wet and red eyes that the memories were harrowing. She worked hard to keep that turbulent past behind her and our kin. She kept her arms open toward her brother and his family, talking to them for hours every week on the phone.

During those estranged times between our two families, I recalled my mother many times speaking vigorously over the phone to her brother. On one occasion, she swore loudly at him in Hungarian. The next minute, she whispered, not wanting Steve and me to overhear. In the end, she banged the receiver down hard after getting angry at something Lali had said.

At that time, I worked to stay clear of our extended family's blast zone. I remained in the den or basement and glued my eyes and ears to the television. I hoped my mother wouldn't bark at me over supper. I prayed I wouldn't hear her crying alone in the kitchen late at night.

I now understood that, during those disgruntled times between Dad and my uncle, it must have been excruciating for her not to be able to hug and kiss her brother, sister-in-law, and niece for months, if not years, at a time.

Hearing about the ongoing fighting between my father and Lali, I felt an ache in my chest and numbness in my heart. I told myself that I should keep a distance from my cousin and her parents.

Over the ensuing years, I never asked my relations about their escape from Czechoslovakia, their time in Vienna, and their immigration to Canada. I never asked my mother for more details about those tumultuous times.

Decades later, I would wonder whether I was protecting Mom or myself from reliving the angst. As with my parents' fighting at home, it was easier to pretend these extended family troubles had never happened.

Mom's voice calmed as she took the last sip of her Sanka. Her tone once again became matter-of-fact. "When things were not good between our two families, instead of coming to see us here in Dorval for holidays, Lali, Martha, and Janet drove to Detroit to see your second cousin Magda."

She stared at us. "You remember my telling you about Magda, the niece of my Cousin Joli. Magda was our only blood relative to survive Auschwitz."

Steve and I nodded.

Mom continued. "Magda and her American husband met in Israel after the war. They got married and moved to Michigan, where he was from originally." She pointed our way. "I don't know if you remember her; she came here once to visit when you guys were small."

Though Steve and I nodded again, I didn't think either of us remembered her.

Mom ended the conversation there. She stood and headed for the sink. She was quiet, and her face expressionless. She focused on her motherly chore, leaving her story on the table for her sons to digest further. Something told me that if we ever talked about her remarkable story again, it would be because she willed it, and only if her astonished sons hungered for more.

Over the ensuing decades, I kept thinking back to Mom's harrowing experiences.

One day, she had been a Slovak Hashomer Hatzair Jewish scout in Košice; the next day, she was a Hungarian Christian seamstress student in Budapest, hiding her heritage behind false papers. One day, she had cowered in a Budapest basement from incessant allied bombings, even living off the meat of a horse that had been killed by a bomb. The next day, she celebrated an end to a brutal war and joyfully reunited with her whole sibling family, finding them alive and intact. One day, she thought she had lost her youngest brother to a forced labour camp; the next day, he miraculously reappeared— his arm, hand, or leg not blown off by a landmine. One day, she had had many cousins to hug, kiss, and cherish; the next day, she had lost most of them to suicides, Hungarian work camps, or a brick factory ghetto and cattle car ride to Auschwitz.

Mom's Budapest home had been liberated by the Soviet army fighting for months through the streets of that city. Soon afterward, she saw her Czechoslovak comrades pulled off a train and sent to a Soviet re-indoctrination camp. She arrived back to her hometown, pleasantly surprised that stray bullet holes were the only physical damage. Then she found out that her family home had become a horse stable, a single photo album the only thing to survive from their prewar lives.

For many, that would have constituted a lifetime of sorrow-filled stories. But for Mom, it didn't end there. She had enjoyed her freedom as a seamstress entrepreneur in her reinstated democracy of Czechoslovakia; then, she saw Czechoslovakia borders closed as a Soviet Iron Curtain descended around her country. A day before, she could have said anything she wanted to anyone; the next day, people started to whisper in their homes and look over their shoulders, fearing detention and deportation by the communists.

She had lived happily with her loving Jewish family in Košice; then she married a Catholic man and left her country for a new life. She had headed to Israel for religious freedom as a Jewish Hungarian brunette; then, she was off to a still anti-Semitic Canada (and not to Australia) as a Christian Slovak bleached blond. She had had a loving relationship with her brother, who saved their family from being rounded up and sent to Auschwitz; then, that relationship was split apart through lost goods in Israel and a knife fight in Vienna.

After escaping Czechoslovakia with the love of her life, my father, they made it through treacherous border crossings—even after being abandoned by their hired guide—and then crossed an ocean together to a free country with fresh opportunities. She worked hard as a domestic and seamstress to help them begin a new life in Canada. She gave birth to and fed us at her kitchen table without complaint. She then saw her husband leave for another woman—being betrayed not just once but now twice.

For nearly two decades, she had concealed her Jewish heritage, her family's Budapest war survival, and her in-law mishigas from her Catholic-raised kids. She chose now, over a hot homeland meal, to reveal her painful history to us.

Though part of me admired my mother for having gone through and survived the atrocities and hardships she did, her story gave me a lifetime of stomach pangs and jaw pains—from gnashing my molars in my sleep. Decades later, I still wondered if she should have recounted so much.

Perhaps she had wanted her children to witness her tumultuous tale, but she failed to realize that she was also placing her lifetime of family burdens within her beloved sons.

* * * *

21

Light at My Tunnel's End?

November 1999.

Nearly a month had passed since my legal consult with my school chum, André Lefebvre, at the law firm of Elliot Trudell. My friend had been a big help to me with my father's clandestine university annuity agreement.

Until then, no one but I, Dad, and the managers at the Global Trade Bank of Luxembourg and the Canadian Supporters of Independent University knew that the charitable annuity's tax deductibility would be bogus. No one else, particularly the Canadian and U.S. tax authorities, and my brother, would know that the annuity's annual income would be untaxed if I played along. All I needed to do was take the annuity payments in cash and keeping my mouth shut about its source.

André had advised that the annuity agreement wasn't binding. I still wasn't sure what I was going to do about it or and how much I would reveal to my brother. I continued to have sleepless nights about that dubious deal.

I had shown André my father's offshore account statements that indicated seven-figure sums. After perusing those damning documents, he arranged an appointment for me with his colleague, Bernard, who was a specialist in dealing with undeclared offshore money.

Tomorrow was to be my first meeting with my new attorney. Not my father, nor my brother, nor even my wife, knew about my conversation with André and my upcoming meeting with Bernard. They thought I was here in

Montreal doing consulting business, but I was here more to deal with my father's decades of underhanded money business.

Memories of my long-deceased mother filled my mind. She had lived a hard life of war survival as a Jew, of escape from a Soviet communist regime, of strife with her sibling, and unending marital conflicts with Dad. She wanted her two sons to get the monetary benefits that she felt she had never had from her husband. She had given her life and given up her family and religion for that man, and she received few benefits in return.

Part of me felt I should honour her by settling my father's offshore shenanigans and include my brother in Dad's hidden stash. Another part of me wasn't sure if my brother deserved my consideration, especially since Dad wanted his offshore money to go only to me.

Either way, I wanted the hidden load off my shoulders. It had been over twenty-seven years since Dad took me to his first hidden money haven in Zurich, Switzerland. I was now sick in my heart, mind, and gut about what I had known and done nothing about.

My mother and brother may have suspected Dad's hidden assets, just as they had known about his other women. But they had no clue as to what I had had the privilege and burden of knowing all these years.

If Dad knew what I was going to do with Bernard tomorrow, he might disown me and block the access I needed to fix his offshore money mess. I had to act prudently and stealthily if I hoped to bring my knowledge of his underground treasure into the light of Revenue Canada. I hoped there would be something left for my brother and me after we'd pay our penance to the government, and no jail time would be involved.

Tomorrow, I would get to know from my newest Elliot Trudell lawyer about how to make Dad's and my peace with the Canadian taxman. But it was still up to me to figure out how I could make peace with both my unsuspecting brother and my burdened conscience.

The latter couldn't stop thinking about my mother.

* * *

The next day.

The air was cold in Montreal. The sky was grey, and the wind brisk and nippy. The trees had lost their leaves to the hard and frosty ground. Snowflakes were falling as I approached the Bank of Commerce building, where Elliot Trudell had its offices. I was wearing my opossum-lined trench coat, what I had worn on frigid days like this when I had lived in Montreal.

I never dared to wear the coat in Boston. My socially-conscious friends and colleagues there wouldn't have understood. I bundled the fur tight around me, the collar high around my neck, but I still felt a bone-penetrating chill.

I was preparing in my mind for my meeting with Bernard. I wondered if he really could help me sort through my father's offshore assets as quickly as André had helped me see the flaw in the clandestine university annuity agreement that Dad had inked eight years earlier.

I didn't want to kid myself. That Independent University annuity agreement was to take effect only after my father's death. For nearly the last three decades, Dad's offshore holdings and earnings had been repeatedly unreported to Revenue Canada. Every April since that sunny summer Swiss day in 1972, Dad committed another crime against his adopted country and province every time he signed his tax returns. He had never disclosed his offshore assets and income.

Over those years, Dad had enticed me with the trappings he and his private business could offer, especially the promise of a pot of hidden money at the end of an offshore rainbow. I was no longer attracted to his style and stash the way I had been. Events of the last years had caused me to wish no longer to follow in my father's finagling footsteps.

I wondered if I could trust Bernard with my case and my tacit complicity in my father's furtive finances. Bernard and I didn't have a shared history as I had with my high school chum, André. Might my new Elliot Trudell lawyer turn out to be the expensive, big-firm lawyer that my entrepreneur father had warned me about and despised?

Bernard and I were to meet at the same large, wood-paneled conference room where my high school chum and I had met a month earlier. For this initial conversation, I wasn't going to show him Dad's offshore Global Trade Bank statements. Instead, I armed myself with a list of questions. I wanted to see what he knew and had to offer about legitimizing my father's hidden holdings.

Unlike André, Bernard entered the conference room within minutes of my arrival. He was tall, dark-suited, graceful in his mannerisms, and as soft-spoken as my school chum was. Bernard's look and demeanor made me wonder if a similar law school mold had produced every Elliott Trudell attorney.

He and I shook hands, and he smiled. "Good to make your acquaintance, Mr. Simkovits." Though I was 45 years old, hearing a "Mr." in front of my surname felt awkward. Usually, I heard only my father being called Mr. Simkovits.

André and I had sat next to the conference room's giant windows with a view of downtown Montreal. This time, Bernard motioned me to sit at one end of the large oval conference table in the middle of the massive boardroom. *I guess I'm a full-fledged client now, and this visit is going to cost me big bucks.*

Bernard spoke first. He had a slight French accent. "André tells me you are a Canadian citizen living in *de* U.S."

"Yes, I've been there over ten years now." I kept my voice friendly, but I didn't want to give long answers. Every minute here could cost me over five bucks.

Bernard's hands were folded on the table while he looked at me. "André didn't tell me much about what brings you to see us today. How can we be of assistance?"

I took a deep breath and spoke carefully. "My father immigrated to Canada fifty years ago. He became a very successful businessman and is now retired." I sputtered, "Over the decades he has lived in Canada, my father has opened several undeclared offshore bank accounts." I didn't say where they were or how much they contained. "He has been accumulating money offshore and hasn't declared any of its income to the Canadian government."

I leaned forward a bit. "My father will be 80 in a few months, and he's not in great health. My brother and I are the sole executors of his estate." I kept my voice firm and steady. "André said that you could tell me what it would take to legitimize his offshore accounts and assets either before or after he passes away."

Bernard paused for a second or two. His eyes and eyebrows hardly moved. He looked directly at me and spoke slowly and deliberately. "Such offshore accounts are not uncommon in Canada. Many wealthy Canadians, especially immigrants like your father, employ them to shelter assets." His voice raised a decibel. "Of course, not paying proper income taxes as a Canadian resident is illegal unless the person officially resides out of the country."

I knew that already but didn't interrupt. The attorney kept his eyes on me and continued. "Unlike in your United States, Canada does not tax a person's worldwide income no matter where the citizen resides. If your father established permanent residency in a tax-free state, like the Cayman Islands or The Bahamas, then the income from those offshore accounts would be tax-free to the extent that those countries maintained their zero-income-tax policy."

Bernard's voice was monotone, and he took his time. "However, because of the complexity of establishing non-residency in Canada, some Canadians choose not to declare the income from their offshore accounts, thereby skirting their tax obligation to Revenue Canada." He raised an index finger, though his hands stayed folded on the table. "But they live with the risk that the government could find out about the money they are hiding."

It was good to know my dad wasn't the only one who dodged income taxes in Canada. I lifted my hand and interrupted. "Bernard, my father once considered obtaining Canadian non-residence status, about fifteen years ago. But that's no longer possible for him with his declining health. What can or should my brother and I do now in our particular situation?"

Bernard didn't flinch. "There are well-established yet somewhat negotiable rules that Revenue Canada performs in such situations. We call it a 'voluntary disclosure.' It is a process that reveals to the government, taxes appropriately, and ultimately legitimizes a Canadian resident's undeclared offshore assets."

Good! What I was trying to do had a name. "Okay, Bernard. Can you tell me more about this voluntary disclosure thing?" My heart beat faster, but I tried not to show it. I held my hands together on my lap. I, too, can play Mr. Cool.

The attorney leaned forward, his arms and hands now placed flat on the table. "The government looks back at three years of tax returns for people who want to declare their hidden income and assets. The taxpayer would have to re-file for those three most recent years, both in their federal and provincial returns. They would need to include all capital gains, losses, and interest earned in any previously undeclared accounts." He kept his eyes on me. I kept mine on him. "There is a customary 18% per annum compounded interest charge on any back taxes owed for those three years.

Wow! That's a steep interest rate. Though I cringed inside, I worked to keep my body as uncommunicative as Bernard's. "Okay," I said.

He went on. "However, there would be no additional tax penalties levied when the taxpayer or their representative," he gestured toward me, "is coming forward voluntarily."

Bernard pointed to himself. "Also, my firm and I could anonymously represent the taxpayer—be it your father, or you and your brother as your father's estate executors—until your arrangement with Revenue Canada would be finalized."

Bernard put his hands back on the table, one palm tilted upward. "Revenue Canada has a special department that handles such voluntary disclosures." He took another breath. "If you and your brother did not like the arrangement that the government offered, my firm and I would not be obliged to declare whom we were representing. You could then take your chances by keeping the money hidden."

He looked at me with fixed eyes. "But if Revenue Canada discovers your father's offshore assets, then the penalties, depending on circumstances, can be very stiff. You could potentially have nothing left after paying the back taxes, interest, and levies."

Gulp! I looked down at the table for a second. *At least it sounds like there'd be no jail time.*

I looked back at him. "Okay, that sounds reasonable. I like having the fallback of pulling out of a government deal if we didn't like it, though I don't think my brother and I would want to keep our father's offshore money hidden." I knew that Steve, once he got wind of Dad's stash, wouldn't allow it to remain under wraps. His religious honesty wouldn't permit him.

I asked the most critical question on my list. "When it's said and done, what portion of the hidden assets do people like my father, or his estate, typically end up paying to the government in back taxes, including the interest?"

Bernard responded without hesitation. "It very much depends on the details of the particular situation, and the final arrangement we would work out with Revenue Canada." He paused for a second. "On average, the taxpayer could potentially be left with 60 to 70% of the total amount declared."

My eyes opened. *That's better than I expected.* Forfeiting in the vicinity of one-third of Dad's offshore wealth seemed fair. That way, the government, Steve, and I would get equal shares.

"However," he added, "it's not unheard of that the number would be just 50% of the original amount."

Ouch! Relinquishing half of what my father had offshore would be an enormous loss. I wouldn't appreciate the government clawing away that much of what he had worked toward for most of his life in Canada.

The tax devil would be in the offshore statement details concealed above a loose ceiling panel in my father's office. I made a mental note to take a closer look at Dad's most recent Global Trade Bank statements.

I wondered how I was going to get a full three years of statements from that bank. Dad destroyed past statements once he got updated ones. I needed my father's permission to ask the bank for documents covering prior years, and Dad would want to know why I wanted them.

I pressed on with my questions, leaving my dilemmas for later contemplation. "Bernard, could we make an offer to Revenue Canada for, let's say, a third of my father's offshore assets? Might they accept such an offer and allow us to walk away with the rest?"

He didn't hesitate as his eyes intensified. "No, unfortunately not. The people at the tax department need to go through their established procedures. They have superiors to which they are accountable, and those superiors wouldn't permit such an informal arrangement. Revenue Canada authorities have established the rules, and we must follow them. No special deals are accepted."

I quickly changed course. "Have you done such voluntary disclosures before?"

His eyes opened wide, but he again didn't hesitate. "I am building that specialty for our firm." He didn't mention how many times he had done such disclosures. "I have an established relationship with the proper authorities at Revenue Canada. When you and your brother are ready, I can open negotiations for you. I do not have to reveal who is coming forward until you accept the agreement with Revenue Canada."

"Okay. And how do you charge for your services to do this kind of work?"

There was no change in his lawyerly tone. "We charge for my time on your file, at a rate of $325/hr." He glanced away and then back at me. "It's hard to know right now how much time it will take without looking at the details of your case. The good thing is that our fees are deductible against the undeclared income in the most recent refiled year." He raised his hand off the table. "We make that part of the agreement with Revenue Canada."

"That's good to know," I said. Though André had told me about the $325 per hour rate, it still took my breath away. My consolation was that it was in cheaper Canadian dollars and fully deductible against my father's offshore income.

I would have liked to have had an estimate of the total cost of our pending project, but I could ask Bernard for such after I showed him Dad's Global Trade Bank statements. I wondered if he wanted to size up the extent of my father's offshore fortune before throwing out a ballpark fee.

The attorney looked at me from across the conference table. "Do you or your brother have direct control over your father's assets at this time?"

I looked down at the table and then back at him. "Right now, no."

That wasn't the whole truth, but it was close enough. I didn't want to get into the complexities over what my father had and hadn't given me control. "I suspect from your question, Bernard, that there is not much we can do until my father passes away, or until my brother and I can gain complete control of his offshore accounts."

He responded, "That's correct." His voice stayed steady. "Until you have legal control over his financial affairs, you could not refile income taxes on his behalf."

My voice hesitated. "But there is one thing I should do soon."

His eyebrow rose. "What is that?"

I felt comfortable enough with André's colleague to divulge an important fact. I also wanted to buy time to digest what I had learned from him. I said, "Even though my older brother is co-executor with me of my father's estate, he knows little about our father's offshore accounts. I need to tell him, and I'll do that soon." But I didn't know how soon that would be. "I'll get back to you after the New Year."

Both of Bernard's eyebrows were now up, but there was no other telling expression on his face. "I understand, Mr. Simkovits."

"Is there anything else I should know about doing a voluntary disclosure?" I asked.

"We have covered the basics, Mr. Simkovits. Everything else depends on the particulars of your situation. I cannot say more until we have dug into the details. When you and your brother are ready, bring me what you can. I will be able to tell you more then."

"My brother may want to meet you personally before we decide to move forward on this."

"That's not a problem. Here is my card." He pulled one from his jacket pocket. "Call my secretary to make an appointment." He looked at me. "As for our time today, because you came through André, I will make a note of it and not send you a bill until we officially get started in this effort. Just leave me your business card, so I have your contact information."

I nodded and handed him my card. "Okay, Bernard. Thank you for your time. I'll be in touch in the new year."

"You are most welcome," he said.

It felt as if Bernard had wanted to say more, but he stopped there. I waited a second or two for him to offer anything else, but he added nothing. His eyes told me that he might be holding back on a question.

I imagined him wondering, *Harvy, how did you and not your brother come to know about your father's hidden assets?* Perhaps his professional etiquette held him back from asking.

Had he asked, I would have responded, *When my dad's voluntary disclosure is behind us, and his assets are scrubbed clean, you and I can go out to have a beer. I can then tell you the whole story of my father's business shenanigans and offshore finagling during his decades in Canada. You might be especially interested in how those Johnny Simkovits survivor seeds, germinated by a brutal war and communist oppression in his home country, grew and blossomed in havens like The Cayman Islands, The Bahamas, and Luxembourg.*

And there was one other thing that's for certain. This survivor son could not and would not live the dual personal and business life that Johnny Simkovits had led. I would not allow myself to follow in my father's furtive footsteps.

I could only hope that my God and the better memories of my mother would help me get through this Johnny Simkovits ordeal.

* * * *

Excerpt –

Book Two:

Survivor Teachings

Trade Trickery

Mechanical hums, swishes, bangs, rumbles, whirls, and whizzes filled the air nearly nine hours each day in my father's Montreal Phono console stereo plant. Factory foremen rushed about and yelled over the noise, "Come here!" . . . "Do this!" . . . "Do that!"

The acrid odors of melting solder flux wafted from the electronic amplifier department. There a wall of women sat in hard metal chairs while they prepared the electrical connections for what Dad calls "the guts" of a stereo unit. An electromechanical wire cutting and splicing machine *CLINKED-CLINK*ED in the background as these "girls" (what my father and the foremen called them) sat tirelessly for the whole workday. They repeated the same intricate hand movements every few minutes until their work was complete.

Their job was to make ready the myriad wires and connections among the Asian radios, cassette and 8-track players, and British changer-turntables that would be placed and wired together within each console stereo box. They chatted in what Dad called *"vimen* talk." He allowed them to gossip away, even listen to the radio, as long as they got their wiring and soldering quotas done well and on time. They always did.

I was among the men positioned along the electronics assembly line. We installed, secured, and connected these staged electronic components into the empty carcasses of vinyl covered, particleboard cabinets. We pushed the simulated hardwood beasts in a single file down the 60'conveyor.

Every four to six minutes, a unit passed from one crewed station to another. We didn't talk much, except to point out a problem seen in a previous guy's work, or if we needed to warn the next guy down the line about something to which he needed to pay attention.

These pressed wood stereo cabinets, up to sixty inches long, were composed of as much industrial glue as they were of wood chips. They had been stacked two-wide and three-high on pallets that employees rolled in from the factory's cabinetmaking and wood finishing departments.

All during the day, employees breathed in the fine sawdust particles of freshly cut pressed wood. They inhaled the full fragrance of the white glue that bound the cabinet together. They smelled the bouquet of toxic spray paint that lingered on the molded-plastic grill that decorated the front of the barren units.

I thanked my stars that I worked here only for short summer stints. I didn't have to take in these toxic odors for fifty weeks a year and half a generation.

I glanced toward the front of the electronics assembly line where two muscular, minimum wage male labourers loaded a stack of cabinets onto the electronics assembly conveyor. I helped out at that station when I wanted upper body exercise.

But today I was filling in for a guy on the line who hadn't shown this morning. Hopefully, he would have a good excuse, like a doctor's note, if he was to avoid an inquisition from his foreman, or worse, from the big boss, my father.

Each stereo unit was handled with care to prevent bangs or scratches that would beget a foreman's shout. Once, while my father had been standing nearby, a worker dropped a console box accidentally onto the floor—perhaps the labourer had been nervous about the boss watching. A fire rose in my father's eyes, and he raised his fist as he bellowed at the perpetrator "I *dun't* know *whaat!* I *looose* my *shhert!*"

The foreman immediately removed the lackadaisical employee from the production line to an area requiring less strenuous work—like flattening empty corrugated boxes for refuse or resale. Being the boss's son, I stayed focused on my job to avoid an angry outburst from my father.

Today, like any day on the production line, pneumatic screwdrivers hummed in random succession, *WHIZ...WHIZ...WHIZ*. My assembly-line compadres were securing turntable motor boards and other electronic components under the cabinet's hinged wooden lid.

A fellow further up the line firmly fastened sets of Czechoslovak-made Tesla speakers on the back of the unit's fabric-lined front grill. Down the line, another employee would make the necessary internal electronic connections, giving life to the modulated current coming from the set of sound equipment when plugged in and powered on.

The veterans among us kept an eye pegged to the office entrance door. We watched out for the big boss who might walk through the plant unannounced. The other day, Dad had caught one Slavic guy smoking on the job. He had motioned crotch-high with his flat hand, and shouted at the worker in mixed English and Ukrainian, "I'll cut off the *yaytsya* [eggs] from between your legs if I catch you doing that again."

The employee stomped out his cigarette quickly and turned his focus back to where it belonged. Though I was standing further down the production line, my father's unpredictable ire sent shivers down my spine.

His outbursts were like a lightning bolt or volcanic eruption. They came with little warning and dissipated as quickly as they flared up, but not before doing their damage. I kept my eyes on my production-line work and was grateful that I wasn't a target.

It was the summer of 1976. I was here on a college break between my MIT bachelor's and master's degree programs. I worked side-by-side with low-wage, Eastern and Southern European, Vietnamese, Middle-Eastern, Pakistani, Haitian, and French Canadian workers—as diverse in cultural background as the imported components that constituted the console stereos. Though most of these folks spoke English or French, the electronics foreman might employ makeshift sign language to show newer immigrants what they needed to do.

Many of these employees had recently arrived in Canada, seeking a better life in a free land. Dad had once told me, "Immigrants know better how to work." He grinned. "You can get good, hard workers right off the boat, as I was when I came here in '49."

Out of this mélange of ethnicity, men stood on pedestals as they looked down on the consoles sitting on the production conveyor. Others crouched down from behind the unit as they performed their recurring routine. It wasn't every day that I got to sit in a chair to plug in the many wire connections inside the bowels of each console carcass as it passed by in monotonous succession.

As I did, every worker repeated their same choreographed procedure a hundred times a day, day after day, week after week, until a 500- or 1000-unit order was complete. The next console or record-player-model run followed right behind.

Some employees here barely eked out a living—perhaps still living with parents or a relative, or crammed into a cheap apartment or boarding house. They were ready to jump jobs at a moment's notice for better pay, if and when it came along.

But others stayed. There was the quiet Greek papa who sat off to one side of the conveyor while he screwed down speakers, *ZZZ…ZZZ…ZZZ*, onto the front grills of the wooden speaker-boxes. Another was the short, thin, muscular Basque senior who pulled the pallet truck, *RUMBLE-RUMBLE-RUMBLE*, down the factory aisles to replenish production-line materials. A third was the Lebanese single mother who sat the whole day soldering wires, *Shh…Shh*, with her fuming soldering gun. All of them would live out their careers as Montreal Phono's own.

Working side-by-side with these long-timers, I got to know them during work breaks. I heard about their immigrant voyages across an ocean, their overseas families they rarely if ever saw, and their children who were the first generation in their family to go to college or even to finish high school. They told of their difficulty in adjusting to our cold and bilingual Quebec, but they saw it as a small price to pay to be able to speak openly about the government. They told me, "Your father has been good to me; he gives me work and pays me okay."

I appreciated their loyalty, work ethic, and quiet character. Being twenty-one, I thanked God for being the boss's son, having to do this kind of factory work only part-time. I was planning to complete my MIT master's degree within a year, then secure a more prosperous and prestigious future in electrical engineering by working elsewhere.

One of the transient workers disrupted the assembly-line monotony with his antics. He was a bean-thin, late-twenties, long-haired, Ukrainian-Canadian, rock-band guitarist. We called him by a nickname, Johnny Guitar.

Johnny's rock career had yet to take off. Having few other skills, and needing to support his rock 'n roll habits, he screwed down radio chassis on the electronics assembly line in between nighttime band performances.

Besides bellbottom jeans, Johnny Guitar wore a big grin. My father told him, "Johnny, you look like a Beatnik."

Johnny retorted, "Better me than you, Mr. S."

My father laughed, for he saw a bit of himself in that always upbeat guy.

Johnny Guitar might come to work weary-eyed and tipsy from a late-night gig. His tiredness might cause his placing his screws crooked or in the wrong hole within a stereo cabinet. Nevertheless, my father enjoyed bantering with him (before or after work, of course) about "screwing other things, like young chicks."

Johnny Guitar and I sometimes worked side-by-side on the assembly line. We talked and joked while standing at our stations, screwing radio chassis onto the console's motor board.

I don't recall what Johnny said that had provoked our fun one day, but Dad unexpectedly walked into the plant from the office. The boss looked our way as he overheard us laugh and snicker.

Johnny and I clammed up, but I could tell my father was not amused. He stood at the front of the line and called over the electronics department foreman. As predictable as the punch clock, Dad raised his fist and screamed his signature shout. "Why are the people playing around and not working? It's *une*-believable! I *dun't* know *whaat!* I *looose* my *shhert* with the stupidity that's going on here!"

Chills went down my spine. The factory floor became quiet except for the humming of pneumatic screwdrivers, the banging of rubber mallets, and the crunching of staples that sealed the packed cabinet boxes. I kept my nose pointed to my motor board screwing and didn't say a word. The foreman stood with a long face and took in Dad's tirade. After the fireworks, Dad turned and headed back to his office.

The foreman came over to Johnny and me. "You guys are getting me into trouble. Stop your screwing around!"

"Sorry," we both said. Johnny Guitar's face looked sincerely apologetic. I suspected he was thinking, *Cool your jets, man. Screwing is our job*, referring to what we were doing with the motor boards. I snickered inside, but my face stayed serious and still.

A moment after the foreman departed, Johnny chuckled softly. He sang and swayed his head to a rock tune. "I *dun't* know *whaaat*....; I *looose* my *shhhert*...., ya babiee..."

I smiled and tried to ignore him, and then double-checked from my vantage point to see whether Johnny's chassis screwing was straight or crooked.

* * *

Over the factory intercom, the office secretary's voice blared, "Harvy, office please; Harvy, come to the office."

Ever since I started high school, I had worked part of my summer breaks in my father's factory. Now, with my MIT engineering bachelor's degree under my belt, I continued to act as a swing person on the production line. I took over an open position when an employee arrived late or needed to leave early, or I helped out if anyone was behind in their work.

I also performed special projects, like testing and repairing electronic components in the electronic staging area. That job gave me practical experience in applying a minuscule amount of my engineering education.

I had been relieved of my assembly line job by the usual worker who crewed that station—after he got a talking to by the foreman for being late. I had begun an electronic repair job when I heard Helen's call.

I knew not to keep her waiting. If it was my father who wanted me, and I didn't get to the office quickly, he'd look at her sternly and ask gruffly, "Where is Harvy? Call him again!"

I walked briskly—but didn't run—toward the front office, which was where my father, at his desk, spent most of his day. If he wanted privacy for a business call or one-on-one meeting, he'd retire to his back office down a hallway.

No partitions separated my father's roost from the six other large, heavy, oak-wood desks situated in that big office. My brother Steve, the company's purchasing agent, sat right behind Dad. Steve faced the wall where a blackboard hung to track merchandise shipments. He was talking on the phone.

Opposite Dad, facing him, sat the production planner, Herb. He had his head down as he looked at production schedules. Beyond Herb, right near the office's front entrance, Helen sat at her L-shaped secretarial desk and was typing away on correspondence. She, too, faced my father. To my father's far-right sat the shipping clerk, Danny, his head down on transportation documents. Though Danny was at the far end of the room, he was still within sighting and hailing distance of Dad.

The company bookkeeper, Jane, sat across the room from Danny, on the other side of the office entrance. She was a slender, middle-aged woman with a shapely body. Dad placed her slightly around a corner to afford her a bit more privacy for her detailed bookkeeping work, and perhaps to keep his roaming eyes away from her well-formed figure.

The remaining desk, next to the factory office door and facing the shipping clerk, was left open for a salesman or truck driver who needed to complete paperwork or make a phone call. Employees could make personal calls from that phone, but only during their lunch break.

When I walked into the office, Helen saw me, raised her hand, and presented a cheerful look. She pointed Dad's way, and her face turned serious. "Harvy, your father wants to see you," she said.

Dad was on his phone. He looked at me, nodded, and held up his hand—a fuming cigarette between his fingers—to let me know to stay put.

I looked at Herb. He glanced up from his work and nodded at me. I nodded back. He then quickly put his eyes back on his production planning sheets. I could tell he didn't want to be disturbed.

I glanced at my brother. He hardly noticed me. His black phone receiver was cradled between his right shoulder and ear as if it were a permanent fixture. His left hand was writing a purchase order as he spoke to a supplier.

I thanked the Lord that I didn't work in this congested office. My butt would get sore from the sitting; my neck would get stiff from continual phone calling; I would choke on Dad and Helen's cigarette smoke. I'd go crazy with the all-day chatter, and I'd get nervous from being in the same room with my father.

I looked around the office as I waited. Prominently displayed on the walls and counters were RCA logos and memorabilia. A picture above the filing cabinets showed RCA's white Nipper dog sitting next to a black phonograph. "His Master's Voice" was the caption. A brass model of the phonograph sat on Dad's desk. These things reminded everyone for whom they were working.

Dad once told me that the RCA head buyer had given him a gold Cross pen and pencil set, with the original round RCA logo attached to its clip. Dad cherished that set and kept it for years in his inside suit pocket. He told me he used those writing instruments at every business meeting he had at RCA's Montreal head office.

Even when he was out of the office, like when he went to RCA, Dad called in at 4:45 to check in with his secretary and foremen. No one dared leave the premises a minute before the five o'clock factory buzzer. If they did, they'd later get a penetrating eye and a "Why were you running away? Did you have a better place to be?" from my father. Unless there was a hospital or family emergency, no one escaped Montreal Phono on Johnny Simkovits's time.

Dad finished his call and turned to me. "Hi, son. Please come with me to my back office. I have an important job for you concerning our recent European trip."

Dad picked out a half dozen red, blue, and black pens from a metal cup on his desk. He also grabbed a pad of notepaper. He gestured for me to follow him, and he escorted me into his private domain, where he had another desk.

From his top desk drawer, he pulled out a small stack of papers clipped together. He put them on the desk and pointed. "These are our cash receipts from our hotel stays, restaurant meals, and gas station fill-ups during our recent trip to Czechoslovakia and Hungary." The receipts had been handwritten—credit card charges were not possible in those communist countries.

We had been on another two-week family trip to Mom and Dad's homeland. From the time of his first trip back to Czechoslovakia in 1968, Dad had established a business relationship with Tesla, a Czechoslovak supplier of acoustic speakers. My father bought Tesla speakers by the tens of thousands, employing them in Montreal Phono's console stereo units. That business arrangement allowed him not only to enter his communist homeland expediently but also to deduct a portion of our overseas trip as a business expense.

Dad spoke calmly. "Son, sit here at my desk."

He remained standing next to me. He demonstrated what he wanted me to do. He took his pens and scribbled vertical lines from each onto the pad. He picked up the receipt on the top of the stack and placed it next to the pad. "First, I want you to match the ink colour on each receipt with the right pen colour."

A handwritten restaurant supper receipt showed "93 Kcs" (Czechoslovak koruna). That was about $9CAD at the official exchange rate received when converting money when entering the country.

Dad retrieved the pen that best matched the colour of the ink on the receipt. He practised writing the number "1" on the notepad. He then placed a "1" in front of the "93," changing the total to "193." He was careful to match the handwriting of the server who had created the tally.

"See what I'm doing," he said. "Do the same with the rest of the receipts. Find simple ways to change the numbers so you can at least double the total." He showed me another example. He altered a "381 Kcs" supper cheque to look like "881 Kcs," again being careful to match the ink color and handwriting that was on the receipt.

He looked at me. "You see how I'm doing this?" He had a soft yet serious look on his face. "I could use your help on this, son."

My eyes opened wide, but I didn't say a word. It occurred to me that what my father was doing was not legit. I nodded and said, "Yes, okay, Dad." I gave his request no second thought. I figured that Dad knew what he was doing and that I was learning his trade tricks.

He continued. "Good! And when you have finished, add everything up on a separate sheet, separating the different types of expenses: hotel, restaurant, and car."

He put a pad of lined paper on the desk in front of me. "To make your accounting easier, keep Czechoslovak korunas and Hungarian forints separate. And, if any of the receipts are typewritten—like some of these hotel receipts are—leave those alone. Just report those amounts as they are."

I nodded again. Dad continued to speak matter-of-factly. "Then convert the koruna and forint into dollars by using the official exchange rate of 10 korunas and 100 forints to one dollar U.S., as you see here on these currency exchange receipts we obtained at those borders." He pointed to our border bank receipts. He then looked at me. "Don't worry about converting the results into Canadian dollars; our bookkeeper will do that later."

Those Iron Curtain countries had forced us, as they did with all tourists, to convert some hard U.S. currency into their local money when entering their country. It was at a measly one-third of the rate that Dad obtained from illegal money changers on the streets of Košice, Prague, and Budapest.

Dad didn't give a second thought about using the more meagre exchange rate for my calculations. That way, our Canadian government would pay for a more substantial part of that communist foreign-exchange enterprise through a more significant Canadian business tax deduction.

As a young adult, I didn't question my dad. I admired his shrewdness and was glad he was showing me his business ropes.

An hour later, I called my father into his back office. I presented a proud smile. "How's this?"

He examined my work, both the doctored receipts and the neat spreadsheet of expense calculations I had created. He responded, "That's good, son." He grabbed the receipts and my tally and headed out the office door. I followed right behind him as he walked to his bookkeeper's desk.

Jane watched as Dad pointed to my spreadsheet. "Here, Jane. Harvy has made the expense calculations for you. Enter this as one amount in your books, and then write me a cheque for the total U.S. dollars you see right here."

She nodded at my father and then looked at me. "Thank you, Harvy, for your work."

Dad turned back to me, a slight smile on his face. "Thanks, son; you can go back to the factory now." I could tell he liked having the Eastern European portion of our family's vacation cost him nearly nothing.

Though Dad's blatant deceit and my part in it sour my stomach today, I had been pleased to do my part to make our European trip a little more cost-effective. Little did I realize at the time what his survivor teachings would cost me in the years to come.

* * *

Acknowledgements

I wish to thank my writing coach, Tom Daley, for his years of dedication to me and my project. Tom saw the potential not only in my story but also in my writing. His writing workshops and personal coaching helped me to tell my turbulent tale in sound and prolific prose.

Close behind Tom are Terri Payne Butler and Barbara Greene. Terri was a source of terrific feedback and great notions for my manuscript, especially in connecting my many family stories to the "surviving a survivor" theme of the whole book series. Barbara, too, helped enormously with her line-by-line copyediting of my manuscripts.

All of them taught me how to become a better writer, and I couldn't have completed my project without them. The quality of this manuscript is a testament to their excellent work with me. Note to Tom: I'm still holding onto that voodoo doll in your likeness.

I also wish to thank my wife and kids for their patience when they lost me for many evenings and weekends over twelve years to my keyboarding in my home office. I hope this memoir will give them understanding as to whom, what, and where I came from, and why I felt compelled to pen this profound, painful, and ever so personal story.

About the Author

For too long, Harvy Simkovits followed in the path of his crafty and conniving patriarch. Harvy's WWII surviving, Soviet communism escaping, Canada immigrating, Montreal business building, government tax skirting, and blatant womanizing father told him, "Harvy, I want you to finish engineering school, business school, and then law school." The family's flamboyant forbearer longed for his second son to become somebody. He then wanted Harvy to come into the family business where he'd brashly say, "*Lassen* to me, son, for I have more experience than you!"

Harvy, a loyal and impressionable youth, heeded his predecessor's wily wisdom for a while. After completing his bachelor's and master's degrees in engineering at MIT, and a stint at Harvard Business School, Harvy realized that he was following his father's designs and not creating his own dreams.

Harvy dropped out of Harvard and discovered his passion in the fledgling field of organization development. After completing another master's degree in that discipline, Harvy enjoyed a twenty-five-year career in management consulting and executive coaching. He helped many owner-managed companies and family businesses not to make the same mistakes that his father and family had made in their business of over thirty years.

Then, in 2005, years after the death of his dad, Harvy felt he had to make peace with his past. He started to write not only about how his charming, hard-driving, and finagling father built his success in Canada, but also about how those qualities had had an insidious impact on their family, the family business, and (of course) Harvy. The second son of Johnny had to reconcile, repudiate, and rectify the moral and ethical dilemmas he faced with his furtive father and the rest of his thorny family so that he could successfully survive his survivor patriarch.

Harvy Simkovits has been writing and publishing stories about his Canadian immigrant family and their family's business since 2005. *Just Lassen to Me!* is Harvy's full-length memoir turned book series. He resides in Lexington, MA, with his wife, two kids, and two cats.

Visit Harvy at his website:
www.HarvySimkovits.com
to read the latest news regarding his memoir series.

Just Lassen to Me!
Book Two: Survivor Teachings (Third Edition)

Available in 2019 in e-book and paperback through most online outlets.

The Johnny Simkovits saga continues in this no-holds-barred second volume of *Just Lassen to Me*. Johnny's second son, Harvy, continues to get immersed in his father's business shenanigans and enmeshed in his offshore money chicanery. We learn how Johnny, having to overcome unscrupulous bosses and crooked partners, got started as a businessman in Canada. As his business grows, the seemingly masterful Johnny gets caught by the authorities for creative but illicit company accounting devices. A big-city lawyer and a made-up money story help him elude criminal charges. More strife works to darken the marriage of Harvy's parents. A second separation rips the family apart.

Harvy tries to distance himself from his parents' conflicts by focusing on college, accumulating degrees, and finding a job outside the family business. Though he resides five hundred kilometers away, he gets dragged back into his father's appalling mischief. The weight of it all comes crashing down while Harvy attends Harvard Business School. But a stunning epiphany pivots him back to face his family and ameliorate his dad's shady dealings.

Will Harvy be able to help his mother, father, and brother heal bitter wounds that have built up for over a generation, or will Johnny's deceptions and deceit get the better of all of them?

With uncompromising candor and wonderful cinematic detail, Harvy Simkovits has written a powerful memoir of culture, character, family dynamics, triumph, and trauma. In Just Lassen to Me, Book One, *the author views his father—at once brilliant and generous, and cruel and deeply flawed—through the eyes of a boy, teen, young man, and mature man. Book Two is a deeper dive into Harvy's journey toward adulthood and the often conflicting agendas of success, his father's approval, self-preservation, and healing his family, body, and psyche. I feel deeply moved, as many will be, by this story of uncommon courage through pain toward truth and personal integrity.* ~ Lawrence Peltz MD, Psychiatrist, author, **The Mindful Path to Addiction Recovery—a practical guide to regaining control over your life**

An emotionally astute sequel. ~ **Kirkus Review**

Just *Lassen* to Me!
Book Two: Survivor Teachings

Harvy Simkovits

An always alluring yet forever finagling entrepreneurial father.
A pair of misled brothers unwittingly pitted against each other.
A son who struggles to reconcile, repudiate, and rectify his family's past.

www.ingramcontent.com/pod-product-compliance
Lightning Source LLC
Chambersburg PA
CBHW022129020426
42334CB00015B/828